P9-AFX-260

SCIENCE ANNUAL

A Modern Science Anthology for the Family

2005

Published 2004 by Grolier Incorporated.

Library of Congress Control Number: 64-7603
ISBN: 0-7172-1582-2
ISSN: 0742-7514

This annual is also published under the title *The 2005 World Book
Science Year* © 2004 World Book, Inc.

Printed in the United States of America.

STAFF

■ EDITORIAL

Editor in Chief
Dale W. Jacobs

General Managing Editor
Paul A. Kobasa

Managing Editor
Maureen Mostyn Liebenson

Contributing Project Editor
Barbara A. Mayes

Senior Editors
Timothy D. Frystak
Kristina A. Vaicikonis

Staff Editors
Andrew Davis
Scott Richardson

Contributing Editors
Rob Knight
Alfred J. Smuskiewicz
Scott Thomas, Managing
Editor, *Year Book*

Editorial Assistant
Ethel Matthews

Cartographic Services
H. George Stoll, Head
Wayne K. Pichler, Manager,
Digital Cartography
John M. Rejba,
Staff Cartographer

Indexing Services
David Pofelski, Head
Aamir Burki, Staff Indexer

Permissions Editor
Janet Peterson

■ GRAPHIC DESIGN

Manager, Graphics and Design
Sandra M. Dyrlund

Senior Designer, Science Year
Brenda B. Tropinski

Senior Designers
Don Di Sante
Isaiah W. Sheppard, Jr.

Contributing Designers
Lucy Lesiak
Sandy Newell

Photographs Editors
Tom Evans
Sylvia Ohlrich

Contributing Photographs Editors
Julie Laffin
Cathy Melloan

Production and Administrative Support
John Whitney

■ LIBRARY SERVICES

Library Services
Jon Fjortoft, Head

■ PRODUCTION

Director, Manufacturing and Pre-Press
Carma Fazio

Manufacturing Manager
Barbara Podczerwinski

Senior Production Manager
Madelyn S. Underwood

Designer/Production Manager
Anne Fritzinger

Print Promotional Manager
Marco Morales

Proofreading
Anne Dillon

Text Processing
Curley Hunter
Gwendolyn Johnson

■ MARKETING

Director, Direct Marketing
Mark R. Willy

Marketing Analyst
Zofia Kulik

■ *This book is dedicated to the memory of Carol Yehling.*

CONTRIBUTORS

Barone, Jeanine, M.S.
Nutritionist and Exercise Physiologist; Free-Lance Health Writer. [**Consumer Science,** *The A, B, C's of Vitamin Supplements*]

Bhattacharjee, Yudhijit, B.Tech., M.A.
Staff Writer, *Science*. [*Engineering*]

Bolen, Eric G., B.S., M.S., Ph.D.
Professor Emeritus, Department of Biological Sciences, University of North Carolina at Wilmington. [*Conservation*]

Brett, Carlton E., M.S., Ph.D.
Professor, Department of Geology, University of Cincinnati. [*Fossil Studies*]

Burchett, Andrew, B.A.
Chemicals and Seeds Editor, *Farm Journal Media.* [*Agriculture*]

Carpenter, Siri, B.A., M.S., Ph.D.
Free-Lance Science Writer. [**Consumer Science,** *Food Fresh? Ways to Tell*]

Chiras, Daniel, B.A., Ph.D.
Mellon Visiting Professor, Colorado College. [*Environmental Pollution*]

Despres, Renee, Ph.D. Free-Lance Writer. [*Medical Research; Psychology (Close-Up)*]

Ferrell, Keith Free-Lance Writer. [*Computers and Electronics; Consumer Science, Getting a Charge Out of Batteries*]

Gadomski, Fred, B.S., M.S.
Meteorologist, Pennsylvania State University. [**Special Report,** *Is the Weather Getting Weirder?*]

Graff, Gordon, B.S., M.S., Ph.D.
Free-Lance Science Writer. [*Chemistry*]

Hay, William W., B.S., M.S., Ph.D.
Professor Emeritus, Geological Sciences, University of Colorado at Boulder. [*Geology*]

Haymer, David S., M.S., Ph.D.
Professor, Department of Cell and Molecular Biology, John A. Burns School of Medicine, University of Hawaii at Manoa. [*Genetics*]

Hebets, Eileen, Ph.D.
Insect Biologist, College of Natural Resources, University of California at Berkeley. [**Special Report,** *Amazing Spiders: Sex, Lies, and Video Watching*]

Hester, Thomas R., B.A., Ph.D.
Professor Emeritus of Anthropology, University of Texas at Austin. [*Archaeology;* **Special Report,** *Saving the Past*]

Hoop, Jinger G., B.A., M.F.A., M.D.
Senior Fellow, MacLean Center for Clinical Ethics; Psychiatric Genetics Fellow, Department of Psychiatry—University of Chicago. [*Drugs* (Close-Up)]

Johnson, Christina S., B.A., M.S.
Science Writer, California Sea Grant College Program, Scripps Institution of Oceanography. [*Oceanography*]

Kilgore, Margaret, B.A., M.B.A
Free-Lance Writer and Teacher. [*Environmental Pollution (Close-Up)*]

Kowal, Deborah, M.A., P.A.
Adjunct Assistant Professor, Emory University Rollins School of Public Health. [*Public Health*]

Levine, Jon E., A.B., Ph.D.
Professor of Neurobiology and Physiology, Director of the Program in Biological Sciences, Northwestern University. [**Science Studies,** *Why Are We Getting Fatter? The Puzzle of Obesity*]

Lunine, Jonathan I., B.S., M.S., Ph.D.
Professor of Planetary Science and Physics, University of Arizona Lunar and Planetary Laboratory. [*Astronomy;* **Special Reports,** *Fantastic Voyage: Discoveries on Mars, Fantastic Voyage: Discoveries on Jupiter*]

Lykken, Joseph D., Ph.D.
Theoretical Physicist, Fermi National Accelerator Laboratory. [**Special Report,** *The Super-Strange World of Superstrings and Extra Dimensions*]

March, Robert H., A.B., M.S., Ph.D.
Professor Emeritus of Physics and Liberal Studies, University of Wisconsin at Madison. [*Physics*]

Marschall, Laurence A., B.S., Ph.D.
Professor of Physics, Gettysburg College. [*Books About Science*]

Maugh, Thomas H., II, Ph.D.
Medical Writer, *Los Angeles Times.* [**Special Report,** *Seeing Beneath Our Skin: Imaging the Body*]

Milius, Susan, B.A.
Life Sciences Writer, *Science News.* [*Biology*]

Milo, Richard G., B.A., M.A., Ph.D.
Associate Professor of Anthropology, Chicago State University. [*Anthropology*]

Morring, Frank, Jr., A.B.
Senior Space Technology Editor, *Aviation Week & Space Technology.* [*Space Technology*]

Moser-Veillon, Phylis B., B.S., M.S., Ph.D.
Professor, Department of Nutrition and Food Science, University of Maryland at College Park. [*Nutrition*]

Murphy, Michael J., M.D., M.P.H.
Assistant Psychiatrist, McLean Hospital; Instructor, Harvard Medical School. [*Psychology*]

Ravilious, Kate, B.A., M.Res., Ph.D.
Free-Lance Science Writer. [**Special Report,** *The Core: New Findings About Earth's Final Frontier*]

Riley, Thomas N., B.S., Ph.D.
Professor, School of Pharmacy, Auburn University. [*Drugs*]

Sforza, Pasquale M., B.Ae.E., M.S., Ph.D.
Professor of Mechanical and Aerospace Engineering, University of Florida. [*Energy*]

Snow, John T., B.S.E.E., M.S.E.E., Ph.D.
Dean, College of Geosciences, and Professor of Meteorology, University of Oklahoma. [*Atmospheric Science*]

Snow, Theodore P., B.A., M.S., Ph.D.
Professor of Astrophysics, University of Colorado at Boulder. [*Astronomy*]

Tamarin, Robert H., B.S., Ph.D.
Dean of Sciences, University of Massachusetts Lowell. [*Ecology*]

Teich, Albert H., B.S., Ph.D.
Director, Science and Policy Programs, American Association for the Advancement of Science. [*Science and Society*]

EDITORIAL ADVISORY BOARD

CONTENTS

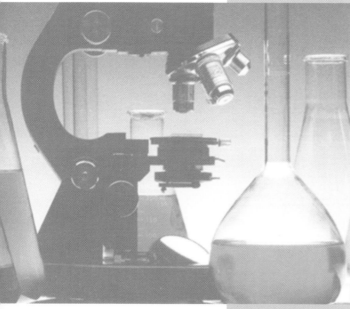

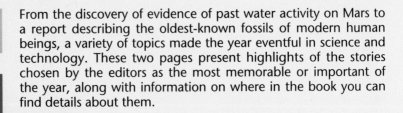

MAJOR SCIENCE STORIES

From the discovery of evidence of past water activity on Mars to a report describing the oldest-known fossils of modern human beings, a variety of topics made the year eventful in science and technology. These two pages present highlights of the stories chosen by the editors as the most memorable or important of the year, along with information on where in the book you can find details about them.

MAD COW DISEASE IN THE UNITED STATES

A dairy cow slaughtered in Washington in December 2003 became the first cow in the United States to test positive for bovine spongiform encephalopathy, or "mad cow disease." An exhaustive search by government inspectors uncovered no other cows with the disease, which had previously crippled the cattle industries of Canada and the United Kingdom. In the Science News Update section, see **AGRICULTURE, page 163.**

GENES AND DEPRESSION

Genes play an important role in determining whether a person will develop depression in response to stressful life events, researchers reported in July 2003. In the Science News Update section, see **GENETICS, page 230, and PSYCHOLOGY, page 254.**

WATER ON MARS

Spirit and Opportunity, twin robotic rovers that touched down on Mars in January 2004, discovered strong chemical and geologic evidence that parts of the Red Planet had once been soaked in water—conditions that may have supported life. In the Special Reports section, see **FANTASTIC VOYAGE: DISCOVERIES ON MARS, page 28.**

8

MASS EXTINCTION CAUSED BY METEORITE?

The largest extinction of animal life in Earth's history may have been triggered by the impact of a massive meteorite 250 million years ago, according to a November 2003 study describing meteorite fragments found in Antarctica. Researchers said in May 2004 that a crater off the coast of Australia may be the site of the impact. In the Science News Update section, see **FOSSIL STUDIES, page 226.**

AFRICAN BEGINNINGS

The discovery in Ethiopia of the oldest-known fossils of modern human beings was reported in June 2003. The discovery supports the theory that all living people are the direct descendants of a small group of people who lived in Africa between about 200,000 and 150,000 years ago. In the Science News Update section, see **ANTHROPOLOGY, page 165.**

OBESITY EPIDEMIC

The U. S. Centers for Disease Control and Prevention reported in March 2004 that obesity was rapidly overtaking smoking as the leading cause of death in the United States. Researchers, physicians, and government agencies as well as individuals and community groups are tackling this "obesity epidemic" with renewed vigor. In the Science Studies section, see **WHY ARE WE GETTING FATTER? THE PUZZLE OF OBESITY, page 120.**

HISTORIC HEAT WAVE

A heat wave of historic proportions caused the deaths of an estimated 35,000 people in central and western Europe in August 2003. Scientists are working to determine if heat waves and other extreme weather events are becoming more common. In the Special Reports section, see **IS THE WEATHER GETTING WEIRDER? page 44.**

CHINA REACHES SPACE

China became the third nation to send a human being into space when *taikonaut* (astronaut) Yang Liwei completed 14 orbits of Earth over a period of 21 hours in October 2003. In the Science News Update section, see **SPACE TECHNOLOGY, page 267.**

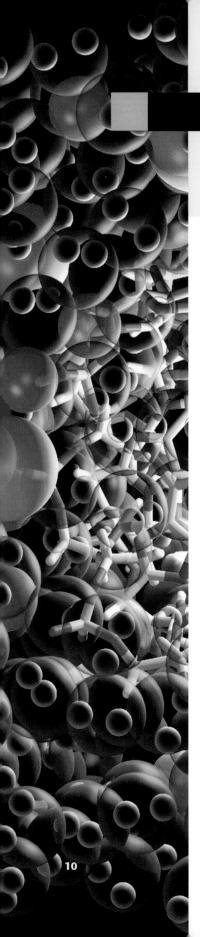

SPECIAL REPORTS

These feature articles take an in-depth look at significant and timely subjects in science and technology.

In the early months of 2004, treasure hunters in Iraq's Dhi Qar province turned the flat floor of the desert into a moonscape of craters. Working at night under bright lights powered by gasoline-fueled generators, the men plundered 4,000-year-old graves from Sumer, the world's first civilization. The looters were seeking the objects—the engraved seals, jewelry, and small statues—buried with the ancient dead. In the process, they broke and trampled what did not interest them. When they were finished, pieces of a large urn littered the floor of one of the hollowed-out craters.

SAVING THE PAST

BY THOMAS R. HESTER

Archaeologists continue to combat
the problem of looting, which
destroys the wealth of information
available from ancient artifacts
and archaeological sites.

Although archaeological looting in Iraq has greatly intensified since
the Iraq War, it represents a pattern that began during the Persian Gulf
War of 1991. The small group of police assigned to protect ancient sites
is sadly outnumbered. The destruction of cultural remains is not, however, just a problem for Iraq. It is a worldwide phenomenon.

On the other side of the world, in the jungles of Central America,
looters, who are often local farmers, use chain saws to cut up large stone
sculptures and burrow into pyramids in their search for treasure-filled
tombs. The archaeologists who carefully excavate 1,000-year-old Maya

TERMS AND CONCEPTS

Antiquities: Objects modified by people in ancient times.

Artifact: A human-made object, often ancient.

Avocational archaeology: Scientifically based archaeological research conducted by people with other careers who work with professional archaeologists.

Black market: An underground or illegal market.

Context: The information linked to an artifact or feature when discovered, especially the geologic layer in which it was found and objects found with it.

Ecofact: A natural object found with artifacts and features that provides clues to how people lived in ancient times.

Feature: A change made at an archaeological site by people and their activities.

Launder: To pass something illegal through many hands until it appears to be legal.

Projectile point: A stone tip of an arrow or spear.

Provenience: The specific records documenting where an artifact was discovered.

Strata: Layers of earth and archaeological material from different time periods.

The author:
Thomas R. Hester is a Professor Emeritus of Anthropology at the University of Texas at Austin.

sites in the region cannot keep up with the pace of the looting. As a result, great segments of Maya heritage have been lost.

In Italy, looters known as *tombaroli* have dug into more than 100,000 ancient graves and tombs in recent years. Many of these burials date to the Etruscan civilization that flourished in the 600's B.C. In Germany, antiquities collectors supply metal detectors to unemployed local farmers so that they can hunt for objects dating from the Bronze Age, a period that lasted from about 1800 to 700 B.C. in central Europe. Authorities recently recovered one of these looted objects, a plate-sized bronze disk that maps the night sky. Dating from about 1600 B.C., the disk was being offered to collectors for $400,000.

Archaeological looting also has risen dramatically in the United States, where looters have turned to backhoes and bulldozers in their search for highly marketable Native American earthen pots and *projectile points* (the stone tips of arrows or spears). In 2003, for example, looters dug into the BA Cave, a 7,000-year-old site in north-central Wyoming. Archaeologists had studied the site, which sits on federal land, in the 1990's. However, they had explored deposits from only the last 3,000 years during which people had used the cave. In their search for Native American objects, the looters destroyed half of the cave deposits, completely destroying the cave's value for future archaeological study. Such destruction tears pages out of the book of human history, preventing archaeologists from acquiring the knowledge they need to make meaningful interpretations of the ancient past.

Archaeological looters are part of an international billion-dollar "industry" that preys on the cultural heritage of many nations. In general, the plundered sculptures and other objects flow from the poorer nations of the world to the richer nations. There, they end up in the hands of private collectors, and even museums, in Europe, Japan, and the United States.

The systematic study of the past

Archaeology is the scientific study of the remains of past human cultures. It employs systematic techniques to excavate and describe cities, farms, camps, and any other place used by people of the past, and so enriches our knowledge of ancient societies.

Archaeologists attempt to analyze the remnants of a past culture with the aim of explaining how people lived in the past. Such evidence consists of *artifacts, features,* and *ecofacts.* An artifact is any object made by human hands—from a small flint projectile point to the largest ancient pyramid. Features are visible disturbances to the earth that provide evidence of past human activities. They may include a cooking pit, the foundations of a building, or a buried irrigation canal. Unlike artifacts, features cannot be separated from their surroundings. Ecofacts are natural objects, such as plant pollen or animal bones, found with artifacts or features. They can provide specific clues about environments in ancient times and what people ate at a particular place. Archaeological looters generally keep only rare and beautiful artifacts that command big prices. In the process of removing such items from archaeological sites, looters often damage or destroy great numbers of artifacts from daily life as well as features and ecofacts.

An archaeological site is any place where people once lived, sometimes for a brief period and sometimes for centuries. Sites may be places where people constructed houses, buried their dead, or used local resources such as lakes and streams. At sites, people may have made tools, huddled around cooking fires, built cities, or constructed great temples.

Hundreds of thousands of such sites exist around the world. They vary from the simple—such as a central Texas campsite containing 11,000-year-old stone tools—to the highly complex—such as the elaborately carved stone and earthen buildings of a Maya ceremonial and political center covering several square kilometers.

A large carving of an animal devouring a man's head was cut away from a Mayan temple in Guatemala, likely with chain saws. Authorities confiscated the 2,000-year-old carving in Brooklyn, New York, in November 1999.

Archaeologists regard all sites as important. A small cave in the Nevada desert used by hunting-and-gathering peoples for 8,000 years is, in fact, as important to the study of its ancient inhabitants as is the rich tomb of an Egyptian pharaoh. Regardless of their size and complexity, sites provide valuable clues about how inhabitants once lived and adapted to their environment.

Archaeological sites are also incredibly fragile. Although looters are often singled out as thieves of the past, both nature and the expansion of modern civilization also destroy great numbers of sites. For example, floodwaters can cut into riverbanks, washing away evidence of ancient villages. In 2003, China began filling the reservoir of the world's largest dam. By 2009, the reservoir will cover not only hundreds of modern cities and villages but also innumerable sites thousands of years old. In the United States, untold numbers of archaeology sites are destroyed annually by quarrying and mining, by the sprawl of housing subdivisions, and by ranchers clearing brush with bulldozers. In cities such as Athens and Rome, air pollution endlessly eats away at ancient monuments.

A man prays to statues of Buddha from the 1500's and 1600's carved into stone on the banks along China's Yangtze River. Flooding resulting from the construction of the Three Gorges Dam will place this and many other archaeological sites under water by 2009.

Why does looting threaten the past?

If there are hundreds of thousands of archaeological sites and if natural forces and an ever-expanding human population are already destroying them, why do archaeologists worry about looters? There are two major reasons. First, the number of looters and the number of sites being looted have grown enormously in recent years. The increase is driven largely by two forces—the skyrocketing prices that antiquities command on international markets and the dwindling prices farmers in developing countries earn for their crops. Most looters in these countries are poor farmers who turn to looting to make extra money. Often, they are hired by middlemen who direct the looters to specific sites and place orders for certain kinds of artifacts.

The second reason why looting has become a serious problem involves the quality of the sites under attack. While all sites are important from a scholarly point of view, not all, in fact, are "created equal." Looters seek the most marketable artifacts—that is, the rarest and most beautiful objects. In their quest, they tend to select, and subsequently destroy, sites of extreme importance. Some of these sites—for example, the Sumerian tombs in Iraq, the Maya ruins in Central America, and temple complexes in Egypt—represent the political, ceremonial, and spiritual capitals of once-great empires. A team of looters, armed with picks, shovels, and even bulldozers, can destroy in one night a site that archaeologists might spend decades excavating, photographing, measuring, and documenting.

When looters break up an Egyptian sculpture to steal only the head, or when they tear into a 1,000-year-old Mimbres burial in a New Mexico pueblo to find highly decorated pottery, the *context* of the artifacts they find and discard is lost forever. Context—information about the spot within the site where an artifact is found—is critical when archaeologists interpret the past. They must have specific data on the artifact's place in time and space. They must record its depth, its location within the site boundaries, and its association with cooking pits, house floors, burials, or any number of features at the site. If context is lost, archaeologists cannot determine whether the fragment of an Egyptian statue was made during the reign of a specific pharaoh, or whether a Mimbres bowl came from a burial. The looted artifact's potential for adding to human knowledge is forever gone. The pieces have become "art objects," valuable to collectors but essentially worthless to scholars.

And what becomes of the other archaeological remains that the looters destroyed to obtain the beautiful, exotic, or exquisitely made artifacts that feed the antiquities market? This is perhaps the most destructive aspect of the looters' work. The rest of that Egyptian statue, with its hieroglyphs and its *cartouche* (name glyphs), is shattered. To steal that Mimbres pot, the looters tore through the floor above the burial. In the process, they cast aside the broken pottery, animal bones, and stone tools they found—all of which are needed to tell the story of the ancient pueblo and its people. As looters shovel out the contents of a cave to find a marketable basket, they discard sharp stone blades that have *residues* (bits of material sticking to the surface). As a result, no specialist will be able to determine which animal or plant species the blade was used to cut or chop. The age of the object and its connection with a particular people who once lived in the cave are lost.

The history of looting

The plundering of archaeological sites has a very long history. In ancient Egypt, the craft workers who built the tombs of the pharaohs often returned later to loot the gold artifacts buried with the royal mummies. Tomb robbing became so widespread that in about 1500 B.C., Egyptian priests removed and hid 40 mummies of pharaohs. The mummies remained hidden until 1881, when Abd-el-Rasul, a well-known Egyptian looter, stumbled over them. After artifacts from these mummies began to appear in Egypt's flourishing *black market* (an underground or illegal market), Abd-el-Rasul was arrested and the mummies were recovered.

In Italy during the Renaissance (a cultural movement that began in the 1300's), wealthy patrons commissioned workers to dig into ancient Roman sites to recover sculpture for use as garden ornaments. The Vatican Museum in Rome has hundreds of such statues that popes paid to have pulled from the ruins of that city. Diggers looking for ancient artifacts outside Naples, Italy, in the mid-1700's discovered an entire ancient Roman city, Pompeii, which had been covered in a volcanic eruption in A.D. 79. Soon, looters employed by the king of the Two Sicilies (a kingdom that consisted of much of southern Italy, including Naples and the island of Sicily) were excavating in Pompeii for sculptures for the king's museum.

Europeans, especially the British, began traveling to Egypt in the 1600's. Many of these travelers bought ancient artifacts or had them excavated to take home as "souvenirs." These early collectors were wealthy, typically aristocrats or members of a royal family. Their collections often became the seeds of such renowned museums as the Louvre in Paris and the Danish National Museum in Copenhagen.

In the early 1800's, an Italian circus strongman named Giovanni Belzoni actually became famous for his plundering of ancient Egyptian sites. Much of his fame rested on his accounts of crunching across mummies to loot tombs and on the number of large sculptures he managed to cart out of ancient Egyptian temples. Belzoni's efforts were often

In this lithograph, Egyptian workers under the direction of Italian archaeological looter Giovanni Belzoni remove the head of a statue of the Egyptian king Ramses II from the ruins of a temple in 1816. Belzoni sent the head to London, where it remains in the British Museum.

sponsored by Henry Salt, the British consul general in Egypt, who shipped the pieces back to Britain. Salt donated the artifacts he had picked up in Egypt to the British Museum in London, which houses one of the world's greatest collections of antiquities.

By the time of Belzoni and Salt, an international market in antiquities had already become well established. Most of the ancient artifacts traded at the time were actually obtained legally and were often removed from the country of origin with that country's permission. During this period, the Egyptian government even allowed massive *obelisks* (four-sided stone shafts with tops shaped like a pyramid) to be removed from ancient Egyptian temple complexes along the Nile. Workers loaded the obelisks, which weighed hundreds of tons, on ships for transport to London, New York City, and Paris, where they remain to this day.

By the second half of the 1800's, European and U.S. museums funded their own expeditions to various countries to secure artifacts for their collections. The leaders of many of these expeditions, such as Flinders Petrie in Egypt in the 1800's, developed methods and techniques for scientific archaeology. Petrie, for example, used different types of pottery and fragments found in the *strata* (layers) at Egyptian sites to help date his discoveries. His research helped establish *stratigraphy* as an essential technique to help study the development and age of deposits at a site.

Prehistoric archaeological materials accumulate in layers in much the same way geological strata are laid down by the forces of nature over vast periods of time. Archaeological strata may consist of soil and decayed vegetable matter, or they may be the products of human activity. For example, the burning of a village would produce a distinct, easily recognizable stratum. Or a layer of gravel atop the refuse from an ancient campsite might indicate a major flood that forced the inhabitants to flee. Archaeological strata provide archaeologists with a kind of time capsule that can be "read"—the most recent period at the top and the most ancient at the bottom.

Looting as an economic enterprise

During roughly the same period that archaeology developed as a scholarly field, wealthy collectors began to specialize in the artifacts of certain regions—ancient Mesopotamia, Egypt, Greece, or Rome—and sought to acquire the finest examples. Many museums actively purchased collections without regard to how the artifacts were obtained. Collectors and museum curators justified the purchase of looted acquisitions with the argument that it "saved" artifacts that would otherwise be lost to looters, deterioration over time, or environmental damage. Some collectors argued that their activities were, in fact, "scholarly" because they developed from a genuine interest in archaeology and the study of native peoples.

The antiquities market became even more competitive in the 1900's when wealthy individuals began buying ancient artifacts as an investment. These individuals collected in the belief that rising antiquities prices would earn them a handsome return on their purchases.

The competition for antiquities did, in fact, drive up prices, which in turn fueled more looting. Experts speculated that the amount of money expended annually on the antiquities market had reached nearly $5 billion by 2000. According to Interpol, an organization that assists police in member nations in international crime investigations, profits from the illegal sale of archaeological specimens ranked third, after drug trafficking and money laundering, by 2001.

Modern-day archaeological looting is a response to an economic demand, much like the situation with the trade in illegal drugs. Would

THE IMPORTANCE OF CONTEXT

The most important element in archaeology is context, the relation of an artifact or feature to the location where it was discovered and to the material found with it. An artifact found and studied in its correct context can reveal valuable information about its age and use. For example, the direction a statue is facing in an ancient temple could help archaeologists determine the significance the statue had. When looters remove an artifact from its site—without carefully documenting its context—essential information is lost forever. Looters raided the Gault Site in Texas for almost 80 years before archaeologists could begin a scientific study. Now archaeologists excavate the site systematically (below). By examining other objects found in context, archaeologists have learned a great deal about the lives of the Clovis people who lived in the area starting about 11,200 years ago.

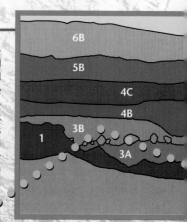

Archaeologists carefully excavate the Gault Site (left), which was occupied by Native Americans from about 9,200 B.C. to the A.D. 1700's. The colored layers in the walls of the pit and in the central column are geologic *strata* (layers), deposits of soil from different time periods. Blue dots connect the strata exposed on one wall of the site to a drawing that depicts details about the depth and composition of the strata.

Colombian farmers grow coca or Afghans raise poppies without the enormous demand for cocaine and heroin in the United States and Europe? As archaeologist Ricardo Elia of Boston University has said, "... the collector is the real looter."

Looters sell their product—the artifacts—to middlemen and earn relatively little money for their labor. The big profits go to the middlemen and dealers. For example, a local villager may get $10 for a looted artifact that a dealer might sell for $10,000. The middlemen smuggle the pieces out of the country of origin and, because this usually violates laws, they often must bribe local officials.

Artifacts pass through a number of hands until they are *laundered* (made to appear legal) so that their origins become hard to trace. Along this journey, an artifact generally picks up a false *provenience*—that is, a false history of an object that includes information on its origins—allow-

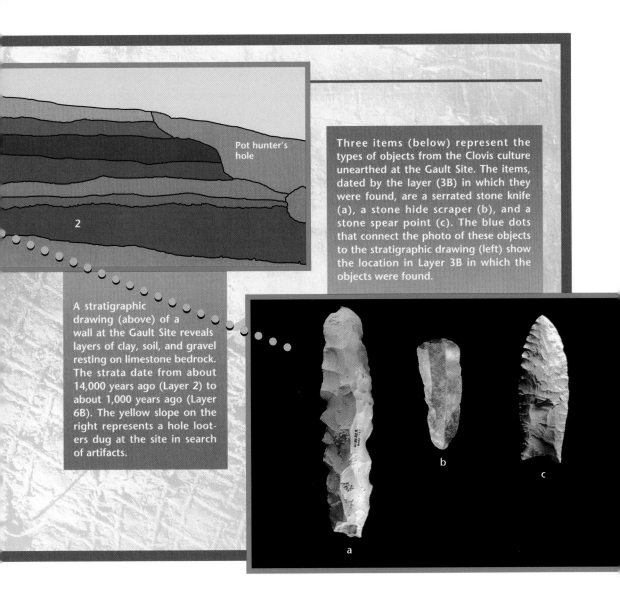

Pot hunter's hole

2

Three items (below) represent the types of objects from the Clovis culture unearthed at the Gault Site. The items, dated by the layer (3B) in which they were found, are a serrated stone knife (a), a stone hide scraper (b), and a stone spear point (c). The blue dots that connect the photo of these objects to the stratigraphic drawing (left) show the location in Layer 3B in which the objects were found.

A stratigraphic drawing (above) of a wall at the Gault Site reveals layers of clay, soil, and gravel resting on limestone bedrock. The strata date from about 14,000 years ago (Layer 2) to about 1,000 years ago (Layer 6B). The yellow slope on the right represents a hole looters dug at the site in search of artifacts.

b

c

a

ing dealers and buyers to evade national and international laws protecting archaeological resources.

Centers of the antiquities trade include Geneva, Switzerland; London; New York City; and Hong Kong. Individual dealers in "ancient art" operating through the black market and auction houses provide outlets for archaeological artifacts. However, many of the artifacts offered by established dealers and auction houses are, in fact, perfectly legal. They may have been a part of a large personal collection for many years and may have been purchased before the enactment of legal statutes prohibiting the removal of pieces of cultural heritage from countries of origin.

However, legitimate dealers and auction houses—whether knowingly or not—also sometimes sell looted antiquities whose origins have been concealed. In early 2004, for example, U.S. federal agents seized a colossal marble bust of the Roman emperor Trajan from its latest owner. That collector had purchased the bust for $276,000 at an auction at Christie's gallery in New York City in December 2003. The person who asked Christie's to sell the bust claimed that it had been inherited from his father in 1932. In fact, the piece had been stolen from an Italian museum in 1998.

In 1992, a New York art dealer sold a bust of the Egyptian pharaoh Amenhotep III for $1.2 million. He had purchased the 3,400-year-old sculpture for $915,000 from a British citizen. Authorities, however, discovered that the artifact had been smuggled out of Egypt by coating it in plastic and painting it black to make it look like something from a souvenir shop.

Legal authorities warn that in such instances, the buyer will lose his or her entire investment. In the mid-1990's, the U.S. Customs Service seized a rare, ancient Greek bowl for which a New York investor had paid $2.1 million. The investor sued. But, the bowl had, in fact, been looted from a site in Sicily and was returned to the government of Italy in 1999. The investor got neither the bowl nor the money back.

Looting and the law

Professional archaeologists believe that hope for ending or, at least, slowing the destruction of archaeological sites exists despite the current grim reality. Many countries have passed legislation outlawing the destruction of archaeological sites and the removal of artifacts from their territory. And governments are increasingly enforcing such laws. A number of countries have established their right to all "cultural patrimony" within their borders. Mexico is one such country, though it still loses thousands of artifacts annually to the looting of palaces, tombs, and pyramids of its ancient civilizations. Mexico also signed a treaty with the United States in 1972 to halt the illegal import of artifacts. Unfortunately, the treaty has been unevenly enforced, and smugglers continue to take valuable objects out of Mexico. In part, the problem stems from lack of training that would enable U.S. Customs agents to recognize illegal artifacts.

Legal attempts to protect ruins and artifacts found on federal lands in the United States date to the Antiquities Act of 1906, which had little impact. In the 1970's, Congress passed the Archaeological Resources Protection Act (ARPA), which has proved to be a more effective weapon against looters. In early 2004, for example, federal authorities charged several individuals under the ARPA for using metal detectors to search for Revolutionary War artifacts at Valley Forge National Historical Park in Pennsylvania.

In the early 1990's, Congress passed another piece of legislation to protect archaeological sites, the Native American Graves Protection and

Repatriation Act. The law essentially stopped the once-flourishing trade in Native American skeletal remains and grave offerings. It has also provided many Native American tribes with the legal power to recover burials and sacred objects excavated from their lands.

The U.S. government, unfortunately, employs too few law enforcement agents to actively pursue violations of these laws. In many cases, one or two National Park Service rangers patrol hundreds of thousands of hectares of land, a situation that makes it physically impossible to stop the looting.

Nations also have banded together to establish treaties to control the worldwide antiquities market. The 1954 Hague Convention, the first of these treaties, included provisions to protect cultural property during war or times of conflict. However, the convention includes a clause allowing its provisions to be waived by "military necessity." The 1970 United Nations Educational, Scientific, and Cultural Organization (UNESCO) Convention on the Means of Prohibiting and Preventing the Illicit Import, Export and Transfer of Ownership of Cultural Property was created, in part, to halt the illegal export of artifacts and to return stolen cultural materials to their countries of origin. About 100 nations have ratified the convention. However, many wealthy nations have been slow to agree to its provisions. The governments of the United States and the United Kingdom did not sign the treaty until

An antiquities shop in Afghanistan displays artifacts looted from Islamic archaeological sites. Looters often destroy such sites in their search for artifacts, which they sell for small amounts of money.

United States Customs agents return a Chinese tomb sculpture from the 900's to Chinese officials in New York City in 2001. Agents seized the marble sculpture, which was stolen in 1994, at a U.S. auction house before it could be sold.

1983 and 2002, respectively. Germany and Japan in 2004 had yet to agree to the convention.

International authorities believe a 1995 treaty—the International Institute for the Unification of Private Law (UNIDROIT) Convention on Stolen or Illegally Exported Cultural Objects—may prove to be the most effective means yet to control the illegal flow of antiquities. The treaty internationalizes the various national laws that affect "market nations," where many collectors live, and "source nations," where much of the looting occurs. But fewer than 30 nations have ratified the UNIDROIT Convention, and the government of the United States has yet to sign on. U.S. officials, however, have acted within the framework of the convention, as in 1997, when customs officials seized a $1.2-million ancient gold platter and returned it to Italy. The United States also has signed cultural property protection agreements with Bolivia, Cambodia, Canada, Cyprus, El Salvador, Guatemala, Italy, Mali, and Nicaragua in an attempt to stem the illegal flow of artifacts from these countries.

Is there a future for the past?

As tools for the enforcement of looting laws have increased dramatically in the past 20 years, the rise of "e-commerce" on the Internet has

made antiquities dealing harder to trace. The U.S. Customs Service has set up a "national cybercenter" to check the Internet for various forms of smuggled goods, including antiquities. Although few prosecutions have resulted, authorities have achieved some success in warning Internet dealers to remove artifacts from sale.

At the same time, the Internet has become an effective tool in the fight against illegal trafficking in antiquities. In 2004, it was used to alert the public to museum thefts and to the movement of illegal artifacts. The International Council of Museums (ICOM) maintains on its Web site a "Red List," a list of examples of artifacts that are systematically being looted because they are in great demand. The list is intended to help museums and dealers avoid illegal merchandise. In May 2003, ICOM issued an emergency Red List for Iraqi antiquities.

The enforcement of international treaties and changes in public perception will slow, but cannot stop, the looting. The economic motive, both for the looter and for the collector, is simply too strong. The struggle to "save the past" is really a struggle with greed, a human motivation that is difficult to overcome.

In the long run, public involvement may be the only truly effective way to slow looting. In recent years, both television and newspapers have increasingly spotlighted site destruction and the activities of art

Artifacts stolen from Mexico and smuggled into Texas cover a table at a training seminar for U.S. Customs agents. Archaeologists at the seminar discussed the kind of antiquities being looted and transported for sale to collectors.

GUIDELINES FOR VISITING ARCHAEOLOGICAL SITES

Sometimes, people who visit public archaeological sites to enjoy and learn from them accidentally damage them. Following these site etiquette guidelines will help reduce damage to fragile sites and preserve the past for the future.

- All the things you see at an archaeological site are evidence of the lives of people who once lived there, so it is important that you do not move or disturb anything. If you see an interesting artifact, you may look at it, draw it, or photograph it, but don't pick it up.
- Don't lean, sit, stand, or climb on prehistoric walls. They can be very fragile.
- Stay on established paths and trails to help control erosion and preserve the site.
- Trash can contaminate the soil of an archaeological site, so be sure not to discard an apple core, banana peel, or similar things on the ground. Food may attract animals, which can be very destructive to sites.
- Be sure to camp away from archaeological sites. Campfires and cigarettes produce charcoal that can confuse the *radiocarbon dating* (a method of determining the age of artifacts) of an archaeological site.
- Pets can be very destructive to archaeological sites—leave your pooch at home.

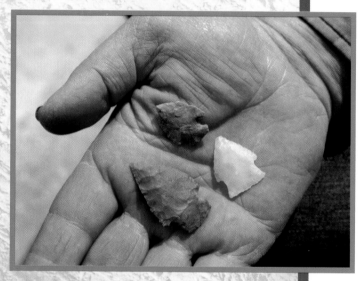

What to do if you find an artifact

- Leave the artifact where you found it. Record as much information as possible about the location and the description of the artifact. It is useful to draw or photograph the object and record its location on a map.
- Share the information you have collected with a professional archaeologist. If you are visiting a state or national park, inform a park ranger, naturalist, or interpreter. Each state has a historic preservation office that records the location of archaeological sites. The Web site of the National Association of State Archaeologists—http://www.uiowa.edu/~osa/nasa/—provides contact information for states. The Government of Canada's Web site—http://www.culturecanada.gc.ca—provides similar information for Canadian sites.

Learn

There are many ways to learn about and get involved in archaeology:

- Join a local or state archaeological society. These groups can provide training in archaeological techniques and introduce you to the kinds of artifacts and sites found in your area.
- Participate in some of the events your state sponsors during its "Archaeology Week" each year. Such events may include site tours, lectures, and hands-on archaeology activities.
- Volunteer! Some areas have programs that use volunteers to monitor sites and record changes to them. Archaeological societies often welcome volunteers to help record, survey, or excavate sites. The United States Forest Service and National Park Service also sponsor volunteer programs.

The Web site of the Society for American Archaeology—http://www.saa.org—features more information about these programs and activities.

These guidelines were adapted from those developed by the U.S. Forest Service.

dealers and artifact collectors. In the United Kingdom and the United States, educational programs on archaeology for the adult public are expanding. Programs in the school system provide the best chance for educating future generations about the damage that looting causes to the study of human heritage. Education, however, takes time. Meanwhile, the accelerated destruction of antiquity continues.

The popularity of *avocational* (amateur) archaeology is a significant development that is helping to create greater public awareness about looting. Avocational archaeologists are people from many careers who share a love for the study of the past and who use professional techniques in their research. In the United States, thousands of people belong to hundreds of archaeological societies, most of which exist to study and publish information on regional sites and artifacts. Similar organizations exist in the United Kingdom. Avocational archaeologists are the "watchdogs" who often report or stop looting. More significantly, their organizations often teach relic hunters and collectors about the scientific importance of archaeological data. As a result, many of these individuals have adopted avocational roles. At least in Western nations, this form of "education" may offer the most effective means of saving the past.

■ FOR ADDITIONAL INFORMATION

Books

Brodie, Neal; Doole, Jennifer; and Renfrew, Colin (editors). *Trade in Illicit Antiquities: the Destruction of the World's Archaeological Heritage.* McDonald Institute for Archaeological Research, 2001.
Green, Ernestine L. (editor). *Ethics and Values in Archaeology.* Free Press, 1984.
Messenger, Phyllis M. (editor). *The Ethics of Collecting Cultural Property: Whose Culture? Whose Property?* 2nd ed. University of New Mexico Press, 1999.
Vitelli, Karen D. (editor). *Archaeological Ethics.* Altamira Press, 1996.

Web sites

Illicit Antiquities Research Centre—www.mcdonald.cam.ac.uk/IARC/home.htm
International Council of Museums Red List—www.museum.or.jp/icom/redlist/
United States Department of State's Bureau of Educational and Cultural Affairs: International Cultural Property Protection—http://exchanges.state.gov/cul-prop/index.html
Texas Beyond History—http://www.texasbeyondhistory.net

■ QUESTIONS FOR THOUGHT AND DISCUSSION

Imagine that you are with a group visiting an archaeological site. Out of view of everyone else, you and a friend find a stone projectile point (sometimes known as an arrowhead) half buried in the ground. Would you dig it out and take it? What would you do if your friend took the artifact and pocketed it? Whom should you tell about your discovery?

Fantastic Voyage:

Discoveries on Mars By Jonathan Lunine

An illustration depicts the rover Spirit as it sits on the surface of Gusev Crater after landing on Mars on January 4, 2004.

In early 2004, a buglike mobile laboratory nicknamed Opportunity helped answer a question that had puzzled scientists for more than 100 years. It provided strong evidence that red, dusty, inhospitable Mars once had pools, rivers, or even lakes of liquid water on its surface. Opportunity was one of two *rovers* (remote-controlled robotic wheeled vehicles) sent to Mars by the National Aeronautics and Space Administration (NASA) to examine rocks and soils to determine possible past water activity.

The exploration of Mars came into something of a golden age in 2004, with three orbiting spacecraft and two roving labs studying the planet. The Mars Global Surveyor and Mars Odyssey, launched by NASA in 1996 and 2001, respectively, continued their orbit of Mars. Their data have ranged from detailed images of the Martian terrain to chemical measurements of the surface. Cameras aboard Mars Odyssey, for example, revealed vast fields of hydrogen—almost certainly bound in water ice—that triggered questions about the disappearance of water and the possibility of life once existing on the planet.

In December 2003, Mars Express became the first European spacecraft to visit the Red Planet. On December 19, Mars Express launched the probe Beagle 2, which landed on December 25 and was never heard from again. Nevertheless, Mars Express has captured many stunning images of some of the planet's unusual surface features. The spacecraft has

The rovers Spirit and Opportunity discover new evidence about the connection between Mars and water.

also found proof of sulfur compounds on the surface—circumstantial evidence of the existence of liquid water in the past.

NASA's two Mars Exploration rovers, however, have taken center stage. Spirit landed in early January 2004 in Gusev Crater. This crater lies at the end of a valley 900 kilometers (559 miles) long that cuts into one edge of the crater. Spirit initially found little evidence of water but, in March 2004, the rover discovered fractures filled with minerals that hint at past water-related activity.

Opportunity landed later in January in a vast dusty plain called the Meridiani Planum, where orbiting instruments had previously detected hematite. This mineral usually forms in the presence of water. At Meridiani, Martian science got a lucky bounce. As Opportunity's airbags struck the surface, the spacecraft careened off in a direction different from its planned path and came to rest inside a small crater, informally named Eagle Crater. At Eagle Crater scientists discovered the evidence they were seeking. Four chemical and geologic lines of evidence convinced scientists that at some point early in the history of the solar system, liquid water flowed across what was once a shallow sea here.

The discovery that Mars once had liquid water has, of course, led to another question about Mars: Has life ever existed on Mars? In June 2003, NASA announced plans to launch the Phoenix Mars Scout in 2007 to study one of Mars's polar regions. Scout's mission will include drilling into Martian ice to search for *organic* molecules (molecules created by living things). NASA also announced plans to send other rovers to Mars in 2009 to search for and possibly collect animal and plant fossils at sites where liquid water may have hosted life. If the missions go as planned, sometime after 2010 the first samples collected by these robotic explorers will return to Earth for study.

An astonishing, 360-degree view of Eagle Crater, Opportunity's landing site, appears in an image created with photographs taken by the rover's navigational and panoramic cameras over three days in January 2004. Opportunity, still sitting near its airbags and ramps, surveys the scene from the center of the image. Tracks in the fine Martian soil show the rover's path as it explored the crater, which is about 22 meters (72 feet) in diameter.

The author:
Jonathan Lunine is a professor of planetary science at the University of Arizona Lunar and Planetary Laboratory in Tucson, Arizona.

Spherical objects, nicknamed "blueberries," cover the floor of Eagle Crater at Meridiani Planum, Opportunity's landing site. Opportunity's chemical analysis of the spheres led scientists to conclude that the blueberries—which are only millimeters in size—consist of hematite, an iron-bearing mineral that usually forms when iron is exposed to water and oxygen. The presence of the blueberries helped convince scientists that water once flowed across the surface of the crater.

Deposits of hematite appear in various colors in a composite image of one section of Eagle Crater. Scientists created the image by combining data from Opportunity's Miniature Thermal Emission Spectrometer (Mini-TES) with an image from Opportunity's panoramic camera. The Mini-TES detects infrared radiation emitted by objects. The red and orange patches represent areas with high levels of hematite, while those colored blue and green have lower levels. The sharp boundary from hematite-rich to hematite-poor surfaces corresponds to changes in the surface texture and color. The hematite-rich surfaces have ripples, suggesting that wind moved hematite there. Opportunity detected little hematite (white) in areas where the rover's airbags compressed the soil as the rover rolled to a stop. Scientists suggested that, somehow, the bouncing of the spacecraft eliminated the signal the hematite emitted.

Tiny waves of wind-blown soil crest and dip across the surface of Gusev Crater in a *false-color* image taken by the rover Spirit. (A false-color image does not show the true colors of an object but uses shades that enhance, contrast, or distinguish details.) The area shown in the image measures about 3 centimeters (1.2 inches) across. Coarse particles on the crests of the waves, photographed by the rover's microscopic imager, helped scientists determine that the waves were created by gentle winds. (Faster winds would have created particles with a more uniform shape.) Such findings are helping scientists learn more about the direction and speed of the winds that help shape the Martian surface.

A rock that was nicknamed "Last Chance" provided scientists with more evidence that Eagle Crater may once have lain along the shore of a sea. The rock, which measures about 10 centimeters tall (4 3.9 inches), consists of thin layers called *cross-laminae* that are only 1.4 centimeters (0.6 inch) thick. On Earth, cross-laminated rock usually forms as mineral grains and other types of sediment settle in layers on the beds of rivers, lakes, or oceans over time. Currents in the water push and shape the sediment so that the cross-laminae, like those in "Last Chance," eventually lie at angles to one another.

Close-up images of "Last Chance," taken by Opportunity's microscopic imager led scientists to conclude that the water that created the cross-laminae flowed from left to right. Tiny, rounded pebbles from "Last Chance" may represent a different type of rock than that in the cross-laminae. These spheres may have been carried along by the water and dropped into the layers as they formed.

1 cm

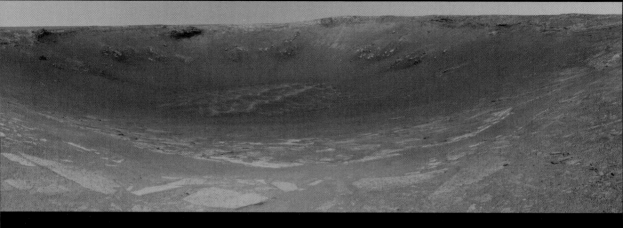

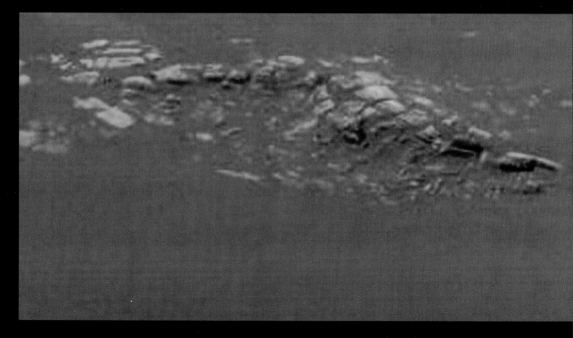

In May 2004, Opportunity reached Endurance Crater (top), a formation the size of a stadium, after roaming across the Martian plains for six weeks. Scientists hoped that the walls

The bottom image, also taken by Opportunity, shows bedrock in Eagle Crater. Scientists hope to use the rock—which they believe is not as deep or as old as the bedrock at Endurance—to

age shows an area about 50 kilometers (30 miles) wide. If the system were on Earth, the entire canyon system would extend the Grand Canyon. The rugged surface features suggest that liquid water eroded parts of the canyon.

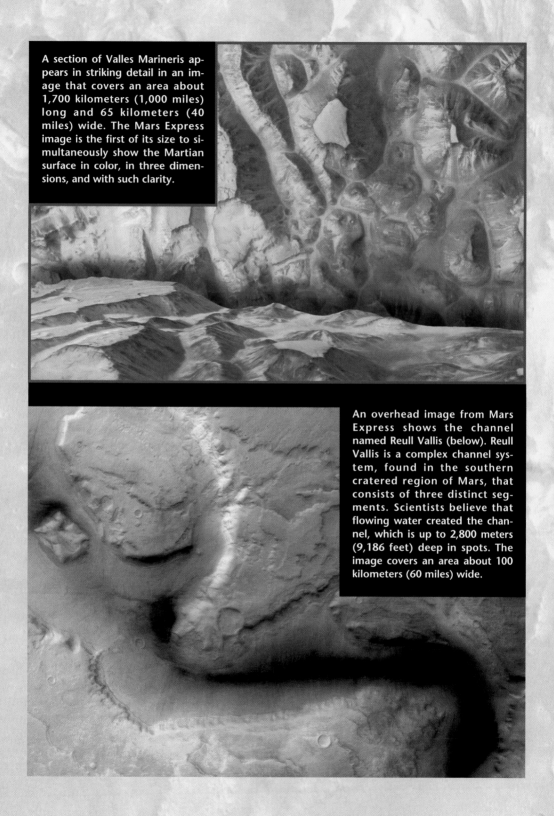

A section of Valles Marineris appears in striking detail in an image that covers an area about 1,700 kilometers (1,000 miles) long and 65 kilometers (40 miles) wide. The Mars Express image is the first of its size to simultaneously show the Martian surface in color, in three dimensions, and with such clarity.

An overhead image from Mars Express shows the channel named Reull Vallis (below). Reull Vallis is a complex channel system, found in the southern cratered region of Mars, that consists of three distinct segments. Scientists believe that flowing water created the channel, which is up to 2,800 meters (9,186 feet) deep in spots. The image covers an area about 100 kilometers (60 miles) wide.

The spacecraft Galileo has captured the wonders of Jupiter as well as those of its moons.

Fantastic Voyage:

Discoveries on Jupiter

By Jonathan Lunine

Spectacular images of monstrous lightning storms, explosive volcanoes, and other amazing phenomena on Jupiter and its moons were beamed from the Galileo space probe for nearly eight years, enthralling scientists and the public. Although a number of spacecraft have explored Jupiter and its moons, Galileo became the first to collect information directly from the planet's atmosphere. The craft also observed Jupiter, the largest planet in the solar system, far longer and in richer detail than any other spacecraft has.

The National Aeronautics and Space Administration (NASA) launched Galileo in October 1989 from the space shuttle Atlantis. The spacecraft, which consisted of a main orbiter and a smaller probe, reached Jupiter in December 1995. On its arrival, the atmospheric probe, which had been released from the main orbiter about five months earlier, floated on two parachutes 200 kilometers (125 miles) through Jupiter's atmosphere. For nearly an hour before disintegrating, the probe endured crushing pressures and extreme temperatures while relaying information about conditions in *Jovian* (Jupiter-related) cloud layers to the main orbiter.

Originally, scientists intended Galileo's exploration of Jupiter and its moons to last for about two and a half years. Galileo performed so well, however, that in 2001 NASA extended the orbiter's mission by two years so it could fly by Jupiter's four largest moons—Io, Callisto, Europa, and Ganymede—to observe and study their different surface features. The main orbiter circled Jupiter 34 times before engineers intentionally crashed it into the planet on September 21, 2003.

Galileo helped scientists solve many mysteries about Jupiter. For example, scientists concluded from Galileo's data that Jupiter's chemical composition resembles what astronomers believe was the original makeup of the sun. Jupiter has roughly the same composition as the sun, but there are variations in the amounts of some of the elements.

Other major findings involved the nature of the water on Jupiter and some of its moons. Previous studies of Jupiter's atmosphere had led

scientists to expect that Jupiter would have water clouds in its atmosphere. To their surprise, scientists found none. However, images taken later by the orbiter revealed the presence of storm clouds that almost certainly held water. This difference, scientists concluded, means that water levels vary across Jupiter. Galileo also found evidence of the presence of liquid water oceans beneath the surface of Europa and deep within Ganymede and, possibly, Callisto. Galileo also found intriguing hints that Europa's subsurface ocean is—like Earth's—full of salt.

Scientists also learned more about the ways in which Jupiter's powerful magnetic field influences the many parts of its system, including its rings and moons. Data from the orbiter's *magnetometer* (an instrument that compares the strength of magnetic fields) revealed that Ganymede and Europa—but not Callisto—have metal cores. Galileo also found that Ganymede, Jupiter's largest moon, generates its own magnetic field, the only moon in the solar system known to do so.

In July 1994, Galileo's images of Comet Shoemaker-Levy 9's collision with Jupiter's nightside atmosphere became the first to document such an impact. On the way to Jupiter, Galileo obtained the first close-up images of an asteroid, Ida, and discovered the first confirmed moon orbiting an asteroid. Galileo's mission was the first detailed orbital study of a giant planet and its moons. Its success paved the way for Cassini-Huygens, an orbiter that NASA launched in 1997 to explore Saturn, which, like Jupiter, has a ring system. Scientists hope that these missions will lead to more explorations of Jupiter and the other outer planets.

The Galileo spacecraft orbits Jupiter in an artist's depiction. Galileo consisted of a main orbiter and an atmospheric probe, which was released as the spacecraft neared Jupiter. NASA named the probe after Italian astronomer and physicist Galileo Galilei, who discovered Jupiter's four largest moons in 1610.

The author:
Jonathan Lunine is a professor of planetary science at the University of Arizona Lunar and Planetary Laboratory in Tucson, Arizona.

A gigantic thunderstorm swirls through Jupiter's turbulent atmosphere in a *false-color* image taken by Galileo in 1996. (A false-color image does not show the actual color of an object but uses different colors to enhance, contrast, or distinguish details.) The white area in the image represents a thundercloud that is about 1,000 kilometers (620 miles) wide and extends 75 kilometers (45 miles) above background clouds—five times larger than thunderclouds on Earth. The higher levels of the cloud, like most other visible clouds on Jupiter, consist mainly of ammonia ice. The red area in the image represents the base of the thundercloud, which extends about 50 kilometers (30 miles) below the bases of surrounding clouds. This thundercloud base almost certainly consists of water, either as liquid or ice.

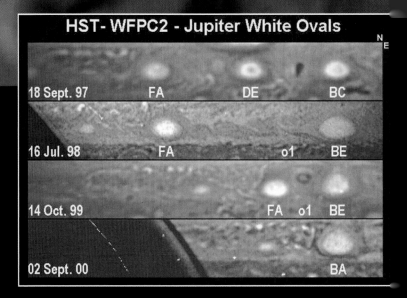

Huge Jovian storms, like the one shown at the top, appear as white ovals that merge into a single massive storm in images taken by the Hubble Space Telescope. Three atmospheric disturbances (above, top three rows) were each 8,000 to 12,000 kilometers (5,000 to 8,000 miles) wide. By September 2000 (bottom row), the remaining storms had combined into one disturbance about 12,000 kilometers wide. The winds in this storm, like other Jovian storms, blow counterclockwise. Evidence from Galileo revealed that heat from the planet's molten rock core powers Jupiter's huge thunderstorms.

Gossamer rings
Main ring
Halo ring
Amalthea
Adrastea
Metis
Thebe

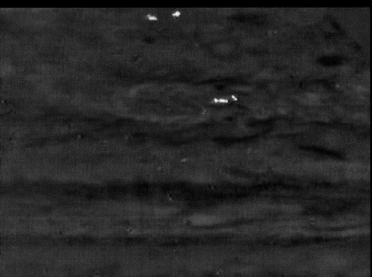

Jupiter's three rings consist of fine dust particles created when meteors strike the planet's four innermost moons, data from Galileo revealed in 1998. Jupiter's main ring is about 30 kilometers (20 miles) thick and more than 6,400 kilometers (4,000 miles) wide. The halo ring has particles that may be 100 times smaller than the width of a human hair. The gossamer rings actually consist of two rings, one embedded within another. Data analyzed by Galileo revealed that the dust in the gossamer rings is the same kind as that found on the moons Amalthea and Thebe, which orbit near this ring.

Jovian lightning storms 10 to 100 times brighter than those on Earth flash on the dark side of Jupiter in an image taken by Galileo in October 1997. Reflected sunlight from Io, Jupiter's volcanic moon, illuminated the clouds, making them visible. Astronomers theorize that the lightning forms in clouds containing water ice because the lightning appears at depths where such clouds would exist. They believe the lightning brightens a large area of the visible ammonia cloud layer lying above it. The storms here are from 1,000 to 2,000 kilometers (620 to 1,200 miles) wide.

Composite images of Ganymede (below) from Galileo reveal the deep depression that divides the moon's older dark areas (left, in the bottom image) from its younger bright regions (right, in the bottom image). Both areas consist mainly of water ice, with the darker terrain containing more rock. Impact craters (shown in greater detail in the top image) are especially common in the dark terrain. The grooves in the bright areas are actually numerous ridges and valleys that separated and stretched.

Ganymede appears to have large, frosty polar caps (inset) that may consist of water ice that is cleaner than that on the rest of the surface or made of another substance that *sublimates* (changes from a solid to a gas) more easily than water does. Measurements by Galileo revealed that the moon has a *magnetic field* (region in which magnetic force can be detected). This magnetic field, which is significantly weaker than Earth's, is the first known to be generated by a moon. The magnetic field suggests that Ganymede has a warm iron core and a layer of melted, salty water beneath its icy crust. Because salts conduct electricity, a salty ocean could generate electric currents that could produce a magnetic field.

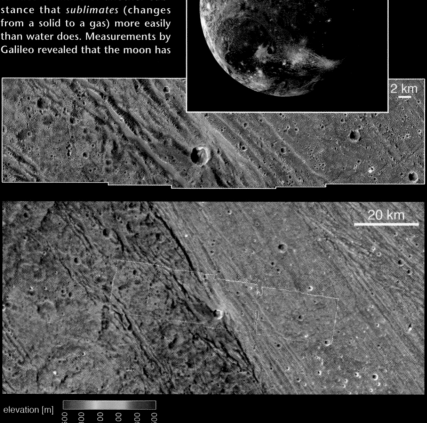

2 km

20 km

elevation [m]
500 300 100 -100 -300 -500

A volcanic *plume* (rising column of gas) erupts from the Masubi region of Jupiter's moon Io, which is about the size of Earth's moon. The plume extends 100 kilometers (62 miles) above the surface of the moon in this image, taken by Galileo in 1999. During Galileo's tour of Jupiter and its moons, a plume has appeared at different locations within Io's Masubi region.

A colorful patchwork of molten rock and sulfur flows from volcanoes that blanket the surface of Io in an image from Galileo (inset). Io has more active volcanoes than any other body in the solar system—perhaps 100 times as many as Earth. The explanation is gravity. Io follows an egg-shaped, rather than a circular, orbit because of the gravitational pull of fellow moons Europa and Ganymede. Jupiter's tremendous gravity pulls and squeezes Io as it orbits the planet. This constant stress has heated Io's interior to the melting point of rock, fueling eruptions of sulfur and silicate material.

Bright spots on the surface of Callisto (inset) represent craters formed by collisions with asteroids and comets. Callisto, the outermost of Jupiter's Galilean moons, has more impact craters than any other body in the solar system. This abundance of craters led scientists to believe that Callisto was a geologically dead world made of rock and ice. However, close-up images taken by Galileo of the surface (below) revealed a puzzling absence of small craters. Scientists believe that the surface is so fragile that the smaller craters are disappearing. They theorize that icy material on the surface is sublimating.

A color-enhanced close-up of Europa (above) taken by Galileo reveals striking details about the ice rafts that cover large areas of the moon's fractured surface. The rafts are areas of icy crust as much as 15 kilometers (10 miles) wide and possibly 100 kilometers (62 miles) thick that have split apart and rotated. Galileo's images of Europa (inset), as well as other evidence, have led scientists to conclude that Europa has an ocean of liquid water beneath its icy crust. Observations suggest that Europa's ocean contains more water than all of Earth's oceans combined. Some scientists have speculated that Europa's ocean may support some forms of life.

Is the Weather Getting *Weirder?*

By Fred Gadomski

During the summer of 2003, weeks of relentless sunshine and a stifling absence of wind pushed temperatures to dangerous levels across central and western Europe. That summer ranked as Europe's hottest in 500 years, researchers at the University of Bern in Switzerland reported in March 2004. London and Paris suffered through their highest temperatures on record. In France, where temperatures exceeded 40 °C (104 °F), the heat—and a lack of air conditioning—led to the deaths of nearly 15,000 people, the Bern researchers said.

The European heat wave followed an unusually cold, snowy winter in much of the world. The average snow cover across the Northern Hemisphere in the winter of 2002-2003 reached its greatest depth since comprehensive record keeping began in the mid-1800's. In India, Nepal, and Bangladesh, cold air surging south from ice-covered Siberia in January 2003 contributed to the deaths of thousands of people who were poorly equipped for the record low temperatures.

TERMS AND CONCEPTS

Atmospheric pressure: The amount of pressure exerted by a column of air in the atmosphere.

Climate: The weather of a place averaged over a long period.

Computer model: An electronic simulation of an object, idea, or phenomenon, such as weather and climate.

Cyclone: A storm with rotating winds of from 63 to 117 kilometers (39 to 73 miles) per hour.

Doppler radar: System used to track the movements of storms by detecting radio pulses reflected off moving raindrops and ice particles in clouds.

Fujita Scale: System used to rank the strength of tornadoes, ranging from F0 (weakest) to F5 (strongest).

Global warming: A gradual warming of Earth that began in the late 1800's.

Greenhouse gases: Gases in the atmosphere that trap the heat energy reflected by Earth's surface, thus warming the atmosphere.

Meteorologist: A scientist who studies weather and climate.

Proxy data: Indirect measurements of some factor that is impossible to measure directly—such as the use of tree rings to analyze climate conditions that existed hundreds of years ago.

Solar radiation: Heat and light generated by the sun.

The author:
Fred Gadomski is a meteorologist at The Pennsylvania State University in University Park, Pennsylvania.

A television correspondent struggles against strong winds and rising waters to file a report in the midst of a hurricane. Americans have seen an ever-increasing number of such dramatic reports since the 1990's as 24-hour cable news channels and other media outlets have expanded their coverage of extreme weather disasters.

Heat waves, cold spells, floods, droughts, tornadoes, snowstorms, and hurricanes all occur regularly, of course. Some weather experts and international scientific organizations, however, argue that these dangerous weather events are becoming more common, as well as more severe. In June 2003, for example, the World Meteorological Organization (WMO), a United Nations agency based in Geneva, Switzerland, reported that "new record extreme [weather] events occur every year somewhere in the globe, but in recent years the number of such extremes have been increasing." The WMO linked this increase to *global warming,* a gradual warming of Earth that began in the late 1800's. The organization warned that continued warming could cause weather extremes to worsen in coming years—with potentially devastating effects on human societies and *ecosystems* (communities of plants and animals) across the globe.

Has the weather really become more extreme? Or is the abundance of readily available weather information only creating a perception of weather running amok? How much do scientists actually know about long-term weather trends? And if the weather really is changing, are human activities to blame? Or is extreme weather just part of the complex but natural rhythm of climate—which refers to weather conditions over long periods?

Before we can even attempt to answer these questions, we need to define *extreme weather.* First, extreme weather is weather that

BETTER WAYS TO STUDY WEATHER

The technological ability of scientists to observe, measure, and analyze the weather has grown substantially since the early 1900's, when researchers often flew box kites to study wind patterns (right).

occurs infrequently, compared with usual day-to-day weather events. In addition, extreme weather causes relatively high levels of human suffering, significant disruptions in commerce, and costly property damage.

Scientists face several challenges in determining if certain weather events should be considered extreme. First, Earth's climate is constantly changing because it is influenced by many complex factors that vary over time. For example, long-term changes in Earth's orbit cause variations in the intensity of *solar radiation* (heat and light) reaching Earth's surface. Second, because of this variability, what was "extreme" at one time may be "normal" at another time. Consider the most recent Ice Age, a period from about 2 million to 11,500 years ago when gigantic ice sheets covered vast areas of what are now Europe and the United States. Today, of course, such conditions would wreak havoc on modern life.

Technological advances in the ways scientists observe, measure, and analyze the weather have also compounded the difficulties in comparing extreme weather events that happened centuries or even decades apart. For most of human history, the process of monitoring and recording weather depended solely on observers who witnessed events firsthand.

Today, computers offer a technologically sophisticated tool for analyzing such weather factors as wind, precipitation, temperature, and air pressure. A *computer model* (simulation) of a hurricane (above, left) shows details of the storm's swirling wind patterns and rising air currents. These simulations help improve meteorologists' understanding of how hurricanes form and move. Such models make it easier for meteorologists at the National Weather Service (above) to predict and track the development of serious storms and to alert the public to possible hurricane landfalls.

If there was no observer, there was no record. Now, because of weather satellites, no important weather event goes unnoticed—not even those in remote parts of the world.

Finally, the revolution in global communications has made weather information much more available today than it was in the past. Harrowing accounts of winter storms, tornadoes, and hurricanes have become a common feature on television newscasts, especially on 24-hour-a-day cable TV news. Because we see more weather coverage and can freely access an abundance of detailed weather information through the Internet, we are aware of more weather events that might be extreme. But this does not necessarily mean that today's weather is more severe than it was in previous decades.

Seeking a greater understanding of weather

How do we make sense of this confusing puzzle? *Meteorologists* (scientists who study weather and climate) seeking to understand the weather take a close look at Earth's complex system of atmospheric circulation. The weather, in the most general sense, is the air in motion. Masses of cool and warm air sink and rise, respectively, and drift from place to place as the atmosphere attempts to even out temperature differences between Earth's polar and equatorial regions.

The study of Earth's atmospheric processes produces a great deal of data on temperature, precipitation, storm strength, and other weather factors. Meteorologists use statistical tools to analyze these data, trying to identify trends in extremes. For example, a statistical analysis of temperature trends would tell a researcher that temperatures have moved into the extreme range if the average temperature over an area increased by a certain percentage above what would be expected to happen by chance alone. Reliable data about the weather over long periods of time and over large areas are essential for such detailed analyses.

Unfortunately, long-term weather records are scarce for most places on Earth. Weather satellites began orbiting Earth only in the 1960's. Even with satellite data, meteorologists still need ground-based observations to determine the effects of weather on Earth's surface—and surface data are very spotty. At least 70 percent of the planet's surface is ocean, where relatively few observations are, or have been, made. Large regions of the land have long been sparsely populated, so there are few weather records for these places. Even in areas with relatively abundant weather measurements, records seldom go back further than 100 years. Furthermore, standards of measurement and the quality of weather instruments vary greatly from one country to another.

To help compensate for this lack of data, some climate scientists use indirect measurements of weather conditions known as *proxy data*. For example, the rate at which trees grow—and the thickness of their

TEMPERATURE DIFFERENCES AND WEATHER

Weather is greatly influenced by the movements of huge masses of air whose motions result from temperature differences in the atmosphere. In general, the weather is stormier and more extreme when these temperature differences are large. In such cases, more energy is available to lift warm, moist air higher into the atmosphere. There, the air cools, and water vapor can condense into clouds, which produce rain and snow.

Winter storms are driven primarily by *horizontal* temperature differences— that is, differences between temperatures in the polar regions and equatorial regions. In the Northern Hemisphere, this contrast between cool air (blue to green) and warm air (yellow to red) is greatest in January, when less solar radiation reaches northern areas than at any other time of the year. As cool air masses move south and warm air masses move north, they often combine into swirling storms that push air high into the atmosphere, where clouds and precipitation form.

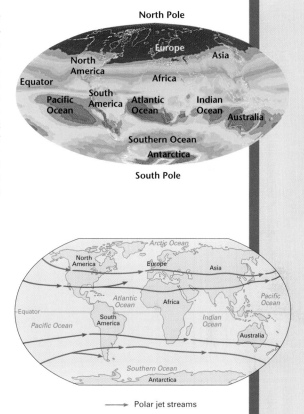

Horizontal temperature contrasts also provide energy for the polar jet streams (blue) and subtropical jet streams (red), bands of fast-flowing air currents that move eastward at high altitudes in both the Northern and Southern hemispheres. The jet streams supply energy to developing storms and help control the directions in which the storms travel.

→ Polar jet streams

→ Subtropical jet streams

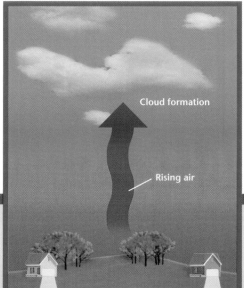

Cloud formation

Rising air

Summer showers and thunderstorms get most of their energy from *vertical* temperature differences—changes in temperature with height. The greater the temperature contrast between the rising warmer air (red) and the higher, cooler air (blue), the higher the air will rise. As a result, more water will condense into rain clouds.

TORNADO TRENDS IN THE UNITED STATES

Meteorologists have observed an increasing number of tornadoes in the United States since 1950. This increase may be due, in part, to improved methods of detecting tornadoes. However, weather data have revealed that the number of the strongest tornadoes—known as F3, F4, and F5 tornadoes—has declined during this time, except for an unexplained peak in the 1970's.

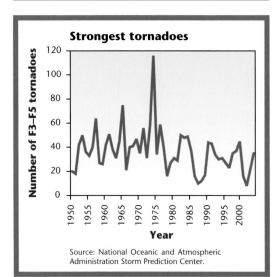

Total tornadoes

Source: National Oceanic and Atmospheric Administration Storm Prediction Center.

Strongest tornadoes

Source: National Oceanic and Atmospheric Administration Storm Prediction Center.

annual rings—depend on temperature and moisture. As a result, measurements of tree rings can be used by researchers to estimate what climate conditions were like at certain times in the past.

Proxy data may also be found in *cores* (cylindrical samples) of ice dug from Greenland and Antarctica and in cores of sediment dug from the ocean floor. Scientists can analyze chemicals in these cores to estimate temperature changes over thousands of years. For example, high levels of carbon dioxide or other *greenhouse gases* detected in ice cores suggest that the ice formed when global temperatures were relatively warm. Greenhouse gases in the atmosphere allow energy from the sun to reach Earth's surface but trap the energy radiated by the surface, thus warming the atmosphere.

By using weather-monitoring satellites and aircraft, ground-based weather stations, computer programs, and other methods, scientists have been able to gather and study reliable data about extreme weather events in various parts of the world. Their findings—covering tornadoes, hurricanes, floods, droughts, winter storms, and excessive heat—offer mixed results. For some types of events, researchers have found that extreme weather is on the rise. For other types of events, extreme weather seems to be decreasing. And for still others, investigators have failed to identify any obvious trend.

Tornado activity in the United States

Tornadoes, the most violent of all storms, have been observed on all continents except Antarctica, though they are more common in the United States than anywhere else. Official records of tornado activity in the United States began in 1950. In the 1970's, researchers at the National Oceanic and Atmospheric Administration's (NOAA) Storm Prediction Center in Norman, Oklahoma, reported an average of 858 U.S. tornadoes annually. The number of observed tornadoes reached 1,000 for the first time in 1973. By the 1990's, the yearly average had risen to more than 1,200 twisters.

At first glance, these figures may seem to indicate a steady increase in the overall number of tornadoes. However, experts note that most of this apparent jump in tornado activity relates to changes in the way tornadoes are observed. In the early 1980's, the U.S. National Weather Service (NWS) in Silver Spring, Maryland, began a program to improve the accuracy of the tornado warnings that its meteorologists issue to the public. As part of this program, the NWS regularly deploys teams to search for signs of tornadoes, assess tornado damage, and classify tornadoes according to a system called the Fujita Scale, which was developed by Japanese-born American meteorologist T. Theodore Fujita. This scale ranks tornadoes with designations ranging from F0 (the weakest) to F5 (the strongest). Since the program began, the number of strong tornadoes—those rated F3 to F5—has shown a slight decline, according to the NWS.

In contrast, the official number of weaker tornadoes—those rated F0 to F2—has risen. In the 1990's, the NWS began deploying a nationwide network of ground and airborne Doppler radar stations to track the movements of tornadoes and thunderstorms. Doppler radar works by bouncing radio waves off moving raindrops and ice particles in clouds and then detecting the reflected pulses. This radar network and the other parts of the NWS's tornado surveillance program have greatly increased experts' ability to identify twisters.

In addition, population in tornado-prone areas has increased steadily since the 1950's. Moreover, home video cameras and cellular telephones have become widespread. As a result, people are spotting and reporting many more tornadoes, especially weaker twisters that probably would have gone unreported in the past.

So, are a greater number of weaker tornadoes actually striking the United States now than in the past? As of 2004, the data failed to confirm that they were.

Hurricanes over the Atlantic

What about hurricanes? Many disruptive and sometimes devastating hurricanes have made headlines since the late 1980's. In 1989, Hurricane Hugo caused $8 billion in damage when it slammed ashore in the Carolinas. Hurricane Andrew ranks as the costliest storm in U.S. history, causing more than $25 billion in damage when it hit Florida and Louisiana in 1992. Hurricane Floyd in 1999 caused the largest evacuation in U.S. history.

The most extensive database on tropical storms focuses on those in the Atlantic Ocean. Tropical storms include *cyclones,* which have rotating winds between 63 and 117 kilometers (39 and 73 miles) per hour, as well as hurricanes, which have winds over 117 kilometers (73 miles) per hour. Information on tropical storms from the 1800's and early 1900's comes from land-based weather observations and the logs of oceangoing vessels. More reliable data on the frequency, intensity, and duration of these storms became available beginning in 1944, with the advent of reconnaissance aircraft. These aircraft fly into hurricanes to collect measurements on such factors as wind speed, moisture levels, and *atmospheric pressure* (the amount of pressure exerted by a column of air in the atmosphere). Since the late 1960's, weather satellites have further improved the ability of meteorologists to detect tropical storms over remote areas of the ocean.

According to the National Hurricane Center in Miami, Florida, fewer tropical storms occurred from 1991 to 1994 than in any other four-year period since the beginning of reconnaissance flights. This period averaged 7.5 tropical storms per year, while the long-term four-year average, as of 2002, was 9.8 per year. The number of the most intense hurricanes—those with winds greater than 177 kilometers (110 miles) an hour—dropped slightly each decade between 1944 and the mid-1990's.

Hurricane activity may follow a multi-decade cycle, climatologist Christopher W. Landsea of NOAA's Atlantic Oceanographic and Meteorological Laboratory in Miami proposed in 2001. Landsea's review of available long-term data on hurricanes of all intensities showed that relatively few hurricanes developed from 1900 to 1920. This was followed by a relatively active period of hurricane development, from the mid-1920's to 1960. From 1960 through the mid-1990's, hurricane activity was on a downward trend again. An increase in observed hurricanes since the mid-1990's may be associated with this cycle. However, because meteorologists have fewer than 100 years of reliable

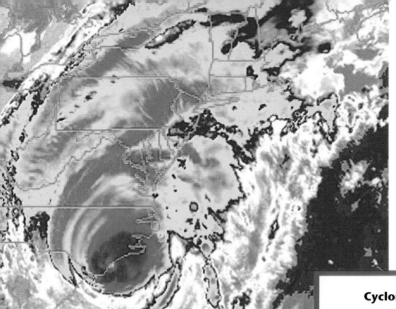

Scientists have not detected any clear trend in the number of tropical cyclones, or tropical storms, per year in the Atlantic Ocean since the 1940's. However, the number of these storms that have developed into intense hurricanes—with winds greater than 177 kilometers (110 miles) per hour—decreased until the mid-1990's. Since then, they have become more common.

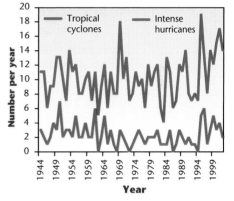

Cyclones and hurricanes

Number per year (0–20), by Year (1944–1999)

Tropical cyclones — Intense hurricanes

Sources: C. Landsea, N. Nicholls, W. Gray, L. Avila, *Geophysical Research Letters*, vol. 23, 1996, pp. 1697-1700; National Hurricane Center.

hurricane data, Landsea's observations cannot be confirmed yet.

Precipitation extremes— floods and droughts

Floods rank as the most dangerous of all natural catastrophes. They cause more than half of all deaths linked to natural catastrophes across the world, and they cause more damage than any other force of nature. In 1998, flooding and landslides resulting from Hurricane Mitch left more than 10,000 people dead in Central America. One of the costliest floods in U.S. history occurred in the Mississippi River Valley in 1993, leading to more than $21 billion in damage.

There are several types of floods. Seacoast floods usually occur when hurricanes or cyclones produce heavy precipitation and the strong winds of these storms drive ocean water onto land. River floods often occur in spring, when snow melts and combines with heavy rains. A third type of flood, called a flash flood, occurs when large amounts of rain fall in narrow waterways or paved urban areas, where the water is not easily absorbed.

The potential for serious river and flash floods may be growing. That is because precipitation extremes in the United States and many other countries seems to be increasing, according to a 2000 report by a team of investigators headed by climate scientists David R. Easterling and Thomas R. Karl of the National Climatic Data Center in Asheville,

North Carolina. The scientists noted that between 1910 and 1996, the number of episodes of intense precipitation—days with at least 50.8 millimeters (2 inches) of rain—increased by about 20 percent in the United States. This change, combined with greater urbanization in *flood plains* (land that borders rivers and is subject to flooding), has put more people at risk of flooding.

An analysis of European precipitation data from the 1900's cited by Easterling and Karl also shows a notable increase in the number of very wet days on that continent. For example, episodes of drenching rains rose in the European part of Russia by almost 4 percent every 10 years between 1936 and 1994. Other areas where heavy precipitation became more common during the 1900's included southeastern Australia, South Africa, northeastern Brazil, and northern Japan. As a result, flooding became more common in many of these areas.

At the same time, data cited by Easterling and Karl showed that other parts of the world are drying out. Heavy-precipitation days became less common in several regions during the 1900's, including Ethiopia,

WINTER STORMS OVER THE UNITED STATES

The frequency and intensity of severe winter storms in the United States decreased from 1970 to about 1990; then they began to increase. Scientists measure the intensity of these storms by their atmospheric pressure. In general, the lower the storm's atmospheric pressure, the more intense it will be.

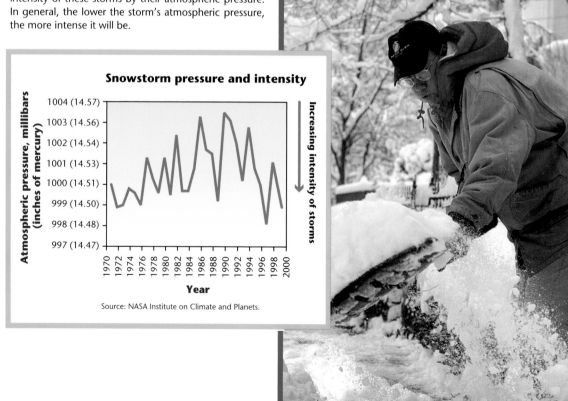

Snowstorm pressure and intensity

Atmospheric pressure, millibars (inches of mercury)

- 1004 (14.57)
- 1003 (14.56)
- 1002 (14.54)
- 1001 (14.53)
- 1000 (14.51)
- 999 (14.50)
- 998 (14.48)
- 997 (14.47)

Year: 1970, 1972, 1974, 1976, 1978, 1980, 1982, 1984, 1986, 1988, 1990, 1992, 1994, 1996, 1998, 2000

Increasing intensity of storms

Source: NASA Institute on Climate and Planets.

Kenya, Thailand, and southern Japan. In addition, a 2004 report by climate scientists at the National Center for Atmospheric Research in Boulder, Colorado, showed that the total global land area stricken by drought more than doubled between 1970 and 2002, from 12 percent to 30 percent. The greatest drying effects occurred in central Asia, the Middle East, and the Sahel region of Nigeria. In short, studies of global precipitation highlight how different parts of the world may be experiencing growing, but opposite, extremes.

Severe snowstorms

Winter storms do not usually cause as much death and destruction as other severe weather events do. However, they disrupt transportation, commerce, and the daily lives of millions of people every year. Meteorologists search for trends in the severity of winter storms in several ways. One way is to count the annual number of *nor'easters,* which are winter storms, often severe, originating off the northeastern coast of the United States. A 1999 report, based on data gathered by climate scientist Robert Davis of the University of Virginia in Charlottesville, examined the number of these storms that had occurred since the early 1940's. The data showed that nor'easters reached their greatest numbers during the late 1960's and early 1970's, then decreased until the late 1980's, when they began to rise in number again.

Some researchers have tried to gauge trends in the severity of winter storms by measuring snowfall. In the late 1990's, meteorologist Paul J. Kocin of the NWS studied several decades of snowfall measurements collected at more than 30 locations in the northeastern United States. He reported that the snowiest seasons of the 1900's occurred during the 1960's, the late 1970's, and much of the 1990's. Many climatologists, however, avoid using snowfall records to judge possible changes in weather, because—due to drifting and other factors—snowfall is among the most difficult weather variables to measure accurately.

Most climatologists prefer to assess winter storms by counting the storms and then plotting their intensity using their atmospheric pressure. In general, the lower the pressure, the more intense the storm will be. In 2001, the National Aeronautics and Space Administration's (NASA) Institute on Climate and Planets identified a drop-off in both the number of winter storms in the United States and in the storms' intensity from 1970 to about 1990. After that, winter storms increased in both frequency and intensity. In 2004, scientists continued to monitor winter storms to determine if this trend was continuing.

High temperatures over the decades

Among all weather events, high temperatures have received some of the greatest attention in recent years. One continuing study of temperatures in the United States was being conducted in the early 2000's by a group of climate experts that included Stanley Changnon and Kenneth Kunkel of the University of Illinois at Urbana-Champaign. These scientists have found that the United States sweated through more excessively hot days during the 1930's than in any decade since then—even taking into account the well-known hot summers of the 1990's. Excessively hot days were defined as days when the temperature reached the highest 1.5 to 3 percent of all temperatures recorded for those days.

Weather data from many sources show that Earth's average temperature rose between 0.6 °C (1 °F) and 1 °C (1.8 °F) during the 1900's. Data have also recorded a build-up in atmospheric levels of carbon dioxide and other greenhouse gases. Most scientists have little doubt that the two developments are linked and that human activities have contributed significantly to the build-up of these gases. The main such

COMPLICATED TEMPERATURE TRENDS

Few weather factors have received as much attention as temperature. A great deal of evidence shows that Earth's average temperature is on the rise. However, temperature trends in the United States present a complex picture.

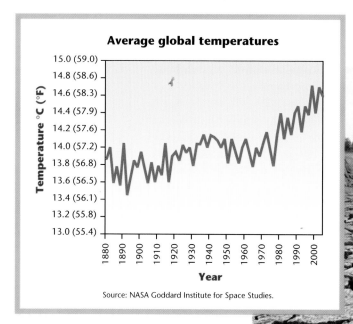

Average global temperatures

Source: NASA Goddard Institute for Space Studies.

Earth's current warming trend began in the late 1800's. Many scientists connect this warm-up to the burning of *fossil fuels* (coal, oil, natural gas), which releases heat-trapping carbon dioxide into the atmosphere.

activity is the burning of *fossil fuels* (coal, oil, and natural gas), which produces greenhouse gases.

Many meteorological *computer models* (simulations designed to mimic the dynamic processes of real weather systems) suggest that the rate of warming observed in the late 1900's will continue or even increase during the 2000's. An in-depth understanding of this process remains incomplete, however. For example, atmospheric levels of carbon dioxide rose steadily through the 1900's. However, data from the NASA Goddard Institute for Space Studies in New York City reveal that temperatures did not follow in lockstep. Average temperatures around the world rose rapidly from about 1910 to 1940, then cooled slightly from 1940 to 1980. Another episode of rapid warming followed, with most of the warmest years occurring in the 1990's and early 2000's.

Will a warming world lead to more extremes?

Some computer models predict global warming will result in more extreme and dangerous weather. Among these models are those from the Intergovernmental Panel on Climate Change, based in Geneva, Switzerland, and the World Water Council, an international water policy organization based in Marseilles, France. According to these models, the coming decades will likely see a growing number of extreme

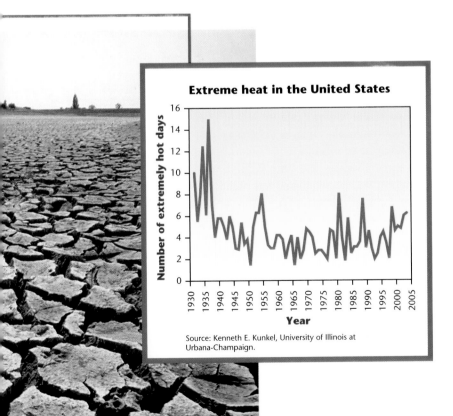

Extreme heat in the United States

Number of extremely hot days

Year

Source: Kenneth E. Kunkel, University of Illinois at Urbana-Champaign.

The United States experienced more extremely hot days—days in which temperatures reached the highest 1.5 to 3 percent of all temperatures ever recorded for those days—during the 1930's than during any other decade. Since then, scientists have found no obvious trend in extreme heat in the United States.

WHAT THE WEATHER MAY HAVE IN STORE

Increasingly severe weather may batter many regions of Earth as global temperatures continue to rise, according to some computer models. These predictions, which carry different degrees of uncertainty, take into account recent observed weather trends, as well as information about ocean currents, precipitation, and other factors that affect weather.

Weather event	Observed trends during the 20th century	Predictions for the 21st century
Higher maximum temperatures over most land areas	Very likely	Very likely
Higher minimum temperatures over most land areas	Virtually certain	Very likely
More heat waves over most land areas	Possible	Very likely
More intense precipitation events over many areas	Likely	Very likely
More wet spells in middle and high latitudes	Likely	Likely
More drought in middle latitudes	Likely	Likely
More intense tropical storms	Unlikely	Likely
More intense middle-latitude storms	Possible	Possible

Sources: D. R. Easterling, NOAA/National Climatic Data Center; Intergovernmental Panel on Climate Change; Munich Reinsurance Group.

weather events, including dangerously intense rainy seasons and flooding in some areas, longer and more severe droughts in other areas, and more killer storms around the globe. In spite of these models, a number of scientists believe that the current state of knowledge about the world's weather is insufficient to say with certainty that most of Earth's weather is becoming more extreme.

Computer models also offer different predictions on the nature of any increase in severe weather. For example, many models predict that warming will occur much more rapidly in polar regions than in the tropics. Such a pattern of warming would reduce the temperature differences between the poles and equator. Because many severe storms derive their energy from these contrasts, the result might be fewer intense storms. On the other hand, on a warmer Earth, more water would evaporate from the oceans and other large bodies of water. The increase in atmospheric water vapor could contribute to heavier rainfalls and snowfalls whenever storms did occur.

A lack of reliable, long-term data will likely hamper scientists' ability to come to any firm conclusions about trends in extreme weather for many more years. Given that reality, why have so many international reports predicted an increase in extreme weather? As with many professionals, two or more weather experts may look at identical information and draw different conclusions. In the absence of indisputable evidence, scientific conclusions may be affected by many factors, including social concerns and political perspectives. Furthermore, many scientists argue that the world cannot afford to wait for all technical disagreements on possible future weather extremes to be settled before taking action to slow global warming, such as by reducing our dependence on fossil fuels.

Improved evaluation of weather extremes will likely come from a greater exchange of weather data between nations, more thorough monitoring of weather conditions throughout the world, and new programs designed to analyze weather trends. For example, the WMO's Data Rescue Project is retrieving, preserving, and evaluating climate data from such developing nations as Vietnam, Rwanda, and Honduras. As these data become available to scientists, gaps in the global climate record will be filled. Another international project, called the Global Climate Observing System, is improving the collection and distribution of weather-related data from the ocean and atmosphere. Climate scientists expect this information to lead to earlier and more accurate detection of weather trends.

No doubt extreme weather will continue to produce dramatic headlines in the years ahead. Weather is a compelling part of the story of life on Earth, with a major impact on social, economic, and ecological conditions. In time, improved observations of the global environment and a better understanding of the forces that shape weather will help answer the two main questions confronting meteorologists in 2004: Is the weather becoming more extreme? And if so, are human beings responsible?

■ FOR ADDITIONAL INFORMATION

Books and periodicals

Easterling, David R. and coauthors. "Observed Variability and Trends in Extreme Climate Events: A Brief Review." *Bulletin of the American Meteorological Society,* March 2000, pp. 417-424.

National Science Foundation. *Forecasting the Future: Exploring Evidence for Global Climate Change.* National Science Teachers Association, 1996.

Wagner, Robert L. and Adler, Jr., Bill. *The Weather Sourcebook.* Globe Pequot Press, 1997.

Web sites

Climate Variability and Predictability—www.clivar.org

Intergovernmental Panel on Climate Change—www.ipcc.ch

National Climatic Data Center: Climatic Extremes and Weather Events— www.ncdc.noaa.gov/oa/climate/severeweather/extremes.html

Storm Prediction Center, National Weather Service—www.spc.noaa.gov

Amazing Spiders: Sex, Lies, and Video Watching

By Eileen Hebets

Imagine allowing yourself to be eaten by your mate to increase your chances of producing offspring. Think about disguising your movements to sound like a twig falling on a web in order to sneak up on your prey. These are just a few of the tactics spiders use to compete in a harsh world.

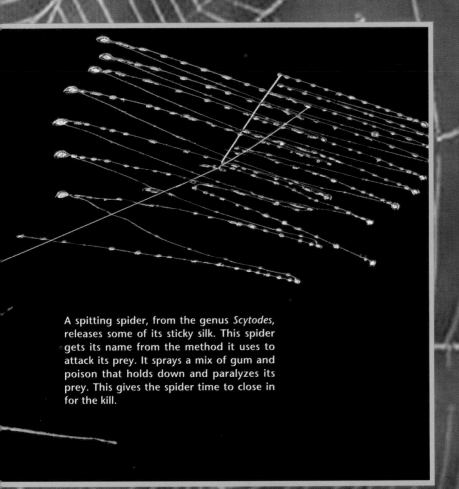

A spitting spider, from the genus *Scytodes*, releases some of its sticky silk. This spider gets its name from the method it uses to attack its prey. It sprays a mix of gum and poison that holds down and paralyzes its prey. This gives the spider time to close in for the kill.

Studying Spiders

TERMS AND CONCEPTS

Aggressive mimicry: A type of behavior in which a predator or parasite gains an advantage by looking like something else.

Arachnid: A member of the group of eight-legged animals that includes spiders, scorpions, and ticks.

Arachnologist: A scientist who studies arachnids.

Cannibalism: Eating one's own kind.

Courtship: Behavior designed to attract a mate for reproduction.

Foreleg: One of the front pairs of walking legs.

Opisthosoma: The rear part of the body of an arachnid.

Pedicel: The part of an arachnid's body that connects the prosoma to the opisthosoma.

Pedipalp: A short, leglike structure near the mouth and fangs of spiders used in reproduction and hunting.

Penultimate: The stage of life just before adulthood in arachnids.

Pheromone: A chemical released by one type of animal that transmits a message to other members of the same type.

Prosoma: The combined head and chest area of an arachnid.

The author:
Eileen Hebets is an assistant professor of insect biology in the College of Natural Resources of the University of California at Berkeley.

bout 400 million years ago, when land animals began appearing on Earth, spiders were among the first on the scene. Before dinosaurs roamed the planet and at a time when most of the continents were clustered together in one huge land mass, spiders were spinning webs.

Scientists have identified at least 35,000 different *species* (types) of spiders. That's more than the number of amphibian, reptile, bird, and mammal species combined. Spiders are also among the most *adaptive* of all animals—that is, they are able to adjust easily to their environment. Spiders live in nearly all of Earth's habitats and on every continent except Antarctica.

Spiders make up the largest group of animals that feed primarily on other animals. Most spiders weave silken webs to trap small insects and other animals as they fly, scurry along the ground, or crawl across branches. Some spiders lie in wait—sometimes in disguise—and then ambush and pounce on their prey. Others stalk their prey first, then spit out sticky silk that pins their prey to the ground so they can go in for the kill.

Such a variety of behaviors fascinates *arachnologists* (scientists who study spiders, scorpions, and related animals) like myself. In recent years, many researchers have discovered that spiders behave in ways that are more complex and intelligent than we had ever suspected.

My own studies have revealed that female wolf spiders can "learn" to choose certain males as mates based on the ornamentation on the males' front legs. Other researchers have learned equally fascinating things about spider behaviors. The discoveries that spiders have memories and the ability to "think" make them good models for increasing our understanding of learning and memory in all animals.

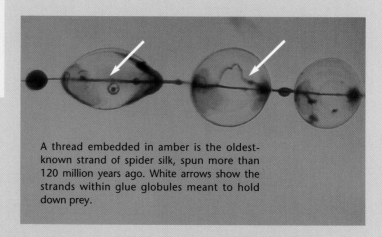

A thread embedded in amber is the oldest-known strand of spider silk, spun more than 120 million years ago. White arrows show the strands within glue globules meant to hold down prey.

AN ANATOMY LESSON

Although spiders differ in color, shape, and size, their bodies consist of the same structures. A few spiders have excellent eyesight. Most spiders, however, rely on touch, vibrations, and chemicals to gain information about their environment. Specialized parts include spinnerets (to spin webs) and fangs (to hold and kill prey).

External anatomy of a spider

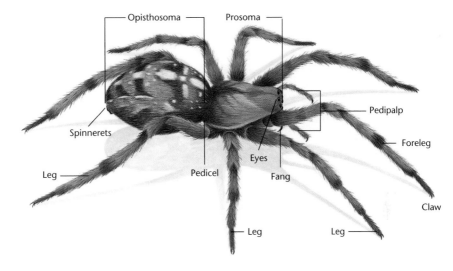

Opisthosoma — Prosoma — Pedipalp — Foreleg — Eyes — Fang — Claw — Leg — Pedicel — Leg — Leg — Spinnerets — Leg

Comparing spiders (actual sizes, including only body length; in order of appearance in Special Report)

	Schizocosa uetzi (male wolf spider), size: 7 mm			*Scytodes* (spitting spider), size: 6–8 mm
	Schizocosa uetzi (female wolf spider), size: 9 mm			*Portia labiata* (jumping spider), size: 7-9 mm
	Latrodectus hasselti (male Australian redback), size: 3–4 mm			*Evarcha culicivora* (mosquito-eating spider), size: 6–8 mm
	Latrodectus hasselti (female Australian redback), size: 10 mm			*Hogna helluo* (wolf spider), size: 24 mm
	Various groups, (Bolas spider), size: 11–14 mm			*Pardosa milvina* (wolf spider), size: 4–11 mm

The Choice Is Hers

arefully, I placed the adult female spider into a clear plastic arena, flipped on a tiny television that sat on one side, and started a videotape. On the screen, my spider star, an adult male, waved his *forelegs* (front legs) in a dance intended to get the female's attention. The female was interested. She slowly turned in circles, eventually settling down in front of the screen—the same way female spiders behave when watching live males.

My spiders belonged to a *genus* of wolf spiders (group of closely related species) named *Schizocosa*. These hairy, ground-dwelling spiders live mainly in the forests of the southeastern United States. Wolf spiders are a popular subject of study for arachnologists because the spiders are easy to capture and work with in the laboratory.

My movie for the female spider was supposed to do more than entertain her. The males of many species of wolf spiders have dark areas on their forelegs, which they often wave at females during courtship dances. I wanted to find out whether these areas of ornamentation affected the females' choice of mates.

In using the television, I was taking advantage of the wolf spiders' sharp eyesight, which they use to hunt, find mates, and avoid predators. In the mid-1990's, Dave Clark, a biology professor at Alma College in Michigan, and George Uetz, a *behavioral ecologist* (a scientist who studies animal behavior) at the University of Cincinnati in Ohio, had discovered that spiders can recognize and make sense of televised images. In other words, they can watch TV.

For my project, I filmed live courtship dances by males from a number of *Schizocosa* species. Then I changed the video images to create three courtship sequences. For the first sequence, the males appeared just as they were, with black or brown areas on their forelegs. For the second sequence, I removed all the ornamentation from the forelegs. For the third sequence, I digitally added black patches of hair to the males' forelegs to emphasize the ornamentation. Then I rolled the film.

While the females watched the various videos, I watched them to see if they were more interested in one type of male than another. *Schizocosa uetzi* females seemed equally interested in all three. I concluded that the ornamentation on male forelegs had no effect on a female's choice of mate for this species. So then why do the males have these areas of ornamentation?

I decided to look to the spiders' natural behavior. In nature, *S. uetzi* males mature, on average, a few weeks before females do. So in late spring, the spiders' habitats teem with mature males and immature females. My hypothesis was that the ornamentation the females see at this time influences their mate choices after they become adults.

THE DATING GAME

Experiments by arachnologist Eileen Hebets (below) have revealed that female wolf spiders use memory to decide on partners. Hebets wanted to see if ornamentation on the males' forelegs played a role in mate selection. In one experiment, Hebets had adult females watch videotapes of males performing courtship dances (right). The ornamentation on the males' forelegs varied—but the females reacted in the same way to all of them.

The second experiment involved pairing adolescent females with adult males with either black or brown forelegs. Hebets enhanced their leg ornamentation with nail polish (below, right). The results showed that adult females tended to mate with males with the same foreleg ornamentation they had seen in adolescence. The experiment showed that spiders learn and remember much better than scientists had believed.

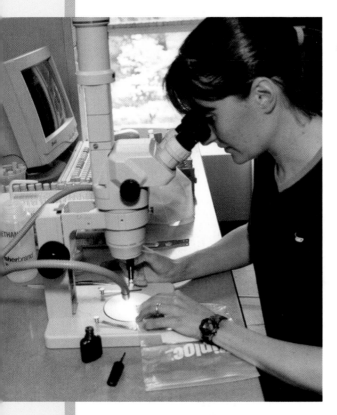

To test this idea, I collected immature females. Then I paired them with one of two groups of males whose forelegs I had painted with nail polish. The males in the first group had black forelegs; the males in the second, brown. I placed the *penultimate* females (females at the stage before adulthood) in a plastic box on a bed of silk from mature females. Then I placed mature males in the box for 30 minutes every other day until the females became adults. Chemicals in the silk fooled the males into thinking they were with mature females and so they began to dance for the immature females.

When the females matured, I paired them with either males that had a familiar foreleg ornamentation or males whose foreleg ornamentation they had never seen. I found that my females were much more likely to mate with males they were familiar with. Specifically, females that had been exposed to males with black forelegs mated with a male with black forelegs about 50 percent of the time. In contrast, females that had been exposed to males with black forelegs mated with a male with brown forelegs only 13 percent of the time. The other 37 percent did not mate.

Interestingly, how well a female knew a particular foreleg ornamentation also influenced the chances that she would eat the male during mating. Female wolf spiders don't eat their mates very often. Usually, they will either mate with a male or ignore him. However, my females ate about 27 percent of their mates if their ornamentation was unfamiliar. This number was much higher than the number of cannibalized males with a familiar ornamentation.

My experiment showed that penultimate *S. uetzi* females are clearly able to recognize and learn details about the appearance of the males of their species. In addition, the females are able to remember this information for more than three weeks until they become adults. Before this experiment, we did not know that spiders could learn and remember so well. Finally, the experiment revealed that spiders may use information they have learned to choose a mate.

This last finding adds to the debate regarding the importance that experience has on *cognition* (the act or process of knowing, including both judgment and awareness). In the past, scientists had believed that most animals choose a mate based on their genetic programming—that is, the pattern of genes they inherit from their parents. However, recent studies have shown that experiences early in an animal's life or even in adulthood may affect an animal's choice of a mate. Specifically, studies have shown that adult females may be influenced by the mating choice of another female. In other words, they will take a second look at a male just because another female seems interested in him. My study on *S. uetzi* shows that even in spiders, social experiences in adolescence may affect mating choices later in life.

A Mate and a Meal

or three hours, the male Australian redback spider had been performing his courtship dance for the huge female sitting nearby. Finally, he moved in, carefully climbed up the female's side onto her abdomen, and began to mate with her. Suddenly, the male—still in the process of mating—flipped over and positioned his abdomen directly over the female's mouth. She quickly responded by sinking her fangs into his body. Then, while mating continued, she slowly began to digest him.

The male's success in mating cost him his life. However, his death was no accident, according to behavioral ecologist Maydianne Andrade of the University of Toronto at Scarborough in Canada. In fact, his death offered great benefits.

Australian redback females are not the only animals that eat their mates during or just after mating, a practice known as *sexual cannibalism*. For many years, scientists assumed that the males were eaten because they couldn't escape fast enough from a hungry female looking for a meal as well as a mate.

Scientists have long known that an animal's urge to reproduce may be greater than its urge to survive. In 1996, Andrade showed that Australian redback spider males make the ultimate sacrifice—their lives.

While studying redback spiders (*Latrodectus hasselti*) in the wild in Western Australia, Andrade observed that female redbacks ate males only during mating. She also found that, although the males always offered themselves to the females during mating, the females ate the males only 65 percent of the time. Finally, she discovered that the females didn't help males perform the flip that put them in their suicidal position.

THE ULTIMATE SACRIFICE

Male Australian redback spiders offer themselves as food to the female during mating in order to ensure that they have offspring. The cannibalized males mate longer and fertilize more eggs than those that are not eaten.

A male redback (in red) positions himself on the female in order to mate.

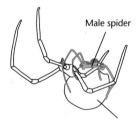

Male spider

Female spider

The male flips onto the female, placing his abdomen directly over the female's mouth.

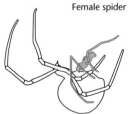

The female digests the male as the mating continues.

A male Australian red-back spider (above, right) approaches a much larger female that has already killed one mate (above, left). In some species, the urge to reproduce may be greater than the urge to survive.

Back in her laboratory, Andrade tried to determine what advantage this suicidal behavior might give the males. First, she allowed male and female redbacks to mate and then measured how long the matings lasted. She found that matings lasted more than twice as long when the females ate their mate than when they allowed the male to go free—about 25 minutes, compared with only 11 minutes.

Second, Andrade counted the numbers of eggs in the egg *sacs* (bags) laid by each female after mating with either a cannibalized or freed male. Again, she found that cannibalized males were more successful, fertilizing an average of 235 eggs, compared with 115 eggs for the freed males. Andrade concluded that males that were able to mate longer were able to fertilize more eggs.

Andrade also found that female redbacks, who may mate with more than one male, were much less likely to mate again if they ate their mate. Sixty-seven percent of the females who ate their mate rejected a second mate, compared with only 4 percent of the females who did not cannibalize their mate. As a result, cannibalized males were more likely to father all the offspring a female had.

In 2002, Andrade reported that the males, who live for only a few weeks, use up their supply of *sperm* (male sex cells) in just one mating. In 2003, she discovered that in nature, more than 80 percent of mature male redbacks die without ever finding a mate. Both studies show that by sacrificing themselves to the females, the males improve their chances of producing offspring during their first—and probably only—mating.

Bait and Switch

olas spiders are clever, efficient hunters. They produce chemicals that resemble the sex *pheromones* (chemical signals) that female moths use to attract males. As a moth flies nearer, the spider identifies its victim by its wing vibrations—and then attacks.

Researchers led by Kenneth Haynes and Kenneth Yeargan, *entomologists* (scientists who study insects) at the University of Kentucky in Lexington, studied a type of bolas spider called *Mastophora hutchinsoni*. This spider hunts two species of moths that give off very different sex pheromones and are active at different times of the night. The researchers discovered that the spider produces a blend of pheromones that appeals to both types of moths. The males of the moth species that feeds earlier find the spider's chemical mix about as attractive as they do their own pheromones. However, the male moths of the species that feeds later are turned off by the blend. To improve its ability to catch prey all night, *M. hutchinsoni* changes its blend as the night passes. At the beginning of the night, the spider produces chemicals similar to both types of moth pheromone. Later in the night, it produces less of the chemical that appeals to the early moths and more of the pheromones that attract the moths that feed later.

LIKE A MOTH TO A FLAME

To capture moths, a bolas spider hangs from a leaf or branch while dangling a single vertical line of silk with a sticky ball at the end. The spider produces chemicals called *pheromones* that attract male moths. As the moth approaches, the spider swings its line and traps the insect on the sticky part. The spider then pulls the moth in for a meal (below).

Jumping to Conclusions

ith its tufts of hair and long, thin legs, *Portia labiata*, a type of jumping spider, looked like just another bit of plant *debris* (garbage) on the forest floor. (Jumping spiders get their name because of their ability to jump from 10 to 14 times their body length to capture their prey.) Even when a female spitting spider came into view, the jumping spider remained still, watching. Unfortunately for *P. labiata*, the female was not carrying an egg sac in its jaws. Jumping spiders usually attack from the front, but this method was too dangerous now. Spitting spiders capture jumping spiders and other prey by sending out a poisonous, sticky silk that paralyzes their victims and pins them to the ground so they can rush in for the kill. But a female carrying its eggs to protect them against predators can't spit unless it first drops the sac. Cautiously, *Portia* began stalking the female—from behind.

The ability to make a decision after analyzing a situation may seem to be unusually advanced behavior for such a small-brained creature as a

THE EYES HAVE IT

Arachnologists believe jumping spiders are such good hunters because of their sharp vision. Three pairs of eyes provide a combined 360-degree field of vision. Their large main eyes can actually determine the shapes, sizes, and colors of objects. Scientists believe these eyes are nearly as complex as human eyes. The evolution of such sharp vision may be one reason jumping spiders have developed such unusual intelligence.

spider. But a jumping spider is no ordinary spider. It uses some of the most clever and flexible hunting strategies known.

P. labiata, also known as the white-mustached jumping spider, bases its hunting strategy on information it collects by watching its prey. In particular, it determines whether its prey is carrying an egg sac. This discovery emerged from research published in 2002. A team of scientists headed by zoologist Robert Jackson of the University of Canterbury in Christchurch, New Zealand, found that when *P. labiata* pursues a spitting spider with an egg sac, it makes a fast, efficient attack from the front. If the jumping spider chases an egg-less spitting spider, however, it takes a safer, roundabout route to come up on its prey from behind.

Making decisions is only one of the re-markably intelligent behaviors scientists have observed in jumping spiders. For example, *Portia* uses *aggressive mimicry* to capture food. Aggressive mimicry is a type of behavior in which a predator gains an advantage over its prey by appearing to be something else, such as dirt, leaves, or even another member of the species it is hunting.

Portia, which does not build webs, often invades the homes of web-building spiders and then stalks the web's owner. The jumping spider uses its legs and abdomen to vibrate the web to imitate the patterns of vibrations that males of the web-building species use as mating signals or even to imitate the vibrations made by trapped insects. The vibrations lure the web-building female out onto the web, making her easy prey for the jumping spider.

A female spitting spider, in the genus *Scytodes*, walks with an egg sac in its mouth to protect it. The presence of the sac helps *Portia labiata*, a spider that preys on spitting spiders, decide on its plan of attack. If *Scytodes* has a sac in its mouth, *P. labiata* is much more likely to attack it from the front because the spitting spider cannot spit. If the spitting spider does not have a sac, the jumping spider attacks from behind.

But the jumping spider's use of web vibrations is even more sophisticated than that, according to a 1996 study by Jackson; Stimson Wilcox of Binghamton University in Binghamton, New York; and Kristen Gentile of the University of Canterbury. The scientists conducted laboratory experiments based on spider behavior they had observed in the wild. They found that *Portia* sometimes disguises its movements by approaching a web when slight breezes—created by the scientists with small fans and other devices—shake the web. *Portia* may also wait to attack until the web owner is occupied wrapping its own prey in its silk.

Even more amazingly, the scientists also discovered that *Portia* is the only animal known to create its own "smoke screens." To disguise its movements, the spider sometimes vibrates the web of the spider it is stalking. These vibrations, the scientists found, are just like those caused by a twig falling on the web.

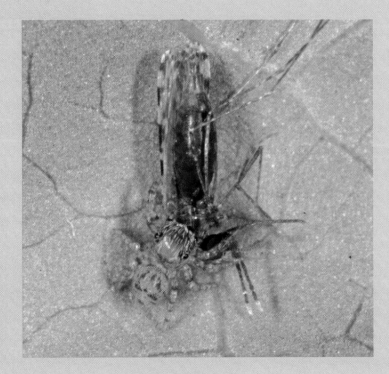

A young "mosquito terminator" (*Evarcha culicivora*) attacks a much larger female mosquito. The terminator preys on female mosquitoes, particularly those filled with blood that it can drain quickly.

The Terminator

varcha culicivora, a type of jumping spider that lives in Africa, likes fast food. It feeds on midges, nectar, and pollen. However, the spider's favorite meal consists of mosquitoes, preferably mosquitoes already filled with blood that it can drain quickly.

In general, spiders feed by using various mouthparts to suck the body fluids of their victims into their stomach. To eat their victims' solid tissue—for example, their internal organs and eyes—spiders first must spray on digestive juices that turn the tissue into a soupy mixture. However, feeding this way may take hours. For example, a large tarantula can reduce a mouse to a small pile of hair and bones, but the process takes about 36 hours, or about a day and a half. *E. culicivora* has been nicknamed the "mosquito terminator" because it picks up a quick meal of blood from mosquitoes that have already collected fluid from other animals, including people.

The mosquito terminator and its unusual eating habits came to the notice of zoologist Robert Jackson in 1995. Since then, Jackson has conducted ongoing field and laboratory research about this remarkable arachnid.

E. culicivora is a rather ordinary-looking spider that has a red face and grows only to about 8 millimeters (0.3 inch) long. The spider caught Jackson's attention because it seemed to prefer female mosquitoes over any other type of food. When he watched the spider feeding in nature, he discovered that 71 percent of the spiders' meals consisted of female mosquitoes that had fed on blood. Jackson found that the smell of blood turns the terminator into a killing machine. He and his colleagues have watched terminators quickly kill as many as 20 mosquitoes in a row.

Why is the terminator so crazy about blood? In the laboratory, Jackson and his colleagues raised a large number of the spiders and fed them different types of food. Then he measured how fast the spiders grew and how long they lived. The spiders that fed on a mixture of blood and other foods ranked first in both these categories. Jackson also found that the spiders that received blood attracted more mates than the spiders that were given other foods.

Finding blood-filled mosquitoes to prey on is one of the most amazing abilities of the terminator spider. The key to the spider's success is its extraordinary eyesight. Laboratory studies have revealed that the spider's vision is as sharp as that of *primates* (a group that includes monkeys, apes, and human beings). In fact, the spiders' vision is so good that it can detect a mosquito hidden among a crowd of other insects.

Exactly how does the terminator spider identify mosquitoes that have fed recently? To find out, Jackson and his colleagues created unusually shaped mosquitoes with body parts from dead mosquitoes. For example, they created mosquitoes with abdomens that were flat or full and mosquitoes with different numbers of legs. Then they mounted the altered mosquitoes on corks and presented them to terminator spiders. They found that the spiders identified blood-filled mosquitoes by their antennae and their abdomen. The antennae of the male mosquito look like tiny feathers, while those of the female— which drinks blood—are much smaller. The spiders preferred mosquitoes with smaller antennae, even if those antennae were attached to a male's body. In addition, the spiders chose mosquitoes with abdomens that stuck out, suggesting that they were full of blood. The experiments showed that the terminator spider can see differences between mosquitoes and then use that information to make decisions about which mosquitoes to attack.

Jackson planned additional research to explore the connection between the spider's sharp eyesight and its thinking ability. Studies of the spider may also provide information to help health experts in their battle against mosquitoes that cause disease.

Playing Defense

I n the cannibalistic world of spiders, predators often end up as prey. For their own defense, spiders have developed many strategies to avoid being eaten and to protect their eggs. One interesting example of defense involves the unusual case of a fly that preys on spiders, described in 2002 by a research team led by behavioral ecologist Craig Hieber of Saint Anselm College in Manchester, New Hampshire. The scientists explored the relationship between the colonial web-building spider (*Metepeira*

THE SPIDER AND THE FLY

Behavioral ecologist Craig Hieber (below) prepares an experiment to investigate how the colonial web-building spider recognizes the approach of the sarcophagid fly (right), which preys on the spider's eggs. The fly vibrates the web so that the spider thinks that it has a meal (right, middle). When the spider comes out, the fly goes after the eggs. Hieber pinned live sarcophagid flies and houseflies to cork and placed them near colonial web-building spiders (right, bottom). The spiders seemed to recognize the sound pattern of the sarcophagid fly's wingbeats.

incrassata) and the sarcophagid (*sar KOFF uh jid*) fly (*Arachnidomyia lindae*), whose young eat the spider's eggs. The scientists found that both the spider and the fly use several tactics to trick or outsmart each other.

The sarcophagid fly attempts to lay an egg on the surface of a spider's egg sac. If the larva can escape detection long enough to dig through the surface of the sac—a process that takes about 15 minutes—it can devour the spider eggs from the inside without the spider ever knowing. In the field in Veracruz, Mexico, the scientists observed that as a sarcophagid fly nears a colonial web-builder's web, the spider begins taking defensive actions. It moves around the egg sac to try to place itself between the sac and the fly. It also uses its mouthparts to search the surface of the egg sac for fly larvae. However, the spider does not take these actions if a different type of fly lands on the web.

The scientists theorized that the spiders could tell approaching sarcophagid flies from other types of flies by the *frequency* of their wingbeats (the rate at which the fly beats its wings). To test this theory, the scientists tied live sarcophagid flies and common houseflies, which don't eat the webbuilder's eggs, to insect pins. Then they placed the flies at random near colonial spiders guarding their egg sacs. Both types of flies beat their wings during the experiment. The researchers discovered that spiders began acting defensively when they were near a sarcophagid fly more often than they did when they were near a housefly. This behavior suggests that the spiders can recognize the sarcophagid fly based on the sound pattern of its wingbeat.

In another example of attack and defense, a sarcophagid fly may vibrate the center of a colonial web-builder's web—where the silk is not sticky—to imitate the vibrations caused by prey struggling to escape the web. Then the fly moves off a short distance and waits for the spider to leave her eggs. The scientist found, however, that after running to check on the vibrations several times and finding no prey, the spider cuts the vibrating line to stop the phony signal. After the fly leaves, the spider repairs the line.

A large wolf spider, *Hogna helluo* (below, right), stalks a smaller wolf spider, *Pardosa milvina*. Scientists have discovered that *P. milvina* takes steps to avoid *H. helluo* only if the larger spider has recently eaten another *P. milvina*. *P. milvina* ignores *H. helluo* spiders that have eaten other types of prey.

Surprising discoveries are showing that the mysterious world far, far beneath our feet may be even stranger than what's been fantasized in novels or in films.

THE CORE:
New Findings About Earth's Final Frontier

By Kate Ravilious

E arth's core is a restless, alien place that has long captured the public's imagination. Many novels and movies have attempted to bring this strange place to life. If we could actually journey to this deep environment, scientists say, we would encounter churning, seething rock melted to a hot fluid by temperatures approaching those on the surface of the sun. We would also witness electrical currents sweeping through the fluid, bubbles of gas exploding, and mountains the size of peaks in the Himalaya collapsing in monstrous avalanches. This is the planet's *outer core*, which fills an area larger than Mars.

Within this nightmarish inferno lies the *inner core*, a spinning ball of iron and rock that is a little larger than Pluto. Hotter even than the outer core, the inner core is squeezed solid by crushing pressures 3.5 million times greater than those at the surface of Earth.

Although the core lies thousands of kilometers below us, it is crucial to life on the surface. The heat, motion, and electricity of the outer core generate a magnetic field around Earth—like that made by a giant

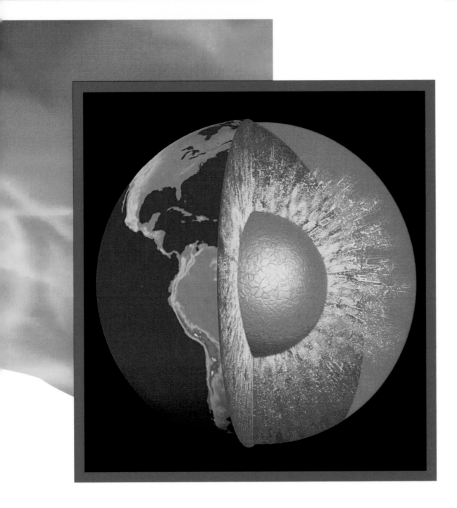

magnet—that acts as an invisible, protective shield. This shield deflects the *solar wind,* a flow of electrically charged particles generated by the sun. Without this shield, the solar wind would enter and sweep away our atmosphere. By preserving our blanket of air, the magnetic field preserves life.

In 2004, scientists were exploring exciting new discoveries about the core. For example, some investigators were following up on findings that the inner core may spin at a faster rate than the rest of the planet does and that it may house an even smaller "inner, inner" core. Other researchers were developing new theories to explain why the core is still so hot more than 4.5 billion years after Earth's formation; how activity within the core influences the magnetic field; and why the magnetic field periodically changes direction.

No intrepid explorers have ever been able to dig a tunnel to the center of Earth and study the rocks along the way. The distance from Earth's surface to the outer core is about 2,900 kilometers (1,800 miles), the

The author:
Kate Ravilious is a free-lance science writer who specializes in the physical and environmental sciences.

approximate distance between Seattle, Washington, and Port-of-Spain, Trinidad and Tobago. Compared with this distance, the deepest hole ever dug—the Kola well in northern Russia—is a mere pinprick. This well penetrates 12.3 kilometers (7.6 miles) into the *crust,* Earth's outermost layer, which ranges between 8 and 40 kilometers (5 and 25 miles) in thickness. The Kola well does not even reach into the *mantle,* a layer of shifting, partially *molten* (melted) rock that extends to the outer core—and on which the crust and continents float.

First attempts to "see" inside Earth

How do scientists study—and how have they already learned so much about—a region of the planet that no one has ever seen? They have been forced to rely on indirect methods to study this subterranean world. Laboratory experiments and mathematical calculations are the oldest of these methods. In 1798, the English chemist and physicist Henry Cavendish accurately calculated Earth's *mass* (amount of matter in an object) based on now-classic laboratory experiments

THE WORLD UNDER OUR FEET

Earth consists of four main layers surrounded by an atmosphere. The surface of Earth is a thin, rocky layer called the *crust.* Below the crust is the *mantle,* a thick layer of solid, partially *molten* (melted) or completely molten rock, depending on depth. The core is divided into an *outer core,* consisting mainly of molten iron, and an *inner core,* almost completely made of solid iron.

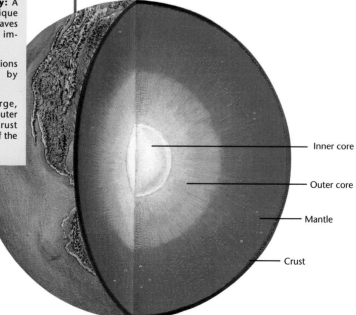

- Inner core
- Outer core
- Mantle
- Crust

using a *torsion balance,* a very sensitive device for measuring forces of push or pull. Cavendish also arrived at a remarkably accurate measurement of Earth's *density* (the amount of mass in a given volume).

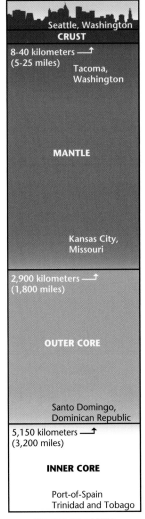

Cavendish's findings proved that Earth is solid—not hollow, as the ancient Greeks believed. He also showed that Earth's average density is greater than the average density of the rocks found on its surface. At first, this difference puzzled scientists. However, they soon realized that the presence of an extra-dense central core inside the planet could explain the difference. They turned to an out-of-this-world source to learn more about the makeup of this core—*meteorites.* These chunks of rock and metal from space that crash onto Earth's surface provide a wealth of information because they—and everything else in the solar system—formed from the same whirling cloud of dust and gas.

By the mid-1800's, scientists knew that some meteorites consist almost completely of iron; others consist chiefly of stone; and still others have nearly equal amounts of both. Scientists began using different types of meteorites as models for different layers of Earth. They concluded that as early Earth cooled from its completely molten phase, iron and other heavy metals sank to the center, forming a dense core surrounded by a lighter, stony crust. The core, scientists deduced, consists of iron and various *alloys* (metallic compounds mixed with other metals). This makeup resembles that of meteorites called chondrites, which may be leftover material from the formation of the planets.

Reading the waves

At about the same time that scientists began studying meteorites for clues to inner Earth, they discovered *seismic waves,* vibrations inside Earth caused by earthquakes. The vibrations travel outward in all directions from an earthquake's point of origin. Instruments called seismometers can record the location, direction, duration, and intensity of these waves.

Over the years, seismic waves have become scientists' most important tool for probing inner Earth. Of particular value are two types of seismic waves called primary (P), or compressional, waves and secondary (S), or shear, waves. P waves squeeze and pull back rock, like an accordion. S waves cause rock to move from side to side, like a snake slithering across the ground. The direction and speed of P and S

HOW FAR IS IT TO THE CENTER?

A journey from Earth's surface to the center of the core would cover approximately the same distance as a trip from Seattle, Washington, on the Pacific Coast, to Port-of-Spain, in the Caribbean island-country of Trinidad and Tobago.

Seattle, Washington
CRUST
8-40 kilometers
(5-25 miles)
Tacoma, Washington

MANTLE

Kansas City, Missouri

2,900 kilometers
(1,800 miles)

OUTER CORE

Santo Domingo, Dominican Republic

5,150 kilometers
(3,200 miles)

INNER CORE

Port-of-Spain
Trinidad and Tobago

CENTER OF EARTH
6,437 kilometers
(4,000 miles)

HOW SCIENTISTS STUDY THE CORE

Because neither explorers nor scientific instruments have been able to travel to the core, scientists have used indirect methods to study this fearsome region.

Geologists work with a *seismometer,* an instrument that measures the location, direction, and intensity of *seismic waves.* These waves, which are vibrations in Earth caused by earthquakes, rank as one of scientists' most valuable tools for probing inner Earth.

waves depend on the characteristics of the rock they are passing through. For example, the waves travel faster through colder, denser material than they do through molten rock. In addition, P waves can travel through both solid and liquid material. S waves, because of their side-to-side nature, can travel only through completely or partially solid material.

In the early 1900's, scientists found that below a certain depth, P waves slow down sharply and bend toward the center of Earth. At about the same depth, S waves disappear or are reflected back to the surface. These findings led researchers to conclude that this depth marked the boundary of the core. They also theorized that the inability of S waves to pass beyond this depth indicated that the core is molten.

Then in 1936, Danish seismologist Inge Lehmann noticed that although P waves slow down as they pass through the core, they still travel faster than they would if the core was composed completely of molten rock. From this evidence, she concluded that the core has a solid center that acts like an expressway for the waves.

Today, seismic research, mathematical calculations, and meteorite-composition studies remain important methods of teasing out information about the structure and chemistry of the core. Scientists also rely on

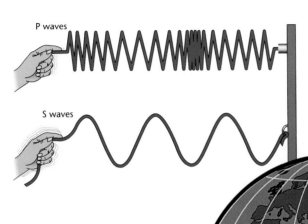

P waves

S waves

Earthquakes produce two main types of seismic waves: primary (P) waves, which squeeze and pull back rock, and secondary (S) waves, which move rock from side to side. The direction and speed of P and S waves vary, according to the type of rock they pass through.

Mantle

laboratory studies that subject various types of rock to high temperatures and pressures in an attempt to mimic conditions in the core. Since the 1980's, however, technological advances, particularly in computers, have revolutionized the study of Earth's interior.

For example, seismic studies took a leap forward with the development of a computer-based technology called *seismic tomography.* This technique resembles a medical imaging system called computed tomography (CT), which uses X rays to produce images of different cross sections of the human body. A computer then converts the cross sections into three-dimensional pictures of a particular organ, muscle, or bone. In a similar way, seismic tomography produces three-dimensional images of Earth's interior using seismic waves instead of X rays. Scientists sometimes feed these images into *computer models,* simulations that allow researchers to create detailed maps of the composition, temperature, pressure, and density of Earth at various depths.

Some of the most important recent studies of the core have been based on seismic research involving the atomic arrangement of the iron crystals that make up much of the core. Some crystals consist of molecules whose atoms have a uniform arrangement. These *isotropic* molecules look basically the same from every direction. In contrast, other crystals consist of molecules whose atoms have an uneven arrangement. The appearance of these *anisotropic* molecules differs

Seismic tomography is a computer-based technique for creating detailed maps of the structure and activity inside Earth. A map of Earth's mantle made with this technique indicates areas where seismic waves traveled at fast speeds (bluish) or slow speeds (yellowish), depending on the density, chemical composition, and temperature of the particular areas.

according to the direction from which they are viewed. For example, from some directions their atoms may seem to be arranged like the aisles of a supermarket viewed from the front of the store—in parallel lines running straight away from the viewer. From other angles, the atoms may seem to follow a crosswise arrangement, like the aisles viewed from the side of the store.

Faster-spinning inner core?

Studies of the arrangement of the core's crystals led in 1996 to a surprising theory about the nature of the inner core. Paul G. Richards and Xiaodong Song, seismologists at the Lamont-Doherty Earth Observatory in Palisades, New York, studied seismic data from 30 years of earthquakes in the South Sandwich Islands in the South Atlantic Ocean. The two scientists noticed that seismic waves from the islands reached seismic recording stations in Alaska (after passing through the core) one-third of a second faster in 1995 than they did in 1967. They concluded that the shorter traveling time resulted from changes in the

EARTH'S GIANT BAR MAGNET

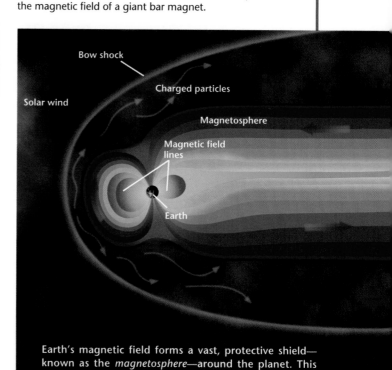

Earth is surrounded by a magnetic field—generated by fluid currents inside the outer core—that is shaped like the magnetic field of a giant bar magnet.

In the magnetic field of a bar magnet, a series of *field lines* of magnetic force flow out of one pole, make a wide curving pattern, and flow into the other pole.

Earth's magnetic field forms a vast, protective shield—known as the *magnetosphere*—around the planet. This shield deflects most of the electrically charged particles streaming from the sun in the solar wind. The solar wind pushes against the force of the magnetosphere, forming a shock wave called the bow shock.

inner core's angle of anisotropy in relation to the planet's surface. In other words, in 1995 the crystals' atoms were more in line with the direction that the waves traveled than they were in 1967. Because of this, the waves were able to move through the crystals more quickly in 1995—just as a person could obviously move through a supermarket more quickly by walking straight down the aisles than by climbing over the shelves.

This change in anisotropy implied, according to Richards and Song, that the inner core rotates at a different rate than the crust does. Calculations by the seismologists suggested that the inner core is rotating eastward a few tenths of a degree per year faster than the crust. This means that every 1,000 years, the inner core makes approximately one complete revolution inside Earth.

Why would the inner core spin more quickly than the rest of the planet? Although scientists are unsure, they have advanced a number of theories. Perhaps the gravitational pull of the moon and sun is slowing the rotation of the upper parts of the planet more effectively than it is the lower parts. Or perhaps the magnetic field generated by the outer core is somehow affecting the movement of the inner core. Yet another possibility, according to some scientists, is that Richards and Song have come to a wrong conclusion and that the inner core is not rotating differently at all. More research will be necessary to settle this issue.

An inner, inner core?

Another big surprise based on estimates of anisotropy came in 2002. Geophysicists Adam M. Dziewonski and Miaki Ishii of Harvard University in Cambridge, Massachusetts, reported evidence for the existence of a previously unknown core within the inner core. The scientists reported that this object lies at the very center of Earth, is approximately 600 kilometers (373 miles) in diameter, and has a different, unknown structure than the rest of the inner core. They speculated that this "inner, inner" core consists of material left over from the original stuff from which Earth formed. If so, the "inner, inner" core would be the oldest unchanged part of our planet.

The road to this discovery began in the early 1980's, when scientists noticed that seismic waves traveling in a northward or southward direction—for example, from Alaska to Antarctica—move faster through the inner core than do seismic waves traveling eastward or westward—for example, from Indonesia to Brazil. The speedy north-south route perplexed scientists until 1986, when Dziewonski and his colleague, John Woodhouse, a geophysicist at Oxford University in the United Kingdom, became the first scientists to propose that the core's iron crystals were oriented in a north-south direction.

Dziewonski and Ishii followed up on this research by combing

ISOTROPY AND ANISOTROPY

Some geologists believe that Earth's inner core rotates faster than the rest of the planet. This theory arose from seismic studies and knowledge of the structure of crystals.

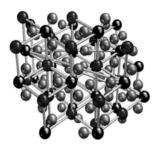

The molecules in crystals may be *isotropic* or *anisotropic*. An isotropic molecule, such as sodium chloride, or table salt (far left), has an orderly arrangement of atoms. It appears more or less the same when viewed from different directions. In contrast, an anisotropic molecule, such as calcium carbonate (left), has an irregular arrangement of atoms. It appears different when viewed from different directions.

through 30 years of earthquake data and examining all the records of seismic waves that had passed through the inner core. They realized that when the waves travel through the very center of the inner core, they travel at a different speed than when moving through the outer regions of the inner core. This led them to conclude that the innermost part of the inner core probably contains iron crystals with a different anisotropy—or some other difference in structure—than the rest of the inner core. However, this conclusion was the subject of debate.

The geodynamo and magnetic field

Although many questions remain about the core, scientists hope that a better understanding of the planet's magnetic field will help answer some of them. The magnetic field is created by electrical currents generated by movements of molten metal in the fluid outer core. Scientists believe that the fluid is stirred as some molten iron *crystallizes* (solidifies) and sinks toward the inner core, while lighter, buoyant elements bubble up toward the mantle. The flowing iron in the stirred, swirling fluid conducts electricity, and the movements of the electric currents give rise to the magnetic field. This process resembles the way an electric current traveling through a wire generates magnetism in an electromagnet. For this reason, geologists sometimes refer to the core as a *geodynamo*. A dynamo is something that changes mechanical energy into electric energy.

In August 2003, G. David Price, a mineral physicist at University College in London, described details about the possible chemical and physical makeup of the geodynamo. He first noted that the outer core must contain a greater proportion of lighter chemical elements than the inner core, because it has a lower density than the inner core. Price proposed that the top contenders for these lighter elements are sulfur,

Seismic waves travel through the anisotropic iron crystals that make up Earth's core at different speeds, based on the direction in which the atoms of the crystal are aligned. To illustrate this point, consider the following: A shopper can move through a supermarket faster by walking down the aisles (above, left) than by absurdly climbing over the shelves (above, right). In the same way, seismic waves can move through iron crystals faster if the crystals are aligned in the direction that the waves are moving. The apparent change in the alignment of the core's iron crystals in relation to Earth's crust implies that the core is rotating faster than the surface.

silicon, and oxygen. He based this proposal on the fact that all these elements are common in meteorites.

Price then used a computer model to analyze the interactions between these various elements as they move about in the core. The model indicated that the crystalline structure of the inner core is too tight for the oxygen atoms to squeeze into. This means that as the outer core's iron crystallizes and falls to the inner core, a great deal of oxygen is left behind to rise up through the outer core. The model suggested that this steady stream of buoyant oxygen is a major factor in stirring up the fluid outer core and driving the geodynamo.

Other information about Earth's geodynamo revealed since the 1990's has come from the work of geophysicists Gary A. Glatzmaier of the University of California at Santa Cruz and Paul A. Roberts of the University of California at Los Angeles. In one of their many findings, Glatzmaier and Roberts showed, through sophisticated computer models, that the rotation of the inner core might contribute to the currents in the fluid of the outer core, thereby adding to the strength of the magnetic field.

Since the late 1990's, the research of geologist David Gubbins of the University of Leeds in the United Kingdom has also advanced scientists' understanding of the geodynamo and magnetic field. Gubbins's maps of the magnetic field over Earth's surface have revealed variations in the strength of the magnetic force. These maps have shown that the magnetic field is strongest beneath oceanic *subduction zones,* areas where an edge of one *tectonic plate* is being forced below the edge of another. Earth's crust is made up of about 30 of these large, rigid plates that carry the continents and sea floor as they drift over the fluid mantle.

To explain his findings, Gubbins reasoned that as a plate is sucked down, some of its crust might break off and tumble like an avalanche down to the edge of the core. These chunks of rock are cool compared to the core, so they may create relatively cool spots on the outside of the outer core. Gubbins proposed that these cool spots might lower the temperatures in the areas of the core beneath them. Material in these cooler areas would tend to sink, creating motions in the mantle that may cause the magnetic field to concentrate in the sinking regions.

Magnetic field flip-flops

Gubbins's studies of Earth's magnetic field have also revealed new information about the phenomenon known as magnetic field reversal. Earth's magnetic field has lines of force that exit the north magnetic pole, curve around Earth, then re-enter the planet at the south magnetic pole. Over time, the magnetic field sometimes changes direction, so that the lines of force exit the south magnetic pole and re-enter at the north magnetic pole. (Today, the magnetic north pole lies near the geographic south pole and vise versa.)

Scientists have found chemical evidence for these magnetic reversals preserved in volcanic rock. Particles of iron and other magnetic elements in volcanic rock are aligned like tiny compasses in the direction of the magnetic field at the time the rock hardened. Studies of ancient volcanic rock have uncovered magnetic particles that are aligned in the opposite direction to today's magnetic field—showing that the south and north magnetic poles switched positions with each other. Such analyses indicate that flips in the magnetic field happen roughly every half-million years—with each reversal taking a few thousand years to complete.

The last flip of the magnetic field occurred about 650,000 years ago. Gubbins's work, however, has revealed that the magnetic field nearly flipped again much more recently. His careful measurements of the orientation of magnetic crystals in volcanic lavas in Hawaii indicated that this near flip happened about 20,000 years ago. The iron crystals seen in volcanic rock from this time partially re-aligned themselves in a new direction—before they switched back to their original alignment. Gubbins theorizes that during such short-lived partial reversals, called *excursions,* the magnetic field might shift in the outer core but not in the inner core. In a complete reversal, by contrast, the field shifts in both the outer and inner core. Gubbins estimates that about 10 excursions happen for every complete flip of the magnetic field.

Physicist Richard Muller of the University of California at Berkeley proposed in 2002 that magnetic reversals might be triggered by bizarre avalanches at the core-mantle boundary. He suggested that as the iron in the outer core crystallizes and falls toward the inner core, the lighter sulfur and silicon minerals in the outer core drift upward and form huge inverted mounds that cling to the upper edge of the outer core. Muller theorized that if one of these accumulated piles should collapse and fall back into the outer core, it could disrupt the currents in the core to such an extent that the magnetic field would temporarily "shut off." Later, when the currents reestablish themselves, the field would turn back on. At that time, it may have either the same *polarity* (direction) or the opposite one. Muller also suggested that the impact of a large asteroid could cause a wave of avalanches in the core, leading to a shutdown of the magnetic field and reversal of polarity.

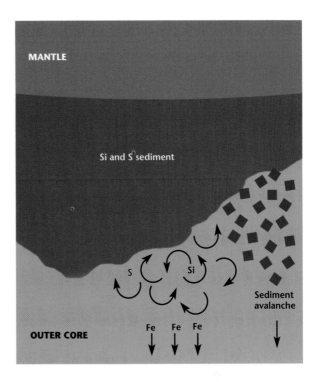

CORE AVALANCHES

Avalanches at the boundary between the outer core and mantle may trigger periodic reversals in the *polarity* (direction) of Earth's magnetic field, according to one theory. As iron (Fe) in the outer core crystallizes and falls toward the inner core, lighter sulfur (S) and silicon (Si) minerals may drift upward and form huge inverted mounds at the boundary. The collapse of these mounds could disrupt the currents in the core, leading to a temporary shutdown of the magnetic field, followed by a reversal of polarity.

Measurements of the present intensity of Earth's magnetic field, made with instruments called magnetometers, suggest that the field is decreasing in strength. This trend may have begun 2,000 years ago. Is the magnetic field going to shut down and then reverse itself soon? Many scientists note that the magnetic field can diminish and then regain its strength. However, if the field does reverse, navigation, communication, and weather satellites might be vulnerable to the charged particles in the solar wind. On the other hand, some computer models suggest that, during a reversal, enough of a magnetic field would remain to protect the atmosphere from the solar wind. Still other models suggest that the interaction of the solar wind with electrically charged atoms in the atmosphere could lead to the formation of a temporary magnetic field.

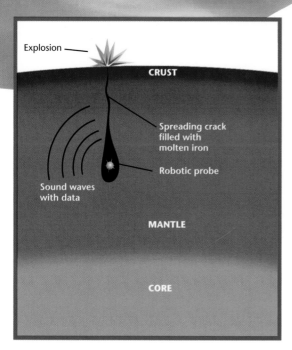

Explosion

CRUST

Spreading crack filled with molten iron

Robotic probe

Sound waves with data

MANTLE

CORE

FANTASTIC JOURNEY?

A robotic probe sinks toward the core in an illustration of a proposal by planetary scientist David Stevenson to study the core directly. Stevenson suggests first creating a crack in the crust with explosives. Molten iron containing the probe would then be poured into the spreading crack. As the probe sinks, it would transmit data on temperature, pressure, and chemistry encoded in sound waves back to the surface.

Earth's mysterious furnace

The continuing existence of the magnetic field seems to require a very fine energy balance, according to computer models. The outer core must remain just warm enough to stay fluid, but not so hot that iron cannot crystallize from the outer core and settle to the inner core. As iron crystallizes, the molecules re-order themselves from a liquid to a solid state, releasing energy and heat—just as water does when it freezes into ice cubes.

The source of the core's heat over the course of Earth's history is one of the greatest remaining mysteries about Earth's center. Scientists have calculated that the crystallization of iron in the core would provide enough heat and energy to keep the outer core flowing for only about 500 million years. This is nowhere near the age of Earth's magnetic field, which has been dated to 3.5 billion years. So scientists believe that the core's heat must have another source—perhaps the decay of certain radioactive *isotopes* (forms of an element).

In May 2003, a research team led by geochemist V. Rama Murthy of the University of Minnesota at Minneapolis proposed that some of the core's heat may result from the continuous decay of a particular radioactive isotope of potassium known as potassium-40. Murthy had previously theorized that radioactive potassium might be a heat source in the core. Subsequent laboratory experiments, however, failed to confirm that large amounts of potassium could move from the mantle to the core at the high temperatures and pressures in the planet's center. Without this movement, potassium could not exist at high enough concentrations to create significant heat.

In 2003, Murthy reported uncovering fundamental flaws in the experimental methods that had been used to test his proposal. He noted that the oil used to grind rocks for the experiments had sucked most of the potassium out of the rocks before any measurements could be made. Murthy found a new way to break up the rocks that didn't extract the potassium. With this problem solved, he was able to model the composition, pressure, and temperature of the core and mantle in the laboratory and show that large amounts of potassium-40 could indeed move into the core. This proved that radioactive potassium was a valid heat source.

Murthy's computer simulations of the core indicated that the decay of potassium-40 might currently provide about 10 percent of the core's heat output, leaving the crystallization of iron as the dominant energy source. Murthy believes that the heat generated by potassium-40 was probably much greater in the past, and that this has made it possible for Earth's core to maintain its heat and magnetic field for billions of years.

Journey to the core

Visiting the core would be the ideal way to learn more about it. But of course, it would be impossible for human explorers to survive the horrific pressures and temperatures there using current technology. In May 2003, David J. Stevenson, a planetary scientist at the California Institute of Technology in Pasadena, proposed the next best thing. He suggested embedding a small robotic probe in large quantities of molten iron and letting it sink through a crack to the core. To get the probe started, an explosion equivalent to a powerful earthquake would split a small section of the planet's crust to a width of about 30 centimeters (12 inches). Then the molten metal containing the probe would be poured into the crack. Stevenson estimated it would take about a week for the probe to reach the core. During that time, it would continually analyze temperature, pressure, and chemistry in the interior and beam the data back to the surface encoded in sound waves. Some scientists have suggested that Stevenson's proposal is preposterous, but he has argued that it is no more outrageous than our robotic exploration of other planets.

In many ways, the core of our own planet remains more alien to us than the surfaces of Mars and Venus. However, scientists continue to work on improving our understanding of how the geodynamo functions, how the core and mantle influence each other, and how and why the magnetic field changes. One day, scientists believe, these and many more secrets of deep Earth will be brought to light.

■ FOR ADDITIONAL INFORMATION

Books and periodicals

Bowler, Sue. "Journey to the Centre of the Earth." Inside Science 134, *New Scientist,* Oct. 14, 2000.

Harris, Nicholas; Gave, Marc (editor); and Hincks, Gary (illustrator). *Journey to the Center of the Earth* (ages 9-12). Reader's Digest, 1999.

Lutgens, Frederick K.; Tarbuck, Edward J.; and Tasa, Dennis. *Foundations of Earth Science.* Third edition. Prentice Hall, 2002.

Lamb, Simon, and Sington, David. *Earth Story: The Shaping of Our World.* Princeton University Press, 1998.

Web sites

Geodynamo—www.es.ucsc.edu/~glatz/geodynamo.html

The Truth About Earth's Core?—www.lbl.gov/Science-Articles/Archive/Phys-earth-core.html

What Is the Mantle?—geology.about.com/library/weekly/aa020898.htm

When North Goes South—www.psc.edu/science/Glatzmaier/glatzmaier.html

Scientists continue to develop new techniques to view the organs and tissues of the body without surgery, providing physicians with better tools to diagnose and monitor diseases.

Seeing Beneath Our Skin:
IMAGING THE BODY

By Thomas H. Maugh, II

For thousands of years, healers and physicians have poked, probed, and squeezed the body to diagnose disease and injury. Seeing *into* the body, however, involved cutting through the skin, which was an extremely risky process. A laboratory accident in 1895 dramatically changed that situation. German physicist Wilhelm C. Roentgen was passing a beam of *electrons* (small, negatively charged particles found in atoms) through a gas-filled tube in his laboratory. He noticed that a nearby screen, which had been coated with chemicals, began to glow whenever he turned on the electron beam. The glow surprised him because heavy cardboard shielded the tube and should have blocked any known form of light or particles emitted from the tube.

Roentgen named his newly found rays *X rays*. He experimented with the rays by placing various objects between the electron beam and the screen and then observing their shadows. Eventually, he placed his wife's

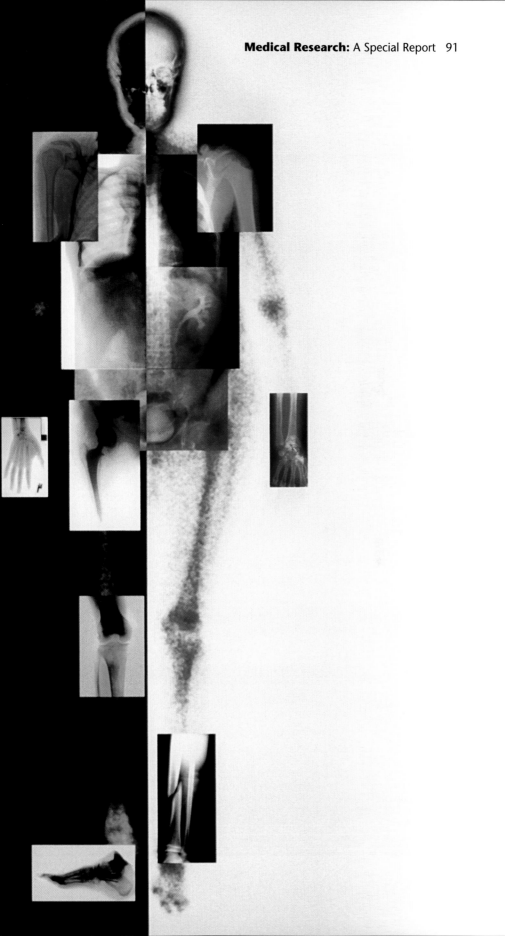

TERMS AND CONCEPTS

Computed tomography (CT): A sophisticated kind of X-ray image that is three-dimensional and in color.

Contrast agent: A substance that increases the effectiveness of an X ray by filling soft tissues so that they show up more clearly in the resulting image.

Fluoroscope: A device that creates a moving X-ray image and projects it onto a television monitor.

Magnetic resonance imaging (MRI): A technique using high-powered magnets to create images of the nervous system and other soft tissues.

Positron emission tomography (PET): A medical imaging technique that uses radiation to produce images of metabolic activity in the body.

Radiologist: A doctor who uses internal imaging techniques to diagnose problems in the body.

Single photon emission computed tomography (SPECT): An imaging technique that is similar to PET, but which creates less detailed images.

Ultrasound: A medical imaging technique that uses high-frequency sound waves to create images of the inside of the body without the use of radiation.

Whole-body scanning: The process of taking a series of CT scans of a healthy patient's entire body in order to look for undiagnosed health problems.

X rays: A type of energy that can pass through skin and create images of the inside of the body.

hand in front of the screen and saw the silhouette of her bones along with the ring she was wearing. Not long after discovering X rays, Roentgen had hit on their most important application—medical imaging. For the first time, physicians had a *noninvasive* way to see the effects of disease and injury inside the body—that is, a way that did not require cutting through the skin.

For most of the 1900's, X rays provided the only means to diagnose broken bones, search for abnormal growths, and locate bullets and other foreign objects. Since the 1970's, however, the growing power of computers and the ability to create rare radioactive *isotopes* in the laboratory have led to the development of a number of new imaging techniques. (An isotope is one of two or more atoms of the same chemical element that differ in the number of neutrons they contain.) Among these techniques are ultrasound, computed tomography (CT), magnetic resonance imaging (MRI), positron emission tomography (PET), and single photon emission computed tomography (SPECT).

Using these techniques, *radiologists* (experts trained in using internal images of the body for medical diagnosis) can not only obtain highly detailed images of extremely small structures within the body but also watch the body at work. For example, radiologists can detect cancerous cells, identify heart tissue damaged by heart attack, and observe the brain in action. Researchers in 2004 were using the techniques to hunt for clues to such mental disorders as Alzheimer's disease and schizophrenia and to monitor the development of multiple sclerosis and other progressive diseases.

Radiologists in the United States perform about 300 million scans each year. Scanning technology, however, comes at a price. The newest MRI and CT scanners cost as much as $5 million each, and individual diagnostic tests may run from $1,000 to more than $4,000. Medical imaging is consuming a growing portion of the more than $1.5 trillion spent on health care annually in the United States. Technology, including diagnostic imaging, accounted for an estimated 12 to 39 percent of the growth in health care spending in the 1990's, according to a 2000 study by the Blue Cross and Blue Shield Association, a Chicago-based organization that finances health care insurance coverage. The study projected that medical technology would account for 25 to 33 percent of spending growth between 2001 and 2005.

Scanning has personal costs as well. As scanners grow more sensitive, their images are increasingly revealing small abnormalities in the human body whose medical significance is unclear. A small spot on the lung, for example, might be a tiny tumor that needs immediate treatment, or it might be a scar or *benign* (non-

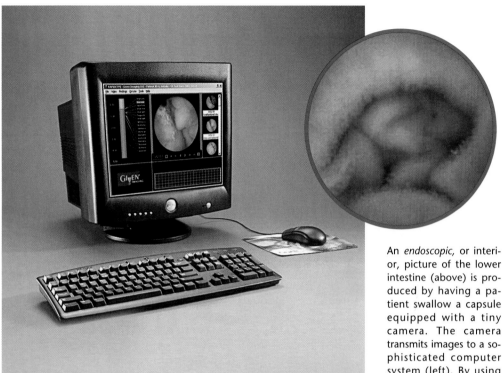

An *endoscopic,* or interior, picture of the lower intestine (above) is produced by having a patient swallow a capsule equipped with a tiny camera. The camera transmits images to a sophisticated computer system (left). By using such images to diagnose potential health problems, physicians can avoid invasive surgical techniques.

cancerous) lump of tissue. Usually, patients and their physicians feel compelled to follow up with further testing and, often, with diagnostic surgery. The growth in the number of such follow-ups has triggered a debate over whether the benefits of some types of scans, particularly whole-body scans, justify their high overall financial cost and the amount of anxiety they often cause.

Researchers fear this is also the case with the search for early lung cancer in smokers using technologies called spiral CT—or its successor, multidetector CT—which can identify *nodules* (masses) smaller than 1 centimeter (0.4 inch) in size on the lungs. Many researchers theorize that most of these nodules are benign and that patients are better off not knowing they are there. In addition, scientific research has never verified whether early detection of lung cancer actually saves lives, though logic would indicate that it should.

In 2002, the National Cancer Institute, a part of the U.S. National Institutes of Health, organized an eight-year trial of 50,000 current and former smokers to determine whether CT scans are more effective than conventional X rays in detecting lung cancer and thus in reducing deaths from the disease. The trial, which is being run at 30 sites throughout the United States, was to conclude in 2009.

The author:
Thomas H. Maugh, II, is a medical writer for the *Los Angeles Times.*

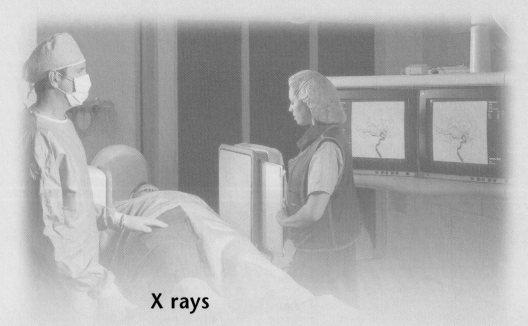

X rays

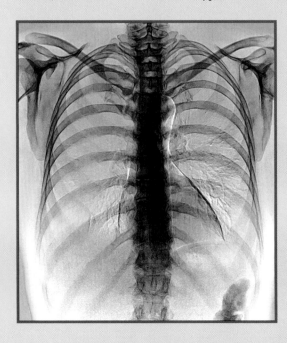

X-ray images of the chest (below) and other parts of the body are produced by passing X rays through a patient's body onto a sheet of film sensitive to the rays. Bones absorb more rays than muscles or internal organs do and so cast the sharpest shadows.

X rays are high-energy electromagnetic waves with a much shorter wavelength than visible light and much greater penetrating power. They are the simplest, least expensive method of producing images of broken or diseased bones and other injuries, dental cavities, and some types of tumors.

The X-ray process is very similar to photography. The patient stands against or lies over the X-ray film. A machine then sends X rays through the body to the film, which records an image called a *radiograph*. Different types of tissue absorb different amounts of radiation. For example, dense tissues, especially bones, absorb most of the radiation beamed on them and so appear as white or light gray areas on the film. In contrast, muscles, the intestines, and other soft tissue allow more radiation to pass through to the film and so appear as dark areas. Foreign objects, such as bullets, absorb more radiation than soft tissue and thus show up very clearly.

To X-ray some types of soft tissue, such as the veins or specific organs, radiologists use a *contrast agent*, a substance that fills the veins or organs, increasing the density and the amount of radiation the area absorbs. Some contrast agents are swallowed, while others are injected, usually into a vein.

A version of radiology called *fluoroscopy* allows physicians to make "X-ray movies" of parts of the body—including the digestive tract or heart—which are in motion. Physicians also use a *fluoroscope* (a device that projects moving X-ray images onto a television monitor) to observe the progress of certain medical procedures. For example, surgeons use a fluoroscope to guide the insertion of a *catheter* (tube) into an artery or to remove foreign objects from the lungs or stomach.

Radiology's chief benefits include its low cost and speed. It is also pain free. Its principal risk is the damage it causes to cells. For example, X rays can damage a *fetus* (developing baby) because its cells are rapidly dividing and growing into specialized cells. X rays can cause *mutations* (changes) in these cells, which may increase the chances of miscarriage, birth defects, or illnesses later in life. As a result, physicians rarely order X rays for pregnant women. In addition, children, whose cells are growing at a relatively rapid rate, are more susceptible to X-ray damage than adults are. Repeated exposure to X rays increases the risk of cell damage. For this reason, technicians stand behind a barrier when operating an X-ray machine. X-ray technicians also often place a lead apron over the parts of a patient's body not being screened.

Researchers have long believed that the risk of damage from a single X ray or fluoroscopy was extremely low because the body quickly replaced any damaged cells. A 2003 study led by radiation biologist Markus Lobrich of the University of Saarland in Homburg, Germany, challenged this belief. In an experiment using human cells grown in the laboratory, the Saarland scientists found that damage caused by low doses of radiation (such as those in dental X rays) actually took longer to repair than the damage resulting from higher levels of radiation (such as those given to cancer patients). The reason for this difference in cell-repair rates is unknown. However, the scientists speculated that the body may not recognize low levels of radiation damage and so may not move to repair them as quickly as it does more serious damage.

Benefits
- Quick
- Painless
- Inexpensive

Risks
- Causes cell damage in patients, especially children
- May damage cells in *fetuses* (developing babies) in pregnant patients

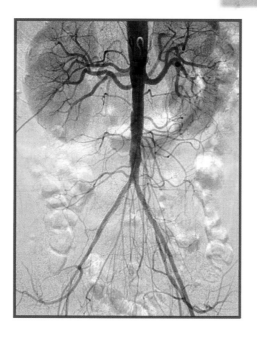

An X ray of an abdomen (left) provides a sharp, detailed image of blood vessels and kidneys. To X ray such soft tissues, radiologists inject a contrast agent, a substance that fills the veins, increasing their density and, therefore, the amount of radiation they absorb.

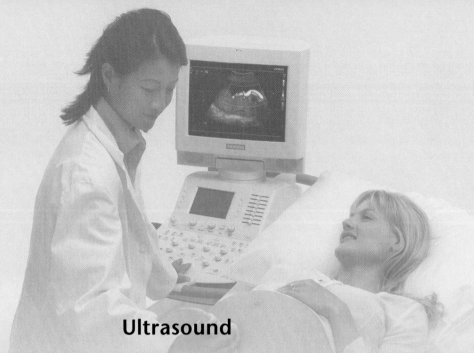

Ultrasound

Ultrasound imaging, also called sonography, uses high-frequency sound waves—well above the frequencies that can be heard by people—to penetrate the body and create images of internal tissue. Because ultrasound does not use radiation, physicians often use the technique to monitor the growth of and detect abnormalities in fetuses. In addition, the technique is widely used for imaging the eyes as well as the liver and other organs in the abdomen and to identify areas of infection and swelling. It is often used to image the breast during needle biopsies, procedures during which a physician inserts a needle into the breast to sample tissue for laboratory testing.

Ultrasound images of internal tissues, such as a human heart (right), are created by penetrating the body with high-frequency sound waves. The waves bounce back each time they encounter a boundary, such as between tissue and bone. A machine measures the elapsed time between release and return (far right). A computer then processes that distance into a two- or three-dimensional image in real time.

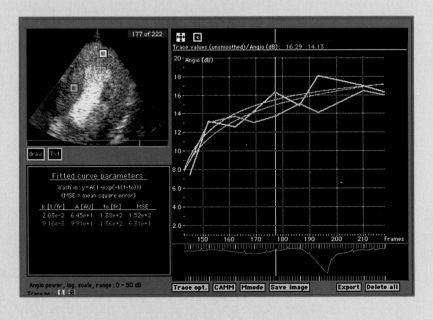

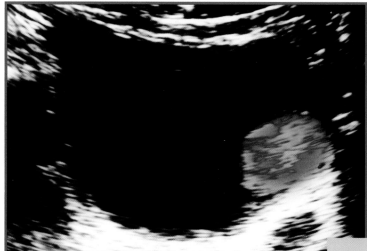

A false-color ultrasound image can help doctors analyze a bladder tumor (shown in color). Ultrasound is highly effective in identifying tumors in a patient's internal organs.

Benefits
- No risk of cell damage in patient or fetus
- Produces images in real time

Risks
- Does not effectively penetrate joints and bones

An ultrasound machine includes a probe, called a *transducer,* which emits very short bursts of sound into body tissue. Some of the waves bounce back each time they encounter a boundary of some sort, such as that between blood and tissue or between tissue and bone. The transducer then collects the reflected waves and measures the elapsed time between the waves' release and their return in order to calculate the distance they have traveled into the body. A computer registers the information from the transducer and processes it into a two-dimensional image of the body part being scanned. The image appears on a television screen for viewing in *real time*—that is, the image appears as it is being created.

Advances in computing power have made it possible to combine two-dimensional ultrasound images into three-dimensional images. These images are especially useful for checking the development of a fetus and identifying cancerous tumors in the breast early in their development.

Radiologists use a specialized form of ultrasound, called Doppler ultrasound, to measure the rate at which blood flows through the heart and major arteries. Doppler ultrasound measures very tiny changes in the frequency of returning signals to calculate how fast blood is moving.

Numerous studies have established that ultrasound is one of the safest imaging technologies available. It is much safer than X rays because the patient is not exposed to radiation. Because ultrasound produces images in real time, the technology has become a common replacement for X rays in certain situations—such as gynecological problems—in the emergency room. However, ultrasound does not provide clear images of bones because bone tissue reflects sound waves.

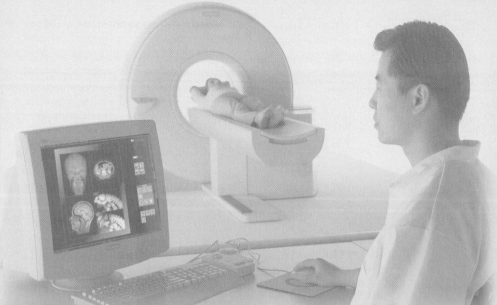

Computed Tomography

Computed tomography (CT) scanning—formerly known as computerized axial tomography (CAT) scanning—is a more sophisticated and expensive form of X-ray imaging. CT scanning can create detailed, three-dimensional images of the soft tissue in the brain, kidneys, liver, lungs, and other organs as well as bony tissue in the limbs, pelvis, and spine. Radiologists commonly use CT scans to diagnose problems of the inner ear and sinuses because the scans can generate detailed images of both the delicate soft tissue structures and very fine bones in these areas. Because CT scans clearly show organ injuries and accumulations of blood inside the body, most emergency rooms in the United States had access to a CT scanner by 2004, so that medical personnel could quickly check accident victims for major injuries and internal bleeding.

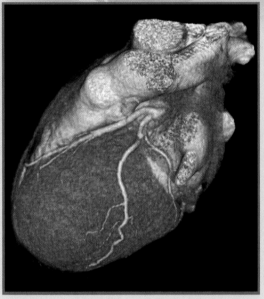

A colorized computed tomography (CT) scan of a heart (above) helps physicians analyze problems with blood flow. A CT scanner is a machine with an X-ray source on one side and a detector on the other. While it rotates around the patient's body, a computer collects data from the X rays and uses them to produce a three-dimensional image.

A CT scanner, which resembles a large ring, is slightly less than 1 meter (3 feet) in diameter. The scanner has an X-ray source on one side and a detector on the other. While the ring rotates around the patient's body, a computer collects data from the X rays and uses them to produce a two-dimensional image of a cross section of the body. A motorized table then moves the patient farther into the machine, and the computer collects data from another cross section. This process is repeated until enough data are collected to combine the images into a three-dimensional image.

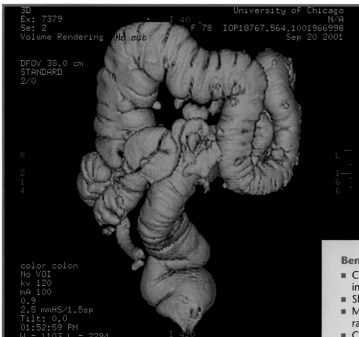

```
3D                                    University of Chicago
Ex: 7379                      I 40                      N/A
Se: 2                              F 78  IOP18767.564.1001966998
Volume Rendering  No cut                          Sep 20 2001

DFOV 38.0 cm
STANDARD
2/0




R                                                      L

2                                                      1
1                                                      6
4                                                      6




color colon
No VOI
kv 120
mA 100
0.9
2.5 mmHS/1.5sp
Tilt: 0.0
01:52:59 PM
W = 1103 L = 2294            I 420
```

Computed tomography scanning provides highly detailed, three-dimensional images of soft tissues, such as the colon (left). Radiologists often use contrast agents, usually iodine-based compounds, to enhance the visibility of such organs.

Benefits
- Creates three-dimensional images
- Shows both bone and tissue
- More sophisticated than X rays
- Can be used during surgery

Risks
- Low levels of radiation pose the same risk that X rays do
- More expensive than X rays
- Some patients may be allergic to contrast dyes used in fluoroscopic CT imaging

Spiral CT is an improvement over conventional CT. The scanner in spiral CT, in fact, travels in a spiral around the patient's body while the table carrying the patient advances continuously. Thus, the scan is completed more quickly, more images can be taken, and the images are more precise because they are made in a continuous motion instead of a series of starts and stops. However, the newest form of CT—called multidetector CT—is better yet. A multidetector CT includes either 4, 8, 16, or 32 detectors instead of just 1, allowing it to take many more images much more quickly and to detect small areas of abnormal cells better than conventional or spiral CT can.

Many procedures conducted using X rays may also be done with CT scans. For example, radiologists may use contrast agents, usually iodine-based compounds, to enhance the visibility of certain organs or disease processes. In addition, a CT scanner can be linked to a fluoroscopy screen. Fluoroscopic CT imaging can help guide surgeons during delicate procedures by enabling them to view internal body structures as well as surgical instruments.

CT scans carry the same risks as radiographs because patients are exposed to low levels of radiation. In addition, some CT patients may suffer a reaction to contrast dyes, though by 2004, newer dyes made side effects less common.

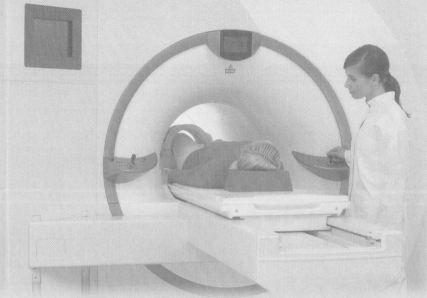

Magnetic Resonance Imaging

Since its development in 1946, magnetic resonance imaging (MRI) has become a useful tool for imaging the nervous system and other soft tissues of the body. Physicians use MRI to diagnose multiple sclerosis, brain tumors, infections in the brain, spine, and joints, and strokes in their early stages. MRI also aids physicians in diagnosing torn ligaments, tendinitis, and other athletic injuries.

MRI is particularly useful for imaging soft tissue because it detects the magnetic properties of the hydrogen in water molecules, which account for two-thirds of the weight of the human body. When hydrogen atoms are placed in a powerful magnetic field and bombarded with radio waves, they emit radio signals that provide information about their surroundings. The strength and length of the signals depend on the properties of the tissue. Using these data, a computer produces two-dimensional images of cross sections of the body.

One version of MRI is functional magnetic resonance imaging (fMRI). Radiologists use fMRI to measure *metabolic activity* (the process of turning food into energy and living tissue) in the brain. When you use a particular area of the brain—to look at an image, for example—more blood flows to that region. The fMRI scanner monitors that increased flow by focusing on a blood component called deoxyhemoglobin. FMRI scans can monitor such changes as the recovery of parts of the brain after a stroke. In addition, researchers use fMRI to study the structure of the brain.

In 2004, researchers were experimenting with a type of MRI called magnetic resonance elastography (MRE). MRE is an advanced version of *palpation* (touching the body with the fingers to probe for signs of injury or disease). MRE measures

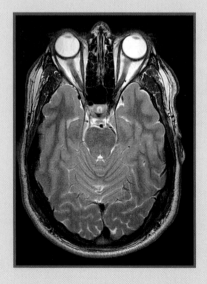

Magnetic resonance imaging (MRI) of a head (below) provides a detailed cross section of the brain, eyes, nasal cavity, and cranium. In MRI, a computer translates signals created by the interaction of a magnetic field and radio waves into highly detailed cross-sectional images.

the stiffness of damaged muscles and brain tissue. Tissues accumulate fluids when they are injured, stretching cell membranes tight and making the tissues feel stiff. The stiffer the tissue is, the greater the damage.

Other adaptations of MRI include MR angiography (MRA) and diffusion imaging. MRA uses MRI technology to view blood vessels. Physicians may use MRA to confirm an arterial *aneurysm* (blood vessel about to burst), for example, so that they can treat it before it causes fatal bleeding. Diffusion imaging allows physicians to see how fluids—particularly water molecules—spread inside organs or tissues. The technique is especially useful in diagnosing strokes at an early stage, when some of the brain damage can still be prevented. (Research in the early 1990's showed that water diffusion slows significantly during the early stages of a stroke.)

Radiologists may use contrast agents with MRI to improve their ability to see specific areas. Unlike the contrast agents used with X rays, which physically block the transmission of the rays, contrast agents used in MRI have magnetic properties that alter the magnetic field in a very small area. In a technique called *MRI with nanoparticles*, for example, magnetic atoms, such as iron or gadolinium, are attached to *antibodies* (immune-system proteins) that attach themselves to tumors or other specific tissues. As a result, those tissues appear much more clearly in the scan. MRI with nanoparticles is particularly useful for identifying very small prostate cancers before they spread.

Because MRI uses no radiation, physicians generally consider it a safe procedure. The contrast agents used in MRI are also less likely to provoke reactions than those used with X rays. Physicians avoid using MRI on people with pacemakers because the machine's magnetic field can damage implanted electronic devices. The metal in other implanted objects, such as screws, plates, and artificial joints, can also interfere with the magnetic field and distort MRI images. In addition, technicians must be especially careful that no metal objects are present in the area around the scanner. Such objects can strike and injure patients when the objects are pulled toward the magnet in the center of the MRI unit at high speed.

A conventional MRI can pose difficulties for some patients. Some people are too big to fit inside the scanner. Others may fear being confined in the scanner for the 20 to 90 minutes needed to complete a procedure. These patients may be scanned with an open MRI. Instead of lying in a narrow, tube-shaped structure, the patient lies on an imaging table with more space around the body. Just above the patient is a large, round mechanism that transmits the electromagnetic waves. Some patients also may be disturbed by the loud noises an MRI machine makes as the magnetic fields interact. Ear plugs and other forms of hearing protection can muffle the noise somewhat.

Benefits
- Excellent for imaging soft tissues such as the nervous system
- More versatile than CT scanning
- Does not use radiation
- Uses safer contrast agents than X-ray imaging does

Risks
- Magnets used in MRI can damage implanted electronic devices, such as pacemakers
- MRI scanner may be too small for some patients
- Patients may fear being confined in the scanner
- Patients may be bothered by loud noises created by the MRI scanner

Positron Emission Tomography and Single Photon Emission Computed Tomography

A colorized single photon emission computed tomography (SPECT) scan of the brain of a person having a migraine (below) reveals areas of high activity (yellow and red) and reduced blood flow (blue and gray).

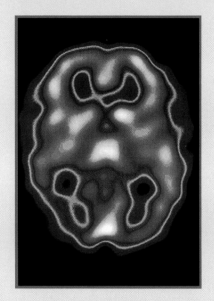

Positron emission tomography (PET) also uses radiation to produce images of the chemical activity of the brain and other body tissues. Unlike other imaging techniques, PET scans do not produce highly detailed images of the body. Instead, they show areas of high metabolic activity, such as a brain tumor with its rapidly growing cells or a specific area of the brain that is in use. The radiation used in PET scans comes from radioactive isotopes injected into the body rather than from an outside source.

For a brain PET scan, the radiologist injects a solution containing glucose and a harmless amount of a radioactive substance into the patient's vein. The radioactive glucose mixes with glucose in the blood and eventually enters the brain. The radioactive glucose gives off *positrons* (subatomic particles identical to electrons but carrying an opposite electric charge) that collide with electrons in brain tissue. The collisions give off *gamma rays* (shortwave electromagnetic radiation). The scanner records the points where these rays emerge. A computer then assembles the data into a three-dimensional representation of the regions emitting the rays. The representation is displayed on a video screen as cross-sectional "slices" of the brain.

PET scans are used most often to detect cancer and to monitor the effectiveness of cancer therapy by determining changes in metabolic activity in tumors. They are also valuable for identifying brain tumors and evaluating memory and seizure disorders that have an unknown cause.

The isotopes used in PET scans are short-lived, so the scanner must be near the *cyclotron* that produces them. (A cyclotron is a machine that accelerates electrically charged atomic particles to high energies.) As a result, patients—particularly in rural areas—often have to travel some distance to reach a medical center that can perform PET scans.

A related technology is called single photon emission computed tomography (SPECT). SPECT, which also uses radiation to image the body, is less sensitive than PET, and SPECT images are less detailed. However, SPECT requires radioisotopes that have a longer life and so can be shipped greater distances. As a result, the technique is more widely available and less expensive. Physicians use SPECT scanning to monitor tissue damage in heart attacks because damaged tissue has little or no metabolic activity.

Because the two techniques allow physicians to study body functions, they can identify alterations in biochemical processes that suggest the presence of disease before actual changes in anatomy are visible on other types of scans. Both PET and SPECT use radioactive chemicals and so pose a risk similar to that associated with X rays. In particular, radiologists advise pregnant women to avoid PET and SPECT scans and suggest these techniques be used for children only when absolutely necessary. PET occasionally gives false results, particularly in diabetic patients whose high blood sugar or insulin levels may interfere with the scan.

Benefits

- Excellent for observing brain activity
- Can be used to identify brain disorders that have no known cause
- Can suggest the presence of disease before it can be seen in other types of scans

Risks

- Not widely available outside major cities
- Uses radiation
- Occasionally gives false results in diabetic patients

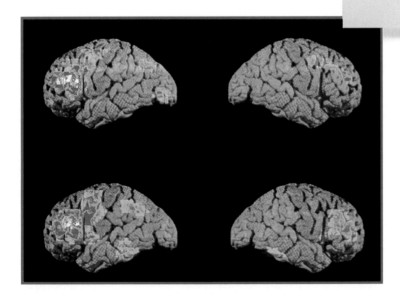

Two colorized positron emission tomography (PET) brain scans of a person with schizophrenia (bottom) compared with those of a healthy brain (top) reveal that different areas are active during the process of speaking. The active areas show up as red and yellow. Schizophrenia is a brain disorder characterized by unpredictable disturbances in thinking.

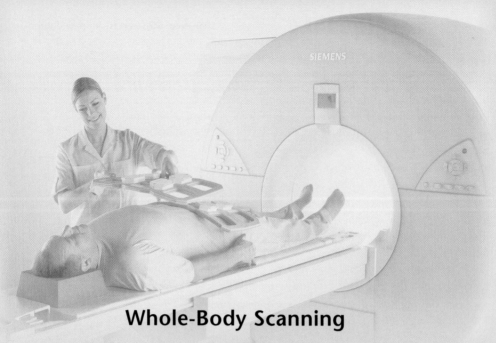

Whole-Body Scanning

One of the most controversial areas of medical imaging is the use of whole-body CT scans on healthy people to look for abnormalities that could represent undiagnosed health problems. The tests, which can cost $800 to $1,000 each, are widely promoted with slogans such as "15 minutes that can save your life." They may not require a referral from a physician.

For the scan, the patient lies on a table that slides into an imaging machine. The machine performs a CT scan, producing hundreds of "slices" of the body. A computer then reassembles the images into an X-ray film that a radiologist can examine.

Many physicians oppose the use of the scans because if the scans are used in healthy people without symptoms, most of the abnormalities that they uncover will be harmless. However, once an abnormality is found, most doctors and patients will feel that it must be investigated with more imaging tests and with procedures such as biopsies. The whole process can be expensive and stressful and can expose a healthy person to such health risks as bleeding and infection from the biopsy or other procedures.

A 2002 study conducted by Giovanna Casola, a radiologist and the chief of body imaging at the University of California at San Diego, analyzed the results of nearly 1,200 people who had whole-body scans. About one-third of the patients required follow-up exams. About 10 percent of the patients were told they had masses that could be tumors. However, only 1 percent of this number actually had a life-threatening condition. In addition, more than 90 percent of suspected lung abnormalities seen on whole-body scans turn out to be benign, according to the Radiological Society of North America.

Whole-body scanning also exposes patients to more radiation than does any other imaging technique. Studies have shown that the radiation exposure from a whole-body scan is about 250 times that from a normal chest X ray and 30 times that from a mammogram. Physicians generally agree that the information gained from a CT scan far outweighs the risks from radiation exposure for people with a known problem. For healthy people, however, the scales tip in the opposite direction. As a result, the Food and Drug Administration, the American Cancer Society, and the American College of Radiology oppose whole-body screening. For the same reasons, insurance companies do not pay for it. Several state health agencies, including those in Texas and Pennsylvania, have banned the scans unless a patient has a physician's referral.

Benefits
- May provide early warning signs of undiagnosed health problems

Risks
- Expensive
- Many abnormalities discovered through whole-body scanning are harmless
- Exposes the patient to a high level of radiation

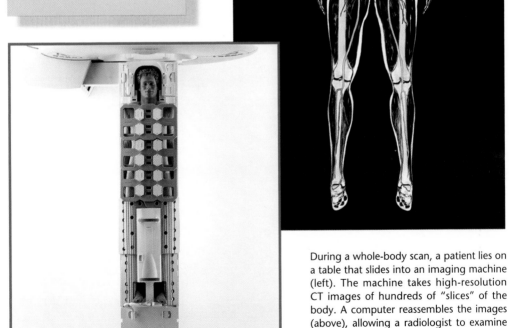

During a whole-body scan, a patient lies on a table that slides into an imaging machine (left). The machine takes high-resolution CT images of hundreds of "slices" of the body. A computer reassembles the images (above), allowing a radiologist to examine the whole body for abnormalities.

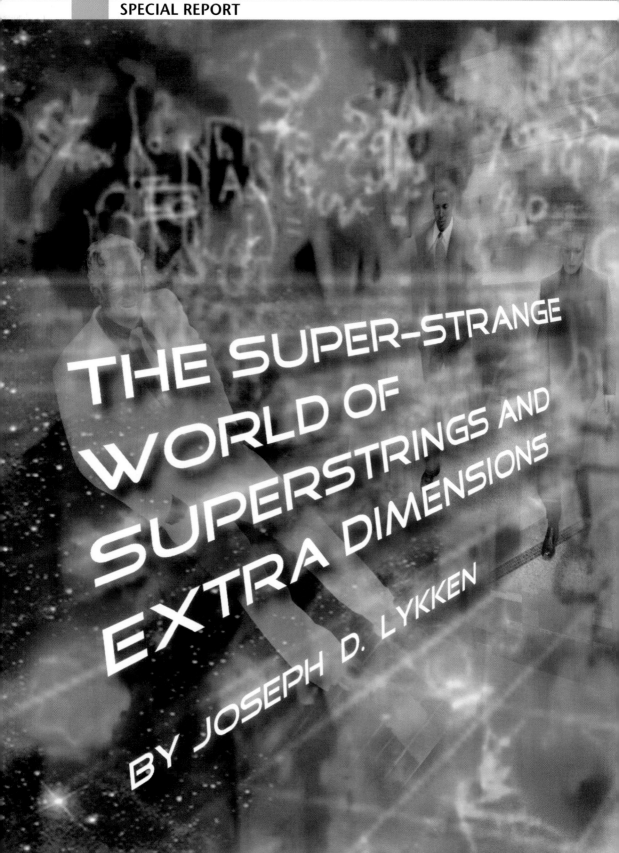

THE SUPER-STRANGE WORLD OF SUPERSTRINGS AND EXTRA DIMENSIONS

BY JOSEPH D. LYKKEN

COULD AMAZINGLY TINY STRINGS OF ENERGY GIVE PHYSICISTS A "THEORY OF EVERYTHING?"

Imagine that you could invent a super-powerful microscope—one so powerful that you could use it to see the tiniest, most basic units of matter. What would you see if you used this microscope to focus on, say, a banana?

After you peeled off the hard, yellow skin of the banana, you would focus on the soft fruit inside. You would see the cells that make up the fruit and, if you focused at a higher power, the tiny molecules and atoms that make up the cells. Your microscope could even see the various kinds of subatomic particles that make up the atoms.

But are there even smaller bits to see through your microscope? Many physicists believe the answer to that question is "yes." They think that subatomic particles themselves consist of incredibly tiny and unimaginably weird loops of energy called *superstrings*, or *strings* (for short). If you could see these superstrings, they would appear to be vibrating, merging, breaking apart, disappearing, and reappearing right before your eyes. And they would be doing this in at least nine different dimensions of space, not just the three spatial dimensions we normally experience—left/right, forward/backward, and up/down.

These seemingly bizarre ideas form the basis of string theory—one of the most important theories in science today. This theory suggests that superstrings form the most basic stuff of everything in the cosmos—from planets to rays of sunlight to coffee cups. Physicists have yet to find experimental evidence that superstrings exist, but complex mathematical calculations suggest that superstrings may be real. Physicists often think and work in mathematical terms before their ideas can be translated into concepts that can be tested in the laboratory. If experiments eventually confirm the existence of superstrings, scientists may have a way to unify all our knowledge about the nature of the universe and the laws that govern it. In 2004, researchers were seeking to determine whether string theory is physics, philosophy, or fantasy.

The author:
Joseph D. Lykken is a theoretical physicist at Fermi National Accelerator Laboratory near Batavia, Illinois.

TERMS AND CONCEPTS

Brane: A giant vibrating surface on which our universe might exist, according to an idea called M-theory.

General relativity: Theory that describes how the force of gravity works.

Grand unified theory: Theory uniting the three forces that affect subatomic particles—the electromagnetic, strong, and weak forces.

M-theory: Theory suggesting that space-time has a total of 11 dimensions.

Particle accelerator: A machine that forces atoms or subatomic particles to collide, producing other particles.

Quantum mechanics: A theory describing the behavior of atoms and subatomic particles.

Quarks: The subatomic building blocks of positively charged protons and electrically neutral neutrons.

Space-time: The combination of the three spatial dimensions of length, width, and height with the dimension of time.

Special relativity: Theory describing how the speed at which time passes varies depending on the position and motion of an observer.

String modes: The various vibration patterns of superstrings that give rise to various kinds of particles.

Theory of everything: Sought-after theory that would unite ideas of the theories of general relativity and quantum mechanics.

Uncertainty principle: Idea in quantum mechanics stating that it is impossible to precisely describe both the location and speed of a subatomic particle at the same time.

Contradiction between two theories

To understand how important superstrings may be to science, it helps to look at the evolution of the theory describing them. Physicists developed string theory in the late 1900's as a way to explain a glaring contradiction between two foundation blocks of modern physics—the theories of *general relativity* and *quantum mechanics.* The theory of general relativity, developed by the German-born American scientist Albert Einstein in the early 1900's, provides a brilliant explanation of the laws that govern the behavior of large things, including planets, stars, and galaxies. Specifically, it describes how the force of gravity works. The theory of quantum mechanics, also known as *quantum theory,* was developed in the early 1900's as well. It offers a precise understanding of the microscopic world of atoms and subatomic particles.

The problem with these two theories is that gravity plays no significant role in the subatomic realm, and microscopic interactions are unimportant when it comes to explaining how a planet orbits a star. So the universe seems to operate according to two separate sets of laws—one for the big, the other for the small. Physicists, who prefer simple, elegant explanations, are convinced that there should be only one set of laws for both big and small.

Space-time warp

Einstein's theory of *special relativity,* published in 1905, set the stage for this puzzle. This theory describes time as a *relative* concept—something that varies depending on the position and motion of an observer. According to special relativity, the passing of time would actually slow down for an individual moving close to the *speed of light,* the speed at which light travels—299,792 kilometers (186,282 miles) per second. (This is the fastest possible speed in the universe.) After scientists discovered that an observer's motion through space influences the passage of time, they realized that time should be added to the list of the universe's dimensions. Special relativity indicates that the three spatial dimensions of length, width, and height are interwoven in a kind of flexible cosmic fabric with the fourth dimension of time. This fabric, called *space-time,* extends throughout the universe. All events that take place in the universe and all locations in the universe are completely embedded in it.

The shape of the space-time fabric is responsible for the force of gravity, according to the theory of general relativity, which Einstein introduced to the world in 1915. The English scientist and mathematician Isaac Newton had developed the original scientific description of the effects of gravity in the 1600's. However, Newton was unable to explain how this force, which holds the planets in orbit around the sun and people on the surface of Earth, actually works.

The theory of general relativity states that all objects in the universe cause the fabric of space-time to *warp* (curve). One popular analogy, for example, compares the sun to a bowling ball. If this bowling ball were placed on a rubber sheet, the sheet would curve downward all around the ball. According to Einstein, the sun warps space-time in the same way. Earth and the other planets orbit the sun because they are caught in the curvature of space-time, rolling around and around the sun the way marbles would roll around the bowling ball on the warped sheet. So, Einstein said, the force we feel as gravity is really the sensation of being caught in the curvature of space-time.

Subatomic strangeness

While Einstein was explaining the movement of planets in terms of general relativity, he and a number of other physicists were also developing quantum theory to describe the structure and behavior of the smallest-known units of matter, including atoms and the particles they are made of. Matter consists of several kinds of elementary particles. Among these are *electrons* (negatively charged particles that orbit the *nucleus* [central part] of an atom); various kinds of *quarks* (the building blocks of the positively charged *protons* and electrically neutral *neutrons* in the nucleus); and *neutrinos*, which have no electrical charge.

One of the strangest ideas in quantum theory is the *uncertainty principle*, discovered in 1927 by the German physicist Werner Heisenberg. The uncertainty principle states that it is impossible to precisely determine both the location and speed of subatomic particles at the same time. This is because the particles are always wildly "jittering" in so-called *quantum fluctuations*. These fluctuations reflect the fact that the particles behave like both flowing waves and little points.

Quantum fluctuations are responsible for many strange phenomena that are difficult—if

PHYSICAL LAWS OF THE LARGE

Mathematical equations developed by Albert Einstein in the early 1900's led to the revolutionary concept of space-time and to an explanation for how gravity works, allowing physicists to understand the behavior of such large objects as planets and stars.

Space-time is a mathematical concept that combines the three dimensions of space—length, width, and height—with the fourth dimension of time. Space-time is usually represented as a grid (above) or a woven fabric.

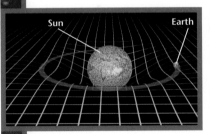

According to Einstein's theory of general relativity, the sun and all other objects in the universe cause the fabric of space-time to *warp* (curve), the way a heavy ball might press into a soft mattress. Gravitation is the effect of that curvature. Earth and the other planets in the solar system orbit the sun because they are caught in this vast "depression" in space-time and cannot escape.

PHYSICAL LAWS OF THE SMALL

Quantum theory, developed by a number of physicists in the early 1900's, provides a comprehensive description of the microscopic world of atoms and subatomic particles.

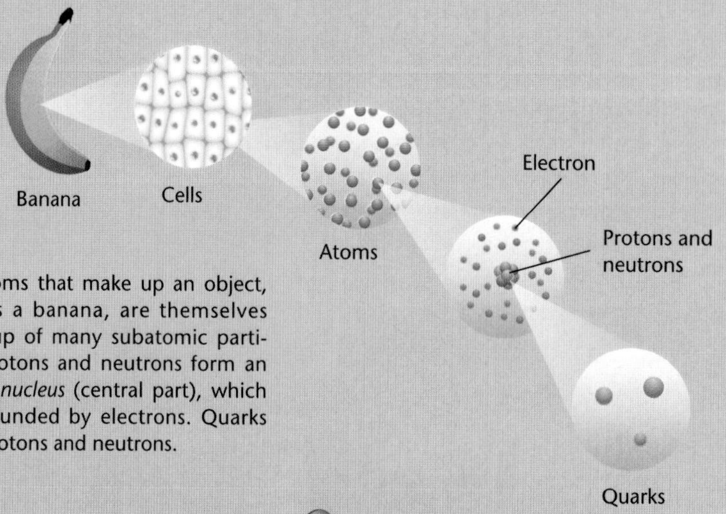

Banana

Cells

Atoms

Electron

Protons and neutrons

The atoms that make up an object, such as a banana, are themselves made up of many subatomic particles. Protons and neutrons form an atom's *nucleus* (central part), which is surrounded by electrons. Quarks form protons and neutrons.

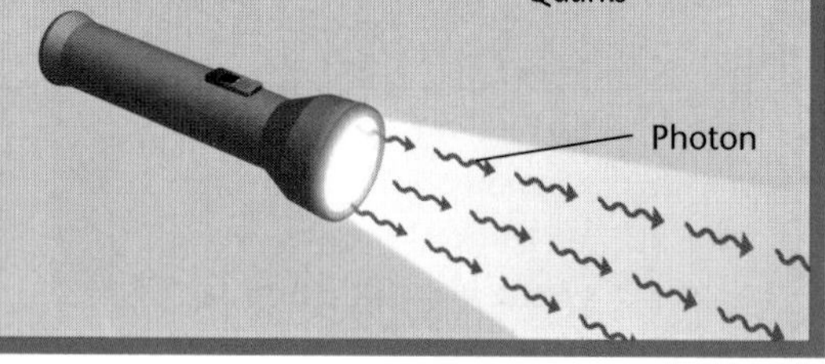

Quarks

Quantum theory also states that all forces are transmitted by particles. For example, the electromagnetic force, which includes light, is transmitted by wavelike particles called photons.

Photon

not impossible—to understand without using mathematics. For example, a moving subatomic particle can actually be considered to travel along many different paths at the same time. If you were subject to the same level of quantum fluctuations, you could walk out of your home in the morning and go to work, the grocery store, your friend's house, and your doctor's office—all at the same time!

Although the phenomena predicted by the uncertainty principle are, for all practical purposes, impossible in our everyday world of the large, physicists are convinced that this is how the world of the very tiny works. Thousands of experiments have provided support for the uncertainty principle and other elements of quantum mechanics. Some of the strongest evidence comes from experiments in which scientists bombard crystals with high-intensity X rays to create images of the atoms that make up the crystals. These images show the atomic structure to have a "fuzzy" nature—due to the quantum fluctuations described by the uncertainty principle.

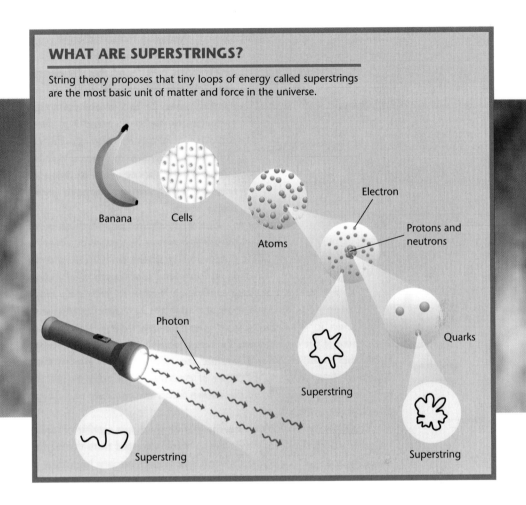

WHAT ARE SUPERSTRINGS?

String theory proposes that tiny loops of energy called superstrings are the most basic unit of matter and force in the universe.

Banana

Cells

Atoms

Electron

Protons and neutrons

Quarks

Photon

Superstring

Superstring

Superstring

Four forces united?

By 1980, physicists had a complete quantum theory describing how all the known elementary particles behave under the influence of all the measurable elementary forces. The elementary forces that affect the subatomic world are the *electromagnetic force,* the *strong force,* and the *weak force.* The electromagnetic force holds electrons in orbit, makes electricity flow through wires, and is responsible for the movement of light and compass needles. The strong force holds quarks together in neutrons and other tiny objects. The weak force is responsible for the behavior of neutrinos and for certain types of *radioactive decay,* in which an element changes into another form of that element or into another element entirely.

Like matter, elementary forces are made of particles. Quantum mechanics describes these particles as microscopic bundles that transmit the effects of the forces between particles of matter. For example, the tiny bundles that transmit the electromagnetic force are called *photons. Gluons*

HOW SMALL IS A SUPERSTRING?

According to string theory, a superstring measures approximately 0.000000000000000000000000000000001 centimeter in length. In size, a superstring compares with an atom the way an atom compares with our solar system.

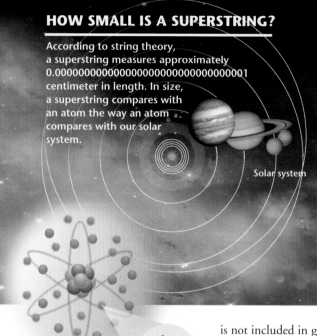

Solar system

Atom

Superstring

transmit the strong force, and *weak gauge bosons* transmit the weak force.

Physicists have found that the electromagnetic, strong, and weak forces are remarkably alike. In fact, at extremely high temperatures, the characteristics of these three forces become indistinguishable. This has led scientists to propose that the forces fall under a single unified theory of nature, called *grand unification* or *grand unified theory.*

But what about the fourth force of nature—gravity? In quantum theory's tidy world of grand unification, gravity sticks out like a sore thumb. Gravitation is not included in grand unification because its effect on a single atom or nucleus is so weak that scientists have never been able to detect it. Why should gravity operate under different rules than those of the other forces? Perhaps it doesn't. Physicists believe that if they could discover a sensible theory of quantum gravity, they would be close to having a "theory of everything." In other words, the same rules would apply to all the known forces and particles, to the large as well as the small.

String theory, as of 2004, was the leading candidate capable of unifying gravity with the other forces. String theory emerged from the mathematical calculations of many physicists and mathematicians beginning in the late 1960's. By the mid-1980's, many scientists were convinced that this bold theory solved the riddle of how general relativity and quantum mechanics could be related.

Super-tiny superstrings

What exactly are superstrings? They actually have a lot in common with the more familiar strings of musical instruments. A superstring, like a guitar string, is *elastic,* meaning that it can stretch and then return to its original shape. Superstrings also have *tension,* meaning that when they are stretched, they can resist. However, superstrings don't need to be plucked like a guitar string to stretch; according to string theory, they can stretch themselves.

A superstring differs from a guitar string in several important respects, of course. First, superstrings are a lot smaller than guitar strings. In fact, they are as small as anything can theoretically be. Physicists believe that superstrings measure approximately 10^{-33} centimeters in length. That's 10 with 32 zeros and a decimal point in front of it. If you were the size of a superstring, an atom would appear to be the size of the solar system! In addition, unlike guitar strings, superstrings are not *made* of some material. Rather, the superstrings themselves *are* the most fundamental things possible. A superstring can be described only as being made of a superstring.

The super-tiny size of superstrings is not their weirdest characteristic, however. According to string theory, they have zero thickness—that is, no thickness at all. In other words, superstrings are like one-dimensional lines that bend, vibrate, and even break and merge with one another.

Both guitar strings and superstrings have certain characteristic vibrations. For a guitar string, vibrations determine how a string sounds when it is plucked. According to string theory, the different vibration patterns of superstrings, called their *string modes,* give rise to the various particles of matter and force. String modes with relatively low energy give rise to particles with little or no *mass* (the amount of matter in an object). High-energy string modes are thought to lead to particles with large mass.

Scientists at first tried to estimate the apparent masses of the lightest possible string modes by using a formula developed by Einstein for calculating the mass of a moving particle. However, the results of these calculations did not make sense. They showed that the superstrings had a *negative mass*—that is, their masses were less than zero. The calculations also indicated that superstrings move faster than the speed of light. Both of these results are impossible according to the accepted laws of physics.

Supersymmetry and extra dimensions

These results might have tempted physicists to conclude that string theory was seriously flawed. Instead, they suspected that their calculations were inadequate to describe string theory. Researchers sought to improve their mathematical formulas by turning to a version of string theory that incorporates *supersymmetry,* which was developed by a number of physicists, including John Schwarz of the California Institute of Technology in Pasadena. The "super" in superstrings comes from "supersymmetry." According to the mathematical formulas of supersymmetry, the apparent masses of the lightest string modes depend on only one thing: the number of spatial dimensions that the superstrings wiggle in. It turns out that when a superstring has nine spatial dimensions to wiggle around in—that is, six more than our usual three—its lightest mode is never negative, and it never violates the cosmic speed limit.

Supersymmetry also sheds light on the two main shapes that superstrings can take—closed and open. *Closed superstrings* take the form of loops, while *open superstrings* have two free ends. Supersymmetry calculations show that the lightest mode of a closed superstring has the expected mass and energy characteristics of the *graviton,* the theoretical particle that

SUPERSTRING MUSIC

Superstrings and the strings of musical instruments, such as guitars, have a lot in common, including *elasticity*, the ability to stretch and return to their original shape. However, superstrings don't need to be plucked like guitar strings; they can play themselves!

Each string on a guitar vibrates in a different way when plucked. The various patterns of the vibrations (below) determine the musical notes that the strings produce.

In a similar way, the vibration patterns of superstrings determine the types of particles the superstrings give rise to. The more energetic the vibrations, the greater the mass of the particles. Increasing energy is shown from top to bottom (right).

Whether a superstring forms a closed loop (top) or has open ends (bottom) also influences what type of particle the superstring produces. For example, physicists believe gravitons are made of closed superstrings, while photons are made of open superstrings.

carries the force of gravity. The lightest mode of an open superstring has the properties of the other force-carrying particles—photons, gluons, and weak gauge bosons.

If string theory works only in a world with at least nine dimensions in space and one dimension in time—a total of 10 space-time dimensions—where are these extra dimensions? And what are they? We are so used to our usual three spatial dimensions that it is virtually impossible to imagine what an extra-dimensional world would be like. According to certain equations of string theory, the six extra dimensions are all around us, at every point in space-time. But they are not noticeable because they are curled up into extremely tiny shapes.

What would these extra dimensions look like if we could shrink to the size of a super-string and see them? Scientists aren't sure, but one possibility is a complex six-dimensional shape called a Calabi-Yau (*kah LAH bee YOW*) space. This shape was named after mathematicians Eugenio Calabi of the University of Pennsylvania in Philadelphia and Shing-Tung Yau of Harvard University in Cambridge, Massachusetts, because their research in a related field helped physicists understand the concept of extra dimensions.

If you were the size of a microscopic super-string and living in a Calabi-Yau space, you would probably be very confused and lonely. You would have so many possible directions to move in that you would find it extremely difficult to get back to your starting point once you wandered away. Because light would spread out so quickly inside this extra-dimensional environment, other superstring-sized beings would become dimmer very rapidly—then quickly disappear—as you moved away. Sound would also fade rapidly, so it would be impossible to hear others unless you were right next to them. In one way or another, you would always be very lost in a Calabi-Yau space.

The idea of 10 dimensions seems truly

bizarre. But why should there be only three dimensions to space? Nothing that we know about in the laws of physics points to three dimensions as the unique or required number. Physicists have developed a mathematical description for geometry and physics in three spatial dimensions. However, these scientists can also write equations to describe a universe with 9 or 10 spatial dimensions. Although such equations do not prove that extra dimensions exist, they do imply that experiments could perhaps confirm their existence one day.

One way to consider the possibility of extra dimensions is to think of a newborn baby who is beginning to explore its world. The baby at first may not realize there are three dimensions. But gradually through experience, the child discovers these previously unknown dimensions. Might we be like young children, merely unaware of dimensions that surround us?

Seeking support for string theory

Despite remarkable theoretical advances and insights, much of the physics of superstrings remains mysterious. In fact, as of 2004, no one had succeeded in using string theory to make precise predictions for real-world experiments. Because of this, not all physicists have jumped on the superstring bandwagon.

Some physicists believe that string theory will never be proved or disproved. One of the more vocal skeptics has been Nobel Prize-winning physicist Sheldon Glashow of Boston University, one of the developers of grand unification. In the opinion of Glashow and some other physicists, string theory has more in common with philosophy than science.

In 2004, physicists lacked the technology to observe superstrings directly. Thus, the challenge for researchers is to test certain predictions of string theory that would, at least, provide indirect evidence that parts of the theory are correct. According to string theory, every type of elementary particle has a closely related "superpartner" particle, called a *sparticle*. Sparticles differ from regular particles in their spin—or lack of spin. For example, an electron spins, but its superpartner, called a selectron, does not. Thus, the discovery of sparticles with predicted spin characteristics would lend support to string theory.

Researchers are seeking evidence of sparticles with *particle accelerators,* large machines that force subatomic particles to collide and then either break apart into smaller particles or join together to form other types of particles. The particles resulting from such collisions trace different paths that are visible in a special detector. By analyzing the length, angle, curve, and other characteristics of a path, scientists are able to determine what type of particle made the path. This is because each type of particle has a certain electrical charge, energy, mass, and *momentum* (the force with which an object moves), and these traits cause the particles to trace the paths that they do.

THE WEIRD WORLD OF EXTRA DIMENSIONS

String theory predicts that there are at least six extra dimensions in the universe—in addition to the four dimensions of length, width, height, and time. However, string theorists do not agree on exactly where—or what—these extra dimensions are.

Certain equations of string theory require that the extra dimensions be curled up and twisted together into microscopic shapes called Calabi-Yau shapes (below) and that these shapes occur at every point on the space-time grid (right). However, these extra dimensions are invisible to us because they are so tiny.

Other equations suggest that the extra dimensions might be infinitely large. We cannot see them because the universe we live in exists on a membrane-like surface called a brane, or a "braneworld" (right). This brane is only a thin slice of the entire "megaverse" in which the extra dimensions lie. According to this idea, other universes on other branes also make thin slices through the multidimensional megaverse. String theory suggests that *gravitons*, the particles that carry the gravitational force, may move from one brane to another.

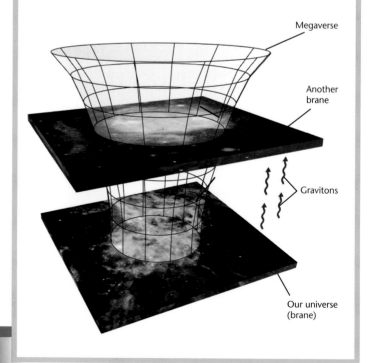

Megaverse

Another brane

Gravitons

Our universe (brane)

Particle accelerators might be able to create the exotic sparticles in the laboratory. Physicists are using the world's most powerful accelerator, the Tevatron at the Fermi National Accelerator Laboratory (Fermilab) near Batavia, Illinois, to try to produce and detect sparticles, as well as other possible evidence for string theory.

Physicists are also using particle accelerators to search for evidence of the extra dimensions predicted by string theory. Although these dimensions are normally hidden from our view, they still might be detected by discovering exotic, heavy particles called Kaluza-Klein particles. These theoretical objects are named after physicists Theodor Kaluza of Poland and Oskar Klein of Sweden, who suggested the possible existence of extra dimensions around 1920.

The expected existence of Kaluza-Klein particles is based on Einstein's formula for calculating the mass of a moving particle. According to this formula, any particles moving in extra dimensions would have a large amount of mass (compared to other known particles); these would be the Kaluza-Klein particles. If these heavy, yet normally hidden, particles really exist, they might be produced and studied in the same particle-accelerator experiments that are looking for the lighter sparticles.

Vibrating "braneworlds"?

Additional evidence for some of the ideas of string theory could come from a related idea known as M-theory. The mathematical equations of M-theory support the concept that superstrings might be more like tiny two-dimensional membranes than one-dimensional lines. M-theory also suggests that space-time has a total of 11 dimensions. String theorist Edward Witten of the Institute for Advanced Study in Princeton, New Jersey, introduced the name M-theory for this 11-dimensional formulation of physics in 1995. Strangely enough, the "M" in M-theory doesn't stand for

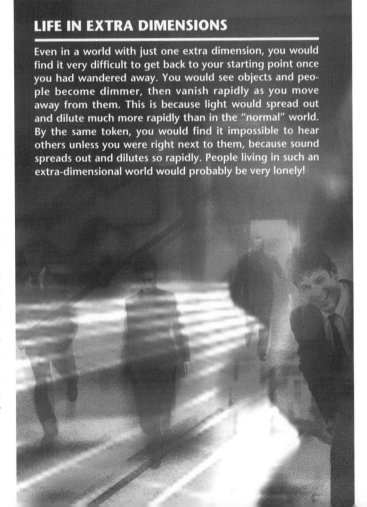

LIFE IN EXTRA DIMENSIONS

Even in a world with just one extra dimension, you would find it very difficult to get back to your starting point once you had wandered away. You would see objects and people become dimmer, then vanish rapidly as you move away from them. This is because light would spread out and dilute much more rapidly than in the "normal" world. By the same token, you would find it impossible to hear others unless you were right next to them, because sound spreads out and dilutes so rapidly. People living in such an extra-dimensional world would probably be very lonely!

LOOKING FOR EVIDENCE

Physicists are using particle accelerators, such as the Tevatron at Fermi National Accelerator Laboratory, to look for evidence supporting string theory. After circling the Tevatron's track (below), beams of subatomic particles collide, producing a shower of new particles.

anything in particular, though some physicists prefer to think of it as standing for "membrane," "mystery," or even "mother of all theories."

M-theory also suggests that our entire visible universe might exist on a giant three-dimensional vibrating membranelike surface called a *brane.* This would help explain why all the proposed extra dimensions are hidden from us: We exist on just one thin slice of a universe with many other dimensions. If so, we cannot see the extra dimensions because they fall outside our so-called "braneworld."

To find evidence of this braneworld, researchers are searching for certain particles that could, theoretically, move between the brane on which our world exists and other possible branes (on which other possible universes exist). M-theory proposes that gravitons would be such particles because, according to the theory's equations, they would not be tightly confined to any one brane. This means that physicists might find evidence of extra dimensions by performing very sensitive tests of gravity over microscopic distances or by producing gravitons in particle accelerators. In 2004, for example, physicists Maria Spiropulu, Greg Landsberg, and their collaborators were using Fermilab's Tevatron particle accelera-

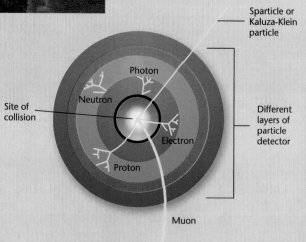

A particle detector inside the accelerator consists of different layers, each of which is sensitive to certain types of particles produced in the collision. Different kinds of particles make different kinds of paths (right), which reflect the charges, energy, momentum, and mass of the particles. For example, physicists expect that a long-lived, charged sparticle or a Kaluza-Klein particle—both of which are proposed by string theory—would make a long, straight path leading out of the detector.

Sparticle or Kaluza-Klein particle

Photon

Neutron

Site of collision

Different layers of particle detector

Electron

Proton

Muon

tor to measure the energy released in particle collisions. They were hoping to find that the energy from some of these collisions was "missing"—that is, less than expected. If gravitons are moving off our brane, they might be carrying this "missing energy" away with them as they disappear into the extra dimensions outside the brane. If researchers eventually detect this energy imbalance, they will have strong evidence for the extra dimensions proposed by string theory and M-theory.

More efforts to find evidence

Yet another way in which physicists are probing for particles associated with string theory is by using nature's own particle accelerators. When high-energy cosmic ray particles, such as neutrinos and negatively charged *muons,* strike Earth's atmosphere, they produce collisions that are much more energetic than any produced by human-made accelerators. These spectacular events and their by-products can be observed on the ground by special cosmic ray detectors, such as the Pierre Auger Observatory, which began operating in 2003 in Argentina. AMANDA (Antarctic Muon and Neutrino Detector Array) and IceCube, two neutrino detectors buried beneath the ice in Antarctica, are also very sensitive to cosmic rays. Some physicists believe that such cosmic ray detectors have an excellent chance of detecting the particles associated with string theory.

Although physicists had yet to find experimental evidence supporting string theory, they had high hopes that their many efforts would soon bear fruit. The unification of all theories of physics under string theory would not spell the end of science by any stretch of the imagination. Nevertheless, it would go a long way toward helping scientists understand the fundamental nature of the cosmos.

■ FOR ADDITIONAL INFORMATION

Books and periodicals
Arkini-Hamed, Nima; Dimopoulos, Savas; and Dvali, Georgi. "The Universe's Unseen Dimensions." *Scientific American,* August 2000, pp. 62-69.
Greene, Brian. *The Elegant Universe: Superstrings, Hidden Dimensions, and the Quest for the Ultimate Theory.* Vintage Books, 2000.
Gribbin, John R. *The Search for Superstrings, Symmetry, and the Theory of Everything.* Little, Brown and Co., 1999.

Web sites
The Collider Detector at Fermilab—www-cdf.fnal.gov
NASA Imagine the Universe! Superstrings—
    imagine.gsfc.nasa.gov/docs/science/mysteries_l2/superstring.html
NOVA The Elegant Universe—www.pbs.org/wgbh/nova/elegant
The Official String Theory Web Site—www.superstringtheory.com

By 2004, obesity had become a major health threat throughout the world. Although scientists had uncovered a variety of social, psychological, biological, and genetic reasons for skyrocketing obesity rates, they remained frustrated in their efforts to find an effective solution to the problem.

WHY ARE WE GETTING FATTER?
THE PUZZLE OF OBESITY

By Jon E. Levine

E pidemic. When people hear this word, they usually think of the rapid spread of *influenza* (the flu) or another highly infectious viral disease among a large number of people. But by the early 2000's, health experts were using the word *epidemic* to describe a different type of threat to millions of people in the United States and other nations. This epidemic, which began in the 1980's, involves a skyrocketing increase in the number of people who are overweight or obese. More shocking is the evidence from medical researchers that children in the United States and other countries with a high living standard are even more likely to be overweight or obese than adults are. In the history of our species, human beings have never been as heavy, on average, as we are now.

In March 2004, researchers at the Centers for Disease Control and Prevention (CDC) in Atlanta, Georgia, reported that obesity was rapidly overtaking smoking as the leading cause of death in the United States. In 2000 (the latest year for which data were available), tobacco use caused 435,000 deaths—18.1 percent of everyone who died. Obesity ranked as the second leading cause of death, killing 400,000 people—16.6 percent of all who died. In addition, by 2004, researchers had linked overweight and obesity to a variety of medical and psychological problems, including a shorter life span. Health experts worried that obesity, which often becomes a lifelong condition, posed a special threat to the well-being and future of today's children.

Many experts predicted that, unless checked, the obesity epidemic would change the ways we travel and work. For example, it could affect the size of seats in cars, airplanes, and waiting rooms; the ability of police and fire departments to find fit employees; and the level of productivity among workers with obesity-related health problems. The epidemic could also lower the overall quality of health care as society struggles to care for huge numbers of people with long-term obesity-related illnesses and with the expense of purchasing such items as heavy-duty wheelchairs and scales that can handle weights up to 360 kilograms (800 pounds).

Why has obesity become epidemic? A variety of researchers are attempting to answer this very complex question. Biologists, for example, are studying how the body normally works to control its weight so they can learn how such control systems may malfunction in people who become obese. Neurobiologists are focusing on the ways the brain governs appetite. In addition, endocrinologists are studying the roles *hormones* (chemical messengers in the blood) play in controlling eating behavior.

Since the early 1990's, researchers have made significant progress in understanding how the brain, liver, fat cells, and pancreas—and the hormones they produce—work to balance the amount of food we eat with the energy we need to live and to control our *metabolism* (the process by which living

Researchers have found that fat cells (shown magnified hundreds of times) play a much more active role in obesity than they had previously thought.

things turn food into energy). Researchers have even succeeded in manipulating *genes* (the basic units of heredity) that play a role in controlling various aspects of appetite to produce animals that become obese. Such work not only sheds light on the body's systems for managing weight but also suggests possible drug treatments for people with obesity. Nevertheless, many pieces of the puzzle are still missing. As human beings evolved over millions of years, our bodies developed systems to protect us from the constant threat of starvation. Are these same systems now sabotaging our attempts to fight obesity?

While biologists pursue the "how" of body weight regulation, many psychologists and sociologists are attempting to understand the "why" behind the obesity epidemic. Why are people heavier, on average, in the 2000's than they were in the 1980's? Data collected by national and international health organizations have shown that obesity is most common in countries with high living standards, though obesity rates appear to be increasing in developing nations as well. Is obesity on the rise because food is so plentiful today? That explanation, most health experts believe, is too simple. Most people in developed nations enjoyed an abundance of food long before the 1980's, when obesity rates began to rise sharply.

Have people simply become too lazy or weak-willed to keep their weight in check? Many experts contend that such a judgment is too harsh, because it places all the blame for the epidemic on people who are overweight or obese and ignores the fact that society tends to judge overweight or obese people harshly. Is obesity a result of a lack of exercise in our modern life style? Are we eating too much sugar or too many *processed foods* (foods preserved for the sake of convenience or safety)? Or are all these factors contributing to the increase in obesity rates? In countries such as the United States, where our popular culture seems to be obsessed with appearance and a desire for an unrealistically lean body shape, the trend towards heavier and fatter bodies is all the more difficult to understand.

Researchers hope that by studying the scope of the obesity epidemic and the biological, psychological, and social roots of the problem they may be able to help those already affected. They also hope their findings can prevent obesity from devastating future generations.

The author:
Jon E. Levine is professor of neurobiology and physiology at Northwestern University in Evanston, Illinois; director of Northwestern's Program in Biological Sciences; editor-in-chief of the journal *Frontiers in Neuroendocrinology*; and a member of the editorial board of the journal *Endocrinology*.

THE OBESITY EPIDEMIC

What does it mean to be *overweight?* At what point does an *overweight* person become *obese?* Both conditions develop from the same cause—too much *adipose tissue,* more commonly known as fat, stored in the body.

The most common tool health experts use to determine whether a person is storing too much fat is called the *body mass index (BMI).* The BMI is based on a mathematical formula developed by Belgian statistician Adolphe Quetelet in the mid-1800's. Quetelet had taken height and weight measurements of a large number of people in an attempt to learn the size of an "average" person. He discovered that, in adults of normal size, weight in kilograms is proportional to height in meters squared. Today, physicians have other ways to measure body fat. However, these methods are more complicated and expensive than the BMI and require specialized medical equipment and personnel.

Many health organizations and other sources of medical information offer charts that make it easy for you to look up your BMI. But you can also calculate your BMI yourself with either of the formulas indicated below. Once you know your BMI, you can determine which of four categories you fall into: un-derweight, normal, overweight, or obese. Then you can determine your risk of developing such obesity-related diseases as high blood pressure, diabetes, and *cardiovascular disease* (diseases of the heart and blood vessels).

The standard BMI chart used by medical professionals classifies adults with a value of less than 18.5 as "underweight." Those with a BMI of 18.5 to 24.9 are in the "normal" range. Adults with a BMI of 25 to 29.9 are considered "overweight." And those with a BMI of 30 or above are classified as "obese." (Having a BMI of 30 corresponds roughly to being about 14 kilograms [30 pounds] overweight.) Physicians caution that the BMI does not take into consideration a person's proportion of fat to muscle. As a result, a very muscular person may be misclassified as obese simply because muscle weighs more than fat. Nevertheless, for most people, a high BMI is a valid measure of unhealthy excess fat.

Unlike BMI values for adults, those for children, teen-agers, and young adults (ages 2 to 20) differ by age and sex. A BMI in the 85th to 95th percentile for a child's age and sex places a child in the "overweight" category. A BMI at or above the 95th percentile indicates obesity.

Evidence that overweight and obesity rates are on the rise in the United States is unmistakable. From 1960 to 1962 and from 1971 to 1994, agen-

THE BODY MASS INDEX (BMI) AND WHAT IT MEANS

The body mass index (BMI) represents the relationship between a person's weight and height. The BMI has become the most common method used by doctors to determine whether a person is overweight or obese.

How to measure your BMI

Many sources of health information offer calculators and tables that adults over age 20 can use to determine their BMI. The U.S. National Institutes of Health provides a calculator and table on the Internet at http://nhlbisupport.com/bmi/bmicalc.htm

You can also figure out your BMI using a simple mathematical formula:

$$BMI = \left(\frac{weight\ in\ pounds}{(height\ in\ inches) \times (height\ in\ inches)} \right) \times 703$$

$$BMI = \left(\frac{weight\ in\ kilograms}{(height\ in\ meters) \times (height\ in\ meters)} \right)$$

According to this formula, a person who weighs 125 pounds and is 5 feet 3 inches tall has a BMI of 22.1.

BMI as a measure of risk

The risk of developing an obesity-related disease increases among adults as an individual's BMI rises.

BMI	Classification	Risk of associated disease
18.5 or less	Underweight	Low
18.5 to 24.9	Normal weight	Average
25.0 to 29.9	Overweight	Increased
30.0 to 34.9	Obese	High
35.0 to 39.9	Very obese	Very high
40.0 or greater	Extremely obese	Extremely high

Source: National Institutes of Health.

CHILDREN'S BMI

A child's BMI is calculated using the same formula as that for adults. However, BMI charts for children 2 to 20 years old organize height and weight information by age because the amount of fat in a child's body changes as he or she grows. These charts also plot levels of fat by gender because girls and boys have different levels of fat at different ages.

Children with a BMI index-for-age below the 5th percentile are considered underweight. Children with a BMI index-for-age in the 85th to 95th percentile are considered overweight. Children with a BMI index-for-age at or above the 95th percentile are classified as obese.

Source: U.S. Centers for Disease Control and Prevention.

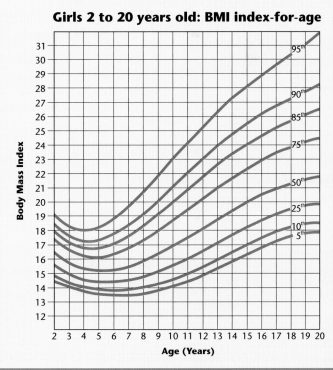

cies of the U.S. government conducted four major national surveys of body weight and body fat levels, including three National Health and Nutrition Examination Surveys (NHANES I, II, and III). NHANES IV began in 1999 and was ongoing in 2004.

The data from these surveys have revealed several remarkable facts. First, the rates of overweight and obesity among adult Americans changed little from 1960 to 1980. Second, since 1980, the rates have risen dramatically. For example, from 1976 to 1980, 46 percent of adults in the United States were classified as overweight or obese. By 2000, that figure had risen to 64.5 percent. A significant rise in the percentage of adults with obesity—30.5 percent in 2000 compared with 14.5 percent in 1980—accounted for most of the increase.

The NHANES studies found that overweight and obesity rates among children and teen-agers also remained relatively stable from 1960 to1980. Beginning in 1980, however, the rates skyrocketed. In 1980, 5.0 percent of 2- to 5-year-olds were obese, compared with 10.4 percent in 2000. Among 6- to 11-year-olds, 6.5 percent were obese in 1980, with the number rising to 15.3 percent in 2000. Five percent of 12- to 19-year-olds were obese in 1980, compared with 15.5 percent in 2000.

Linked to the epidemic in childhood obesity was an increase in the number of children with Type 2 diabetes. Type 2 diabetes is a serious health condition in which the body is unable to move a sugar called glucose, used for energy, out of the bloodstream and into the cells. This condition used to be known as adult-onset diabetes because it usually developed in chronically overweight or obese adults. Because of the increase among children, health experts have largely stopped using that term.

By the early 2000's, NHANES researchers had confirmed that the obesity epidemic was affecting all social, economic, and ethnic groups in the United States. NHANES IV indicated that among children, though, rates had risen faster among Mexican American and non-Hispanic black teen-agers.

Obesity rates were also on the rise throughout the world, in industrialized and developing countries alike. In 2003, more than 1 billion adults worldwide were overweight and at least 300 million of them were obese, according to the World Health Organization (WHO), an agency of the United Nations based in Geneva, Switzerland.

The American Obesity Association (AOA), a group headquartered in Washington, D.C., that promotes research and advocacy on obesity issues, also found that obesity affects some ethnic groups more than others. The key seemed to be exposure

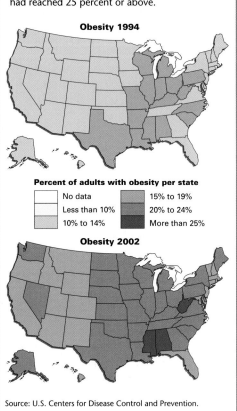

OBESITY RATES RISE

Maps of obesity rates by state from 1994 and 2002 record the skyrocketing increase in obesity among adults in the United States. In 1994, only 16 states reported that at least 15 percent of their residents were obese. By 2002, all 50 states reported obesity rates of at least 15 percent. Twenty-nine states reported that 20 to 24 percent of residents were obese. In three states, obesity rates had reached 25 percent or above.

Obesity 1994

Percent of adults with obesity per state

No data	15% to 19%
Less than 10%	20% to 24%
10% to 14%	More than 25%

Obesity 2002

Source: U.S. Centers for Disease Control and Prevention.

to a typical Western lifestyle. Such a lifestyle includes a decrease in physical activity and an increase in consumption of foods high in sugar and fat. Australian Aborigines, Pima Indians in Arizona, and native Hawaiians experienced a higher growth in obesity rates than other ethnic groups did after adopting a Western lifestyle, the AOA found.

In several developed countries, according to WHO, obesity-related medical problems accounted for a rising percentage of total health care costs. In the United States, for example, such costs reached $75.1 billion—or 7 percent of total health care costs—in 2003, according to researchers at the CDC and at a nonprofit group called RTI International in Research Triangle Park, near Durham, North Carolina. Most public health officials were convinced that these figures would continue to rise.

ENERGY IN/ENERGY OUT

Everyone knows what it feels like to be hungry or full. Most of us feel these sensations several times a day. Many people assume that we feel hungry—and develop an *appetite* (a desire to eat)—because our stomach is empty. But this is not always the case. We are usually no more hungry at breakfast, for example, than we are at lunch or dinner, even though the time between dinner and breakfast is normally longer than the time between breakfast and lunch or between lunch and dinner. Likewise, shortly after dinner, we might catch sight of our favorite dessert and want to eat again, even though our stomach is still digesting the food we ate.

If we do not develop an appetite just because our stomach is empty, then what determines when and how much we eat? Researchers have long known that appetite depends on other factors as well. These include time of day; social conditions, such as whether we're eating alone or in a group; the way we feel emotionally—if we are stressed or bored, for example; the availability, smell, and taste of food; learned eating habits; and our activity and exercise schedules. Biological factors also affect our appetite. For example, the act of eating prompts the intestines to release a number of *hormones* (chemical messengers), including cholecystokinin (CCK). CCK signals the brain that the stomach is getting full and that it's time to stop eating.

Does our body weight depend only on our responses to these short-term cues for eating? This is unlikely. Researchers note that the amounts and kinds of food we eat can vary dramatically from day to day. Yet, for some of us, body weight remains relatively stable over months or years at a time.

Since the 1950's, numerous experiments have established that laboratory animals remain at about the same body weight over long periods, even when they can eat as much as they want. In 1996, for example, researchers led by clinical nutritionist Michael W. Schwartz of the University of Washington in Seattle monitored the weight levels of three groups of rats over several weeks. The rats in the first group followed a normal diet, eating as much as they wanted. The second group of rats received much less food than those in the first group. Finally, researchers force-fed the rats in the third group much more than they normally ate.

After a few weeks, the rats that continued to eat as much as they wanted remained within their normal weight range. Not surprisingly, the rats on a reduced diet either gained less weight than the free-feeding rats or lost weight. Finally, as expected, the force-fed rats gained weight. When the researchers then allowed all three groups of rats to eat as much as they wanted, they made some surprising discoveries. They found that the rats that had been on a reduced diet soon weighed as much as the rats that had eaten as much as they wanted throughout the experiment. The force-fed rats

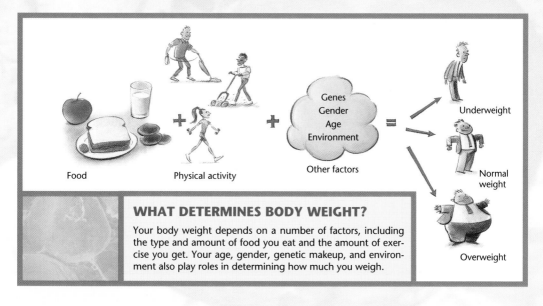

Food   Physical activity   Genes / Gender / Age / Environment — Other factors   Underweight / Normal weight / Overweight

WHAT DETERMINES BODY WEIGHT?

Your body weight depends on a number of factors, including the type and amount of food you eat and the amount of exercise you get. Your age, gender, genetic makeup, and environment also play roles in determining how much you weigh.

quickly lost the weight they had gained, choosing not to overeat, even though they had that option. In other words, all of the rats returned to their previous weight when they were allowed to eat according to their own body's desires.

The Schwartz experiment supported the theory that animals have a *set point* (a preferred body weight) that is established by their genetic makeup and maintained by internal biological processes that researchers still do not fully understand. According to this theory, any forced change in an animal's eating habits—whether dieting or overeating—prompts the body to take steps to return the animal's weight to its set point.

Many researchers believe that each person also has a set point and the biological control systems for maintaining it. They point out that some people can maintain a stable weight for years with little effort. In contrast, most people who lose weight on a diet eventually gain back most of it unless they continue to eat less food than they used to eat.

But what biological systems control set points? How do they work? And, most important of all, why don't they prevent people from becoming overweight or obese in the first place? Although scientists can't answer all of these questions yet, they have begun to make progress on some of them.

The answers may lie in a concept called *energy balance*. When we eat, we take in energy in the form of *calories* (the amount of energy a food yields when it is completely used by the body). As we walk, work, or engage in other physical activities during the day, we use up some of this energy. Our bodies also use energy to keep our internal temperature at a normal level and our various organ systems working.

If we take in more energy than we use—for example, on Thanksgiving Day—we store the extra energy in fat cells and the liver. In this case, we have a *positive energy balance*. In times of *negative energy balance*—when we may not be able to eat as often or as much as we need—we call on our stored fat. In this way—at least for a time—we have a supply of readily available energy.

For some people, the amount of energy they take in and the amount they use up match closely, even if they tend to overeat at times. In other words, these people, like most animals, seem to maintain a *neutral energy balance*—they neither gain nor lose weight over long periods of time.

By 2004, researchers had discovered some key information about this adjustment process, though much remained unknown. Researchers know that the balancing process begins when energy, in the

form of fat and a sugar called glucose, enters the bloodstream. These nutrients come from two sources—the *gastrointestinal tract* (the stomach and intestines) after a meal has been digested and the stores of energy in the liver and fat cells.

The brain and the liver monitor and control the amount of glucose and fat entering the bloodstream. Both organs can detect glucose and fat levels in the blood at any given time and can signal this information to each other through a system of nerves. When the liver and brain detect low levels of glucose and fat in the blood, they act to reverse the drop. For example, the liver may release more of its stored glucose, while the brain may stimulate the appetite. Scientists agree that the purpose of the adjustment processes is to safeguard the body from dangerous reductions in energy. Tissues that depend almost exclusively on glucose to function—such as the brain—are, therefore, safe from a potentially deadly drop in energy levels called *hypoglycemia*. (Many people fear that they may become hypoglycemic by missing a meal. However, in healthy people, the liver and several hormones ensure that enough glucose is pulled from its stored forms so the blood always has enough glucose.)

Some people, however, seem unable to maintain a neutral energy balance for very long. For these people, eating an extra 10 calories per day—about one-third of a small cookie—may cause a weight gain of about one-half kilogram (1 pound) per year. Over decades, such a tiny but steady weight gain may lead to obesity. So why can some people eat a whole cookie every day and still not gain weight? Researchers believe their bodies must have some way of matching the energy they take in with the energy they use.

Research during the 1990's confirmed what scientists had long suspected—that body fat and weight are regulated by hormones that are released in proportion to the amount of fat our bodies have stored. In other words, if we try to lose weight by eating less, these hormones signal us to eat more so that our fat stores do not fall too low. Ideally, if we begin eating too much, the hormones should signal us to stop, because our fat stores are already at a required level.

One of the most important of these newly discovered control hormones produced by fat cells is called leptin. Identified in 1994 by molecular geneticist Jeffrey Friedman and colleagues at Rockefeller University in New York City, leptin acts as a messenger from fat cells to other tissues, including the brain. Researchers think that leptin levels rise and fall according to the amount of fat stored in the

WHAT CONTROLS WHEN—AND HOW MUCH—WE EAT?

A number of *hormones* (chemical messengers) produced in different parts of the body play a major role in determining how much we eat and how much we weigh over time. The hormones travel to parts of the brain called the hypothalamus and the brain stem, which send out signals of hunger or fullness. For example, ghrelin (Ghr) is released by cells in the stomach when it is empty, triggering signals that make us feel hungry. Levels of peptide YY (PYY), produced in the digestive tract, rise during a meal, making us feel full. Cholecystokinin (CCK), produced by the intestines during a meal, slows down the rate at which food leaves the stomach, also sending a "stop eating" signal to the brain and making us feel full. Researchers think that a drop in leptin, which is produced by fat cells, keeps the body from losing weight during times of starvation by stimulating the hypothalamus to send out hunger signals and by slowing the rate at which the body uses energy. Insulin, made in the pancreas, suppresses appetite.

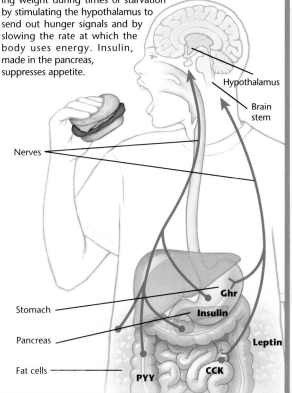

Hypothalamus

Brain stem

Nerves

Ghr

Stomach

Insulin

Pancreas

Leptin

Fat cells

CCK

PYY

eating behavior and weight according to a feedback system, much like the heating system in your home. As the temperature in your house falls below the set point on the thermostat, the thermostat registers the drop and signals the furnace to turn on. The furnace heats the air until the air reaches the temperature designated on the thermostat, at which point the thermostat stops calling for heat. In this way, the thermostat monitors the temperature in the house and adjusts the amount of heat the furnace is putting out to maintain a particular temperature over time.

Similarly, an increase in the amount of food you eat or a decrease in the amount of energy you use over time leads to an increase in the amount of fat stored in your body. As your fat levels rise, your body makes greater amounts of leptin and insulin. Rising leptin and insulin levels trigger the brain to send out signals lowering appetite and increasing the amount of energy your body is burning.

On the other hand, dieting or increasing your physical activity over time reduces the amount of fat stored in your body. As a result, the body produces less leptin and insulin. The hormones are not as effective in reducing appetite, and you eat more. In addition, your body burns less energy.

How do leptin and insulin cause us to have a bigger or smaller appetite? By the early 2000's, neurobiologists and *endocrinologists* (scientists who study hormones) had identified several groups of cells in a part of the brain called the hypothalamus that may be the targets of leptin and insulin. These cell groups make *receptors* (cells that are sensitive to a particular substance) to which leptin and insulin attach. After leptin and insulin have attached to the receptors, the cells release *neurotransmitters* (chemical substances that send messages between nerve cells). The neurotransmitters carry messages to other areas of the brain, either increasing or decreasing the desire to eat.

Researchers have identified a number of neurotransmitters made and released in the hypothalamus that very powerfully regulate eating. One of the most important is neuropeptide Y (NPY), which increases appetite in rats. Other neurotransmitters, such as a group called the melanocortins, suppress appetite. Many scientists are attempting to develop drugs that either stimulate or inhibit the receptors that produce specific neurotransmitters and thus provide effective new treatment options for obesity.

body. They also think that leptin signals the brain that it is time to start or stop eating.

A second important advance was the demonstration by Schwartz, as well as other researchers such as Stephen J. Woods of the University of Cincinnati in Ohio and colleagues, of the importance of insulin in eating behavior. Insulin, a hormone produced by the pancreas, is best known for helping to move glucose from the bloodstream into body cells. Schwartz, Woods, and others demonstrated that insulin also functions as a messenger to the brain, signaling the body to stop eating.

Researchers have theorized that in people who can maintain a normal weight, the body controls

HOW DO WE BECOME OBESE?

Why do people become overweight or obese? Researchers agree that the simple answer to this question is that most overweight or obese people take in more energy from food than they spend in maintaining their body systems and engaging in physical activity. In short, they either eat too much, exercise too little, or both. A more difficult question—one that remained unanswered in 2004—was: Why are greater numbers of people becoming heavier today than at any other time in recorded history?

Scientists have found evidence that a person's weight is normally controlled within very precise limits by *hormones* (chemical messengers), such as leptin and insulin, and by brain cells that regulate appetite and energy use. Do these biological control systems break down in overweight and obese individuals? If so, how do the systems become damaged? Although researchers were hotly debating these questions in 2004, all agreed that some combination of genetic and *environmental* (social and psychological) factors must be involved.

Researchers had long suspected that body weight is, to some degree, an inherited characteristic. Leaner parents tend to have leaner children, and heavier parents, heavier children. However, researchers believe that a person's environment during childhood and adolescence also affects body weight. Thus, someone may become heavier than other people of the same age because of inherited genes that *predispose* him or her (make him or her susceptible) to becoming heavier. At the same time, an individual's family may serve meals high in calories and rarely participate in physical activities.

One way that researchers have tried to prove the existence of genetic predispositions to overweight or obesity has been by conducting studies of body weight among relatives. Among them is a now-classic 1986 study of twins by psychiatrist Albert J. Stunkard of the University of Pennsylvania in Philadelphia and his colleagues. The researchers found that identical twins, who share all their genes, were much more likely to be overweight or obese to the same degree than were fraternal twins, who share only about 50 percent. The research strongly supported the idea that weight is genetically determined to some degree.

The results of another study by Stunkard and his colleagues in 1990—this one of twins who had been adopted and raised apart—proved even more convincing. The researchers found that the weights of the adopted children more closely matched the weights of their biological parents than those of their adoptive parents.

Exactly which genes may predispose an individual to obesity is still the subject of intense research, though scientists have linked a number of genes to the condition. One of the most closely studied is a gene that *encodes for* (instructs the body to produce) the hormone leptin. Leptin acts in the brain to reduce appetite and increase the amount of energy the body uses for maintenance. In 1997, for example, a team of researchers at the University of Cambridge in the United Kingdom studied two cousins whose weight had been normal at birth but who had become extremely obese at a young age. Both children had abnormally low levels of leptin in their bloodstream. The researchers theorized that the cousins' low leptin levels made them feel constantly hungry and caused their bodies to use less energy than normal.

When the researers analyzed the cousins' genes, they found that the children had inherited a *mutated* (changed) leptin gene that left them with virtually no active leptin circulating in their blood. After the children were injected with leptin, they began to eat dramatically less, and their body weights returned to a normal level for their age.

Genetic studies of obese individuals, however, have revealed that few have a known mutation in their leptin gene, its *receptor* (the site in the brain to which leptin attaches), or in any other known gene that governs the body's ability to balance appetite with energy output. Fewer than 6 percent of severely obese children, for example, have been found to have *any* type of genetic defect associated with obesity.

In fact, throughout the 1990's, researchers hoping to link obesity with low leptin levels continued to find exactly the opposite. Studies revealed that most people who have become obese have *high* leptin levels. This is consistent with researchers' findings that the amount of leptin in the bloodstream depends on the number of fat cells present in the body. Scientists began to suspect that the bodies of obese people may not be responding to leptin's appetite-suppressing signals. In other words, people who become obese may be *leptin-resistant.* Researchers believe that because, for most people, neither the leptin gene nor its receptor is flawed, leptin resistance is caused by some other defect along leptin's route to the brain. As of 2004, that defect had not been discovered.

The fact that a defective leptin gene has not proved to be the cause of all obesity does not rule out the possibility that obesity may depend upon the interaction of several different genes. It is also possible that the most significant genes that cause obesity have yet to be identified.

In their search for other genetic causes of obesity, some scientists looked for clues in the early days of human history. For example, in 1962, geneticist James Neel of the University of Michigan at Ann Arbor introduced the "thrifty gene" theory. This theory proposes that early human beings in certain parts of the world may have faced situations that favored the survival of individuals with specific types of genes. Because people often faced the threat of scarce food resources, those individuals whose bodies tended to store fat in times of abundance—even to the point of obesity—were more likely to survive during times of famine than people whose bodies remained lean.

In the mid-1990's, molecular geneticist Jeffrey Friedman of Rockefeller University in New York City revived the thrifty gene theory by suggesting that some of these genes may be increasing our resistance to leptin. If this is true, the descendants of fat-storers—people who carry thrifty genes and who now live a sedentary Western lifestyle with abundant, calorie-dense food—would be expected to become obese at high rates.

In fact, this appears to be the case among the Pima Indians, a Native American group whose members live in both Arizona and Mexico. The Pima living in Arizona were subsistence farmers until about the 1940's, when they began to adopt a Western lifestyle. The Pima living in Mexico continued to practice subsistence agriculture into the 2000's.

Researchers with the U.S. National Institutes of Health, who have been studying the groups since the mid-1960's, found that the Arizona Pima have developed obesity at alarming rates, while Pima in Mexico are more lean. Thus, genes that promote efficient energy storage in times of an uncertain food supply may become less useful—and even detrimental—in a modern, food-rich society.

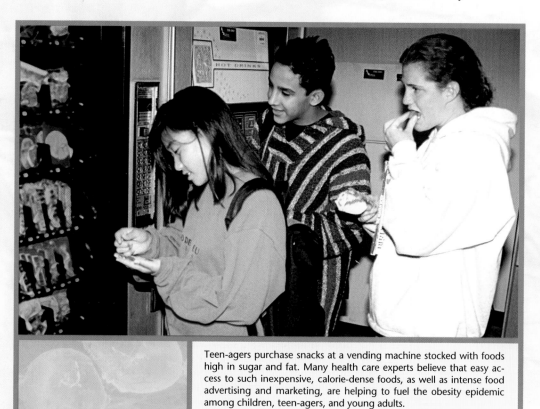

Teen-agers purchase snacks at a vending machine stocked with foods high in sugar and fat. Many health care experts believe that easy access to such inexpensive, calorie-dense foods, as well as intense food advertising and marketing, are helping to fuel the obesity epidemic among children, teen-agers, and young adults.

Nutrition experts believe that a gradual increase in portion sizes has contributed to the rise in obesity in the United States. An average serving of French fries in the 1950's weighed about 68 grams (2.4 ounces), about one-third the weight of an average serving of fries in the early 2000's.

By contrast, Friedman has theorized, early human beings who lived in another part of the world—an area of abundant food called the Fertile Crescent (part of what is now known as the Middle East)—may have developed genes that protected them against obesity. Being obese under such circumstances increased the chances of dying from health complications related to obesity or from becoming the easy prey of a wild animal. As a result, an individual's chances of becoming obese in today's affluent societies may depend upon whether he or she inherited genes from hunter-gatherer/subsistence farmers or Fertile Crescent-dwelling ancestors.

All of these research findings suggest a link between genes and obesity. However, the rapid increase of obesity in affluent nations since the 1980's suggests that environmental factors must play a major role as well. Scientists know that genetic mutations normally do not occur in large groups of people within such a short period of time. As a result, they agree that environmental factors—and the way such factors interact with genetic predispositions—are largely to blame for the current epidemic of obesity.

How has our environment changed since the 1980's to make obesity much more common? Some experts, such as James O. Hill, director of the Center for Human Nutrition at the University of Colorado Health Sciences Center in Denver, blame the social environment in the United States and other industrialized nations. They believe that this environment encourages overeating and discourages exercise. They also believe that an abundance of energy-dense, inexpensive foods is a major contributor to the obesity trend. In affluent countries, the food supply has become incredibly diverse, providing thousands more food choices than people ever had before, including processed, packaged, and prepared foods that are often high in fat, sugar, and calories.

Intense marketing—particularly advertising campaigns aimed at children—adds to the incentive to eat these high-calorie packaged foods. According to the World Health Organization (WHO), such marketing encourages overconsumption, especially in children.

Another factor that has contributed to overeating, according to nutrition experts, has been the remarkable increase in food serving sizes. An average serving of French fries in the 1950's, for example, weighed about 68 grams (2.4 ounces), the same as the "small" size of the early 2000's.

A detailed study of portion sizes served in takeout restaurants, fast-food outlets, and family restaurants was conducted by nutritionists Lisa R. Young and Marion Nestle at New York University in New York City. The study compared the size of serving sizes provided by those restaurants with portion sizes approved by the U.S. Department of Agriculture (USDA). The researchers reported in 2002 that cookies served in the restaurants were 700 percent larger than USDA standard sizes. In addition, cooked pasta exceeded standards by 480 percent, and steaks exceeded USDA recommended servings by 224 percent.

Social scientists also believe changes in family lifestyles have affected our diets. Since the 1980's, the number of households with a non-working parent has decreased significantly. As a result, time-pressured families eat out more often, buy dinner from fast-food restaurants more frequently, and prepare more meals using packaged ingredients—all of which generally contain more fat and sugar than a typical home-cooked meal. According to the USDA, food consumed outside the home accounted for an average 34 percent of a family's food budget in 1970. By the late 1990's, such purchases consumed

47 percent of a family's food budget. As a result, convenience, rather than nutrition, has become the most important element in food preparation.

Some psychologists have studied the role that emotional factors play in the development of overweight and obesity as well. Sometimes, weight loss or weight gain is a sign of mental depression. Researchers do not yet know why or how depression affects eating, nor do they understand how anxiety affects it. However, some researchers think that eating—particularly consuming so-called "comfort foods" that are high in sugar and fat—may help reduce anxiety. For example, a team at the University of California in San Francisco led by physiologist Norman Pecoraro reported in 2003 that rats placed under stressful conditions sought out high-energy foods such as sugar and lard about 24 hours later. After the animals ate, the level of stress hormones in their bodies decreased. Perhaps, then, the stress under which many people in the Western world live is helping to fuel the obesity epidemic.

Sedentary lifestyles have also become more common since the 1980's, and most scientists agree that this environmental change has played a major role in the current obesity epidemic. Today, our bodies need only a fraction of the energy our ancestors did in order to complete our daily tasks and provide ourselves with food. Yet, our bodies' energy-balancing mechanisms have not changed. The result is we are taking in enough energy to perform strenuous physical activities that we no longer perform and then storing the excess as fat.

In addition, we spend much of our free time engaged in nonphysical activities, such as television watching, playing with video and computer games, and surfing the Internet. Many working parents require their children to stay inside after school for safety reasons, preventing them from riding bikes, skating, and playing sports with friends. The increasing distances at which families live from one another—and from activities and entertainment—have led people to drive more and walk less. All of these social trends have produced new generations of children and adults who spend very little time being physically active.

In general, scientists agree that for most people, genes are not destiny. People who eat a healthful diet and get plenty of exercise can usually maintain a healthy body weight, regardless of their genetic inheritance. In a society where people tend to eat too much and exercise too little, however, a genetic predisposition to obesity may make the difference between maintaining normal weight and carrying too many extra pounds.

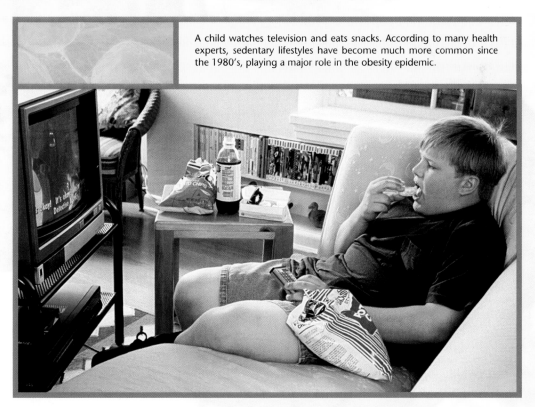

A child watches television and eats snacks. According to many health experts, sedentary lifestyles have become much more common since the 1980's, playing a major role in the obesity epidemic.

THE DANGERS OF EXTRA POUNDS

Some of us may decide to lose excess weight because we want to look better, perhaps for a special event or in preparation for swimsuit season. But for people who are overweight or obese, excess fat is more than a cosmetic concern; it is a serious health problem.

Numerous studies have shown that obesity greatly increases a person's risk of developing such life-threatening diseases as diabetes, hypertension (high blood pressure), heart attack, stroke, and cancer. By 2000, obesity had nearly surpassed tobacco use as the leading preventable cause of death in the United States. Some scientists have predicted that the average life span of Americans, which had risen steadily throughout the 1900's, may begin to decline as increasingly overweight or obese children reach adulthood and middle age during the 2000's.

Young people whose BMI values categorize them as overweight or obese may not show signs of cardiovascular or metabolic diseases for many years. (Cardiovascular diseases are those related to the heart or blood vessels. Metabolic diseases affect the system of chemical processes by which the body nourishes, maintains, and regulates itself.) Not all these children are destined to develop a cardiovascular or metabolic disease. However, data from many epidemiological (population) studies link a higher BMI in childhood to a higher-than-normal risk of developing such diseases—and at an earlier age than might be expected.

Some scientists, including pioneer obesity researcher George Bray at the Pennington Biomedical Research Institute in Baton Rouge, Louisiana, have argued that obesity itself is a disease. Bray theorizes that obesity, like mental depression or hypertension, develops because of a complex interplay between genes and a "toxic" environment. Bray describes the toxic environment for obesity as one filled with highly caloric and easily accessible foods.

By the early 2000's, most obesity researchers agreed with Bray that overweight and obesity result from multiple causes, not just a failure of willpower or a personal weakness. They now consider obesity a condition based, to a significant degree, on a defect in brain chemicals that directs the body's unconscious and powerful drive to defend an unhealthy weight—even at the cost of disease and disability. The extreme difficulty most obese people face in trying to lose weight and to maintain that weight loss reflects the strong biological forces that must be overcome to reverse this condition.

Researchers believe that the basic pathology (damage to cells and tissues) of obesity begins when we take in more energy as food than we use up. Our bodies store that excess as fat in adipocytes (fat cells), which enlarge to accommodate the additional fat. When the adipocytes reach their maximum size, they begin to multiply. But, in their enlarged state, they produce several substances that promote diseases, many scientists believe.

One unwelcome consequence of enlarged adipocytes is that they produce too many free fatty acids (FFA's). FFA's are fats that circulate in the blood. They form during a process called lipolysis, in which the body breaks down the fat molecules inside fat cells. Lipolysis releases the energy stored as fat into the blood so that the body can use it.

Although they do not understand the reasons why, researchers believe FFA's may contribute to

---

HEALTH CONSEQUENCES OF OBESITY

People who are overweight (BMI of 25.0 to 29.9) or obese (BMI of 30 or above) are more likely to develop health problems than are people of normal weight, according to the U.S. National Institutes of Health. These conditions include:

- High blood pressure
- High blood cholesterol
- Type 2 diabetes
- Insulin resistance, glucose intolerance (higher-than-normal levels of blood sugar)
- Coronary heart disease
- Angina pectoris (sudden heart pain)
- Congestive heart failure
- Stroke
- Gallstones or cholecystitis (inflammation of the gall bladder)
- Osteoarthritis (wearing away of the joints)
- Obstructive sleep apnea and other respiratory problems
- Some types of cancer (such as endometrial, breast, prostate, and colon)
- Complications of pregnancy
- Poor female reproductive health (such as menstrual irregularities, infertility, irregular ovulation)
- Bladder control problems
- Kidney stones
- Psychological disorders (such as depression, eating disorders, and distorted body image)

Source: U.S. Centers for Disease Control and Prevention.

DIABETES RATES SKYROCKET

Maps of the United States in 1994 and 2002 reveal a dramatic increase in cases of Type 2 diabetes among adults. In 1994, only 2 states reported that at least 6 percent of their adult residents had this condition. By 2002, the number of states with this rate of Type 2 diabetes had risen 1,500 percent, to 29.

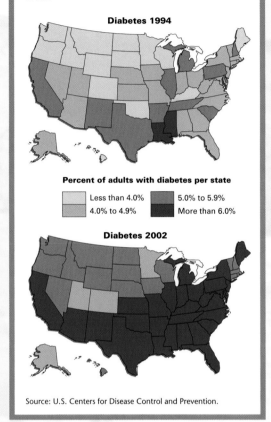

Diabetes 1994

Percent of adults with diabetes per state

Less than 4.0%
4.0% to 4.9%
5.0% to 5.9%
More than 6.0%

Diabetes 2002

Source: U.S. Centers for Disease Control and Prevention.

University of Tokyo independently identified a protein called adiponectin that appears to increase the effectiveness of insulin and, therefore, decreases insulin resistance. According to the researchers, as people become more obese, their adipocytes produce less adiponectin.

Insulin resistance and diabetes, in turn, may contribute to the development of cardiovascular diseases, such as *arteriosclerosis* (hardening of the arteries), heart attack, and stroke. A class of molecules called cytokines, some of which are made by adipocytes, has negative effects at high levels as well. For example, several cytokines can act in the liver to increase production of such molecules as C-reactive protein (CRP), which causes *inflammation* (swelling). Researchers have known since the 1980's that inflammation plays a role in the build-up of fatty deposits called plaques in blood vessels, increasing a person's chances of having a heart attack or stroke. Enlarged adipocytes also produce molecules that, at high levels, increase a person's likelihood of developing blood clots that can lead to a stroke.

Obesity can increase a person's risk of developing hypertension as well. Enlarged adipocytes appear to release higher levels of a protein called angiotensinogen, which in turn is converted to a protein called angiotensin. Angiotensin increases blood pressure.

Researchers have discovered that a certain type of obesity—called central, or abdominal, obesity—has a stronger link to metabolic and cardiovascular disease than obesity does in general. Thus, two obese people can have the same BMI value, but a person who carries more fat in the abdomen—one with a so-called apple-shaped figure—has a greater chance of developing an obesity-related disease than someone who carries more fat in the thighs or buttocks—one with a so-called pear-shaped figure.

Researchers are trying to learn why this is so. Many scientists suspect that some of the fat in the abdomen may be stored in the liver itself. Such fat may be especially dangerous because its location allows adipocytes to send fatty acids and inflammatory molecules directly into the liver. There, these products raise blood pressure, increase the production of triglycerides, and interfere with the liver's ability to regulate glucose. Other researchers believe that abdominal adipocytes themselves may have unique properties that make them more dangerous. They may, for example, release more products that can increase insulin resistance or arteriosclerosis, compared with other adipocytes.

several harmful effects. FFA's may interfere with the liver's ability to store *glucose* (blood sugar). In a healthy body, the liver stores glucose until cells need it to fuel their activities. FFA's may also hamper the liver's ability to respond to the hormone insulin, preventing the liver from removing glucose from the bloodstream. This results in a dangerous build-up of glucose that may lead to Type 2 diabetes. (Type 1 diabetes, which begins in childhood, occurs when the body does not make enough insulin. That condition is not related to obesity.)

A high level of FFA's may be just one way in which obesity leads to *insulin resistance* and Type 2 diabetes. (Insulin resistance is a condition in which the cells do not use insulin properly. People with untreated insulin resistance often develop Type 2 diabetes.) In 2001, researchers at Albert Einstein College of Medicine in New York City and at the

For decades, researchers have recognized that central obesity is the core feature of a *syndrome* (group of symptoms) that includes insulin resistance, excess levels of insulin in the body, *glucose intolerance* (higher-than-normal levels of blood sugar), hypertension, elevated blood fats, and high levels of inflammation. This cluster of symptoms was originally called "Syndrome X," but in 1998, the World Health Organization suggested that the term "metabolic syndrome" be used to describe the condition. In 2002, epidemiologist Earl Ford at the Centers for Disease Control and Prevention in Atlanta, Georgia, and his colleagues estimated that about 22 percent of U.S. adults—at least 47 million people—have the syndrome. Metabolic syndrome increases the risk of developing heart disease, coronary artery disease, and Type 2 diabetes.

Although most people are aware that obesity increases the risk of diabetes and cardiovascular disease, few realize that excess weight also increases the chances of developing other diseases, including cancer. Epidemiologist Anna Bergstrom at the Karolinska Institute in Stockholm, Sweden, and her colleagues reported in 2001 that weight gain in adulthood—more than about 10 kilograms (22 pounds) after age 20—can increase the risk of breast, colon, prostate, gallbladder, endometrial, and kidney cancers.

Some scientists speculate that obesity may increase cancer risk because the presence of adipocytes may encourage production of more hormones—such as insulin and estrogen—that stimulate cell growth and division. The more often cells divide and grow, the more chances there are for mistakes to occur in new DNA molecules, and the greater the chance for cancer-causing genetic mutations to arise. Other scientists have suggested that fat cells may increase the risk of cancer because they can serve as storage depots for toxic chemicals, which may in turn damage genetic material and cause cancer to develop.

Obesity may also lead to the development of *osteoarthritis* (wearing away of the joints), especially in the knee. Many researchers had found that the higher an individual's BMI, the greater the risk for developing this painful and debilitating disease.

Scientists in France reported in 2003 that they may have uncovered a reason for that connection. The researchers looked for fat-cell products, such as leptin, in the *cartilage* (tissue that cushions the joints) and *synovial fluid* (lubricant found in the joints) of obese people with osteoarthritis. They found that the leptin levels in the subjects' synovial fluid rose with BMI. They also discovered a relation-ship between the amount of leptin in the joints and the extent of destruction in the cartilage. The researchers suggested that leptin may promote joint inflammation. The physical stress of movement about a joint that bears excess weight may also increase the incidence of osteoarthritis in obese individuals.

Besides physical illnesses, researchers have found a connection between obesity and poor mental health. According to the American Psychiatric Association, children and teen-agers who are obese are at increased risk for emotional problems well into adulthood. In some cases, such problems may lead to abnormal eating patterns. In others, obesity may lead to increased stress.

Finally, some researchers have proposed that obesity may be a self-propelling disease. In other words, the more food a person eats, the more fat that person's body accumulates. The longer the fat is there, the more the body accepts that level of fat as "normal" and the harder it defends against attempts to lose it. In addition, the more weight an individual gains, the more difficult it becomes to adopt an active lifestyle that would naturally help combat continued weight gain. Such people may well benefit the most from new drugs that may be developed to break this vicious cycle.

A DANGEROUS COMBINATION

Obesity, particularly abdominal fat, is one health risk in a cluster of risks known as metabolic syndrome. People with this syndrome have a higher-than-normal risk of developing heart disease, coronary artery disease, and Type 2 diabetes. A person with three or more of the following risk factors is considered to have metabolic syndrome.

1. Abdominal obesity: waist circumference greater than 102 centimeters (40 inches) in men and greater than 88 centimeters (35 inches) in women;

2. Fasting blood *triglycerides* (fatty substances in the blood): equal to or greater than 150 milligrams per deciliter (mg/dL);

3. Low levels of *high-density lipoprotein* (HDL, the "good" cholesterol): less than 40 mg/dL in men and less than 50 mg/dL in women;

4. High blood pressure: equal to or greater than 130/85;

5. High fasting glucose: equal to or greater than 110 mg/dL.

Source: *The Third Report of the National Cholesterol Education Program Expert Panel on Detection, Evaluation, and Treatment of High Blood Cholesterol in Adults,* 2002.

FIGHTING OBESITY

Americans have grown increasingly overweight and obese at a time when society has grown increasingly aware of the importance of a healthful diet and regular physical exercise. This situation has left many researchers and health care professionals convinced that small, unhealthy changes that people have made over the years because of time pressures—such as eating at fast-food restaurants and driving instead of walking—had become incorporated into a lifestyle that was contributing to obesity. For people who are genetically predisposed to overweight and obesity, these changes have been a prescription for disaster.

How can individuals resist this toxic environment? How can society promote a culture that poses less risk to children, who are vulnerable to lifelong obesity? And which medical solutions can help people who are already overweight or obese?

The place to begin, many researchers suggest, is with the body mechanisms that operate without our conscious awareness to control the amount of energy we take in and the amount we use up. In April 2004, two teams of researchers reported on their studies of the nerve pathways in the brain known to control appetite in mice. One team, led by neurobiologist Richard Simerly of the Oregon National Primate Research Center in Portland, found evidence that these circuits form during the first few weeks of life. Mice specially bred without the ability to make the appetite-suppressing hormone leptin had fewer nerve pathways for leptin to reach the brain than did the mice that experienced a natural rise in leptin shortly after birth.

In human beings, this rise in leptin occurs before birth. The nerve pathways created during this process are then used by leptin throughout a person's life to regulate appetite. The researchers theorized that people who had been exposed to lower-than-normal levels of leptin before birth—and therefore developed fewer leptin pathways—may be leptin resistant throughout their lives and have trouble maintaining a normal weight.

The second team of researchers, led by molecular geneticist Jeffrey Friedman at Rockefeller University in New York City, studied brain *synapses* (connections between nerve cells) in mice. The team found that, compared with normal mice, leptin-deficient adult mice had fewer synapses in the brain circuits that reduce appetite and more synapses in the circuits that increase hunger signals. However, when the researchers injected the leptin-deficient mice with leptin, the number of brain synapses in the circuits controlling appetite increased while the number of synapses prompting hunger signals decreased. Thus, the researchers found that though the circuits cannot be totally rewired later in life, they can be modified. Both teams' findings support previous studies suggesting that the earlier in life an individual becomes overweight or obese, the more difficult it becomes to achieve a healthier body weight.

Many researchers now believe that an individual's lifestyle—the amount a person eats and his or her level of physical activity—may "program" the energy balance centers of the brain to defend a certain body weight. Thus, regular overeating and underexercising in childhood may program the brain to maintain the same unhealthy behavior into adulthood without an individual's awareness.

As a result, many researchers contend that parents, physicians, and others involved in children's health should aggressively treat childhood overweight and obesity. They argue that children and their parents must learn the dietary and lifestyle factors that can lead to obesity and the steps they can take to avoid or reverse these conditions. Children are bombarded by advertising and marketing that psychologically pressure them to consume more calories than they need and to use less energy than they should. Many health care experts believe children should be showered with just as much information and encouragement to eat a healthful diet and become more physically active.

Several government agencies provide information on a healthful lifestyle in books or pamphlets or on the Internet. For example, the Food and Nutrition Information Center of the U.S. Department of Agriculture publishes information to help people determine the number of calories they should eat each day. The center recommends choosing a balanced diet based on the government's Food Guide Pyramid. Such a diet is high in complex carbohydrates (especially whole grains) and includes several daily servings of fruits and vegetables. According to the center, everyone—except children under the age of 2—should follow a diet that is low in saturated fat, cholesterol, and sugar and that contains moderate amounts of total fat.

Researchers have documented successful efforts by people to consciously alter their lifestyle and "train" their unconscious energy balance systems to defend a healthy body weight. In 1993, James Hill, the director of the Center for Human Nutrition at the University of Colorado Health Sciences Center in Denver, and Rena Wing, professor of psychiatry at Brown University in Providence, Rhode Island, founded a registry that tracks about 3,000 successful dieters. The registry includes only those individuals who have lost at least 30 pounds and kept the weight off for more than one year.

How did these people succeed? The successful dieters had four things in common. They followed a low-fat diet. They monitored their weight and food consumption closely. They ate breakfast. And they exercised for at least one hour each day. The successful dieters also understood that adopting a healthier lifestyle requires time, patience, and repetition. For most people, the support and cooperation of family and friends is also important. Family members must understand that "blame and shame" are not helpful to those attempting to make such a change in their lifestyle.

Contrary to the messages promoted in the media, there are no quick or easy ways to reduce body fat. Few—if any—weight-loss products deliver on such promises. Libraries and bookstores overflow with books and tapes that promise special knowledge to help dieters lose weight and maintain a normal weight. Many nutritionists and other health care professionals, however, dismiss these regimens as gimmicks that—at best—produce only small and temporary weight loss.

One weight-loss plan that has attracted many dieters in the United States but generated considerable controversy among physicians is a low-carbohydrate diet advocated by cardiologist Robert C. Atkins, who died in 2003. The diet allows people to eat as much fat and protein as they want while severely restricting their intake of carbohydrates, including those from fruits and vegetables.

Most low-carbohydrate diets contradict the low-fat diet recommended by U.S. government health agencies. The Food and Nutrition Information Center, for example, recommends that most adults get no more than 30 percent of their daily calories from fat. Many physicians fear that people who follow a high-fat diet over the long term may develop cardiovascular disease.

Many physicians also believe that low-carb diets are no more effective for weight loss than other diets are. They contend that people who follow such diets lose weight only because they take in fewer calories than they used to. For example, some researchers have noted that people tend to eat less at a meal that contains small amounts of carbohydrates (such as bread) simply because few of us enjoy eating fat all by itself.

Several studies of low-carb diets confirm these beliefs. For example, health services researcher Dena M. Bravata of Stanford University in California and her colleagues reported in 2003 on their review of 107 studies of low-carb diets that had been published between 1966 and 2003. The researchers found that people who lost weight on a low-carb diet did so by limiting the total number of calories they took in and by maintaining the diet for a significant length of time.

In addition, two studies reported in May 2004 by researchers at Duke University in Durham, North Carolina, and at Philadelphia Veterans Affairs Medical Center compared people who followed a low-carb diet with those who followed either a low-fat or moderate-fat diet. The studies found that while low-carb dieters lost more weight during the first six months of the diet, by one year there was no significant difference in the amount of weight lost by the three groups.

As of 2004, most health care professionals be-

A group of dieters attends a weight-loss support meeting. Researchers have noted the importance of friends and family who encourage people to lose weight, rather than offer "blame and shame." Researchers have also found that successful dieters continually practice behaviors that contribute to a healthful lifestyle.

FIGHTING FOR CONTROL OF YOUR BODY

Many dieters who successfully lose weight find it very difficult to keep the weight off over the long term. When we diet, our bodies may perceive us to be in danger of starvation—as some groups of human beings often were in our early history. As a result, the body works to regain the level of fat we maintained before the diet. The bodies of most people, researchers say, have not developed ways to limit weight gain in times of plenty.

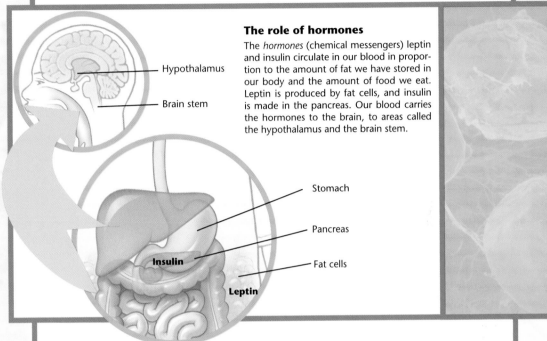

The role of hormones

The *hormones* (chemical messengers) leptin and insulin circulate in our blood in proportion to the amount of fat we have stored in our body and the amount of food we eat. Leptin is produced by fat cells, and insulin is made in the pancreas. Our blood carries the hormones to the brain, to areas called the hypothalamus and the brain stem.

Hypothalamus

Brain stem

Stomach

Pancreas

Insulin

Fat cells

Leptin

Maintaining normal weight

As we eat, leptin and insulin signal the brain to shut down other signals that stimulate appetite and to activate signals that suppress appetite. We feel full and stop eating. At the same time, the hormones also increase the rate at which our body burns energy. In this way, our body maintains a balance between the calories we take in and those that we use up. Our fat levels remain the same, and we neither gain nor lose weight.

Losing weight

When we cut back on the amount of food we eat, we lose fat stores and so produce less leptin and insulin. The lower levels prompt the hypothalamus to send out signals urging us to eat and instructing our bodies to conserve energy. The low hormone levels also decrease the signals that normally suppress appetite. The increase in hunger signals and decrease in appetite-suppressing signals make it very hard for a dieter to cut back on the amount of food eaten, as the body fights to maintain its level of fat stores.

Gaining weight

Most people who are overweight or obese have high levels of leptin and insulin in proportion to the amount of fat they have stored in their body. For reasons that researchers do not yet understand, however, the leptin and insulin do not trigger the stop-eating signals that they should. Researchers think that the signaling mechanisms of overweight people may be defective or that diets high in fats and carbohydrates may cause people to eat more before the signals take effect. In either case, the extra calories are stored in fat cells and people gain weight.

lieved that "a calorie is a calorie"—that is, weight loss depends less on the type of diet a person follows and more on limiting calories in general. These professionals continue to promote three familiar energy equations governing body weight. When we consume more calories than we use, we gain weight. When we use as many calories as we take in, our weight stays the same. And when we consume fewer calories than we use, we lose weight. In practice, this means, first, limit the total number of calories you consume so that they are less than or equal to the calories you normally use. Second, maintain a balanced diet that includes adequate nutrients, vitamins, and minerals. Third, engage in enough physical activity each day to burn off any extra calories you consume.

The most difficult challenge in this process is to make conscious decisions that override the pressures of our environment and our own desire for sweet, fatty foods. Eating out at fast-food establishments that promote large portions of foods high in fat and sugar has become a part of many families' routine. Any individual strategy for preventing overweight and obesity must, therefore, include a limit on the number of meals per week a person eats at such restaurants as well as a watchful eye on the number of calories consumed.

Nutritionists also agree that we should limit the amount of processed foods that we eat. Such foods typically contain many calories from fat and sugar but provide only small amounts of important vitamins and minerals. Many processed foods are also high in salt, which can increase the risk of developing high blood pressure. By reading the labels of packaged foods, people can find out how many calories a particular portion contains and what proportion of the food is fat.

Nutritionists also caution against consuming too much high-fructose corn syrup. This high-calorie sweetener, introduced in the 1970's, became a common ingredient in many foods—particularly soft drinks—in the 1980's. Many physicians believe that children's preference for soft drinks rather than milk, water, and other healthful fluids may be contributing to the development of childhood obesity. In January 2004, the American Academy of Pediatrics, headquartered in Elk Grove Village, Illinois, recommended that schools stop making soft drinks available to their students.

In addition to changing their eating habits, people who want to lose weight should consciously increase the amount of energy they spend. They should change their lifestyle to incorporate that higher level of physical activity. Many people are

A dieter records the food she has eaten in a food diary. Such diaries may also include space for information on the circumstances under which the food was eaten. Doctors have found that people sometimes eat because of such feelings as stress or boredom, rather than because of physical hunger. Becoming aware of such habits and replacing them with more healthful ones can help people to lose weight.

reluctant to even consider such changes because they think they need to exercise rigorously every day to lose weight. Major weight loss generally requires regular, sustained exercise. Even simple changes in our routines, however, can increase the number of calories we use in a day. For example, reducing the time spent watching television and playing video games and increasing the time devoted to gardening, bicycling, walking, and other activities can lead to significant health benefits.

In 2003, James Hill and his colleagues demonstrated how small indulgences can add up to large weight gains over time and, similarly, how small changes in physical activity levels can counteract them. Hill's team analyzed the weight gain reported by people in two eight-year surveys. The researchers learned that the study participants had gained an average of 6 to 7 kilograms (14 to 16 pounds) over that time, about 1 kilogram (1 to 2 pounds) per year. Hill and his colleagues calculated that each person gained the weight by increasing the number of calories consumed by a mere 100 or so per day.

Closing this "energy gap," according to Hill, can be as easy as walking an additional mile— about 2,000 to 2,500 steps—each day or eating about 100 calories less—the equivalent of three bites of a typical fast-food hamburger. To encourage people to walk more, Hill founded a program called America on the Move, which urges everyone to walk 10,000 steps a day.

Although individual effort is essential to weight loss, a person cannot fight the obesity epidemic alone. Health care providers increasingly believe that the problem must be addressed at community and societywide levels as well. Many communities are mobilizing behind efforts to create more healthful school breakfast and lunch programs and provide all children with quality physical education programs. They are also working to create opportunities for physical activity at work sites and in community centers and park districts.

At the national level, public interest groups have begun campaigns to encourage the food industry to serve reasonable portions of their products. The groups also want fast-food outlets to increase the number of low-calorie, nutritious foods they offer. Many of these groups point out that their movement bears a strong resemblance to the relatively successful anti-smoking campaigns that were launched in the 1960's. These campaigns resulted in major changes in Americans' views on tobacco use and improved the overall health of American society.

The best treatment for obesity, of course, is to prevent it from occurring in the first place. However, for people who are already obese, changes in behavior often prove insufficient to combat the disease. As a result, health professionals and pharmaceutical companies are exploring new drug treatments. In particular, advances in the study of brain hormones are driving the development of drugs that may effectively control appetite in obese patients.

The search for effective anti-obesity medications has experienced several setbacks, resulting mainly from the drugs' undesirable side effects. The most widely publicized problems occurred with fen-phen, a combination of the drugs fenfluramine and phentermine. The U.S. Food and Drug Administration took fen-phen off the market in 1997 after discovering that as many as 35 percent of patients taking the medication developed defects in the valves that control the flow of blood through the heart.

Physicians believe that new anti-obesity drugs are difficult to develop because many of the biochemicals that regulate eating and metabolism are also involved in other body processes. Researchers have found it difficult to identify drugs that affect only food intake or energy expenditure.

Not surprisingly, the FDA had approved only two anti-obesity drugs by mid-2004. Both caused

Students at an elementary school help themselves to fruit as part of an effort to teach children about a healthful diet. Many health care experts believe that schools must play a major role in fighting the obesity epidemic.

unwanted side effects. A drug called orlistat, approved in 1999, blocks the action of *lipases*, fat-digesting *enzymes* (molecules that speed up chemical reactions in living things). This process prevents the gastrointestinal tract from digesting and absorbing about one-third of the fat in a meal. However, orlistat can cause cramping, diarrhea, and an oily intestinal discharge. In addition, according to a major study published in 2002, the drug produced an average weight loss of only about 5 kilograms (12 pounds) over 6 to 12 months, compared with an average 3-kilogram (6-pound) weight loss for people who dieted without taking orlistat. The FDA approved patients' use of orlistat for up to one year.

Another drug, approved in 1996 for treating obesity for up to one year, is sibutramine, which suppresses appetite. It belongs to a family of amphetaminelike chemicals and can produce a decrease in body weight of 5 to 10 percent. The drug's side effects may include insomnia, dry mouth, and constipation as well as small increases in blood pressure and heart rate.

Despite these difficulties, scientists in 2004 had reason to be optimistic about the development of new anti-obesity drugs. For example, in the early 2000's, researchers learned that the hormone leptin works in the brain, in part, by sending out *melanocortins*. This group of *neurotransmitters* (chemical messengers in the brain) can suppress appetite. Some scientists believe that a drug that can activate melanocortin *receptors* (cells sensitive to a chemical) might provide a way to trigger leptin's appetite-suppressing action.

Another possible idea for drug development involves an ezyme called AMP-activated protein kinase (AMPK). This enzyme, which is regulated by leptin, monitors energy in cells. A study reported by endocrinologist Barbara Kahn at the Beth Israel Deaconess Medical Center in Boston in March 2004 showed that AMPK also affects appetite. Researchers hoped that drugs targeting AMPK may be effective for people who are leptin resistant.

Other scientists, such as endocrinologist Matthias Tschop at Lilly Research Laboratories in Indianapolis, were studying ghrelin, a hormone discovered in 1999. Produced in the stomach, ghrelin signals the brain that the stomach is empty and it is time to eat. Several scientists were exploring the possibility of developing drugs to block the effects of ghrelin and, thus, reduce the intensity of the hunger signal.

In May 2004, cancer biologist Wadih Araup and colleagues at the University of Texas M. D. Anderson Cancer Center in Houston opened up another avenue for fighting obesity. The researchers already knew that blood vessel cells, called endothelial cells, differ according to the type of tissue in which they are located. Using this "molecular zip code" for blood vessels that supply fat cells, the researchers designed a drug that locates those blood vessels and triggers their endothelial cells to self-destruct. When they injected obese mice with this drug, the mice returned to their normal weight even while continuing to eat the same amount. Such an approach will require many more years of research and testing in animals before it could ever be attempted in people.

Perhaps the most drastic treatment sought by obese patients in 2004 was *bariatric surgery*, a term that applies to several types of operations. The most commonly performed bariatric surgery in the United States—and the one considered the most effective—is gastric bypass surgery. In this procedure, a surgeon seals off most of the stomach, leaving only a portion about the size of an egg. The surgeon also reroutes part of the small intestine so that food from the tiny stomach bypasses a large segment of the intestine, reducing the number of calories the body can absorb.

Most physicians consider bariatric surgery a last-resort remedy for obesity, to be used only for people who are dangerously obese and only when all other weight-loss attempts have failed. The procedures involve the risk and pain of major abdominal surgery. They also force individuals to change their eating habits drastically because they may become violently ill if they overeat. In addition, people who have had gastric bypass surgery may develop nutritional deficiencies because their shortened intestine absorbs fewer nutrients.

People who have had bariatric surgery can lose a significant amount of weight—more than 45 kilograms (100 pounds) in many cases. However, studies have reported conflicting evidence about how many of them keep the weight off and for how long. Some surgeons estimate that 5 to 20 percent of their bariatric surgery patients regain the weight. Some people—usually those who have not had psychological or nutrition counseling—begin to gain weight again after surgery by eating frequent, small portions of calorie-dense foods. For those people, despite the drastic measures taken to force them to eat less, the same unconscious appetite-control mechanisms that led to their obesity may sabotage their efforts.

HOPE FOR THE FUTURE

Most health experts believe that the epidemic of overweight and obesity is not likely to end any time soon. They believe that we live in a "toxic" environment—one filled with an unlimited choice and supply of high-calorie foods and little, if any, incentive to increase our level of physical activity. People who are genetically predisposed to overweight and obesity are especially susceptible to these pressures, which are unlikely to go away.

Despite these disturbing predictions, many scientists believe that the long-term outlook for success in battling the problem is promising. Many segments of society have already recognized the scope of the epidemic and have gone into action. Many researchers are extremely optimistic that in the coming years, they will develop medications to aid in the treatment of obesity. We can expect to gain much more insight into the mechanisms by which overconsumption and/or underactivity may lead to changes in brain circuits and learn how these changes may, in turn, contribute to energy imbalance. Understanding how the body's energy balance system malfunctions may help us develop better strategies for preventing obesity.

Many social scientists think that even greater benefits will come from research on the environmental factors that encourage obesity. Rather than attempting to combat the obesity-promoting effects of the modern environment, they hope to change the environment itself. By identifying the key elements that have helped the obesity epidemic to grow, they hope to change society itself in ways that will reduce the "toxicity" of our environment.

Educational programs, government policies, and even legal strategies may be expanded to aggressively counteract the obesity-promoting culture of Western societies. Because we live in a free society, organizations face limits on the extent to which they can influence individual behavior. Nevertheless, a determined group of health advocates can make a difference, just as they did in the anti-smoking campaign that has extended and improved the lives of millions of Americans.

Real progress in preventing and treating overweight and obesity will probably require some combination of scientific advancements in understanding brain chemistry and drug development as well as education and grass-roots pressure for social change. The first steps in combating these problems, however, have already been taken. We have recognized the scope and seriousness of the problem, realized that it is approaching crisis proportions, and begun to make efforts to address this serious health threat. Biomedical researchers, physicians, social scientists, and health advocates agree that the fight against overweight and obesity has begun in earnest.

A family takes time to run together along the beach. Families who make conscious choices to incorporate physical activities into their life, health care experts say, are teaching their children valuable habits that should help them maintain a normal weight into adulthood.

CONSUMER SCIENCE

Topics selected for their current interest provide information that the reader as a consumer can use in understanding everyday technology or in making decisions—from buying products to caring for personal health.

Our mobile world would be less mobile if we didn't have batteries. These portable sources of electricity enable us to make telephone calls while walking down the street, work on a computer while on board an airplane, and record our heart's activity on a portable electrocardiograph as we sit in the comfort of our home. Batteries power so many modern conveniences that we often aren't aware of them until our flashlight does not light, our cellular phone fails to work, or our watch stops ticking. And of course, many birthdays have been thrown into turmoil because parents neglected to buy batteries for their children's new electronic toys.

At least 4 billion batteries are sold annually in the United States. While the need for batteries has grown larger, however, the size of some batteries has gotten smaller. In 2004, researchers were on the verge of developing microscopically small batteries—and looking for ways to make them even smaller and more powerful.

Such modern technological wonders are a far cry from the first practical battery assembled by Italian scientist Alessandro Volta in 1799. His device, which became known as the *voltaic pile*, consisted of a layered stack of zinc and silver disks separated by linen cloth soaked in salt water. Volta theorized that a chemical action resulting in an electric current would take place in a moist material that came into contact with two different metals. He also theorized that the salt would *conduct* (transmit) the current. His successful experiment produced the first source of steady electric current.

Throughout the 1800's, other scientists refined Volta's device, producing smaller, more powerful batteries. By the 1900's, batteries were becoming widely used.

Modern batteries come in a variety of sizes, shapes, and powers. The Inter-

Getting a Charge out of Batteries

national Electrotechnical Commission, an organization headquartered in Geneva, Switzerland, establishes performance standards for electrical, electronic, and related technology, including most types of batteries. The commission also certifies that batteries produced by manufacturers who belong to the organization meet these standards.

Most batteries used by consumers have essentially the same parts and use the same basic process to convert chemical energy into electrical energy—that is, electricity. This electrochemical reaction occurs inside a *cell,* a unit containing all the chemicals and parts needed to produce an electric current. Some batteries consist of a number of electrochemical cells connected together in series to produce a higher operating *voltage.* Named for Volta, voltage is the strength of electrical force, measured in volts.

Batteries have become an irreplaceable part of everyday life, powering nearly every type of portable device and many other modern conveniences.

Within each cell are two electrodes, also known as terminals. The positively charged terminal is called a *cathode*. The negatively charged terminal is called an *anode*. A battery's voltage depends on the metals used for its electrodes. A battery also contains an *electrolyte*, a chemical substance that conducts the electric current inside the cell.

When you switch on a battery-powered device, such as a flashlight, *electrons* (negatively charged subatomic particles) begin to move quickly within each battery. Switching on the flashlight amounts to completing an electric *circuit* (pathway) that includes the battery terminals and the bulb. The current circulates through the battery and the flashlight, making the bulb work.

Batteries come in two main types—disposable and rechargeable. Disposable batteries, also called primary batteries, are the most common type of battery for everyday use. Most disposable batteries are known as *dry cells* because they use a nonspillable, jelly-like or pastelike electrolyte.

Rechargeable batteries, also called secondary batteries, are commonly used in such devices as laptop computers and cellular telephones. Most rechargeables are *wet cells*—that is, they contain a liquid electrolyte.

As their name indicates, disposable batteries provide power only until their chemical charge is exhausted. At that point, they must be thrown away. There are four types of disposable batteries, classified according to the metals used in their electrodes. They are alkaline, carbon-zinc, lithium, and air batteries.

Alkaline batteries, one of the most common types of batteries, have electrodes made of zinc and manganese-oxide. Their name refers to the strong alkali solution, potassium hydroxide, used in them as an electrolyte.

Carbon-zinc batteries, also called standard carbon batteries, have electrodes made of zinc and carbon. An acidic paste between the electrodes serves as the electrolyte.

Household items such as flash-lights, radios, and remote controls typically use alkaline or carbon-zinc batteries. Because they last from five to eight times longer, alkaline batteries may be more economical than carbon-zinc batteries for devices that require high amounts of current.

Lithium batteries, also called button batteries, have lithium metal anodes and produce more than twice the voltage of an alkaline cell. They are used in cameras, pacemakers, watches, and calculators because they have a very long service life.

Air batteries have a zinc anode and a potassium hydroxide electrolyte. Because an air battery requires oxygen from the air or atmosphere for its electrochemical reaction to occur, it can operate only where the atmosphere is controlled. Air batteries are commonly used in hearing aids because the humidity and temperature within the ear canal remain constant.

Dry cell disposable batteries are highly popular with consumers—and with good reason. Because of industry standards, they are generally dependable. They are also affordable—usually costing less than $1 each—and easy to buy at a wide variety of retail locations. Dry cell disposable batteries also have a long *shelf life*—that is, they keep their energy-producing capacity for years if unused.

The affordability and long shelf life of disposable batteries, however, is offset by their short active life. Once the electric cell loses most or all of its power, the battery is "dead" and must be replaced. Moreover, even a battery not in use will slowly begin to lose some power as the chemicals degrade. To slow this self-discharge, experts suggest placing batteries in a plastic bag and then keeping the batteries at a low temperature, for example, inside a freezer.

A battery's active life depends on the device the battery is powering. This may range from dozens of hours for flashlights, portable radios, and other devices that use relatively little power to only a few hours in such devices as compact disc players, which require more energy to spin the disc.

Over years of use, a battery-powered device may require hundreds of dollars' worth of disposable batteries. For this reason, some people prefer using rechargeable batteries. Like disposable batteries, rechargeable batteries offer consumers a variety of shapes and sizes to fit their electronic needs. The energy drained from rechargeables can be recovered by recharging.

In order to revitalize some rechargeable batteries, consumers must remove the battery from its device and place it in a recharging unit that is plugged into an electric socket. Recharging time varies for different batteries. Most rechargers include meters that indicate when the battery is fully recharged.

Rechargeables have electrodes that contain chemicals that can be returned to their original chemical state by reversing the electrochemical reaction that produces power. When such a

battery is placed into a recharging unit, the charger sends a reverse current through the electrodes. The reverse current is delivered at a higher voltage, which is used to re-form the chemicals at each electrode. Once the battery voltage is increased to its charged state, it can be removed and used again.

There are three main types of rechargeable batteries: nickel-cadmium, nickel-metal hydride (Ni-MH), and lithium-ion. Nickel-cadmium batteries, also called Ni-Cad batteries, have electrodes made of nickel-hydroxide and cadmium and use potassium hydroxide as the electrolyte. Ni-MH batteries use a nickel-hydroxide cathode, an alloy of a rare earth metal (M) with nickel for its anode and a potassium hy-

Types and uses of batteries

Batteries come in a variety of shapes and sizes to fit numerous consumer needs. Each type of battery has advantages and disadvantages that should be considered before purchase.

Disposable	Type/Shape	Advantages	Disadvantages
Alkaline	AA, AAA, C, D, N, 9V	Moderate energy storage; affordable; long shelf life	Energy supply can be drained quickly in high-power devices or equipment
Lithium	Button, cylindrical	High power output; long shelf life; low temperature performance	High cost; energy supply can be drained quickly in high-energy devices or equipment
Carbon-zinc	AA, AAA, C, D, N, 9V	Low cost; long shelf life	Poor performance at lower temperatures; performance diminishes as power drains from the battery
Air	Button shape	High energy output; long service life	Can operate only in a controlled atmosphere; low power

Rechargeable	Type/Shape	Advantages	Disadvantages
Nickel-cadmium (Ni-Cad)	Cylindrical	Strong performance at high and low temperatures	Energy declines quickly with use; low energy capacity
Metal hydride	Cylindrical, rectangular	High energy storage	High cost; easily damaged by overcharging
Lithium-ion	Cylindrical, rectangular	High energy storage; light weight	High cost; performance gradually diminishes as power drains from the battery

Critically reviewed by Christopher S. Johnson, Staff Chemist
Electrochemical Technology Program, Argonne National Laboratory, Argonne, Illinois.

droxide solution for the electrolyte. Lithium-ion batteries use an anode made of any one of a number of carbon-based materials. The cathode is made of a cobalt, manganese, or nickel oxide that includes lithium. Lithium offers the highest energy-producing potential at the lightest weight.

Although rechargeables generally cost more than disposable batteries, their cost is offset by their ability to be reused repeatedly. Their energy can be renewed—perhaps hundreds of times—for only a few cents' worth of electricity each time. As a result, rechargeables are more environmentally friendly.

The energy storage capacity of a battery depends on the amount of stored chemicals in the electrodes that can undergo electrochemical reaction

Nanotubes, shown highly magnified, are being used to develop microscopic electrodes. The tubes are only 1/10,000 the width of a human hair.

and the voltage of the cell. Batteries with more chemicals or a higher voltage will have a larger energy content. Because of their engineered, specialized construction, rechargeable batteries can typically discharge their energy much faster than disposables, allowing them to provide higher power. For this reason, they are often used in portable power tools that require large amounts of energy to accomplish their tasks. Battery-powered drills and screwdrivers, for example, require the extra strength and higher rate of energy discharge that Ni-Cad batteries provide.

Camcorders, cellular telephones, and computers normally use Ni-MH batteries or lithium-ion batteries.

Although rechargeable batteries can be repowered numerous times, they still have a limited life span because, eventually, their chemicals lose their ability to conduct electricity. In addition, rechargeable batteries slowly discharge their stored energy even if they are not being used. For this reason, manufacturers recommend charging these batteries fully before using them for an extended period if you will not have access to an electric outlet.

Some batteries, such as Ni-Cad batteries, may lose some of their voltage if they are recharged after their energy has been only partially discharged. Many electronics experts suggest fully discharging and recharging a battery every two months to avoid such a problem.

Rechargeable batteries also carry a small risk of fire or explosion. During the recharging process, some heat is released. Some rechargeables contain chemicals that are flammable. If a battery *short-circuits*—if two electrodes come into direct contact with each other—as it is recharging, the battery and its chemical contents may start to overheat. If the heat is not released, the battery will begin to vaporize its chemicals and quickly force heat from the container. A spark can cause these vapors to ignite.

The voltage of the electric current used to recharge the battery must also match the battery's specifications to avoid a potentially hazardous situation. This is especially important when traveling outside the United States. The electric current in other countries may carry a higher voltage and so may damage your battery.

In 2004, researchers continued to search for ways to make batteries more powerful and efficient as well as longer lasting. Because batteries operate through electrochemical reactions, much of the research is flowing from a scientific field called *materials science* (the study of the physical properties of materials). For example, scientists have been experimenting with the mix of lithium transition-metal oxides as electrodes in lithium-ion batteries to make them more powerful.

Many of the most promising avenues of investigation involve *nanotechnology,* the precise manipulation of individual atoms and molecules to create larger structures. Nanotechnology involves engineering on an incredibly tiny scale. A nanometer is 0.000000001 meter (1/25,400,000 inch), or about 1/10,000 the width of a human hair.

Nanotechnology may lead to the development of tiny machines that are visible only under a microscope. Such machines will require batteries many times smaller and more powerful than the smallest batteries currently being produced.

In 2004, for example, several teams of researchers, including engineers at the University of California at Los Angeles (UCLA), were trying to create a battery measuring only 1 millimeter in diameter. A battery this size would be much smaller than hearing-aid batteries, which—at 1 centimeter in diameter—are the smallest batteries currently available. The UCLA battery uses "nano-electrodes" that, in tests, have proved to be as much as 100 times more powerful than standard-sized electrodes.

Other researchers are exploring different avenues. Scientists at Royal Philips Electronics in Eindhoven, the Netherlands, announced in early 2004 that they had developed a new generation of curved batteries that will allow engineers to build electronic devices in shapes and sizes that are currently impossible. Some batteries, such as lithium-ion batteries containing liquid electrolytes, need a strong metal case to keep the stack of electrodes inside pressed firmly together. Typically, the battery case is shaped like a rectangle or a cylinder. These shapes, in turn, dictate the shape of the device using the battery.

Instead of packing the electrodes into a case, the Dutch researchers made holes in the electrodes and filled the holes with a *polymer* (plastic or

Battery Do's and Don'ts

Because batteries are so common, we may forget that they are self-contained chemical reactors and that their contents can be harmful under certain circumstances.

- The chemicals that provide the battery's energy source are safely sealed within a metal or plastic container at the factory. Over time, however, battery casings may develop leaks because of abuse or degradation. Leaking batteries should never be used and should be discarded as soon as proper disposal can be arranged.

- You should avoid placing batteries in trash bound for landfills, especially if they are leaking. Chemicals inside a battery can burn the skin. Environmentalists also argue that the chemicals can leak into the ground and contaminate water. Many communities offer toxic waste disposal locations where drained batteries may be deposited safely. Other communities collect drained batteries and other potentially harmful waste on designated days. Many stores that sell batteries also collect drained batteries for disposal.

- Certain types of batteries may explode if they overheat. To protect yourself, never recharge a disposable battery. Batteries should never be exposed to open flames, disposed of in fires or incinerators, or stored in areas where the temperature may exceed 37 °C (100 °F). Batteries should likewise be kept free from moisture, which may cause a metal battery casing to corrode and leak. You should never carry a battery loose in your pocket, as contact with coins or other metal objects may cause the battery to short-circuit and overheat.

- Never use batteries different from those recommended by the manufacturer of a particular battery-operated device.

- Batteries that are no longer useful should not be stored together. While they may lack sufficient charge to power their intended devices, drained batteries nonetheless retain some energy. If they come into contact with one another, they could generate enough heat to become a fire hazard.

other material whose molecules consist of long chains made up of many smaller molecules). The polymer held the stack together, allowing the battery to be molded into various shapes.

In the little more than 200 years since Volta assembled his battery, the technology of this device has developed tremendously. No doubt future batteries will make even today's most advanced technology look outdated in comparison. Until that day, however, our high-tech world will continue to depend on the low-tech battery.

◾ Keith Ferrell

Food Fresh? Ways to Tell

If your hamburger is green, your milk lumpy, your tomatoes fuzzy, or your fish slimy, you don't need to think twice before throwing them away. Likewise, a pungent odor can alert your nose to spoiled food. But sometimes spoilage isn't so obvious.

Spoilage is not necessarily dangerous to your health, but it does involve a deterioration in the appearance, flavor, nutritional value, or odor of food. It usually occurs after food has passed its *shelf life* (the amount of time that food is at its best quality).

Food may spoil or become contaminated for a number of reasons. For example, pests, such as insects and rodents, can contaminate food and in-

troduce disease by leaving behind waste material. Chemical reactions within food involving *enzymes* may cause deterioration. Enzymes, which are proteins produced by cells, influence chemical reactions within plants and animals. For example, the enzymes that exist naturally in a banana cause the fruit to soften and ripen. Over time, these enzymes also cause it to become mushy and turn black.

Chemical changes also cause food to become *rancid* (develop an unpleasant taste or smell). Rancidity results from the breakdown of the molecular chains that make up the fatty acids in fats. This process creates compounds called aldehydes.

The most common cause of food spoilage, however, is microorganisms, including bacteria, mold, and yeasts. Bacteria produce enzymes and other chemicals that cause food to begin to *decompose* (break down). Mold, a type of fungus, spreads along and beneath the surface of food by forming a network of microscopic reproductive structures called spores. The spores spread the mold growth through the food, causing it to spoil. Some yeasts, through a process known as *fermentation,* produce alcohols and other compounds that cause food to taste or smell unpleasant.

All food contains microorganisms unless it has been *sterilized* (treated to kill germs). Microorganisms can thrive at many different temperatures. However, research has shown that they grow best in a warm climate, usually between 4 and 60 °C (40 and 140 °F). Some bacteria that cause spoilage or disease can thrive even in refrigerated environments, though cooler temperatures generally slow the growth of most microorganisms.

When you remove food from the refrigerator, bacteria already present in the food can quickly adapt to the warmer conditions and begin reproducing. Numerous studies have shown that some bacteria start multiplying rapidly after only a few hours in a warm environment.

Spoiled food is not necessarily dangerous to your health. In fact, many foods develop an unpleasant taste before becoming a health hazard. This is not true in all cases, however. Certain types of bacteria, such as *Salmonella, Campylobacter, Escherichia coli (E. coli),* and *Staphylococcus,* produce *toxins* (poisons) that can cause foodborne illness, commonly called food poisoning. Even foods that do not look, smell, or taste spoiled may, in fact, contain these *pathogenic* (disease-causing) microorganisms.

Each year, 6.5 to 33 million people in the United States become ill from foodborne illnesses, according to the Centers for Disease Control and Prevention in Atlanta, Georgia. An estimated 9,000 of these individuals die. Health experts estimate that foodborne diseases result in as much as $6 billion in medical expenses and lost productivity at work each year.

Food poisoning may be mild or severe. Symptoms may include chills, diarrhea, fatigue, fever, headaches, muscle pain, nausea, and stomach pain. The symptoms of foodborne illness usually begin within a few hours of eating contaminated food, though some symptoms may not appear for as long as three weeks.

Some foodborne illnesses may be extremely dangerous. Botulism, caused by the bacterium *Clostridium botulinum,* is often fatal to human beings. Botulism, which affects the nervous system, results from improperly canned or preserved food. It is especially dangerous because the bacteria may reach life-threatening levels before changes in flavor or odor are noticeable. For this reason, the U.S. Food and Drug Administration (FDA) cautions consumers never to use food from cans that are bulging or rusted or from jars that are cracked or have loose or bulging lids. Consumers should also avoid canned food that has a foul odor when opened.

To help protect consumers from becoming ill from their products, food manufacturers determine a food's shelf life by conducting a variety of tests. For example, food scientists keep products at a warmer temperature or expose them to more light than they would normally experience during distribution and storage. Scientists then measure how long the food maintains its flavor, odor, appearance, and texture before spoiling.

Federal law also requires manufacturers to assess the nutritional content of infant formula and baby food over time when determining shelf life. Some manufacturers measure the nutritional content of other products as well.

To further shield consumers from spoiled food, manufacturers put product dates on many items. The United States has no national system of food dating. However, at least 20 states require product dating for some foods, such as milk and seafood.

According to the Food Safety and Inspection Service at the U.S. Department of Agriculture (USDA), there are two general types of food-product dating, open dating and closed dating. Open dating systems use a calendar date to label perishable foods such as dairy products, poultry, meat, and eggs.

Federal regulations require that the date must be accompanied by one of the following phrases: "Sell-By," "Use-By," or "Best if Used By." "Sell-By" dates indicate the last date on which the product may be sold. They allow additional time for the product to be stored and used at home before it spoils. "Use-By" and "Best if Used By" dates tell consumers how long they can expect a food product to remain at its peak quality in terms of taste and nutrition.

"Use-By" and "Sell-By" dates are not purchase or safety dates, the FDA notes. Foods stored at unsafe temperatures or under unsanitary conditions, for example, may spoil sooner.

Calendar dates used for poultry, meat, and eggs must include both the month and day of the month, according to federal regulations. The labels

Refrigeration and freezer storage tips

Most food should be well preserved if handled properly and stored in a refrigerator kept at 4 °C (40 °F). The U.S. Food and Drug Administration recommends that if a product has a "Use-By" date, consumers should follow that date. If a product has a "Sell-By" date or no date, consumers can avoid spoilage by using the following guidelines to cook or freeze the product.

Product	Refrigeration	Freezer
Mayonnaise, commercial (refrigerate after opening)	2 months	Do not freeze
Store-prepared or homemade egg, chicken, tuna, ham, macaroni salads	3 to 5 days	Does not freeze well
Milk	5 days	1 month
Swiss, brick, processed cheese	3 to 4 weeks	Does not freeze well
Eggs, fresh in shell	4 to 5 weeks	Do not freeze
Eggs, raw yolks or whites	2 to 4 days	1 year
Hamburger, stew meat	1 to 2 days	3 to 4 months
Ground turkey, veal, pork, lamb	1 to 2 days	3 to 4 months
Ham, fully cooked, whole	7 days	1 to 2 months
Ham, fully cooked, slices	3 to 4 days	1 to 2 months
Hot dogs (opened package wrap)	1 week	1 to 2 months
Hot dogs (unopened package wrap)	2 weeks	1 to 2 months
Lunch meats (opened package wrap)	3 to 5 days	1 to 2 months
Lunch meats (unopened package wrap)	2 weeks	1 to 2 months
Bacon	7 days	1 month
Smoked breakfast links, patties	7 days	1 to 2 months
Sausage from pork, beef, chicken, or turkey (uncooked)	1 to 2 days	1 to 2 months
Fresh steaks	3 to 5 days	6 to 12 months
Fresh chops	3 to 5 days	4 to 6 months
Fresh roasts	3 to 5 days	4 to 12 months
Fresh chicken or turkey, whole	1 to 2 days	1 year
Fresh chicken or turkey, parts	1 to 2 days	9 months
Fried chicken	3 to 4 days	4 months
Cooked meats and meat dishes	3 to 4 days	2 to 3 months
Lean fish	1 to 2 days	6 months
Fatty fish	1 to 2 days	2 to 3 months
Cooked fish	3 to 4 days	4 to 6 months
Fresh shrimp, scallops, crawfish, squid	1 to 2 days	3 to 6 months

Source: U.S. Food and Drug Administration Center for Food Safety and Applied Nutrition.

placed on frozen foods and other products with a longer shelf life must also display the year. Retailers may not remove or change dates that have been placed on products by a federally inspected manufacturer.

Closed dating is the second type of food-product dating. Many food manufacturers use closed dating systems on canned or boxed foods that have a long shelf life. These systems, sometimes called coded dating systems, employ a series of letters and numbers that refer to the date the food was processed. The code allows manufacturers to track products during shipping, rotate stock, and locate products in the event of a recall. Such codes, however, are meaningless to consumers. The USDA warns consumers against misinterpreting them as freshness dates.

Food preservation is both an ancient practice and a modern, evolving science. Preservation methods help extend a food's shelf life by halting or slowing the growth of microorganisms or by preventing chemical reactions that may cause rancidity or other forms of spoilage. Some commonly used methods of food preservation include drying, curing, canning, cold storage and freezing, aseptic packaging, freeze-drying, the use of additives, and irradiation.

Some of these methods are very old. Prehistoric peoples were probably the first to discover the merits of *drying* (removing the moisture from food to prevent spoilage). *Curing* (adding salt or other ingredients to remove moisture and slow spoilage) also dates to ancient times.

Canning, which involves sealing food in airtight containers that are heated, became widely used in the early 1800's. Refrigeration and freezing evolved in the 1800's from such older cold-storage methods as leaving food outside during the winter; storing it in caves during the summer; or packing frozen food in ice, sometimes using sawdust to insulate the ice and slow its melting.

Other preservation methods, including aseptic packaging and freeze-drying, appeared in the 1900's. Aseptic packaging involves sterilizing food and then packaging it in a sterilized container. Freeze-drying involves removing water from food while the food is frozen. Compared with canning, aseptic packaging requires less heating time. Heat can damage flavor and nutrition. Therefore, food preserved by aseptic packaging stays more flavorful and nutritious. Aseptic packaging is most commonly used for preserving beverages and other liquids.

Because freeze-drying does not involve heating the food, the food is left structurally intact at a molecular level, leaving the taste, texture, and nutritional value relatively unchanged. Because of the expense of the process, freeze-drying is often limited to such foods as dried soup mixes, instant coffee, and some fruits.

Additives are substances added to foods to prevent spoilage as well as for a variety of other reasons. For example, some additives stop the growth of microorganisms in such foods as bread and other baked goods that cannot be processed by canning or other preservation methods.

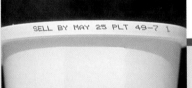

Since ancient times, additives such as sugar and vinegar have been used to prevent spoilage. But the use of chemical additives has grown explosively since the early 1900's with the increased popularity of processed foods.

Irradiation involves exposing food to radiation to kill bacteria and control molds and insects. It kills microorganisms with little effect on food's taste, texture, appearance, or nutritional value.

The U.S. government has approved the use of irradiation for a few foods, including wheat flour, fruits and veg-

Mark your calendars

Manufacturers often use *open dating* (calendar dates) on food products to help merchants determine how long to offer products for sale. The U.S. government does not require open dating on any product except infant formula and some baby food. However, many states require food suppliers to date some products, chiefly meat, poultry, eggs, and dairy products.

Types of dates

- **"Sell-By" date:** Tells the store how long to display the product for sale. Consumers should purchase the product before the "Sell-By" date.

- **"Best if Used By (or Before)" date:** Indicates the last date at which the product can be expected to provide its best flavor or highest quality. This is not a purchase or safety date.

- **"Use-By" date:** Marks the last date at which the product will be at peak quality if held under proper transit and storage procedures.

Source: United States Department of Agriculture's Food Safety and Inspection Service.

The "Sell-By" date on a package of sour cream alerts retailers and consumers to the last date on which the product can be sold. This date allows additional time for the item to be stored before use.

Keeping your food fresh

Most food preservation methods prevent spoilage by cooling or heating food, removing moisture, or adding chemicals to slow microbial growth. The most common methods in commercial use include:

- Refrigeration (at or below 4 °C [40 °F]).
- Freezing (at -17 °C [1 °F]).
- Canning (sealing food in airtight containers then heating to kill microorganisms).
- Pasteurization (heating liquids, such as milk, to a temperature high enough to destroy microorganisms and inactivate certain enzymes).
- Aseptic packaging (sterilizing food and packaging it in a sterilized carton or bag).
- Drying (removing the moisture from food to kill most bacteria present).
- Curing (adding salt, spices, or other ingredients to remove moisture and slow microbial growth).
- Freeze-drying (removing water from food while the food is frozen).
- Adding chemicals that slow food's decay (such additives may be either manufactured synthetically or drawn from such natural food sources as herbs and spices).
- Treatment with ionizing radiation (X rays, gamma rays, or electron beams) to kill microorganisms and inactivate enzymes.

Critically reviewed by the United States Department of Agriculture.

The blue color of a sensor in a package of shrimp alerts customers that the shrimp are spoiling. The yellow sensor shows the color for fresh shrimp. A dye in the sensor reacts with gases given off as the food decomposes.

etables, and poultry and meat. But because many people are wary of this method and the radiation involved, it is not a popular food preservation technique in the United States.

In 2004, scientists were continuing to explore new ways to preserve food without compromising its quality. One method in limited use in the United States involved subjecting food to very high pressure—up to 1 million pascals (145 pounds per square inch)—to destroy microorganisms. High pressure processing can be used either for liquids or for solid food that is at least 80 percent water.

Another development in food preservation is *modified atmosphere packaging,* in which food is packaged in an environment intended to slow microbial growth. For example, carbon dioxide or other gases that do not promote microbial growth may be pumped into sealed packages.

Researchers were also studying ways of using high-intensity light and ultrasound to preserve food. Still another process under development involves passing high-voltage electric currents through foods kept at low temperatures. These methods can be used alone or in combination with traditional preservation techniques.

Despite the best efforts of scientists, manufacturers, retailers, and consumers, it is not always possible to tell through smell, taste, or sight whether food is spoiled. Therefore, scientists are continuing to experiment with methods of monitoring the freshness and safety of food without relying on sensory clues.

One method involves labeling packaged foods with "time-temperature indicators," adhesive tags that change color if the packages reach an unsafe temperature. The color change signals to retailers and consumers that food has been kept at an inappropriate temperature during storage and transportation.

Researchers have also designed chemically treated sensors that can detect bacterial growth or the chemicals released by decomposing food. For example, scientists at the FDA have developed a plastic disk about the size of a U.S. quarter that can be inserted into packages of frozen seafood or vegetables. An organic dye in the sensor reacts with gases given off as the food decomposes, causing the disk to change color. The specific color of the sensor indicates the extent of the food's deterioration. Research into this technology was still continuing in mid-2004.

From ancient methods to modern innovations, food preservation has made it possible for people to enjoy a wide variety of fresh foods. Ongoing research may help ensure that consumers have even safer, more abundant choices. ■ Siri Carpenter

A hungry, blood-sucking mosquito can ruin outdoor fun and expose people to potentially harmful diseases.

Itching for Answers: Preventing Mosquito Bites

Anyone who enjoys being outside in the summer knows the story. You are at a family barbecue or an early evening baseball game. Maybe you hear the high-pitched whine first. Maybe you just feel a sudden sharp pinch on your skin. Or perhaps you feel nothing—until a small, red lump on your skin starts to itch. Your blood has just become a meal for a mosquito.

Mosquitoes can do more than ruin a good time. Some types of mosquitoes spread dangerous or fatal illnesses to people and animals. Among these diseases is West Nile virus. Unknown in the Western Hemisphere until 1999, this virus had claimed more than 200 lives in the United States by mid-2004. Worldwide, at least 700 million people each year fall prey to mosquito-borne illnesses, including West Nile virus, *encephalitis* (a life-threatening brain inflammation), malaria, and yellow fever.

The adult males and females of many mosquito species feed on plant nectar. The females of most species, however, including *Culex pipiens*—a common mosquito in North America—need the blood of people or animals, both warm-blooded and cold-blooded, to nourish the development of eggs inside their body.

As hard as you may try, you may not be able to avoid being targeted by a blood-feeding mosquito. That's because mosquitoes have a highly efficient, three-pronged system for locating victims.

First, you can attract mosquitoes just by breathing. Mosquitoes that feed on blood use sensory organs on their antennae to detect carbon dioxide, a gas exhaled by people and animals. These sensors help the insects follow a vapor trail to its source. Some species can detect carbon dioxide vapor as far as 30 meters (100 feet) away from their potential victim. Second, mosquitoes detect lactic acid on the skin. Lactic acid is a compound produced mainly by muscles during exercise. Third, body heat lets a mosquito know that a meal is near.

All living, breathing things should, in theory, stand the same chance of being attacked by mosquitoes. That is not the case, however. Mosquitoes find certain species more attractive than others and even some people tastier than others.

Why mosquitoes prefer some people over others has been a topic of research at the Agricultural Research Service (ARS), a part of the U.S. Department of Agriculture. Scientists have long known that your breath and perspiration contain an assortment of more than 300 chemicals. Studies conducted by the ARS Mosquito and Fly Research Unit and other researchers have revealed that some people appear to have a combination of these chemicals that makes them irresistible to mosquitoes. The research has shown that it is possible for one person in a room filled with hungry mosquitoes to get 10 bites while another person standing next to him or her gets 100 bites. The exact combination of chemicals mosquitoes find most appealing, however, continued to be the basis of experiments in mid-2004.

Unlike a dog, a mosquito does not really "bite," because the insect cannot open its jaws. Rather, female mosquitoes use a tubelike body part called a *proboscis,* which extends downward from the mosquito's head. Inside are six *stylets,* which are like tiny needles. The stylets are covered and protected by the *labium,* which is like a lower lip.

When a hungry mosquito finds its victim, it places the proboscis against the skin, then inserts the stylets as the labium bends and slides out of the way. The mosquito injects saliva into the wound through channels formed by the stylets. The saliva keeps the blood from clotting, improves the blood flow to the biting site, and acts as a local anesthetic, allowing the mosquito to feast more easily.

Sometimes mosquitoes must feed on blood from more than one victim because the insects are shooed away before they can drink their fill. An undisturbed mosquito, however, may drink for as long as five minutes. After the mosquito has filled up, it slowly pulls the stylets out of the wound, the labium slips back into place over them, and the insect flies away. A female mosquito can drink more than its own weight in blood. A blood-fed mosquito may weigh 2.75 milligrams, compared with an unfed mosquito, which may weigh 1.9 milligrams.

How a mosquito "bites"

A female mosquito pierces a victim's skin with six sharp, needlelike parts called *stylets* hidden within the insect's *proboscis,* a tubelike body part. As the mosquito pushes the stylets down, they curve and enter a blood vessel. The *labium* (lower lip) slides out of the way.

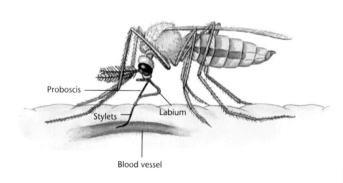

Proboscis

Stylets

Labium

Blood vessel

A red, itchy mosquito bite is actually an allergic reaction to mosquito saliva.

Mosquito bites itch and swell because most people are allergic to mosquito saliva. The saliva activates the body's immune system, causing it to produce *antibodies* (proteins that destroy bacteria, viruses, and other invaders or make them harmless). The saliva and the antibodies, in turn, cause the body to release a flood of *histamine,* a chemical found in certain body cells. Histamine causes tiny blood vessels to expand, which produces swelling in the tissue around the bite. The swelling irritates specialized nerves in the skin, causing the bite to itch. Histamine also causes these nerves to signal the brain that you are under mosquito attack.

Although research continued in 2004, mosquito researchers and *dermatologists* (physicians who treat skin diseases) now have a better understanding of why a mosquito bite itches. Scientists once theorized that an itch travels along the same nerve pathways to the brain as pain sensations do. But in 1997, researchers from the University of Erlangen-Nuremberg in Germany and the University of Uppsala in Sweden discovered this is not the case. Using electric probes and electrodes inserted into bundles of sensory nerves in human volunteers, the researchers identified nerve fibers devoted solely to transmitting itchy sensations.

This finding led to studies of how these itch nerves transmit sensation. In 2000, for example, researchers at the Technical University of Munich in Germany injected tiny amounts of histamine beneath the skin of volunteers. The injection mimicked a mosquito bite. Then the researchers scanned the brains of the volunteers using *positron emission tomography* (PET). PET is a technique used to produce images of the chemical activity in the brain and other body tissue as it occurs.

The PET scans showed activity in parts of the brain responsible for interpreting sensation as well as areas involved in planning and initiating movement. Areas of the brain used to process information on pain and pleasure also became active. More specific

Bypassing bites

Preventing mosquito bites involves a little common sense and some planning. But the effort can ward off the hungry insects, saving you from painful itching and reducing the risk of mosquito-borne disease.

- **Apply insect repellent** containing DEET (*N,N-diethyl-meta-toluamide*) to exposed skin when you go outdoors. Follow the directions on the package.

- **Cover up.** Whenever possible, wear long sleeves, long pants, and socks when outdoors. Light-colored clothing can help you see mosquitoes that land on you. Mosquitoes can bite you through thin clothing, so spraying clothing with an insect repellent containing DEET will provide extra protection.

- **Be aware of peak mosquito hours.** The hours from dusk to dawn are peak mosquito biting times for many mosquito species. Use repellent and protective clothing during the evening and early morning, or consider avoiding outdoor activities during these times.

- **Drain standing water.** Mosquitoes lay their eggs in standing water. Limit the number of places around your house where mosquitoes can breed by getting rid of objects that hold water. Change the water in outdoor pet dishes frequently and replace the water in birdbaths weekly. Also, drill holes in tire swings so water drains out. Keep wading pools empty and on their sides when not in use.

- **Install or repair screens.** Some mosquitoes like to come indoors. Keep them outside by having well-fitting screens on both windows and doors.

Source: United States Centers for Disease Control and Prevention.

information on how an itch can activate areas of the brain responsible for both emotion and rational thought remained a topic of research in 2004.

In addition to itchy, swollen skin, mosquitoes may leave behind germs. Some of these germs are dangerous. Scientists have identified at least 20 different viruses that mosquitoes can transmit to people and animals. Most of these disease-causing viruses thrive in regions surrounding the equator, where the climate is hot and moist. Mosquito-related diseases include dengue, which can cause intense headaches and fever, and yellow fever, which sometimes causes victims to go into a coma and die.

Yet another mosquito-borne disease is malaria, which is caused by a *protozoan* (one-celled organism). The protozoan enters the mosquito along

Spraying your clothing or skin with a chemical repellent can discourage mosquitoes from landing.

with the blood of an infected victim and then reproduces in the mosquito's stomach. From there, the young protozoans find their way into the mosquito's saliva. The mosquito transmits the disease to other people when it bites them. Malaria kills millions of people each year in Africa, Southeast Asia, and South America.

Mosquito bites also spread West Nile virus, which has become one of the most familiar mosquito-borne diseases in the United States. Scientists began documenting the virus in Africa, western Asia, and the Middle East in 1937. They first detected West Nile virus in the Western Hemisphere in 1999.

West Nile virus is carried chiefly by birds. When a mosquito bites an infected bird, the virus can enter the insect's salivary glands. When the infected mosquito bites a person or animal, it may inject the virus into the victim's bloodstream.

There are no foolproof ways of protecting yourself from mosquito bites, short of locking yourself inside your house. Even then, mosquitoes may find their way inside through broken windows, torn screens, or open doors. However, there are ways to reduce your risk of getting bitten.

Natural methods of repelling mosquitoes include limiting the amount of time you spend outdoors from dusk to dawn—prime feeding hours for most mosquitoes—and wearing long sleeves and long pants to cover as much skin as possible.

Biological controls may also be useful. Some scientists suggest using bird feeders to attract purple martins and other birds that feed on mosquitoes to heavily infested areas. But some experts argue that such natural predators do not eat enough mosquitoes to significantly dent the mosquito population. Certain types of fish, such as guppies, eat mosquito *larvae* (young) and can be used in ornamental ponds or pools. Other researchers recommend adding *Bacillus thuringiensis,* a bacterium that kills mosquito larvae, to ponds and pools.

Eliminating unwanted standing water can be a major step in controlling mosquito populations, according to officials at the U.S. Centers for Disease Control and Prevention (CDC) in Atlanta, Georgia. Because mosquito eggs need a source of moisture to survive and hatch, female mosquitoes like to lay their eggs in or near the water, including swamps and salt marshes. Bird feeders and fountains as well as pools of water that collect in old tires, cans, rain barrels, gutters, the bottoms of boats, or hollow tree stumps can serve as breeding grounds.

Sometimes a stronger approach is needed to keep mosquitoes at bay. Chemical *insecticides* kill mosquitoes outright. People can spray small amounts of insecticide in houses and garages to help control mosquitoes indoors. Workers in cities or towns may spray a thick mist of an insecticide into fields, forests, or gardens to kill mosquitoes in larger areas outdoors.

Chemical repellents discourage mosquitoes from landing. Repellents come in sprays, lotions, and creams that can be applied to the skin or clothing. They are also available in sprays that can be used outdoors to reduce mosquito attacks in backyards and other relatively small areas.

Repellents work as they evaporate. As the repellent's molecules hover in the air, they "confuse" the nerve cells on a mosquito's antennae that detect carbon dioxide or lactic acid. With its "radar" jammed, the mosquito cannot lock on its target and, so, flies away.

The chemical *N,N-diethyl-meta-toluamide*, popularly known as DEET, is the most effective ingredient in repellents, according to numerous studies, including some by the U.S. Department of Agriculture, the CDC, and many consumer publications. DEET, which was first developed in the 1950's, is found in almost every popular brand of insect repellent.

Most scientists agree that a product containing about 30 percent DEET, applied thinly and evenly to all exposed skin, should provide protection to a person for about three hours. Products with higher DEET concentra-

tions may be appropriate for people in areas swarming with mosquitoes or areas where the insects are known to carry a disease.

Scientific studies have failed to show that such "natural" remedies as *citronella*, an oil extract of the lemon-scented citronella grass; soybean oil; or peppermint oil offer much protection against mosquitoes. The same is true for electronic bug "zappers." These devices use light to produce heat to attract insects and electricity to electrocute them. Various studies conducted by U.S. universities have shown such devices electrocute a wide variety of harmless, night-flying insects but very few biting female mosquitoes.

Studies are still evaluating the effectiveness of another type of device usually known as a mosquito trap. Mosquito traps are made by several manufacturers and thus vary somewhat in features and technology. All of them use a stream of carbon dioxide, often mixed with other chemicals found in human or animal breath and scents, to lure mosquitoes in. Then, the mosquitoes are killed by such methods as electrocution or being trapped until they dry out and die. Studies by such groups as the U.S. Coast Guard have shown that mosquito traps seem to decrease the number of mosquitoes in an area.

Battling mosquitoes is normally just an inconvenience. Given the potential for contracting disease, however, a little prevention can go a long way toward showing mosquitoes a "closed" sign at the diner.

■ Tim Frystak

DEET facts
What is DEET?
■ DEET (*N,N-diethyl-meta-toluamide*) is a commonly used chemical insect repellent.

■ DEET is one of the few repellents that can be applied to human skin or clothing.

■ DEET does not kill insects but repels them from treated areas.

How does DEET work?
■ DEET probably affects an insect's ability to find a source to feed on. Scientists believe that it interferes with the ability of receptors in mosquitoes to sense chemicals that are produced by people and animals.

What products contain DEET?
■ Aerosol products intended for use on human skin and clothing.

■ Liquid products for use on human skin and clothing.

■ Skin lotions.

■ Towelettes, wristbands, and other products.

■ Products for use on animals.

How toxic is DEET?
■ Scientists believe that DEET poses little danger to humans when properly applied to the skin or clothing.

Source: United States Centers for Disease Control and Prevention.

The A, B, C's of Vitamin Supplements

Consumers can purchase a wide variety of vitamin and mineral supplements. Before taking supplements, however, consumers should check with their physician.

Vitamin supplements are big business. Health-conscious Americans spend more than $6 billion on supplements each year. In 2003, the *American Journal of Preventive Medicine* reported that more than half the adults in the United States use a vitamin or mineral supplement.

People take vitamin supplements for a variety of reasons. Some may want nutrient insurance that they think diet alone can't supply. Other people rely on supplements in the belief that supplements can preserve or improve their health and prevent such chronic diseases as cancer, heart disease, and osteoporosis. According to a study reported in January 2004 by researchers at the Fred Hutchinson Cancer Research Center in Seattle, Washington, supplement users tend to have better diets and tend to be better educated, less likely to be overweight, and more likely to be physically active than those who do not take supplements.

Vitamins are chemical compounds that are essential for good health. They work by increasing the speed of *enzymes,* molecules that convert food into energy and living tissues, among other functions. Unlike minerals, vitamins are

organic substances (produced by living things).

Scientists divide vitamins into two main groups—fat-soluble and water-soluble. The fat-soluble vitamins—A, D, E, and K—dissolve in fats. Water-soluble vitamins—B complex and C—dissolve in water. In general, water-soluble vitamins must be taken regularly because the body cannot store these nutrients in significant amounts. Excessive amounts of these vitamins usually wash out of the body in urine and sweat. The body stores excess amounts of fat-soluble vitamins in its fatty tissues, sometimes for long periods.

Scientists have identified 13 vitamins. Five of these are produced in the body itself. People must get the others either from food or from supplements.

Vitamin supplements come in many different forms, including tablets, capsules or soft gels, powders, liquids, sprays, and lozenges. Some tablets are designed to dissolve under the tongue. Vitamins may also come in the form of gummy candy, jellybeans, or chewables, which may be easier for children to take.

Consumers can buy a wide variety of vitamin formulas. One-a-day vita-

Vitamins essential for human health

Vitamin	Sources	Recommended dietary allowance	
		Children (ages 1-10)	Adolescents and adults
A (retinol)	Butter, carrots, dark green leafy vegetables, eggs, fish liver oil, liver, milk, sweet potatoes, deep yellow fruits and vegetables.	300-600 µg RE	600-900 µg RE (males) 600-700 µg RE (females)
Thiamine (B$_1$)	Legumes, nuts, organ meats, pork, whole grains, yeast, enriched breads, most vegetables.	0.5-0.9 mg	0.9-1.2 mg (males) 0.9-1.1 mg (females)
Riboflavin (B$_2$)	Cheese, fish, green vegetables, liver, milk, poultry.	0.5-0.9 mg	0.9-1.3 mg (males) 0.9-1.1 mg (females)
Niacin	Fish, liver, enriched breads, lean meat, whole grains.	6-12 mg NE	12-16 mg NE (males) 12-14 mg NE (females)
B$_6$	Eggs, fish, nuts, organ meats, poultry, whole grains.	0.5-1.0 mg	1.0-1.7 mg (males) 1.0-1.5 mg (females)
Pantothenic acid	Almost all foods; made by intestinal bacteria.	2-4 mg*	4-5 mg*
B$_{12}$	Eggs, fish, meat, milk, milk products, poultry.	0.9-1.8 µg	1.8-2.4 µg
Biotin	Egg yolk, kidney, liver, nuts; made by intestinal bacteria.	8-20 µg*	20-30 µg*
Folic acid	Fruit, legumes, liver, green leafy vegetables.	150-300 µg	300-400 µg
C (ascorbic acid)	Cantaloupe, citrus fruits, potatoes, raw cabbage, strawberries, tomatoes.	15-45 mg	45-90 mg (males) 45-75 mg (females)
D (cholecalciferol)	Eggs, salmon, tuna, fortified milk; made in the skin in sunlight.	5 µg*	5-15 µg*
E (tocopherol)	Almost all foods, especially margarine, olives, and vegetable oils.	6-11 mg TE	11-15 mg TE
K	Leafy vegetables; made by intestinal bacteria.	30-60 µg*	60-120 µg* (males) 60-90 µg* (females)

µg=micrograms; mg=milligrams; RE=retinol equivalents; NE=niacin equivalents; TE=tocopherol equivalents

*Adequate Intake (AI). The AI is a value based on experimentally derived intake levels or approximations of observed mean nutrient intakes by a group or groups of healthy people. Because there is less information on which to base allowances, these figures are not classified as RDA's.

Source: The National Academy of Sciences. Courtesy of the National Academy Press, 2000, 2001.

mins refer to *multivitamins* (supplements that contain various vitamins and, often, a number of minerals). Some vitamins are designed to meet the special needs of certain groups. A multivitamin for women of childbearing age, for example, may contain more than the recommended amount of folic acid because this vitamin protects against birth defects of the central nervous system in *fetuses* (developing babies). Formulas for men contain little or no iron because

men don't menstruate. Iron is an important part of red blood cells, which are normally shed each month by women of childbearing age.

The Food and Nutrition Board of the National Academy of Sciences, an organization that serves as a scientific adviser to the U.S. government, sets the Recommended Dietary Allowances (RDA's) for vitamins. RDA's are estimated amounts of various nutrients that a healthy person needs each day to avoid

Eating healthful foods, such as fruits and vegetables, is the best way to get all the nutrients important to good health. Even the best multivitamin cannot replace a healthy, balanced diet.

a deficiency and maintain good nutrition. The board also issues a standard called Adequate Intakes (AI's) for certain nutrients when scientists lack enough evidence to establish an RDA. RDA's and AI's are part of a larger category of standards called Dietary Reference Intakes (DRI's). DRI's also include guidelines that define the maximum daily amount of a particular vitamin a person can take and not develop a problem from overdosing.

The labels on vitamin supplements display a Daily Values (DV's) percentage. This figure represents the amount of the recommended daily intake for each nutrient in one supplement. The DV represents the highest RDA or AI recommended for a particular nutrient.

In 2003, the Institute of Medicine at the National Academy of Science recommended that the U.S. Food and Drug Administration (FDA) change the DV's to reflect the needs of the average person. Currently, DV's are based on RDA's established in 1968 for whichever segment of the population requires the highest level of a certain vitamin or mineral. The panel reported that although the DV's cover almost everyone's needs, they also overstate the needs of 97 to 98 percent of the population. The panel suggested that the FDA use census data to determine the proportions of various

life stage groups in the U.S. population and establish a single DV by combining the DRI's of these groups. (DRI's are based on 13 life stage groups, including children ages 4 to 8 years and males and females in the following age groups: 9 to 13 years, 14 to 18 years, 19 to 30 years, 31 to 50 years, 51 to 70 years, and older than 70 years.)

If the FDA adopts these changes, the recommendations for some nutrients would be much lower. For example, the DV for vitamin B_{12} would drop by two-thirds.

The FDA does not consider vitamin supplements to be drugs. As a result, vitamin manufacturers, unlike drug manufacturers, are not required to submit to the FDA the results of clinical studies proving their products' effectiveness and safety. To remove a supplement from the marketplace, the FDA has to prove it is unsafe.

In March 2003, the FDA proposed new regulations that would require vitamin manufacturers to provide accurate labels. For example, the regulations would help ensure that supplements contain the ingredients and amounts stated on the label. The regulations are also designed to ensure that supplements do not contain such harmful contaminants as glass, bacteria, and lead.

When it comes to vitamin supplements, health care experts say, more is not necessarily better. Research suggests that taking excessive amounts of vitamins can increase the risk of health problems. For instance, a 2002 study by scientists from the Harvard School of Public Health provided evidence that too much vitamin A may increase the risk of hip fractures. Other research has shown that taking too much vitamin D may cause weakness, loss of appetite, and constipation. Excess amounts of vitamin B_6 may cause nerve damage.

Large doses of certain vitamins may also interfere with the absorption of other nutrients, reduce the effectiveness of some medications, and cause false readings on lab tests. For example, high doses of calcium may reduce the absorption of iron. Too much vitamin E may increase the risk of bleeding in people taking blood-thinning medication. High levels of vitamin C may produce false results in many different lab results, including blood- and urine-glucose tests.

At the same time, some research suggests that taking doses above the minimum daily requirements can prevent or reduce the risk of some chronic diseases, including cancer and heart disease. Some scientists believe large amounts of certain antioxidant vitamins, such as vitamins A, C, and E, can prevent cell damage that may result in premature aging and degenerative diseases, including Alzheimer's disease, cancer, and heart disease. Antioxidants block the effects of unstable molecules called free radicals. Some studies have linked diets rich in antioxidants with a reduced risk of cancer, heart disease, cataracts, and other diseases common among the elderly.

Other studies have suggested that folic acid and vitamins B_6 and B_{12} may reduce the risk of heart disease. These vitamins appear to lower levels of homocysteine, a chemical that injures blood vessels. People with high levels of homocysteine may have a greater risk for heart disease. A 2003 study by the U.S. Preventive Services Task Force, an independent panel of experts in disease prevention and primary care, concluded, however, that there was little evidence to support the use of vitamin supplements to prevent cancer or heart disease.

Most health experts agree that vitamins can't replace a healthy diet. But consumers who decide to take vitamin supplements should take several steps before making their purchase. They should choose products with a USP stamp on the label. This stamp ensures that the manufacturer followed standards established by the U.S. Pharmacopeia (USP), an independent organization that sets content and safety standards for drugs and dietary supplements.

Consumers should also check the package for an expiration date. Over time, vitamins can lose their potency, especially in hot and humid climates. And unless instructed by their physician, consumers should choose a multivitamin with no more than 100 percent of the recommended DV's.

■ Jeanine Barone

Who needs vitamin supplements?

Health care officials believe that most people can benefit from the daily effects of a multiple vitamin. However, supplements may provide an added benefit to certain groups of people. There are also times during a person's life that vitamin and mineral supplements can complement a normal diet.

- People with alcoholism may benefit from a multivitamin to counteract some of the effects of alcohol abuse, which is often accompanied by poor diet.
- Dieters may develop certain vitamin and mineral deficiencies by avoiding certain foods or food groups.
- Elderly people often suffer from decreased levels of vitamin D and vitamin B_{12} as the result of normal aging.
- Patients with deficiency diseases or absorption disorders may need a physician to prescribe specific doses of vitamins and minerals.
- Pregnant and lactating women benefit from increased doses of folic acid.
- Smokers—in particular, heavy smokers—may benefit from increased doses of vitamin C to maintain healthy levels of the vitamin.
- Teen-agers may fill nutritional gaps with a multivitamin containing minerals.
- Women may benefit from extra calcium and iron.

Critically reviewed by the American Dietetic Association.

SCIENCE NEWS UPDATE

Contributors report on the year's most significant developments in their respective fields. The articles in this section are arranged alphabetically.

AGRICULTURE

United States Secretary of Agriculture Ann M. Veneman announced on Dec. 23, 2003, that a dairy cow slaughtered in Moses Lake, Washington, on December 9 had tested positive for bovine spongiform encephalopathy (BSE), also called "mad cow disease." The announcement was the first report in the United States of the disease that had previously crippled the cattle industries of Canada and the United Kingdom.

The U.S. Food Safety and Inspection Service immediately recalled 4,700 kilograms (10,400 pounds) of meat from 20 animals slaughtered with the BSE-infected cow. At the same time, the Department of Agriculture (USDA) Animal and Plant Health Inspection Service launched an investigation to track the source of the infected animal. The investigation determined that the sick cow had come from a herd in Alberta, Canada, and was imported into the United States in August 2001.

BSE is a degenerative disease affecting the brain of cattle. Scientists believe that deformed proteins called *prions* transmit the disease. Although prions are not alive like viruses or bacteria, they can change normal, healthy proteins into abnormal ones. It takes several years for BSE symptoms to show up in cattle, and prion infection can be detected only after the animals have been killed.

People who eat infected nerve tissue in beef products may develop, in time, a similar brain-wasting disease known as variant Creutzfeldt-Jakob disease. Scientists believe that this fatal condition is a form of Creutzfeldt-Jakob disease, a rare human disease caused by prions.

After the BSE finding was announced, domestic beef sales in the United States plummeted and foreign buyers banned U.S. beef imports. To rebuild confidence in U.S. beef, USDA officials in March 2004 announced an improved one-year surveillance program to begin on June 1, 2004. Inspectors were to test 268,000 slaughtered adult cattle selected through a sophisticated sampling method. Previously, inspectors tested about 40,000 cattle per year. Meat products from the animals are to be released into the food supply only if they test negative for BSE. The

MAD COW DISEASE SCARE

Tagged and quarantined cows nibble at feed on a Washington state dairy farm in late December 2003. The animals were suspected of having been exposed to "mad cow disease" through contaminated feed. One animal from the herd tested positive for the disease on December 9. Many of the animals from the herd were later destroyed.

AGRICULTURE continued

testing program is designed to detect with 99-percent certainty one BSE-infected cow in a pool of 10 million animals.

Insect-killing bacterium. The discovery of a bacterium that can kill several crop pests was announced in December 2003 by a team of scientists working for the USDA Agricultural Research Service (ARS) in Beltsville, Maryland. The bacterium, *Chromobacterium suttsuga,* produces *toxins* (poisons) that kill Colorado potato beetles, corn rootworms, diamond-back moths, silverleaf whiteflies, and green stinkbugs. Crop damage and control costs for these and other insects susceptible to *C. suttsuga's* toxins cost U.S. farmers an estimated $3 billion each year.

The ARS team, led by microbiologist Phyllis Martin, theorized that *C. suttsuga* must produce multiple insect toxins because it affects more than one insect species. Lab experiments and preliminary field tests supported this hypothesis. The researchers planned follow-up field tests.

The development of a new, nonspecific biological control is significant because insect pests often develop resistance to chemical insecticides. The researchers predicted that *C. suttsuga* would become an important agent in the arsenal of insect controls available to farmers and other agricultural interests.

Agriculture cools south Florida. The conversion of natural wetlands to farms in south Florida during the 1900's caused a slight but significant cooling of the local climate, according to a study released in November 2003. The study was conducted by

CHILLY FLORIDA FARMLAND

Computer-generated land use maps of south Florida from a November 2003 study reveal stark changes during the 1900's. Before 1900 (below, left), marshes, swamps, and bogs (shown in pink, red, and brownish-yellow, respectively) dominated the landscape. By 1993 (below), the predominant color had become light yellow, representing cropland. The study concluded that the local climate in south Florida has cooled slightly due to the dramatic loss of wetlands.

Florida pre-1900's

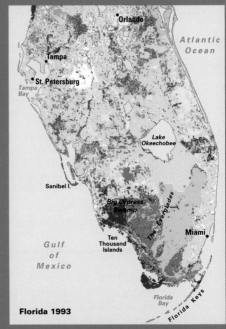

Florida 1993

climatologists Roger A. Pielke, Sr., and Curtis H. Marshall of Colorado State University in Fort Collins, Colorado; and Louis T. Steyaert, a remote sensing scientist from the U.S. Geological Survey in Greenbelt, Maryland.

During the early and middle 1900's, engineers drained wetlands and diverted rivers in southern Florida. Farmland replaced wetlands as farmers moved south to escape the occasional winter freezes farther north.

The researchers used a weather-modeling computer program to compare land use and temperature data for the region from two different periods: before 1900 and the 1990's. The program indicated that temperatures during 1990's freezes would have been slightly warmer and freezing periods would not have lasted as long if wetlands had not been replaced by farmland.

This outcome suggested that farmers, in seeking a warmer climate, had actually caused a cooling trend. The researchers theorized that wetlands provide a buffer against extremes of cold. During the day, bodies of water absorb heat, moderating rising temperatures. At night, they release heat, tempering nighttime cooling. Land, however, heats up and cools down faster than water, providing little buffer against cold extremes.

Pielke noted that climatologists have long studied the effects of such *greenhouse* (heat-trapping) *gases* as carbon dioxide on climate. The Florida study, he asserted, showed that scientists also should consider the impacts of land use when evaluating climate change.

Genetically modified crop area. The amount of cropland worldwide planted with *genetically modified* (GM) crops grew by 15 percent between 2002 and 2003. That finding appeared in a report published in 2004 by the International Service for the Acquisition of Agri-Biotech Applications in Ithaca, New York.

Crops are considered GM (also called transgenic or biotech) when scientists add or change specific genes to improve such traits as resistance to insects or tolerance of herbicides. Such crops often produce bigger yields while enabling farmers to apply fewer or more carefully targeted chemical controls.

In 2003, 7 million farmers in 18 countries grew 67.7 million hectares (167.3 million acres) of GM plants, according to the report. Two major agricultural producers, Brazil and the Philippines, entered GM production during that year. In 2002, 6 million farmers in 16 countries had grown 58.7 million hectares (145 million acres) of GM crops.

Farmers started planting large areas of GM crops in 1996 with the introduction of insect-resistant corn and herbicide-resistant soybeans. Since then, other GM crops have become available, including insect- and herbicide-resistant cotton and herbicide-resistant canola, a crop that produces seeds from which oil is extracted. ■ Andrew Burchett

ANTHROPOLOGY

When and where modern human beings—*Homo sapiens*—first appeared ranks as one of the most important questions in anthropology. In June 2003, an international team of researchers announced a major fossil discovery that points firmly to Africa as the cradle of *H. sapiens.*

The researchers discovered the fossil skulls of two adults and a child, as well as other bones, at a site in Africa known for its spectacular fossil finds. The fossils dated from between 160,000 and 154,000 years ago, making the finds the oldest-known fossils of modern human beings. The scientists said the skulls revealed surprising secrets about the be-

havior and beliefs of our earliest direct ancestors.

The researchers who made the discovery were led by paleoanthropologists Tim White of the University of California at Berkeley and Berhane Asfaw of the Rift Valley Research Service in Addis Ababa, Ethiopia. They found the fossils near a village called Herto, in the Middle Awash River Valley of Ethiopia. Since the 1990's, this valley has yielded numerous fossils of human ancestors dating back millions of years.

The sediments in the Middle Awash River Valley contain large deposits of volcanic ash and rocks, which, in turn, contain large

ANTHROPOLOGY continued

amounts of *radioactive isotopes* (forms of elements that break down over time into other elements at uniform, known rates). Measurements of the ratios of such isotopes in rocks allow scientists to calculate highly accurate dates for fossils deposited in the rocks. The use of this technique enabled White, Asfaw, and their colleagues to obtain reliable dates for the fossils found at Herto.

Two of the fossil skulls are from adult males, one of which is almost completely preserved. The third skull is from a child about 6 or 7 years old. The researchers described the skulls as having several similarities to those of modern people. For example, the fossils have high, rounded foreheads, in contrast to the lower foreheads seen in skulls of Neandertals and other pre-modern humans that existed at the time. The widest point of the nearly complete male skull is high on the sides, in contrast to Neandertal skulls, which are widest across the middle. In addition, the face of this skull, though large and broad, is relatively flat, as in modern people.

The scientists described some features of the Herto skulls as *archaic*—that is, displaying physical characteristics common to earlier human beings. For example, the skulls have prominent brow ridges and angled *occipital bones* (the part of the skull that rests against the spinal column). One of the skulls has an *occipital crest,* a ridge at the back of the skull that some human ancestors possessed.

This combination of modern and archaic features, the researchers explained, indicates that the individuals at Herto were not fully modern. Instead, they were likely a transitional form between pre-modern and fully modern people. Because of this, White and Asfaw assigned the fossils to a new subspecies of early modern people called *Homo sapiens idaltu.* (*Idaltu* means *elder* in the Afar language of Ethiopia.) White and Asfaw proposed that *H. sapiens idaltu* was the immediate African ancestor of *H. sapiens sapiens*, the subspecies of modern people.

In addition to providing insights on evolution, the Herto fossils also revealed a major surprise about prehistoric human behavior, according to the researchers. All the skulls displayed fine, sharp cut marks made by stone tools. The scientists noted that these marks resemble the marks produced when skin and soft tissues on a body are carefully removed after an individual's death. In certain cultures today, including native tribes in New Guinea, this kind of defleshing is usually part of ritualistic practices performed on the dead in which the skull is cleaned to be used in ceremonies honoring tribal ancestors. Supporting this idea, according to the research team, is the fact that the Herto skulls appear smooth and polished, as though they had been handled frequently after they were defleshed. This conclusion suggested to the investigators that the people at Herto conducted ceremonies of a symbolic nature previously documented only among fully modern human beings.

At Herto, the scientists also found the bones of various animals. Among these were the bones of a butchered hippopotamus that was found next to stone tools—suggesting that the people of the site ate these huge water mammals. The hippo bones also indicated that the prehistoric site lay near the shore of an ancient freshwater lake. Zebra and wildebeest bones in the same deposits suggested that open grasslands also lay nearby.

Many anthropologists noted that the report by White and Asfaw supports the idea that all living people are the direct descendants of a small group of human beings that lived in Africa between about 200,000 and 150,000 years ago. Scientists expected that the discovery of the skulls would prompt increased research at Herto and throughout East Africa for other fossils that might reveal additional details about the rise of modern human beings.

Weaker jaws led to bigger brains? A *mutation* (change) in a gene that controls the growth of jaw muscles may have led to the remarkable enlargement of the brain in human ancestors over 2 million years ago. A team of researchers at the University of Pennsylvania in Philadelphia and the Children's Hospital of Philadelphia reported this finding in March 2004. The report of the team, led by surgeon Hansell Stedman, marked the first time that a change to a specific gene had been linked to an observable event in the fossil record.

Nonhuman primates—monkeys and

KENNEWICK MAN RULING

Scientists may study the skull and other 9,300-year-old remains of an individual known as Kennewick Man, a U.S. court ruled in February 2004. Northwest Native Americans had argued that the remains, discovered in Washington in 1996, represented one of their ancestors and, thus, should be turned over to them for burial. In its ruling, however, the court said that examinations of the bones failed to prove that the skeleton is that of a Native American.

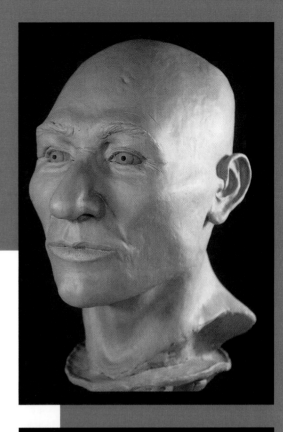

apes—have large, powerful jaw muscles. Their *braincases* (the upper part of the skull) are small compared with the human braincase. As a result, massive jaw muscles may cover the entire top of their skull, even extending to bony crests above the top of the skull. These powerful muscles act like strong rubber bands, placing tension on the bones of the skull. This arrangement of large, strong muscles keeps the braincase—and, therefore, the brain—from growing larger.

Stedman and his colleagues showed that human jaw muscles are only about one-eighth the size of the corresponding muscles in macaque monkeys, chimpanzees, and gorillas. Rather than covering the top of the skull, human jaw muscles typically cover only about three-quarters of the sides of the skull.

The investigators determined that the reason for the small jaw-muscle size in people seems to be a unique version of a gene called MYH16, which lies on *chromosome 7*. (Human beings have 23 pairs of chromosomes, the tiny structures in cells on which genes lie.) In monkeys and apes, the MYH16 gene *codes for* (instructs the body to produce) a protein known as myosin heavy chain, which helps the large jaw muscles of these primates to contract. In people, however, MYH16 does not function. The researchers confirmed that MYH16 is inactive in people by analyzing samples of *DNA* (deoxyribonucleic acid, the molecule that makes up genes) obtained from individuals in many countries. Although the gene was present in all the people, it played no role in the contraction of jaw muscles.

The inactivation of MYH16, the researchers said, explains why human jaw muscles are smaller and weaker than those of our nonhuman cousins. They proposed that, over

Kennewick Man's skull (plastic casting, below) suggests that he had facial features (clay model, above) similar to those of the present-day Ainu, a group that lives in Japan. This finding challenges commonly held ideas about the origin of Native Americans.

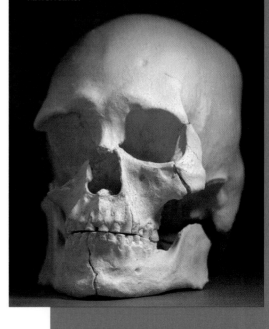

ANTHROPOLOGY continued

time, the reduced size and strength of jaw muscles in human ancestors relaxed the tension and pressure placed on the skull. This allowed the skull and the brain to grow larger.

Considering the average rate at which genetic mutations are believed to accumulate in animal species, Stedman and his colleagues calculated that the distinctively human form of MYH16 appeared roughly 2.4 million years ago. That date corresponds closely to the age of the earliest known species of genus *Homo*— *Homo habilis.* The scientists noted that the fossil record reveals that earlier species thought to be ancestral to *Homo,* such as australopithecines, had skulls more like those of chimpanzees, with large faces, small braincases,

and powerful jaws. Since the appearance of *Homo,* the brain has nearly tripled in size. Furthermore, the fossil record shows that brain growth in *Homo* occurred along with a reduction in the size of the jaws and teeth.

But how did early human beings survive without the ape-sized jaw muscles that had been so important to their ancestors? Developmental biologist Pete Currie of the Victor Chang Cardiac Research Institute in Sydney, Australia, suggested in March 2004 that changes in diet may have favored the mutation of the human MYH16 gene. For example, he said, human ancestors may have begun processing food by hand—by chopping, pounding, or mashing—to make it easier to chew. As a result, they no longer needed strong jaws.

First Americans not from Siberia?

Revised dates for the Ushki Lake archaeological site in northeastern Siberia have cast doubt on the idea that the first settlers of North America traveled across the *Bering Land Bridge* between 18,000 and 17,000 years ago. The Bering Land Bridge was dry land connecting present-day Siberia and Alaska during the last *Ice Age* (a period when ice sheets cover vast regions of land), which ended about 11,500 years ago. At this time, sea levels were lower because glaciers held much of the world's water. The new dates appeared in research published in July 2003 by anthropologist Ted Goebel of the University of Nevada at Reno and colleagues at Texas A&M University in College Station and the Russian Academy of Sciences in Moscow.

Anthropologists have long believed that human beings spread into the Americas from Siberia and that these migrants stopped at the Ushki Lake site before crossing the land bridge to Alaska. Scientists believe those ancient Siberians were the ancestors of the *Clovis people,* people known primarily from stone *projectile points* (stone points for arrows and spears) found at sites in North America dating back to 13,600 years ago. (The name *Clovis* comes from Clovis, New Mexico, near the site where Clovis points

NEANDERTALS NOT OUR ANCESTORS?

A comparison of more than 1,000 skulls of modern human beings, Neandertals, apes, and monkeys indicated in January 2004 that Neandertal skulls differ too much from modern human skulls for Neandertals to have been our ancestors. Anthropologist Katerina Harvati of New York University based this conclusion on measurements of 15 cranial and facial features for Neandertals (red lines) superimposed over those for modern human beings (green lines).

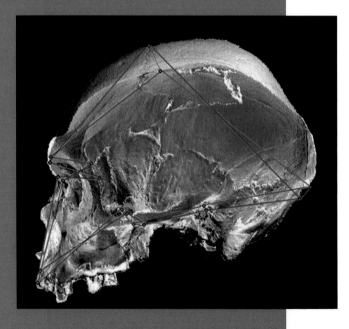

were first discovered.) Previous archaeological excavations supported the belief that Ushki Lake was a stopping point. Those excavators used *radiocarbon dating,* a technique that measures the *decay* (breakdown) of a radioactive isotope of carbon in fossils and other artifacts, to date the human use of the site at 16,800 years ago. Most anthropologists agreed that the period between 16,800 and 13,600 years ago would have given the Clovis people plenty of time to spread throughout the Americas.

The dates obtained by Goebel and his colleagues, however, showed that the Ushki Lake complex is almost 4,000 years younger than had previously been estimated. Goebel said that the previous dates were probably inaccurate because they had failed to control for contamination caused by geological carbon

deposits that were older than the artifacts at the site. In correcting for such contamination, Goebel's team concluded that the Ushki Lake site was occupied no earlier than 13,000 years ago. This date would rule out Ushki Lake as a way station because the site is only 600 years younger than some Clovis sites.

The researchers noted that, although the earliest migrants could not have come from Ushki Lake, they might have come from some other site in Siberia or from somewhere else entirely. Many anthropologists said that this study contributes to a growing body of evidence suggesting that early Americans came from several different ancestral populations that migrated to the Americas by several different routes—some over land and some across the sea.   ■ Richard G. Milo
See also **ARCHAEOLOGY.**

ARCHAEOLOGY

Three beautiful animal figurines, whose discovery was reported in December 2003, represent some of the earliest examples of prehistoric carvings ever found. The mammoth-ivory figurines, which have been dated to about 33,000 years ago, were found in Germany by a team of archaeologists led by Nicholas Conard of the University of Tubingen in Germany. Conard said the artifacts also may be the earliest evidence of *shamanism* (a system of beliefs that explores connections between the visible world and the spirit world).

The scientists found the figurines, which are about 2.5 to 5 centimeters (1 to 2 inches) high, at Hohle Fels Cave in southwestern Germany. The objects lay deeply buried in a layer of earth that also contained broken stone tools and other artifacts identified as belonging to a group of people who were part of the *Aurignacian culture.* This prehistoric culture, which existed in Europe between 40,000 and 28,000 years ago during the *Upper Paleolithic Period* (late Stone Age), is known mostly from its stone and bone tools. The Paleolithic Period lasted from about 2 million years ago to about 8000 B.C. Most archaeologists believe that the Aurignacian people belonged to the same species—*Homo sapiens*—as modern human beings do.

SEE ALSO THE SPECIAL REPORT, **SAVING THE PAST,** PAGE 12.

Archaeologists had previously discovered several Aurignacian mammoth-ivory carvings at four other caves in Germany. However, those figurines represent a more recent period than do the carvings from Hohle Fels Cave.

One of the figurines described by Conard appears to be a creature that is half man and half lion. The archaeologists said it shows great detail in the lionlike head and upper body and in the human lower torso. A second figurine is a skillfully carved water bird, possibly a cormorant, that appears to have its wings folded back as if it was making a dive. The bird has an elongated neck, distinctive eyes, and finely engraved feathers. The third figurine is that of a horse—or possibly a bear—with intricately carved eyes, mouth, and nostrils. The investigators noted that all the figurines are very smooth, indicating that they had been polished by repeated handling.

Conard and archaeologist David Lewis-Williams of the University of Witwatersrand in Johannesburg, South Africa, concluded that at least two of the figurines were used in cere-

ARCHAEOLOGY continued

monies related to shamanism. The shaman leading such ceremonies is a person who is believed to have powers that come from direct contact with the supernatural, often in dreams or trances. Practitioners of shamanism believe that human spirits can transform into animal forms. Conard and Lewis-Williams noted that the half-lion and half-man figurine might represent a shaman undergoing such a transformation. The diving water bird, they added, might represent the passage between the visible world and the spirit world.

Early evidence of fire. Three studies reported in 2003 and 2004 shed light on the controlled use of fire by early human beings—and possibly even by human ancestors. The studies examined evidence of what may be the oldest controlled use of fire ever found as well as other evidence that may represent the oldest-known use of fire in Europe. The prehistoric fire makers lived between about 1.5 million and 250,000 years ago.

The discovery of the earliest-known instance of the controlled use of fire was announced in March 2004 by paleontologists Bob Brain and Francis Thackeray of the Transvaal Museum in Pretoria, South Africa. These scientists attributed a group of burned animal bones unearthed in 1.5-million-year-old deposits in South Africa to either an early type of human known as *Homo erectus* or to *Australopithecus* (sometimes called *Paranthropus*) *robustus,* an early humanlike creature. A number of scientists, however, questioned this conclusion.

Brain and Thackeray based their conclusion on a study of the bones conducted by chemist Anne Skinner of Williams College in Williamstown, Virginia. The analysis was performed to distinguish between charring caused by natural fires, which typically reach temperatures of 300 °C (572 °F), and charring caused by controlled cooking pits, whose fires may reach temperatures of 600 °C (1,112 °F). Skinner used a laboratory technique called electron spin resonance to analyze highly reactive atoms called *free radicals.* These atoms are produced by a variety of processes, including radiation damage and fire. Each kind of free radical absorbs or reflects certain colors of light, producing a group of colors known as a *spectrum* or *light signature.* Analysis of this spectrum revealed the types of free radicals in the bones and, thus, the type of process that produced them.

The scientists concluded that the charring on the bones was produced by the high temperatures usually achieved only in cooking hearths. A number of other experts, however, said that additional evidence was needed to confirm that human beings or humanlike creatures used fire so long ago.

A more widely accepted report of early fire

PREHISTORIC MASTERPIECES?

Archaeological artifacts described in 2003 expanded the evidence that prehistoric people created sophisticated artwork tens of thousands of years ago. The reported objects came from various sites in Europe.

A small figurine of a water bird appearing to make a dive is one of three 33,000-year-old animal figurines carved from mammoth ivory whose discovery was reported in December. Archaeologists at the University of Tubingen in Germany said the figurines, which were found in a cave in southwestern Germany, may have been created by some of the first modern human beings to move into what is now Europe.

use was reported in April 2004 by archaeologist Naama Goren-Inbar of Hebrew University in Jerusalem, Israel. Her team discovered evidence dating to 790,000 years ago of the controlled use of fire at a site in northern Israel called Gesher Benot Ya'aqov. The scientists said the fires could have been made by *H. sapiens* or either of two other human species believed to have existed at that time— *H. erectus* and *H. ergaster*.

Goren-Inbar described finding small clusters of scorched flint artifacts, burned seeds, and charred wood at several locations at the site. She noted that a natural fire would have left signs that it had swept across a wide area at the site. The isolated clusters of burned artifacts, however, suggested small, controlled hearth fires. Goren-Inbar proposed that early human beings may have used the fires for cooking, warmth, or even protection against wild animals.

Another report of early fire use came in October 2003, when workers constructing a road near the town of Salisbury in southern England cut into a site that was occupied from

Flint found in a French cave that had been inhabited by Neandertals appears to have been shaped about 32,000 years ago to resemble a human face, French experts in prehistoric art said in December. The experts, from the Museum of Prehistory of Grand-Pressigny and the French National Centre for Scientific Research in Paris, argued that an animal bone had been pushed through the "nose" of the flint to represent eyes. However, some archaeologists doubted that the shape was deliberately made.

Engravings carved into the stone walls of a cave at Creswell Crags in central England represent the earliest-known examples of cave art in the United Kingdom, according to a July report. The carvings, which include those of a type of wild goat called an ibex (below) and two birds, were dated at 12,000 years old by a research team that included independent archaeologist Paul Bahn and archaeologist Paul Pettitt of Oxford University in England.

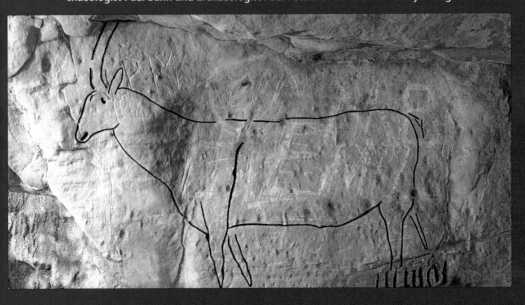

ARCHAEOLOGY continued

about 300,000 to 250,000 years ago. Helena C. Penny, county archaeologist for the Salisbury district, described the site as the remains of a Paleolithic riverside camp with large deposits of wood charcoal, which was produced in wood-burning hearths. The fire makers were probably an early form of *H. sapiens,* according to the archaeologists who investigated the find.

Penny said archaeologists also found bones of horses and more than 40 flint hand axes, tools used to split open animal carcasses. The archaeologists linked the hand axes to the *Acheulian culture,* which is most notable for producing large, pointed chopping tools in much of Africa and Europe between about 1.4 million and 200,000 years ago. Archaeologists had never found such axes with fire pits in England. The researchers concluded that the prehistoric fire pits had been used for cooking meat from the horses whose bones were found at the site. They also suggested that people might have used the fires for warmth, as the climate at that time was very cold.

This discovery marked the earliest-known evidence for the controlled use of fire in England. The scientists added that the find might even represent the earliest-known controlled use of fire in Europe.

Native Americans in Vermont. A discovery reported in September 2003 filled a gap in archaeologists' knowledge about early American Indian settlements in Vermont. Archaeologist John G. Crock of the University of Vermont in Burlington announced the discovery of Vermont's first-known *late Paleo-Indian settlement* (a settlement in North America existing between 10,000 and 9,000 years ago). Although archaeologists had previously found evidence of human settlements in Vermont dating to 11,500 years ago, the lack of evidence from the late Paleo-Indian period had suggested to some investigators that people had temporarily abandoned this part of the country for about 1,000 years. The new find, near the town of Colchester, proved that what is now Vermont was, in fact, continuously occupied during this time.

A team led by Crock uncovered the settlement site during an archaeological survey conducted prior to the construction of a highway off-ramp in the area. State and federal laws require such surveys as a way to discover archaeological sites before they are destroyed by major construction projects.

The archaeologists carefully sifted through the soil deposits to recover any artifacts. This work revealed several fragments of long, stone spear points for killing animals. These points were similar in shape to the *Agate Basin* spear points—a style known from Late Paleo-Indian sites elsewhere in the United States, as far away as Wyoming. The investigators also uncovered scrapers and other tools for stripping hides from animals.

Crock's team concluded that early Native Americans seem to have used the site— dubbed the Mazza Site after property owner Sam Mazza—as a camp for hunting and working hides. They said the camp was probably occupied for a few days or, at most, a few weeks. The researchers noted that the fragmented spear points probably represent spear shaft tips that were broken during hunting.

No animal bones were preserved in the soils, so the archaeologists were unable to identify the types of animals hunted near the Mazza Site. However, they said the most likely prey in this area at that time were such modern mammal species as deer.

Further analysis of the stone spear points revealed signs of trade between the late Paleo-Indian peoples of modern Vermont and New Hampshire. The Mazza Site spear points were made from a type of stony material found about 150 kilometers (93 miles) east of the Mazza Site.

Viking burial in England. The first strong evidence of long-term Viking settlements in what is now England was described in February 2004 by archaeologist Simon Holmes of the Yorkshire Museum in York. Holmes announced the discovery of a possible Viking *burial ship* dating to the 800's in the northeastern part of England. The Vikings often buried individuals with their possessions in such ships to carry the souls of the dead to the afterlife.

Both historical records and archaeological evidence had previously indicated the presence of Vikings in England during the 800's. That evidence, however, had pointed only to brief raids—not to the establishment of actual settlements. Holmes argued that the elaborate burial ship suggested that a true Viking settlement existed in England.

Local people using metal detectors discovered the burial ship in December 2003. They reported to the Yorkshire Museum that they had found more than 100 artifacts, including a dozen ancient iron nails, several silver coins, and a belt buckle. After carefully analyzing the finds, museum archaeologists concluded that the items represented Viking possessions destined for use in the afterlife. The iron nails provided the main evidence for this conclusion. The archaeologists said the nails were "clinch nails," a type the Vikings used with metal washers to build *longboats*. Longboats, also called *longships*, were narrow, highly maneuverable Viking ships used during voyages on the high seas. The Vikings also used these ships to bury important individuals.

The scientists did not fully excavate the site but used metal detectors to trace the locations of the clinch nails underground. The survey showed that the nails spread across an area about 30 meters (98 feet) in length. This was the typical length of a longboat.

The investigators identified a number of other artifacts at the site. For example, they found silver pennies dating to the reign of Alfred the Great, who ruled in what is now southwestern England between 871 and 899. They also found coins from this time linked to King Burgred of Mercia, an area that occupied what is now central England. One of the most surprising findings was a silver *dirham,* a type of Arabic coin that the scientists said was probably minted in ancient Baghdad, in present-day Iraq. The coins are evidence that the Vikings in England had links to a widespread trade network. Other finds at the site included fragments of two swords and two sets of weighing scales. Holmes concluded that the artifacts indicated that the burial was that of a Viking merchant or trader.

Mummies in Siberia. New insights about a little-known, complex culture that existed 1,000 years ago south of the Arctic Circle in Siberia were reported in January 2004. The insights came from unusually well-preserved bodies found in an ancient cemetery known as Zeleniy Yar, which lies along the Poluy River in northwestern Siberia. A group of archaeologists led by Natalia Fedorova of the Ural branch of the Russian Academy of Sciences excavated the mummies, which had been naturally preserved by the *permafrost* (frozen soil) in the region.

Fedorova described 34 shallow burials. The bodies in some of the graves lay in fragments, with shattered skulls and other broken bones. Fedorova noted that the ancient Siberians might have damaged the bodies intentionally in the belief that this act would prevent the dead from producing spells. However, she said it was more likely that the bodies were disturbed by grave robbers or even by the digging of new graves.

The archaeologists reported that five of the bodies in the cemetery were in an excellent state of preservation. The ancient Siberians had first wrapped these bodies in

GOLD TEETH TRIBE

Teeth with tiny drilled holes packed with gold foil adorn an ancient human jawbone uncovered by farmers in a village in Myanmar (Burma). The bone, reported by Chinese archaeologists in July 2003, was the first fossil evidence supporting written historical records describing a so-called "Gold Teeth" tribe that lived in the area between Myanmar and the Chinese province of Yunnan more than 1,000 years ago.

ARCHAEOLOGY continued

the skins of reindeer and bear as well as blankets made from the fur of beaver and wolverine. They then placed the shrouded bodies in log coffins. In the burials, archaeologists found various artifacts, including iron knives and silver medallions. The researchers also found evidence—such as arrow points in eye sockets and stab wounds—that some of the individuals had died in battle.

In their most remarkable find, the archaeologists described how several bodies had been buried with copper masks or plates covering their faces. Copper plates entirely covered the body of one male mummy. Many of the bodies also had small copper hoops binding the animal skins they were wrapped in. In addition, the scientists uncovered the remains of a metalworking shop where copper, iron, and silver items had been made. The researchers suggested that the metal masks, plates, and other items buried with the bodies might have been intended to serve some sort of protective function in the afterlife.

Fedorova pointed out that these findings were clear signs that a culture with complex beliefs and sophisticated technology existed in this part of the world 1,000 years ago. Archaeologists had believed that such an advanced culture did not arise in northwestern Siberia until hundreds of years later.

Yet another surprising discovery at the site indicated that the people of this subarctic culture engaged in long-distance trade. The evidence included several bronze bowls of a style that had been made in Persia (modern Iran) during the 900's and 1000's.

Hanoi's ancient citadels. In what may be one of the most important archaeological discoveries ever made in Vietnam, government archaeologist Tong Trung Tin reported the excavation of buried citadels in the capital city of Hanoi in December 2003. The citadels were built on top of each other, like layers in a cake. According to Tong, the oldest citadel is at least 1,400 years old, while the youngest dates to French colonial times in the 1950's.

Although a citadel is usually thought of as a fortress built to protect a city, the citadels in Hanoi also served as centers of political and economic activity. Vietnamese scholars had long speculated that these lost structures were buried in Hanoi, but the precise location of the structures was not confirmed until the excavations began in 2003.

Tong reported that some of the citadels spread across areas up to 140 hectares (346 acres). Although much of this site remained unexcavated as of mid-2004, Tong's team reported a number of finds that revealed a great deal of information about life inside the citadels. Among these finds were sophisticated drainage systems, walls of brick imported from China, and countless pottery objects and ceramic fixtures—many of which are decorated with birds and dragons.

Museums encourage looting? In October 2003, world-renowned archaeologist Lord Colin Renfrew of Cambridge University in England accused several museums in the United States of encouraging the destruction of archaeological sites. According to Renfrew, these institutions acted like "rogue museums" that purchased artifacts from the *looting* (untrained and illegal excavation) of sites around the world.

Renfrew noted that collectors who are patrons of these museums may believe their purchases of illicit artifacts are providing the artifacts with a "home" that protects the specimens from war, vandalism, or neglect. However, he said, such purchases are likely to encourage even more looting and fuel the commercial destruction of antiquity.

Renfrew cited the African country of Mali as a place where some of the worst cases of archaeological looting have occurred. Numerous ceramic figurines and other archaeological treasures have vanished from sites in Mali dating back to the A.D. 300's. These looted sites represent a culture that is almost unknown to scholars. Because the key archaeological sites have now been destroyed, scholars will be unable to carry out the systematic excavations needed to investigate and understand this lost culture.

Fortunately, Renfrew added, many museums in the United States have adopted strict guidelines that prevent the purchase or donation of looted artifacts. But he and other scholars emphasized that many other institutions around the world need to act to prevent looting and protect archaeological sites.

■ Thomas R. Hester

See also **ANTHROPOLOGY.**

ASTRONOMY

A revolution in the exploration of the planet Mars occurred in 2004. Spirit and Opportunity, two *rovers* (remote-controlled robotic vehicles) launched by the United States National Aeronautics and Space Administration (NASA), made history in early 2004 as they explored two areas of that planet thought to contain evidence that liquid water once existed there. Opportunity's site yielded both chemical and physical evidence of the presence of water in the past.

Also in 2004, NASA's Mars Global Surveyor, an orbiting spacecraft launched in 1996 that provides global views of surface features, continued to find locations on Mars where *gullies* (deep channels) developed in young terrain. These features suggest that liquid water continued to flow on Mars as recently as hundreds of thousands of years ago.

Destructive forces. The Milky Way Galaxy is slowly devouring another galaxy by means of its greater gravitational force, according to a report published in November 2003 by a team of astronomers led by Nicolas Martin of the Strasbourg Observatory in Strasbourg, France. The discovery confirmed the theory that the Milky Way is adding to its own *mass* (amount of matter) through cannibalization.

SEE ALSO

THE SPECIAL REPORTS, FANTASTIC VOYAGE: DISCOVERIES ON MARS, PAGE 28.

FANTASTIC VOYAGE: DISCOVERIES ON JUPITER, PAGE 36.

This cannibalization is due to a property called gravitational force. Gravitational force acting on an object tends to decrease as distance increases. Thus, the moon pulls harder on the side of Earth near it than on the side away from it. The difference between gravitational forces acting on opposing sides of a body is called a *tidal force*. Although tidal forces can stretch an object as large as a planet, Earth is too rigid to be pulled much out of shape. Earth's fluid oceans, however, are pulled into swells that give rise to tides.

In some cases, tidal forces are so strong that they can pull apart another celestial body. The Milky Way Galaxy is one such case. Surveying the sky in *infrared light* (long wavelengths of energy that are associated with heat), the researchers plotted the positions of

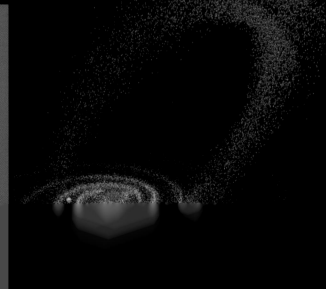

HUNGRY GALAXY

The Milky Way Galaxy (blue) devours a smaller, older galaxy (red) with its stronger gravitational force, shown here in an artist's depiction of a discovery reported in September 2003. This dwarf galaxy, called the Canis Major Galaxy, is the closest galaxy to our own. The finding confirmed the theory that the Milky Way has grown—and continues to grow—by cannibalizing other galaxies. Astronomers estimate that the mass of the Milky Way has grown by about 1 percent through this process.

ASTRONOMY continued

cool and, thus, older stars throughout the Milky Way and found a concentration of stars near the constellation Canis Major. Detailed mapping of these stars revealed a link with a previously discovered *streamer* (ring) of old stars surrounding the Milky Way.

The scientific team used mathematical models to study how the clump and ring formed. The researchers discovered that the Milky Way's tidal force is ripping apart a small galaxy in the Canis Major constellation. This destruction is leaving a concentration of old stars near Canis Major while forming a streamer of stars encircling the Milky Way.

By destroying the galaxy that is closest to it, the Milky Way is adding stars to its own bulk. The existence of the Canis Major Galaxy—which has about 1 billion stars—suggests that the Milky Way formed, in part, by absorbing smaller galaxies. So far, the Canis Major Galaxy may have contributed as much as 1 percent to the Milky Way's mass.

A tenth planet? The discovery of an object orbiting the sun beyond the planet Neptune was reported in March 2004. The body, named Sedna after the Inuit goddess of the ocean, resides well beyond the *Kuiper Belt*, a region of icy bodies believed to be left over from the formation of the planets. Sedna, with a diameter of about 2,000 kilometers (1,200 miles), is almost the same size as Pluto.

A team of astronomers, led by Michael Brown of the California Institute of Technology in Pasadena, observed Sedna in both *visible light* (light consisting of waves that can be seen) and infrared light. These observations, made using the Hubble Space Telescope, the Spitzer Space Telescope, and the Hale Telescope on Mount Palomar in California, allowed the scientists to determine the size and brightness of Sedna.

The scientists determined Sedna's orbit by measuring its movement against the sky over three years. They found Sedna has an oval orbit. At its *perihelion* (closest approach to the sun), Sedna comes within about 13 billion kilometers (8 billion miles) of the sun. This amount is approximately three times Pluto's perihelion distance.

Some scientists theorize that Sedna is a member of the *Oort Cloud*, a huge area of comets and larger bodies that surrounds the

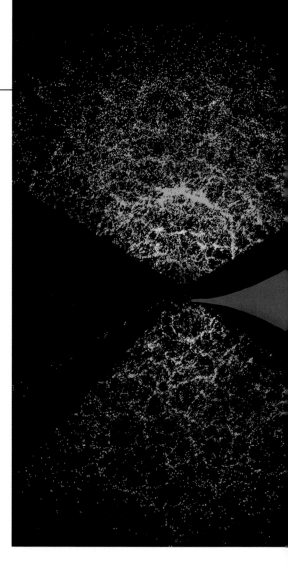

solar system. Scientists had believed that the inner edge of the cloud was no more than about 1.5 trillion kilometers (1 trillion miles) from the sun. The existence of Sedna, whose orbit takes it as far as 130 billion kilometers (80 billion miles) from the sun, suggests that the inner edge of the cloud may be that close to the sun.

Astronomers found Sedna's red color interesting. After Mars, Sedna is the reddest celestial body in the solar system. To some astronomers, this color suggests that Sedna has an abundance of carbon-bearing compounds on its surface that cosmic rays have gradually changed to a reddish crust. Sedna also seems to brighten and darken in a regular way that suggests it may rotate on its axis and that it may have a companion moon. Observations have not revealed the presence of a moon, however, leaving Sedna's change in brightness something of a mystery.

The most precise depiction of the architecture of the universe ever made (left) appears in a map published in November 2003 by scientists involved in the Sloan Digital Sky Survey (SDSS). This map, which covers 6 percent of the sky, shows the location of 205,443 galaxies up to 2 billion light-years away. The map confirmed the existence of *dark matter* (the invisible substance that makes up most of the matter in the universe) and *dark energy* (which makes the universe expand more and more rapidly).

The SDSS created the 3-D map using a 2-D template (above). Using pictures of galaxies, the SDSS used software to measure the shape and brightness of astronomical objects. The scientists then determined the distances to objects to plot the points in three dimensions.

Sedna's discovery is placing a new emphasis on attempts to determine the definition of a planet. Some scientists wonder if Sedna, like Pluto, is a planet. On the other hand, Pluto's orbit and size suggest that it may be the largest-known member of the Kuiper Belt and Oort Cloud. As a result, scientists may have to reclassify Pluto as a "leftover." If so, the solar system would have eight planets and a host of debris.

A deep field. A team of astronomers led by Massimo Stiavelli of the Space Telescope Science Institute in Baltimore released the latest image of the Hubble Ultra Deep Field in March 2004. The image is the farthest—and earliest—view of the universe ever taken.

The first Hubble Deep Field image, released in 1996, revealed several hundred faint galaxies in a region of the sky that looked dark when viewed through ground-based telescopes. That image, made by combining many time exposures from the Hubble Space Telescope, showed dim galaxies at very great distances. It has provided astronomers with information about the earliest periods during which galaxies formed.

However, the most recent image reveals objects up to four times as faint. These galaxies may be so remote that astronomers are seeing them from a time when the universe was only 300 million years old, or 2 percent of its present age. The findings have led many scientists to reconsider their ideas about the size and age of the universe.

The latest images of the field are the results of advanced technology. Recently, astronauts installed the Advanced Camera for Surveys, which offers very fine *resolution* (image sharpness), aboard the Hubble Space Telescope. Astronomers hope to use the image to understand the earliest times in the universe, including the "dark ages," when stars reheated the universe after the *big bang* (the violent explosion that most scientists believe gave birth to the universe).

Liquids on Titan. Evidence of liquids on the surface of Saturn's moon Titan was reported in October 2003 by a team of astronomers led by Donald Campbell of Cornell University in Ithaca, New York. Titan is the largest moon in the solar system after Jupiter's Ganymede and is the only moon with a *dense* (thick) atmosphere.

Astronomers think that Titan has lakes, if not seas, that consist of methane, ethane, and other *hydrocarbons* (carbon-hydrogen compounds) because its atmosphere is rich in methane. They have learned that ultraviolet sunlight in Titan's upper atmosphere breaks apart the methane molecule, which consists of four hydrogen atoms surrounding a carbon atom. Some of the hydrogen escapes, and the remaining carbon and hydrogen combine to make hydrocarbons. These compounds fall to Titan's surface. There, some of the compounds mix with methane as liquids, even at the very frigid surface temperature of –178 °C (–288.4 °F). If this process has been taking

ASTRONOMY continued

place over the entire age of the solar system, scientists speculate, Titan must have reservoirs of methane on or just below the surface that replenish the atmospheric methane lost in the chemical reactions. Lakes or seas of methane might serve as reservoirs for the hydrocarbon molecules.

Titan's atmosphere prevents astronomers

EXTRASOLAR MAGNETIC FIELD

A planet 270 times as massive as Earth creates a hot spot on the surface of the star HD179949 in an interpretive illustration of a finding reported in January 2004. Canadian scientists concluded that a moving area on the star's surface that is 700 times as warm as surrounding areas is evidence of the first orbiting planet with a magnetic field discovered outside the solar system.

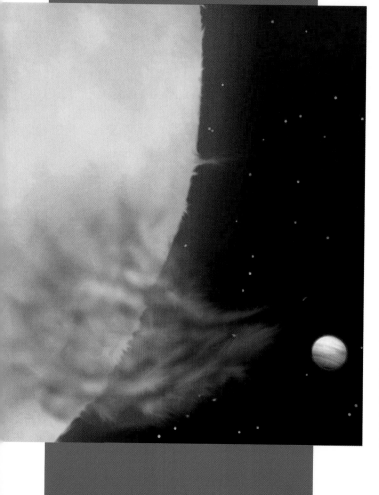

from seeing the surface with optical telescopes. To test the idea of hydrocarbon seas, the researchers relied on *radio telescopes*, which focus radio signals onto a receiver instead of collecting light from a distant object.

The researchers used the Arecibo radio telescope, the world's largest radio telescope, located in Arecibo, Puerto Rico. The researchers also used the Green Bank Telescope in Green Bank, West Virginia.

The astronomers transmitted radio signals from Arecibo that bounced off Titan's surface; the two telescopes received the echo approximately two hours later. The scientists then analyzed the strength of the signal to determine the brightness of Titan's surface at radio wavelengths. They also analyzed the reflection to determine whether it was *diffuse* or *specular*. A diffuse signal is one that has been scattered from a rough surface, while a specular reflection is sharper and comes from a mirrorlike surface. Specular reflections tend to come from very smooth ice or from a liquid that has not been disturbed greatly by wind.

Scientists knew that Titan might have liquid hydrocarbons and smooth water ice. Some hydrocarbon molecules are fluid even at the low surface temperatures found on Titan. The Voyager I spacecraft, which flew by Titan in 1980, found that Titan was made of rock and water ice. Some of the water ice at the surface might have melted in the recent past, creating a smooth surface that would produce specular reflections.

Infrared observations of Titan's surface, however, found that the amount of water ice on Titan's surface was much smaller than that required to explain the specular reflections, which cover 50 to 75 percent of the surface. Therefore, the presence of liquid hydrocarbons ranks as the best explanation for most of the specular reflection. If the scientists interpreted the radar data correctly, Titan is the only other celestial body in the solar system besides Earth to have stable surface liquids.

Spitzer Space Telescope. Astronomers gained an important new window on the universe in August 2003 with the successful launch of a new orbiting observatory that is tuned to infrared wavelengths of radiation. The spacecraft, called the Spitzer Space Telescope, completed a long-standing NASA goal of employing "Great Observatories" to observe the sky at all possible wavelengths. The other observatories in this group are the Hubble Space Telescope, the Compton Gamma Ray Observatory, and the Chandra X-ray Observatory. Although Hubble and Chandra are still in operation, Compton completed its mission in 2000.

The new telescope is named for Lyman Spitzer, considered the father of space-based astronomy for having first advocated the launch of orbiting telescopes in the 1940's. Spitzer also played key roles in the development of several orbiting observatories, including Hubble.

Cold matter—such as matter in space—emits most of its radiation at infrared wavelengths. Therefore, astronomers need infrared telescopes to clearly observe cold interstellar gas and very distant galaxies. While some infrared radiation reaches the ground, Earth's atmosphere blocks most wavelengths, a development that makes orbiting observatories necessary. The Spitzer Space Telescope carries instruments for obtaining both the infrared images and *spectra* (bands of visible light or any

SPIDER, SPIDER, BURNING BRIGHT

Previously hidden newborn stars emerge from the dust surrounding the Tarantula Nebula in a color-enhanced image of the nebula taken by the Spitzer Space Telescope (foreground) in January 2004. The telescope, launched in August 2003, detects *infrared* (heat) rays, which can penetrate the clouds of dust and gas surrounding regions where new stars are being created. At the center of the nebula lies a compact cluster of stars that is up to 100 times as massive and emits 100,000 times as much energy as the sun.

ASTRONOMY continued

other kind of electromagnetic radiation) of astronomical objects and phenomena.

By mid-2004, the telescope had made several groundbreaking findings. In May 2004, Spitzer spotted what NASA called the youngest planet ever discovered. The planet is at least 1 million years old. However, in astronomical terms, the planet is extremely young. For example, Earth is 4.5 billion years old.

The observatory has also confirmed the common presence of *protostars* (developing stars). With the telescope focused on a group of stars at the core of a distant *nebula* known as RCW49, astronomers discovered more than 300 newly forming stars in May 2004. A nebula is a mass of dust particles and gases or a cloudlike cluster of stars that occurs in interstellar space. Each protostar has a swirling disk of stellar dust, which is ideal for the formation of new solar systems. In addition, Spitzer data showed that planet-forming areas around stars contain enough ice to produce oceans.

A very distant galaxy. Scientists determined the greatest distance yet found for any galaxy, according to a March 2004 report by a team of astronomers led by Jean-Paul Kneib of the Midi-Pyrenees Observatory in Toulouse, France. This galaxy is 13 billion *light-years* away from Earth. (A light-year is the distance light, which moves at 299,792 kilometers [186,282 miles] per second, travels in a year.)

Astronomers use the *redshift* of a galaxy to find its distance. Redshift is a stretching of the wavelengths of visible light or similar radiation sent out by a cosmic object. Because the universe is expanding, the farther away a galaxy is, the faster it is receding from Earth and the greater its wavelength shifts.

The scientific team measured an enormous redshift for the new galaxy. The light from the new galaxy has shifted so much that the visible light it emits reaches Earth in the form of infrared radiation, an alteration of about eight times its original wavelength. The enormous redshift means that the researchers are observing this galaxy when the universe was only about 700 million years old, or 5 percent of its present age. At about this time, the first stars and galaxies were forming, astronomers believe.

Spinning black holes. *Black holes*

formed by the collapse of matter are likely to spin rapidly, but measuring the speed of this rotation is difficult. A black hole is an area in space where matter is so concentrated that not even light can escape its gravitational field. In September 2003, a team of astronomers led by Jonathan Miller of the Harvard-Smithsonian Center for Astrophysics in Cambridge, Massachusetts, reported the finding after studying three *stellar* (star-related) black holes in the Milky Way Galaxy.

Stellar black holes form when massive stars collapse after running out of nuclear fuel and when large quantities of matter fall together at the heart of a large system. Stellar black holes are usually a few times as massive as the sun. However, supermassive black holes, such as the one in the galaxy known as RXJ1242-11, have masses hundreds of millions of times as great as that of the sun. Scientists believe that supermassive black holes form as a result of galaxy formation.

Astronomers have developed methods for figuring out the rotation rates of black holes. Scientists cannot observe a black hole directly because the void traps any light that approaches it. However, they can observe the orbital motion of gas just outside a black hole. If the black hole is rotating rapidly, the orbiting gas can exist closer to the black hole than if there is little or no rotation. By measuring wavelength shifts in X-ray emissions from gas close to black holes, astronomers can deduce how close the gas is to the hole, and, therefore, how rapidly the black hole is rotating.

Using data from both the Chandra X-ray Observatory and the XMM Newton X-ray Observatory—launched by the European Space Agency in 1999—Miller's team calculated that gas orbits as close as 32 kilometers (20 miles) to the black holes XTE J1650-500 and GX 339-4. This finding indicates that both areas are spinning very rapidly. On the other hand, a similar analysis showed that gas surrounding Cygnus X-1, the first black hole ever discovered, orbits no closer than 160 kilometers (100 miles). This result suggests that Cygnus X-1 spins very slowly, if at all.

The Milky Way's black hole. A huge black hole at the center of the Milky Way Galaxy rotates at the rapid rate of once every 11 minutes, according to a finding published in November 2003 by a team led by Reinhard Genzel of the Max Planck Institute for Extraterrestrial Physics in Garching, Germany.

Astronomers believe that the Milky Way black hole contains approximately 3.6 million times the amount of mass in the sun. Many galaxies contain supermassive black holes at their centers.

The scientists calculated both the mass and the rotation rate of the black hole using measurements of X-ray emissions from gas orbiting close to the black hole. The team found that the gas orbits close enough to suggest that the black hole is spinning rapidly—about once every 11 minutes. Scientists hope to use spin rates to analyze how black holes affect the matter and space surrounding them.

A hungry black hole. Tidal forces can destroy stars, according to a report published in February 2004. A team of astronomers led by Stefanie Komossa of the Max Planck Institute for Extraterrestrial Physics uncovered evidence that a black hole is tearing apart and partially swallowing a star.

The scientists used images from two orbiting telescopes, in addition to photographs from an earlier space-based observatory, to observe the destruction of a star. Images from the Chandra X-ray Observatory showed that the powerful burst of X rays came from the

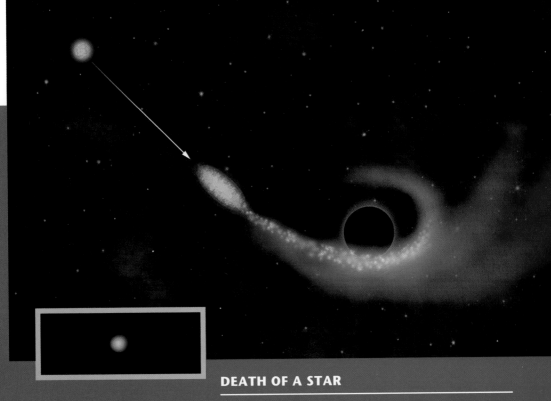

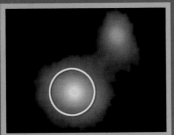

DEATH OF A STAR

A supermassive black hole at the center of a galaxy rips apart and partially swallows a star that is too close (above) in an artist's rendering of data reported in February 2004. Observations made with three telescopes, including the Earth-orbiting Chandra X-ray Observatory, revealed an outburst of X rays (left, above) near the center of the galaxy. Images of the same area (white circle, left) made using an optical telescope showed no signs of the outburst. Scientists reported that the outburst occurred when gas from the destroyed star became very hot as it fell into the black hole.

ASTRONOMY continued

very center of RXJ1242-11, which the astronomers knew to be the location of a supermassive black hole. Scientists also used images from the XMM-Newton Observatory.

Astronomers had seen other dramatic flares from galaxies, but this was the first studied with the very sharp image resolutions of Chandra and XMM-Newton, which detects a wide variety of wavelengths. Chandra showed the RXJ1242-11 event occurred in the center of a galaxy, where the black hole resides. Data from the XMM-Newton revealed the criteria expected for the surroundings of a black hole, ruling out other possible astronomical explanations. In addition, the astronomers used photographs from ROSAT, an X-ray observatory no longer in operation that was developed through a cooperative program among Germany, the United States, and the United Kingdom, to confirm the sudden outburst of X-ray energy. This sudden X-ray explosion occurred because gas from the star became compressed and *superheated* (heated to a very high temperature) as it fell toward the huge void.

The scientists' analysis of the X-ray event showed that a star with about the same mass as the sun came too close to the black hole and was torn apart by tidal forces. Only about 1 percent of the star's mass actually fell into the black hole. However, that was enough to produce a strong X-ray emission.

Astronomers had long theorized that occasionally stars wander too close to supermassive black holes and are ripped apart by tidal forces. The event in RXJ1242-11 provides the best evidence yet for such a phenomenon.

■ Jonathan Lunine and Theodore P. Snow

ULTRA DEEP

The farthest and oldest galaxies ever observed appear in the latest image of the Hubble Ultra Deep Field, released in March 2004. Astronomers created the image by combining many time exposures from the Hubble Space Telescope. The galaxies are so remote that they appear as they did when the universe was only 300 million years old, or 2 percent of its present age.

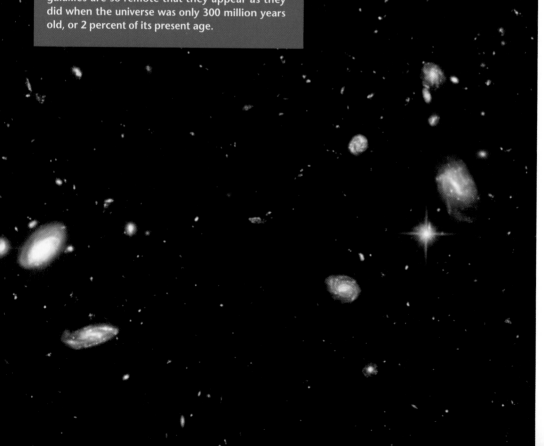

ATMOSPHERIC SCIENCE

The first hurricane ever recorded in the South Atlantic Ocean formed off the coast of Brazil in March 2004. The storm struck Brazil's southern coast on March 28, causing some loss of life and considerable damage. Brazilian weather forecasters named the hurricane "Catarina" after Santa Catarina, the Brazilian state in which it made landfall.

Previously, weather forecasters had tracked a few tropical storms in the South Atlantic, but none of the storms had ever reached *hurricane* strength. A hurricane has sustained winds of at least 119 kilometers (74 miles) per hour in tightly wrapped bands around an *eye* (center).

Tropical storms form only over tropical or subtropical ocean waters with surface temperatures of at least 25 °C (80 °F). Warmth increases the rate of evaporation from ocean surfaces, producing moisture-laden updrafts. If winds at various elevations above the ocean surface are too light to interfere with the spiralling updrafts, a storm begins to grow and thrive. Tropical storms may strengthen into hurricanes when atmospheric conditions remain favorable for several days or weeks.

Meteorologists had long ago concluded that the South Atlantic did not provide the conditions favorable for hurricane development. Although South Atlantic waters are warm enough for such development, prevailing winds above the ocean surface are usually too strong or they blow at cross currents—a phenomenon called *wind shear*. The strong wind shear prevents the formation of most tropical storms and usually tears apart any storms that do form.

The unprecedented South Atlantic hurricane developed from a low-pressure center originating over South America. On March 20, this weather system moved off the coast of Brazil, traveling eastward several hundred kilometers out to sea. There it remained nearly stationary for several days, reorganizing and gathering strength due to an unusual absence of strong winds aloft. By March 26, satellite photos indicated that the storm had become a full-fledged hurricane.

The hurricane then headed westward and, in the early hours of March 28, crossed the southern coast of Brazil near the town of

SEE ALSO THE SPECIAL REPORT, **IS THE WEATHER GETTING WEIRDER?** PAGE 44.

Torres, inflicting major damage. Three people were killed and more than 2,000 people were left homeless by the storm. On-shore wind measurements confirmed that Catarina was a category 1 hurricane, the weakest type of hurricane.

North American meteorologists, experienced in tracking hurricanes, assisted their Brazilian counterparts in tracking Catarina as it neared land. The North Americans found, however, that their computer-based hurricane forecasting models did not perform well in predicting storm development in the South Atlantic. Forecasters, both north and south, said they would need to rethink their assumptions about South Atlantic hurricanes and develop new tools for forecasting such storms.

Arctic thawing. Extensive thaws in *permafrost* in northern Sweden were reported in February 2004 by researchers at Lund University in Sweden. Permafrost is ground that remains frozen year-round to considerable depths. It exists mainly in Arctic and subarctic regions of the Northern Hemisphere.

Widespread thawing of permafrost in Arctic regions could release quantities of methane gas into the atmosphere and accelerate *global warming*, some atmospheric scientists have theorized. Global warming is the gradual increase in the temperature of Earth's surface that began in the late 1800's.

Biogeochemist Torben R. Christensen and other scientists based at Lund University's GeoBiosphere Science Centre studied long-term climate and environmental records from the Abisko region in subarctic northern Sweden. Of special interest to the researchers was the condition of permafrost in the region.

In permafrost regions, a thin top layer of soil, called the *active layer,* may thaw briefly in summer. In stable Arctic and subarctic climates, the active layer thaws and refreezes in an annual seasonal cycle that maintains equilibrium in the permafrost.

The Lund University study, however, showed that permafrost in the bogs of

ATMOSPHERIC SCIENCE continued

Sweden's Abisko region is undergoing dramatic changes. The active layer has become progressively thicker since 1970, and permafrost has disappeared altogether in some locations.

The rapid thawing of permafrost exposes partly decayed plant matter called *peat* to water, resulting in a chemical reaction that releases methane gas into the atmosphere. Methane is 25 times more potent as a *greenhouse gas* than carbon dioxide. Many scientists believe that greenhouse gases, which trap heat within Earth's atmosphere, are causing global warming. Carbon dioxide, a by-product of burning fuels, is the most abundant greenhouse gas.

At a particular Abisko bog called Stor-

dalen, researchers detected an increase of 20 to 60 percent in methane emissions between 1970 and 2000. They attributed the increase to a dramatic reduction of permafrost in the bog.

The cycle of arctic thawing and methane buildup could set up a *positive feedback* to the global climate system. A positive feedback occurs when a change (such as Arctic thawing) produces an effect (warming of the atmosphere) that, in turn, magnifies the change. Because of positive feedback, the release of significant quantities of methane into the atmosphere could accelerate the rate of global warming.

According to the researchers, further studies are needed in the circumpolar region of the Northern Hemisphere to determine whether the Abisko findings represent a widespread trend. If so, says Christensen, Arctic thaws may already have become a significant contributor to global warming.

Hitting bottom. On July 17, 2003, a team of scientists drilling through Greenland's ice cap struck bedrock. The achievement capped seven years' work in one of the most inhospitable places on Earth—the continental glacier that covers Greenland. To reach bottom, workers drilled through 3,085 meters (10,000 feet) of solid glacial ice.

The scientists, participants in the North Greenland Ice-Core Project, shipped the ice cores from the bottom of the ice cap to the Niels Bohr Institute in Copenhagen, Denmark. There, researchers planned to saw slices from the cores and send them to scientists all over the world for further study.

Ice from the bottom of the drill hole is more than 120,000 years old. Air bubbles trapped in the ice are expected to yield important clues about Earth's atmosphere during alternating warm periods and ice ages that have spanned the existence of the ice. Such clues could help scientists understand atmospheric changes that are occurring now.

In addition, glacial meltwater from beneath the huge ice cap froze to the tip of the drill bore, providing researchers with a glimpse into a surface layer never seen before. Biologists speculated that

GREENLAND ICE DRILL

Members of the North Greenland Ice-Core Project view the muddy tip of an ice core pulled from the bottom of Greenland's ice cap in July 2003. Over the course of the seven-year project, researchers drilled through 3,085 meters (10,000 feet) of ice to collect information on Earth's atmosphere for the past 120,000 years. The brownish color of the exposed ice indicates that it was water from the bottom of the glacier that refroze as the drill was extracted. In general, glacial ice cores look like ordinary clear ice.

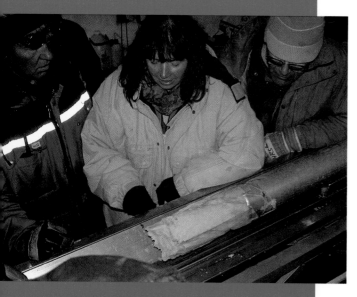

1930'S DROUGHT EXPLAINED

A traveling wall of dust (above) sweeps over Stratford, Texas, during the "Dust Bowl" drought of the 1930's that devastated the interior of the United States. A study reported in March 2004 that unusual sea-surface temperature patterns in the Atlantic and Pacific oceans caused a high-pressure system that normally sits in the North Atlantic to shift eastward (left). As a result, tropical winds that usually cross the Gulf of Mexico and carry moisture into the interior of North America blew farther south instead.

the meltwater might contain rare microbes long isolated from other life forms.

Dust Bowl explanation. The devastating drought in central North America in the 1930's—commonly known as the "Dust Bowl" drought—resulted mainly from temperature changes in the waters of the Atlantic and Pacific oceans, a study reported in March 2004. The study was conducted by meteorologist Siegfried Schubert and colleagues at the National Aeronautics and Space Administration (NASA) Goddard Spaceflight Center in Greenbelt, Maryland. It indicated that cooler-than-normal temperatures in Pacific waters and unusually warm temperatures in Atlantic waters shifted normal wind patterns and diverted moist winds away from the Great Plains.

From 1931 through 1939, the Great Plains experienced an exceptionally severe drought. From east Texas and the lower Mississippi

Valley north to the plains of Canada, rain and snow fell infrequently. The land dried out and loose topsoil blew away. Dust storms swept across affected areas. Severe drought conditions strained a regional economy already devastated by the Great Depression, a worldwide economic slump that also occurred in the 1930's.

The Schubert team used data in ship records from the 1930's to construct a temperature profile for tropical regions of the Pacific and Atlantic oceans during this period. They used these data profiles to run computer-based climate models. The models predicted rainfall patterns that closely matched actual precipitation patterns observed across the Dust Bowl region in the Great Plains during the 1930's.

The researchers reasoned that the unusual temperature patterns in the tropical Atlantic

ATMOSPHERIC SCIENCE continued

and Pacific oceans disrupted weather patterns over interior North America. Under normal ocean conditions, much of the moisture that falls as rain or snow on the Great Plains comes from the Gulf of Mexico.

Winds circling clockwise around a large high-pressure system centered near Bermuda in the Atlantic, called the Bermuda High, pass over the warm tropical waters of the Gulf of Mexico, absorbing water vapor. These winds turn northward and flow into the interior of North America. There the moisture-laden winds produce clouds and rain. In the 1930's, however, ocean conditions displaced the Bermuda High eastward. As a result, normal air flow across the Gulf of Mexico was disrupted and the supply of moisture to the Great Plains fell sharply.

Ozone depletion culprit. Scientists working from a NASA research plane flying high above the Arctic in winter observed for the first time chlorine dimer (*DY muhr*), a rare molecule long suspected of being one of the chief culprits in ozone depletion in the atmosphere. The scientists, led by Rick Stimpfle, senior project scientist for Harvard University's Division of Engineering and Applied Sciences in Cambridge, Massachusetts, reported their findings in February 2004.

Ozone is a molecule consisting of three oxygen atoms bonded together rather than the two bonded atoms found in molecular oxygen. Ozone molecules block harmful ultra-violet radiation from the sun, protecting life on Earth.

Chlorine dimer is the common name for ClOOCl, two molecules of chlorine monoxide (ClO) chained together. ClO consists of one chlorine atom and one oxygen atom. Manufactured chemical products called chlorofluorocarbons (CFC's) circulating in the atmosphere provide chlorine for ClO formation.

In the ultraviolet-drenched upper atmosphere, the chlorine dimer molecule absorbs sunlight and breaks apart, freeing two chlorine atoms to react with two ozone molecules. This reaction produces free oxygen and two more chlorine monoxide molecules, which are then available to form a new chlorine dimer. Thus, an ongoing cycle of chemical reactions repeatedly breaks down ozone, leading to ozone depletion.

Since the 1970's scientists have observed ozone depletion in the upper atmosphere, especially in Antarctica, where a large area of depletion—known as the "ozone hole"—appears annually. Scientists have long known that CFC's are the source of chlorine in ozone depletion. However, they suspected that chlorine dimer played a key role in the chain of chemical events leading to ozone depletion. Although CFC manufacturing has been widely banned since the 1990's, the chemicals may persist in the atmosphere for decades. ■ John T. Snow

See also **ENVIRONMENTAL POLLUTION.**

■ BIOLOGY

The case of the vanishing vultures in Pakistan has been partially solved, according to a February 2004 report by veterinary microbiologist J. Lindsay Oaks of Washington State University in Pullman. Oaks and an international team of scientists presented evidence pointing to an unusual killer: a common, aspirinlike medicine for farm animals.

Farmers in Pakistan rely on vultures to dispose of dead livestock. Wildlife managers in neighboring India noticed a decrease in the bird's population during the mid-1990's.

SEE ALSO THE SPECIAL REPORT, AMAZING SPIDERS: SEX, LIES, AND VIDEO WATCHING, PAGE 60.

Since then, the region's population of the Oriental white-backed vulture, once a common bird, has plummeted by 95 percent. Wildlife managers also saw the numbers of two other vulture species, the slender-billed and the long-billed, fall dramatically.

At first, biologists wondered if a new disease accounted for the mysterious population crashes. However, when the researchers dissected the vultures, they found white spots on the birds' internal organs, a symptom of kidney failure. The researchers tested the dead birds for poisons known to cause kidney damage but found no evidence of such poison.

The scientists then checked veterinary suppliers in Pakistan for livestock drugs known to cause kidney problems in birds. Among the possibilities, diclofenac, used to relieve pain and swelling, seemed the most likely.

The researchers then fed a carcass treated with diclofenac to captive vultures. Several of the birds died of kidney failure. The dissected vultures had the same kind of chalky deposits seen in the wild birds.

Conservation groups have called upon manufacturers of diclofenac as well as governments of countries throughout Asia, Africa, Europe, and the Middle East to ban the use of this drug for veterinary medicine. The discovery that a drug is responsible for the vultures' drastic decline offers hope that the birds' population may recover.

Soybeans punish cheaters. Soybean plants depend on bacteria on their roots for nitrogen, and if the bacteria do not produce their share of the nutrient, the plants "punish" the bacteria, probably by withholding oxygen from them. That finding was reported in September 2003 by Toby Kiers, a graduate student at the University of California at Davis, and her colleagues. The study explained why bacteria that produce lower-than-normal amounts of nitrogen have not crowded out other strains.

Soybeans, like many other kinds of *legumes* (plants that give rise to pods), harbor bacteria in little *nodules* (lumps) on their roots. The bacteria benefit by tapping into the plant to obtain oxygen and carbohydrates. The plants benefit because the bacteria take nitrogen from the air and convert it to a form that the plants can use.

As nitrogen production increases, so does the physical toll on the bacteria. Scientists had identified "cheater" strains that produced less nitrogen. Kiers speculated that these strains

SNAIL FARMERS

A marsh periwinkle, *Littoraria irrorata*, rests on a leaf (below, inset). In December 2003, Brian Silliman of Brown University in Providence, Rhode Island, and Steven Newell of the University of Georgia Marine Institute on Sapelo Island, reported that the snail actually cultivates edible fungi (below). Other animals engage in fungal farming, but this is the first time scientists have observed an animal outside the insect kingdom conducting this activity. The snail bites long gashes down leaves of marsh plants. The wounds are soon populated with fungi, which the snail eats.

ought to have extra energy to overwhelm strains that produce more nitrogen. However, this has not occurred.

The scientists tried to solve the puzzle by placing soybean roots in containers with environments that were either normal or nitrogen-free. The nitrogen-free atmosphere prevented the bacteria from producing nitrogen for the plants. The researchers found that the plants responded to the decrease in nitrogen production by sabotaging the bacteria by choking off oxygen.

They found that the bacteria that were forced to cheat reproduced only half as well

BIOLOGY continued

as the more productive strains in the normal environment. The researchers speculated that soybeans protect their mutually beneficial relationship with bacteria by preventing the cheater strains from growing well.

Coral slime. The mucus released by corals plays a major role in providing nutrients for other sea creatures, according to a March 2004 report. A team of scientists led by microbiologist Christian Wild of the Max Planck Institute for Marine Microbiology in Bremen, Germany, showed that this mucus helps explain why coral reefs have so many organisms living on them.

Mucus protects corals from drying out when water levels drop. It also traps and carries off debris that might smother the animals. However, scientists did not know why so much extra material was made and apparently lost into the open water.

At Heron Island in Australia's Great Barrier Reef, the researchers studied the mucus produced by a major group of hard-bodied corals in the *genus* (group of closely related species) *Acropora*. Like most corals, *Acropora* depends on algae that live in its tissues for some of its energy. The algae provide the energy by transferring carbon to the coral. However, these corals expend about half of the carbon that the algae produce in releasing mucus. In a typical day, 1 square meter (10.7 square feet) of *Acropora* can produce 4.8 liters (1.3 gallons) of mucus.

The researchers found that the mucus is not really lost. More than half the mucus immediately dissolves in the reef water. Water currents drive the mucus into the lagoon in the center of the reef, where sand filters it. Microorganisms in the sand consume it, releasing nutrients for other reef creatures.

The mucus that does not dissolve immediately traps bacteria, algal cells, and small carbonate particles floating in the water, quickly and significantly increasing its carbon and nitrogen content. Currents eventually push these strings of mucus and the additional material back into the lagoon. The material that does not dissolve sinks to the bottom, becoming part of the lagoon sediment and providing food for the creatures that live there.

PATERNAL BABOONS

A father baboon shelters his offspring as another young baboon nears. In September 2003, a group of biologists announced the results of a study showing that father baboons are much more likely to side with their young when they are involved in disputes with other juveniles. The researchers followed 73 such conflicts over a three-year period, and in 69 of the situations, the fathers sided with their young. Scientists theorize that such paternal care might be a long-established trait for *primates* (the family of mammals that includes people and monkeys).

Rolling dung by moonlight. A type of dung beetle from South Africa has become the first animal known to determine its line of movement by *polarized* moonlight, according to a July 2003 report by Marie Dacke, a zoologist at Lund University in Sweden. Polarized light has rays that are aligned in a particular direction instead of being spread out in all directions.

Some animals, including honey bees, use the polarization patterns of sunlight to orient themselves as they move. Dacke wondered if dung beetles, in particular the African beetle *Scarabaeus zambesianus*, used the polarization patterns of moonlight as well.

Dung beetles crowd around fresh piles of animal droppings and compete to roll away a ball of the product. The males use the dung balls to attract females and to provide food for their offspring. With so much importance riding on the dung, competition among males becomes extremely aggressive. A male's best strategy in this scramble is to roll his trophy away in a straight line, the most efficient path for avoiding competing beetles.

To see if the polarization of moonlight affected *S. zambesianus*, Dacke set out a pile of dung. The beetles rolled dung in a relatively straight line until researchers covered them with a polarizing filter that shifted the orientation of moonlight by 90 degrees. Then the beetles shifted direction, making a nearly 90-degree turn. They then moved in a relatively straight line once again.

That shift, according to Dacke, suggests that the beetles' movement depended on the polarization of moonlight. The researchers theorized that being able to navigate by moonlight enables the beetles to extend their foraging time and, ultimately, to improve their chances for survival.

Females finally discovered. In February 2004, Jeyaraney Kathirithamby, a research fellow at Oxford University in England, reported finding a female of an insect species known only from males for 94 years. *DNA* testing by Spencer Johnson of Texas A&M University in College Station identified a female *Caenocholax fenyesi*, a parasite that lives inside other insects. DNA (deoxyribonucleic acid) is the molecule genes are made of.

For over a decade, scientists had thought that they had identified the female of this species. However, DNA analysis determined that these females belonged to related species.

Finally, Kathirithamby discovered the real female *C. fenyesi* in 2002 while collecting crickets that lived near fire ants, the hosts for the male.

As part of its life cycle, a very young male finds an ant in which to live. Eventually, the parasite grows wings and bursts out of the ant's body to fly around looking for females.

The female parasite is much different physically from the male: She never develops wings or even legs. She mates and gives birth through a little patch of her tissue that pokes through the outer surface of the host's abdomen. She does not leave the host, even after it has died.

As far as entomologists knew, the sexes find their hosts independently. However, with the discovery of the female, scientists planned to investigate if entering an ant or cricket determines the gender of the parasite. Researchers can also attempt to figure out how these parasites might inspire new pest controls. The *C. fenyesi* males, for example, attack fire ants, which cause painful stings. When a parasite attacks a male fire ant, the male ant cannot reproduce. The mere presence of the parasite does not allow the ant's reproductive organs to develop because the parasite occupies the ant's entire abdomen.

Song splits. The ongoing debate about how the feathered parasites known as indigobirds actually develop new species received new information from an August 2003 report by biologist Michael D. Sorenson of Boston University in Massachusetts. Indigobirds lay their eggs in the temporarily untended nests of certain other species, particularly firefinches. The nests' actual owners then tend the indigobird egg as their own.

In the 1960's, researchers suggested that indigobirds divided into different species when a host species split into different subgroups. However, in the 1970's, Robert B. Payne, a professor of behavioral ecology at the University of Michigan in Ann Arbor, proposed that the indigobirds evolved into different species later than the firefinches did and that bird songs were key factors in the splits.

New species usually develop because a physical barrier, such as a mountain range, separates an animal population. Over time, the two groups become so different that they develop into different species. However, scientists are looking for animals that evolved into new species without geographic influences, a phenomenon known as *ecological speciation*.

BIOLOGY continued

In an older study of indigobirds, Payne and colleagues focused on young indigobirds nesting with two host species. The first was the red-billed firefinch, a common indigobird target. The second was the Bengalese finch, a species the indigobirds would never meet in the wild. As the male indigobirds grew up they imitated the songs of their foster parents, as they do in the wild. When the males sang songs to court the females, the female indigobirds preferred males with songs like those they heard in their foster nests, even if the nest belonged to the Bengalese finch.

From this result, Payne thought that indigobirds could form a new species by laying eggs in the nest of an unusual host species.

split apart no earlier than 500,000 years ago. However, the firefinches split into multiple species some 7 million years ago. That time difference led scientists to conclude that the evolution of different species of the target birds led to the development of new indigobird species. The new findings suggest that indigobirds apparently can divide into different species without the need for a geographical barrier.

Fungi protect chocolate. Cacao trees, which produce beans processed to obtain chocolate, may get disease-fighting help from fungi inside their leaves, according to a December 2003 report. Tropical ecologist A. Elizabeth Arnold of Duke University in Durham, North Carolina, and her colleagues reported that leaves full of harmless fungi, called *endophytes*, can fight off diseases better than fungus-free leaves.

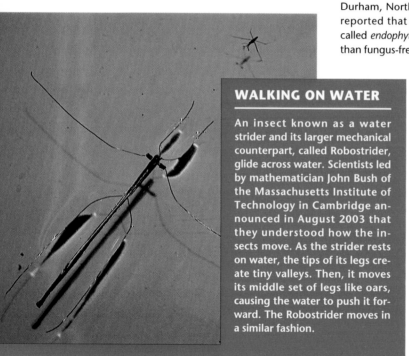

WALKING ON WATER

An insect known as a water strider and its larger mechanical counterpart, called Robostrider, glide across water. Scientists led by mathematician John Bush of the Massachusetts Institute of Technology in Cambridge announced in August 2003 that they understood how the insects move. As the strider rests on water, the tips of its legs create tiny valleys. Then, it moves its middle set of legs like oars, causing the water to push it forward. The Robostrider moves in a similar fashion.

Scientists have discovered that every type of plant tested has some kind of fungus living among its leaf cells. In grasses, the fungi help the plants by making them less appealing—and even toxic—to animals. Before Arnold's work, though, no one had found a fungus-related benefit for broad-leaved trees.

Arnold collected seven vigorous fungal strains from wild Panamanian cacao trees. She then put them on some of the leaves of fungus-free cacao seedlings. Last, she infected these plants with a *Phytophthora* microbe that causes one of the three main diseases affecting cacao.

Indigobirds accepted the songs of their new foster parents and preferred birds with identical backgrounds. Eventually, he theorized, the two groups developed differently enough to become different species.

In 2003, Sorenson, Payne, and their colleagues analyzed DNA from 10 species of indigobirds and their target species. The researchers estimated that the species had

The leaves infected with friendly fungus lost only half as much of their area to the disease as those without the fungus. In addition, they were more likely to survive, the researchers reported. According to Arnold, her research might lead to the use of fungi to fight disease in commercial cacao crops.

■ Susan Milius

See also **ECOLOGY.**

■ BOOKS ABOUT SCIENCE

These 16 important new books about science are suitable for the general reader. They have been selected from books published in 2003 and 2004.

Archaeology. *Ancient Wine: The Search for the Origins of Viniculture* by Patrick E. McGovern traces the history of one of the oldest and best-loved human foods. McGovern, head of the Molecular Archaeology Laboratory at the University of Pennsylvania in Philadelphia, reports how new techniques of biological and chemical analysis have made it possible to obtain information from such trace evidence as the dried *residues* (remains) of wine in ancient pots. These new methods are sensitive enough to reveal even the recipes for ancient wines. (Princeton University Press, 2003, 360 pp. illus. $29.95)

Astronomy. *Lonely Planets: The Natural Philosophy of Alien Life* by planetary scientist David Grinspoon examines where life may exist in the universe and what it might be like. By the end of the 1900's, spacecraft had explored much of the solar system, and astronomers using telescopes had discovered more than 100 planets orbiting nearby stars. Grinspoon describes possible sites of extraterrestrial life and discusses strategies that may help scientists learn whether these worlds are inhabited. (HarperCollins, 2003, 464 pp. illus. $25.95)

Sunquakes: Probing the Interior of the Sun by solar astronomer J. B. Zirker provides an account of the new science of *helioseismology* (the study of the interior of the sun by analyzing its surface vibrations). The sun's interior is not only impossible to see but also so hot that no existing space probe could venture there. But just as geologists can "see" inside Earth by analyzing how Earth shakes during earthquakes, so astronomers have been able to infer conditions inside the sun by observing the constant patterns of shaking on its turbulent surface. (The Johns Hopkins University Press, 2003, 288 pp. illus. $29.95)

Biology. *Mutants: On Genetic Variety and the Human Body* by biologist Armand Marie Leroi argues that human beings born with genetic *mutations* (changes) can help reveal the inner workings of *DNA* (deoxyribonucleic acid, the molecule genes are made of). Although scientists unraveled the human genetic code in 2003, they are only beginning to understand how our genetic inheritance is controlled by different parts of the code. Leroi shows how scientists have been able to match a number of genetic abnormalities with flaws in DNA. (Viking Press, 2003, 448 pp. illus. $25.95)

For Love of Insects by ecologist Thomas Eisner explores the many ways bugs interact chemically with their environment. Detailed photographs illustrate Eisner's descriptions of his more than 40 years' work researching insects all over the world. Among the many odd species he has studied are scorpions that defend themselves with sprays of vinegar as well as bombardier beetles, which shoot out drops of boiling liquid. He also describes blister beetles, which secrete corrosive fluids that are poisonous to most other animals but that seem to make the male beetles more attractive to females of their own species. (Harvard University Press, 2003, 448 pp. illus. $29.95)

General Science. *A Short History of Nearly Everything* by travel writer and humorist Bill Bryson explains in simple terms a

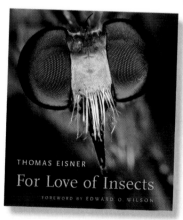
THOMAS EISNER
For Love of Insects
FOREWORD BY EDWARD O. WILSON

BOOKS ABOUT SCIENCE continued

range of topics in the natural sciences, from the big bang to the rise of human beings. Although he is not a trained scientist, Bryson provides insightful descriptions of how scientists know the age of the universe and the size of Earth, as well as what they have learned about the origins of life and the evolution of the human species. Many of the explanations include interviews with the eminent scientists whose work is described. (Broadway Books, 2003, 544 pp. $27.50)

Geology. *Meteorites, Ice, and Antarctica: A Personal Account* by geologist William A.

METEORITES, ICE, AND ANTARCTICA
A personal account
WILLIAM A. CASSIDY

Cassidy describes his hunt for meteorites in the snowy wastes of Antarctica. The meteorites include pieces of rock from the moon, Mars, and even distant asteroids. These meteorites provide direct evidence of

what the surfaces of other planets are like and the material from which the early solar system was formed. A chunk of rock found in Antarctica in 1984 may even contain evidence of fossil life forms from Mars. (Cambridge University Press, 2003, 364 pp. illus. $30)

History of Science. *The Book Nobody Read: Chasing the Revolutions of Nicolaus Copernicus* by astrophysicist Owen Gingerich describes his 30-year hunt for early editions of Polish astronomer Nicolaus Copernicus's 1543 book *On the Revolutions of the Heavenly Spheres*. The work challenged Aristotle's theory of an Earth-centered universe with the theory that the sun is the center of the solar

system. Historians had believed that few people had read the book when it was published. But Gingerich's study of *annotated* copies of the book—that is, books with handwritten notes from readers in the margins—reveals an entirely different story. (Walker & Company, 2004, 320 pp. illus. $28)

The Curious Life of Robert Hooke: The Man Who Measured London by historian Lisa Jardine recounts the life of one of the most brilliant and influential minds in London during the late 1600's. Hooke's accomplishments included fundamental discoveries in physics, chemistry, and biology. In addition, he, along with fellow architect Christopher Wren, designed and rebuilt London after the city's Great Fire of 1666. However, Hooke is not as well known as his contemporary, English astronomer and mathematician Isaac Newton, partly because Newton, a bitter enemy of Hooke, did his best to discredit him. (HarperCollins, 2004, 432 pp. illus. $27.95)

Mathematics. *When Least Is Best: How Mathematicians Discovered Many Clever Ways to Make Things as Small (or as Large) as Possible* by engineering professor Paul J. Nahin explores how mathematicians find the smallest values of quantities and use these "minimization" techniques to solve a variety of important problems in the real world. Using examples based on high school geometry, algebra, and calculus, Nahin explains how mathematicians have calculated the orbits of planets around the sun, the path of light through a lens, the curve followed by wires strung between power lines, and the shapes of soap bubbles. (Princeton University Press, 2004, 370 pp. $29.95)

Medicine. *Scurvy: How a Surgeon, a Mariner, and a Gentleman Solved the Greatest Medical Mystery of the Age of Sail* by free-lance writer Stephen J. Bown traces the gradual recognition that this serious illness is caused by a nutritional deficiency. On long ship voyages hundreds of years ago, sailors deprived of fresh fruits and vegetables that contained vitamin C would sicken and die horrible deaths. No one knew what to do about it until the mid-1700's, when a ship's surgeon learned that a daily dose of lemon juice could prevent scurvy. By the 1900's, vitamin C, in the form of pills or fruit juice, put an end to the disease. (St. Martin's Press, 2004, 256 pp. $23.95)

Natural History. *Monster of God: The Man-Eating Predator in the Jungles of History and the Mind* by nature writer David Quammen examines several animal species that still pose a threat to human beings in remote areas of the world. He researches the lions of India's Gir Forest, the bears that roam the woodlands of Romania, the saltwater crocodiles that rule the wetlands of northern Australia, and the Amur tigers that occasionally seize dogs from residents' yards in eastern Russia. Quammen points out that wilderness regions have dwindled to so few that it is really the "man-eaters" who are endangered. (W.W. Norton & Company, 2003, 384 pp. $25.95)

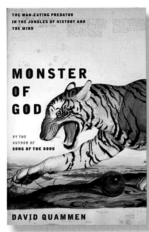

Going Wild: Adventures with Birds in the Suburban Wilderness by naturalist Robert Winkler proves that bird watchers don't have to travel to exotic places to see wild nature—it comes to them on the wing, even in the land of freeways and shopping malls. Winkler describes more than 25 years of his adventures with common and unusual birds—as well as a wide variety of other wildlife—in suburban Connecticut. (National Geographic Press, 2003, 208 pp. $16.95)

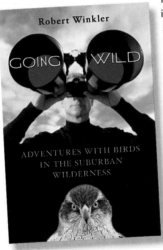

Physics. *The Fabric of the Cosmos: Space, Time, and the Texture of Reality* by physicist Brian Greene explores modern scientific theories about the structure and origin of the universe. Greene is the author of a 1999 book and companion television series about *quantum theory* called *The Elegant Universe.* (Quantum theory is a set of laws in physics that govern the behavior of atoms and subatomic particles.) In this follow-up book, Greene uses analogies based on familiar experiences to explain such concepts as the string theory of fundamental particles, time travel, and the inflationary theory of the expanding universe. (Knopf, 2004, 576 pp. illus. $28.95)

Psychology. *Descartes' Baby: How the Science of Child Development Explains What Makes Us Human* by psychologist Paul Bloom investigates how the development of our childhood sense of self is related to our sense of our physical bodies. (French philosopher Rene Descartes claimed that the world was made up of matter and spirit.) Bloom's study of the mind/body interaction from birth to maturity reveals how human beings develop a sense of the reality of the outside world, how they learn to value other human beings, and how they develop a set of moral values and religious beliefs as well as conceptions of what is humorous, disturbing, and comforting. (Basic Books, 2004, 304 pp. $26)

Technology. *Lost in Space: The Fall of NASA and the Dream of a New Space Age* by Greg Klerkx presents a critical review of the last three decades of the United States National Aeronautics and Space Administration (NASA). Klerkx, a former manager of the SETI Institute (SETI stands for search for extraterrestrial intelligence), argues that NASA's problems go far deeper than the loss of the space shuttle Columbia in 2003. Since the last astronaut walked on the moon in 1972, Klerkx charges, the space agency has spent too much money on such unproductive missions as the international space station and placed too much reliance on such unwieldy spacecraft as the space shuttle. Ultimately, Klerkx argues, the space program needs to regain the ideals of exploration and innovation that characterized the earlier race to the moon. (Pantheon Books, 2004, 392 pp. $27.95)

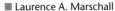 Laurence A. Marschall

CHEMISTRY

The development of a new family of crystals that can store huge amounts of hydrogen gas may advance the use of low-cost, nonpolluting hydrogen power, according to a report published in February 2004. Chemists Omar M. Yaghi of the University of Michigan at Ann Arbor and Michael O'Keeffe of Arizona State University in Tempe created a new family of *porous crystals.* Such crystals have networks of holes that look like diamonds on the outside but are mostly empty space on the inside.

In their report, the chemists suggested the crystals might be used like sponges to absorb large volumes of hydrogen gas. Further development of the crystals could lead to the replacement of *fossil fuels* (coal, oil, and natural gas) with hydrogen. The burning of fossil fuels releases carbon dioxide and other *greenhouse* (heat-trapping) gases into the atmosphere.

Scientists have long known how to obtain molecular hydrogen by splitting water molecules with electricity in a process called *hydrolysis.* When molecular hydrogen reacts with molecular oxygen, the reaction gives off energy in the form of heat. The only by-product of the reaction is water. Currently, this hydrogen-fueled reaction can take place inside *fuel cells* and other devices that convert chemical energy into electrical energy. Researchers believe that such devices have the potential to serve as a major energy source for automobiles and homes, among other purposes.

A number of serious problems plagued the development of hydrogen-based energy as of 2004, however. One of the chief problems was scientists' inability to devise a way to safely and economically store the hydrogen. Normally, hydrogen is a chemically "bulky"gas that takes up a lot of space. For example, storing a useful amount of hydrogen in a regular-sized automobile fuel tank using current technology requires either squeezing the gas at very high pressures, which makes it highly explosive, or cooling it to temperatures near absolute zero (-273.15 °C [-459.67 °F]), which is extremely impractical and expensive.

According to Yaghi and O'Keeffe, the porous crystals they developed might be able to pack large amounts of hydrogen in their internal spaces at conditions close to normal atmospheric pressure and room temperature.

The crystals, named MOF (metal-organic framework)-177, consist of clusters of molecules containing zinc atoms bonded to rings of carbon. The clusters form a three-dimensional structure with the greatest *internal surface area* (the sum of all internal flat spaces) ever seen in a porous crystal. In fact, if 1 gram (0.035 ounce) of the new crystal could be disassembled and laid out flat, its total surface area would cover 4,500 square meters (48,400 square feet)—almost the size of a football field.

The scientists calculated the crystals' internal surface area by measuring how much nitrogen the material could absorb. Although the chemists were encouraged by the results, they noted that the crystals still might not have enough surface area to store the large amounts of hydrogen gas needed for practical energy applications. Nevertheless, the researchers theorized that they might be able to modify the method they used to create the MOF-177 crystals for use with other chemical substances to produce new materials with greater surface areas and gas-trapping abilities.

Left-handed molecules of life. An August 2003 report from scientists at Purdue University in West Lafayette, Indiana, shed light on the question of why all the molecular building blocks of life are "left-handed." Twenty kinds of these building blocks, called *amino acids,* make up the proteins that comprise the tissues of all living things. All amino acids in living things exist in only one of two possible arrangements, called *isomers.* Chemists refer to the naturally occurring amino acid isomers as "left-handed" because the atoms in the molecules twist toward the left. This orientation is also known as *left-handed chirality.* Right-handed amino acid isomers, which twist in the opposite direction, have been produced in the laboratory.

The Purdue investigators, led by chemist R. Graham Cooks, proposed that billions of years ago, a compound called serine might have been the first amino acid to have developed left-handed chirality. The scientists reached this conclusion by studying how serine compounds react chemically with other serine compounds as well as with other amino acids. The chemists found that when left-handed serine reacts with itself, the process al-

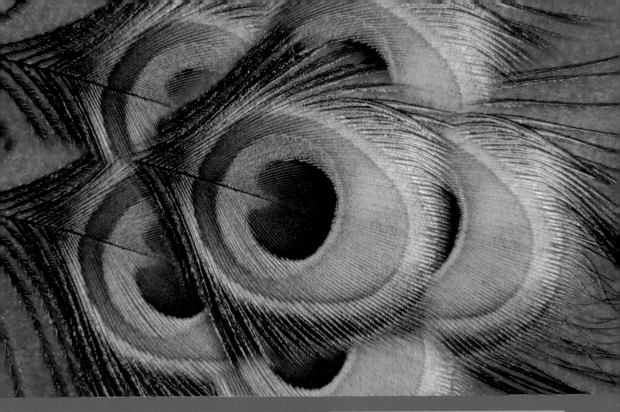

PEACOCK COLOR SECRETS

The beautiful colors of peacock feathers result from the light reflected by microscopic structures in the feathers, according to an October 2003 report by physicist Jian Zi and his colleagues at Fudan University in Shanghai, China. The researchers described how the *barbules* (small "branches") on the feathers consist of crystal structures that include rods of the pigment melanin (inset). The number and spacing of these rods determine which wavelengths of light the barbules reflect, and these factors, in turn, determine which colors result. A feather's crystal structure reflects different wavelengths, depending on the angle from which the feather is viewed.

ways produces clusters of left-handed isomers. In contrast, when serine reacts with other kinds of left-handed amino acids, it forms clusters of both left- and right-handed isomers. The new left-handed isomers then form chemical bonds with other amino acids—but only with those having left-handed chirality.

Cooks and his colleagues concluded that early in Earth's history, there may have been equal amounts of right- and left-handed amino acids. However, some force may eventually have chemically altered the orientation of some right-handed serine clusters, momentarily changing them into left-handed clusters. The chemists suggested *polarized light* (light made of waves vibrating in only one direction) as a candidate for that force.

The scientists said that once the right-handed serine became left-handed, a sort of snowballing process could have taken place. The left-handed serine clusters would have formed strong bonds with other kinds of left-handed amino acids. As the left-handed amino acids got used up in these bonds, any remaining right-handed amino acids would have transformed themselves into left-handed isomers because of the principle of *chemical equilibrium*. According to this principle, chemical products and *reactants* (substances acted upon in chemical reactions) have a natural tendency to maintain constant ratios in a solution. In time, the result of such chemical reactions would be that all remaining amino acids had left-handed chirality.

CHEMISTRY continued

Switch-on wettability. A new type of material with a surface that can change from water-repelling to water-attracting at the flick of an electric switch was described in research published in March 2004. Materials scientists Tom Krupenkin of Lucent Technologies' Bell Labs in Murray Hill, New Jersey, and Shu Yang at the University of Pennsylvania in Philadelphia said their discovery could have applications in chemistry research, communication technology, electronics, and other areas.

Most surfaces either absorb water or repel it. According to Krupenkin and Yang, the new material has the unique ability to shift its properties because of the way it is constructed. The material consists of a flat surface with millions of tiny stalks of silicon sticking out of it. The stalks are coated with a water-repelling *polymer* (a compound in which each molecule consists of two or more simpler molecules strung together). When viewed under a microscope, the material resembles a row of neatly mowed grass. Each "blade" of this "grass" is about 1 *nanometer* (a billionth of a meter, or roughly 100,000 times smaller than the width of a human hair) in size. The developers named their material *nanograss*.

The scientists said that when they deposited a droplet of water on the top of the silicon stalks, it sat there or rolled around without penetrating to the surface below. However, the application of a small electric charge altered the surface area of the stalks under the droplet. This caused the droplet to sink to the underlying surface at the spot where the charge was applied. The researchers also found that applying heat to selected points on the nanograss had a similar effect—causing droplets of water to sink in and wet the surface where the heat was applied.

The researchers envisioned several potential uses for their material. For example, if an overheated silicon computer chip had a nanograss surface, droplets of liquid could be sent to a hot spot on the chip to cool it so that the chip would not be destroyed. The material might also find applications in ultrafast *optical switches* (light-based electric switches), such as those used in fiber-optics technology, to switch signals from one circuit to another. In such an application, liquid droplets moving onto the nanograss surface of an optical switch would alter the properties of the surface, causing the switch to turn on or off.

Yet another possible application, according to Krupenkin and Yang, would be the use of the nanograss material in "lab-on-a-chip" devices, thumbnail-sized silicon wafers with microscopic channels through which chemical solutions flow. Using the nanograss to manipulate the flow of chemicals in such a device might make it possible to conduct thousands of chemical reactions at once.

Two new "superheavy" elements. A joint team of Russian and American scientists reported in February 2004 that they had created two *superheavy chemical elements* never seen before. Superheavy elements have atoms with massive *nuclei* (central cores) that contain positively charged protons and electrically neutral neutrons. The new elements were chemically unstable, *decaying* (breaking down) into lighter elements within less than a second of their creation. Still, they lasted longer than most other superheavy elements. This finding suggested to scientists that the atoms might be close to the "island of stability," a theoretical group of superheavy elements that, scientists believe, would be chemically stable and would survive long enough for in-depth research.

The creation of the new elements, which awaited official confirmation as of mid-2004, was announced by investigators at the Joint Institute for Nuclear Research in Dubna, Russia, and the Lawrence Livermore National Laboratory in Livermore, California. The elements had *atomic numbers* (the number of protons in the nucleus) 113 and 115. Uranium, with atomic number 92, is the heaviest natural element that is chemically stable. Most elements with higher atomic numbers can be created only in *particle accelerators,* machines in which atoms or subatomic particles collide and then break apart or join together to form other types of particles. The heaviest artificial element that experts had confirmed as of mid-2004 was darmstadtium, with atomic number 110.

The scientists made the new elements in a particle accelerator by shooting a beam of calcium atoms (atomic number 20) into a stationary target of americium (atomic number 95). In a few cases, the researchers found that the nuclei of these two atoms merged to form a larger nucleus, which proved to be element 115. That element, in turn, decayed into element 113. The researchers were able to identify these elements based on the types of particles ejected during the decay process, which could have come only from elements with these atomic numbers.

Most scientists involved in researching superheavy elements said the report of elements 113 and 115 made it more likely that a chemical island of stability actually exists. A stable superheavy element, according to some mathematical calculations, might exist around atomic number 120 or 126. Chemists believe that a superheavy element of this weight might be stable enough to react chemically with other atoms. This development could give chemists the opportunity to evaluate the properties of novel compounds.

The chemists assigned the temporary names *ununtrium* to element 113, and *ununpentium* to element 115. The International Union of Pure and Applied Chemistry assigns permanent names to newly discovered elements after additional research duplicates the initial discovery. Other superheavy elements awaiting confirmation in 2004 were elements 111, 112, 114, and 116. ■ Gordon Graff

See also **ENGINEERING; PHYSICS.**

COMPUTERS AND ELECTRONICS

A wave of destructive and disruptive *computer viruses* and *worms* dominated the attention of the computer industry during the second half of 2003 and the first half of 2004. Computer viruses are small pieces of software code that can damage computer files. Worms are a type of computer virus that can make copies of themselves and then forward those copies to e-mail addresses stolen from infected computers.

Viruses and worms have many purposes. Some are intended to disrupt businesses. Others are designed to steal sensitive private information such as computer passwords and credit card or bank account numbers.

Both viruses and worms take advantage of security weaknesses that allow the unwanted code to enter computers and computer networks. Because tens of millions of computers are linked through the Internet, an effective virus or worm can spread around the world in a matter of hours.

Such was the case with MyDoom, a virus spread by e-mail that in January and February 2004 became the fastest-spreading and most destructive virus ever released. Within hours of its appearance on the Internet, MyDoom had infected more than 300,000 computers across

SMART SHOE

A running shoe designed by sportswear company Adidas, headquartered in Herzogenaurach, Germany, uses a sophisticated electronic system to sense its environment and change its physical properties. The shoe features a tiny battery-powered sensor, a microprocessor, and an electric motor that allow the shoe to adjust the amount of cushioning it provides, depending on a runner's preference and surface conditions. Such adjustable cushioning will reduce the amount of stress on a runner's knees, company officials said.

COMPUTERS AND ELECTRONICS continued

the world and had become incorporated into 1 in 12 e-mails, experts estimated. The virus allowed *hackers* (the authors of viruses and worms) to access infected computers and use them for their own purposes, including storing illegal software and sending junk e-mail.

By the end of the virus's first week of circulation, MyDoom had inflicted damages in excess of $38 billion on businesses worldwide. Financial analysts attributed the costs to the negative impacts of disrupted communications as well as the costs of removing the virus from infected computers and installing software to protect against further infections.

In August 2003, a worm known as MsBlast infected more than 250,000 computers. In April and May 2004, a worm known as Sasser infected more than 1 million computers. At the end of one week of havoc inflicted by Sasser, a German teen-ager confessed to creating the worm and was arrested.

Many of the security holes exploited by worms and viruses are found in the Windows family of software produced by the Microsoft Corporation of Redmond, Washington. Windows is an *operating system,* the central program that makes it possible for the computer to run other types of programs; send and receive e-mail; access the Internet; and perform many other tasks. Because Windows is the most widely used computer operating system in the world, its security flaws have global implications for business, education, government, and personal computer users.

Software makers such as Microsoft fix security holes in their programs by distributing protective software, called *patches,* for specific viruses and worms. Installing the patches is an important task for both business and personal computer users. Software manufacturers often release patches before hackers can exploit a particular security flaw. Many computer users, however, fail to install the patches, leaving their machines vulnerable to infection. Infected machines then compound security problems by serving as bases from which infections can spread more widely.

Another line of defense against infections is anti-virus and anti-worm software. Just as with patches, however, users must properly install and constantly update the software to defend against new viruses and worms.

Even these measures cannot provide total protection against infection. Hackers work quickly, sometimes introducing new creations within hours of discovering a security hole.

ELECTRONIC PAPER

Flexible, paper-thin circuitry developed by Philips Research Laboratories in Eindhoven, the Netherlands, is being used to develop a bendable computer display. The Cambridge, Massachusetts-based company E Ink developed an electronic ink containing black and white pigments that rise to the surface of the ink when voltage is applied. The two companies collaborated to design the mini-monitor, which consists of a laminated electronic sheet containing electronic ink and flexible circuitry. The companies unveiled the first consumer application in March 2004.

Also, hackers produce variations of these programs at a startling rate, using software code modifications to overcome newly installed defenses. In the case of the Sasser worm, four variations appeared in Internet traffic within days of the original version's debut.

Fighting back against spam. Another computer problem that continued to be a costly annoyance in 2003 and 2004 was unwanted e-mail, often called *spam.* Junk e-mails, frequently used to advertise products, had by 2004 become the most common type of e-mail by far. Internet experts estimated that spam made up 15 percent of all e-mail communications.

Much of the spam is simply an annoyance that clogs e-mail boxes and steals time from computer users who must remove it. Some spam has a more sinister intent, however. Some spam e-mailers use their communications to promote financial scams. In a technique called *phishing,* they send out what appear to be legitimate requests from well-known companies and institutions for financial information. Once in possession of consumers' private financial data, phishers use the information to defraud their unwitting victims. According to analysts of Internet traffic, the volume of phishing e-mails swelled from fewer than 1,000 in September 2003 to more than 215,000 in March 2004.

In an attempt to reduce the volume of spam, the United States House of Representatives in December 2003 passed a law requiring bulk e-mailers to clearly identify their communications as advertisements. The law further mandated that the e-mailers give recipients an opportunity to have their names removed from mailing lists if they desire.

To reduce spam's heavy volume, businesses routinely purchase and install software designed to block out unwanted e-mail on company computers. This response, of course, adds to the companies' costs of doing business.

Tiny disk drive. In January 2004, Toshiba Corporation of Tokyo, Japan, announced the development of the world's smallest hard disk drive. The new drive measures barely 2.2 centimeters (0.85 inches), about the size of a quarter or a postage stamp. The device is capable of holding up to four gigabytes of data—enough space to store a full-length motion picture, hundreds of albums of music, or thousands of photos.

The drives were scheduled to go into production in late 2004, Toshiba officials said. Industry experts speculated that the powerful miniature drives would spur the development of new features in such small electronic devices as cellular telephones and wristwatches.

Faster transistors and chips. In November 2003, researchers at the University of Illinois at Urbana-Champaign announced they had fabricated a transistor that operates at 509 *gigahertz* (a measure of processing speed). At that speed, the *transistor* outperforms the world's fastest transistors by more than 10 percent.

Transistors are tiny electronic devices that can switch between "on" and "off" states, providing the basis for manipulation of the 1's and 0's that underlie all digital processing. Computer chips, the components that run such digital devices as computers, calculators, and cell phones, are packed with millions of transistors.

Conventional transistors are fabricated from silicon and germanium. The Illinois researchers achieved their device's increased performance by using indium phosphide and indium gallium arsenide, which, the researchers said, can support more current than silicon and so process data faster. Also, because the new transistors are smaller, they are able to charge and discharge faster.

University of Illinois engineers achieved another breakthrough by designing and fabricating the first light-emitting transistor. Announced in January 2004, the new transistor uses *photons* (the particles that form light) to produce "on" and "off" pulses for digital processing. Although the breakthrough remained experimental, it could have an immense impact on digital applications, experts said. Conventional, electron-based transistors are limited by the heat that electron flow generates. A light-driven transistor is not subject to such limits.

Meanwhile, researchers continued to improve the processing power of conventional silicon-based transistors. In September 2003, researchers at IBM of Armonk, New York, announced the development of a new manufacturing process that could increase transistor speed by as much as 60 percent. The process uses a technology called *strained silicon,* which involves layering silicon on the "wafer" base of the transistor in a way that boosts the speed of the electrons in the super-thin top layer.

Radio frequency identification. Wal-

COMPUTERS AND ELECTRONICS continued

Mart Stores, Inc., of Bentonville, Arkansas, the world's largest retailer, began testing a new shipping technology called *radio frequency identification* (RFID) in May 2004. The company announced plans to require all manufacturers and shippers sending goods to Wal-Mart to equip their goods with RFID chips by 2005.

In RFID shipping, every unit is tagged with a wireless-enabled computer chip. An RFID-equipped pallet of merchandise broadcasts its location constantly so that both shippers and recipients can monitor its progress from its point of origin to its destination.

Advocates of the technology say RFID companies will be able to simplify their bookkeeping and tracking procedures and manage inventories of goods more efficiently. For example, shippers will be able to assign priorities to shipments based on local consumer demand simply by issuing instructions from a computer. Although implementing the technology is costly, increased efficiencies in the distribution of goods among stores will lead to bigger profits, advocates predicted.

In its May 2004 trial, Wal-Mart tagged shipments of 21 products going to 7 destination stores with RFID chips. The test paved the way for nearly 100 Wal-Mart suppliers to implement the technology by January 2005, said Simon Langford, manager of the retail giant's RFID strategy.

Although business analysts touted the benefits of RFID practices, the technology also has significant security implications. If containers shipped by sea are equipped with RFID chips, computers will be able to take over many of the monitoring and tracking functions currently handled by security personnel at the various ports of entry around the world. In many of those ports, security staffs consist of too few personnel and are becoming increasingly overwhelmed by the number of shipping containers entering daily.

Some industry analysts foresee broader applications of RFID. The technology could be applied not only to shipping units but also to individual items. Individually tagged items could send data about their location before purchase as well as their location and other data about consumers after purchase. Industry watchdog groups, however, warn that this use

of RFID capabilities would represent a dangerous intrusion into consumers' privacy.

iTunes anniversary. Apple Computer of Cupertino, California, celebrated the first anniversary of its highly popular iTunes service in April 2004. The service, which enables consumers to download music—entirely legally—from the Internet, had sold more than 70 million songs since its April 2003 debut. The iTunes service has created a large and growing market for legal music downloads, many of them played on Apple's iPod music device. A new version of that device, the iPod Mini, proved so successful in early 2004 that some consumers were forced to wait weeks for delivery.

Before iTunes, music industry executives regarded the transfer of digital music files over the Internet as a violation of copyright laws. Under these laws, the owners of copyrights for videos, books, music, and other items—called *intellectual properties*—must receive payment each time a work is copied. Many Web sites illegally posted thousands of music files, prompting music publishers to sue the sites' owners and, in some cases, the computer users who downloaded the songs. Licensing arrangements between Apple Computer and music publishers form the basis of the iTunes service.

Lightglove computer control. In January 2004, Harmonic Research, Inc., of Manassas, Virginia, introduced the Lightglove, a wireless device designed to control computers by hand motions. The new product eliminates the need for such traditional pointing devices as a mouse or joystick.

The wrist-worn Lightglove unit uses light beams to "read" miniscule hand and finger movements. The device communicates by radio waves with a *base station*, a plug-in box that interfaces with a computer's standard USB port. The base station relays motion data to controller software in the computer, which translates the data into cursor action on the screen. Harmonic Research said researchers designed the Lightglove to meet the needs of people whose physical disabilities, including those caused by disease or injury, limit their ability to use traditional pointing devices.

Industry experts predict that the technology will have a number of other applications as well. Because the light beams that record the hand movement are sterile, the Lightglove could be used in operating rooms, laboratories, and other environments that must be kept free of contamination. Still other applications might include the use of light beams for video game control; remote control of robots; and *gesture recognition,* the ability to decode hand motions, including those used in sign language.

Telephone television. In November 2003, the Sprint Corporation of Overland Park, Kansas, and MobiTV of Berkeley, California, announced a joint venture to provide cell phone television to Sprint customers who have Sanyo and Samsung cell phones with color screens. MobiTV developed the software that turns the phones into small television receivers capable of displaying live broadcasts.

Sprint was to provide the service network for the specialized service add-on. Industry analysts said that the service would appeal to consumers who want short-term entertainment while in transit or waiting for buses or trains.

New humanoid robot. In September 2003, the Sony Corporation of Tokyo introduced a humanoid robot called QRIO—short for *Quest for cuRIOsity*—designed to do many things that people do. QRIO walks upright on two legs; identifies and overcomes obstacles in its path; recognizes faces; and carries on conversations, drawing on a vocabulary of 60,000 Japanese words. It can receive and speak e-mail as well as take digital photos through its eyes.

According to robotics experts, QRIO is the most sophisticated humanoid robot yet introduced to the public. The robot employs advanced software, high-speed microprocessors, and numerous sensors that enable it to interact with the environment in a very humanlike fashion. Sony officials did not provide a timetable for marketing QRIO.

■ Keith Ferrell

■ CONSERVATION

O rnithologists discovered a new species of blue seedeater, a type of finch, in Venezuela just as construction for a dam destroyed the bird's only known habitat, according to a report published in July 2003. (Ornithologists are scientists who study birds.) Miguel Lentino and Robin Restall of the Phelps Ornithological Collection in Caracas, Venezuela, discovered the bird, which they named *Amaurospiza carrizalensi,* on Isla Carrizal, an island in the Caroni River. Several other species of blue seedeaters live in South America. However, their habitat lies on the other side of the Andes in Colombia and Ecuador. *A. carrizalensis,* known informally as the Carrizal seedeater, has a larger bill and different plumage than other species.

The Carrizal seedeater's island home lies in an area where a major hydroelectric dam is under construction. Workers have cleared Isla

FROG FIND IN INDIA

Purple and plump, this frog made news when its discovery was announced in October 2003. Biologists found the frog in a remote region of southern India. Named *Nasikabatrachus sahyadrensis,* the frog represents the first new frog species discovered since 1926. It is distantly related to a group of frogs—now living in the Seychelles, islands off the east coast of Africa—that has existed for about 175 million years. Researchers theorized that the two species became separated when India drifted away from Africa more than 100 million years ago.

CONSERVATION continued

Carrizal of a dense forest of spiny bamboo where the birds lived. As a result, the new species faces the possibility of extinction at the very time of its discovery. The electric company building the new dam is helping conservationists search for other patches of spiny bamboo in the Caroni River basin to determine if Carrizal seedeaters might be relocated and saved.

Wind farm bird threat. Windmills at Altamont Pass in California are killing large numbers of migratory birds and violating federal and state laws protecting the birds, according to a lawsuit filed in January 2004 in a United States District Court in San Francisco. Lawyers for the Center for Biological Diversity, a conservation group based in Tucson, Arizona, argue that the permits required to continue operating the wind farm should not be renewed until the killing is reduced. The deaths of the birds may violate such federal laws as the Migratory Bird Treaty Act and the Golden Eagle Protection Act as well as state laws, the suit argues.

The Altamont Pass wind farm, located east of San Francisco Bay, is the world's largest collection of electricity-generating wind turbines. Nearly 7,000 huge, propeller-bladed turbines dot the windswept hills. The windmills power turbines that produce energy for California without burning fuels. Coal and oil, when burned, are major sources of air pollution. Despite the environmental benefits, the windfarm is located on a major migration route for such birds of prey as eagles, hawks, kestrels, and owls.

As the turbine blades spin, they inevitably strike and kill some of the birds. According to federal law enforcement officials, who dispose of the bird carcasses, the kill rate is about 1,000 birds per year. Biologists estimate that the turbine blades have killed at least 22,000 birds since the wind farm started operations in the early 1980's. Of special concern to environmentalists are the roughly 100 golden eagles killed each year. The golden eagle is protected under California state law. Jeff Miller, a spokesperson for the Center for Biological Diversity, characterized Altamont as "a death zone for eagles and other magnificent birds of prey."

Representatives for the power companies

operating the wind turbines say that the companies have worked closely with the U.S. Fish and Wildlife Service and the California Energy Commission to develop ways to reduce bird deaths at Altamont Pass. Steve Stengel, spokesperson for a subsidiary of Florida-based FPL Group, which operates some 2,000 turbines at Altamont, listed several steps taken to protect the birds. They include installing screens, painting rotor blades, and attempting to control rodent populations around the turbines to make the area less attractive to birds of prey.

However, the Center for Biological Diversity and other environmental groups demanded that the companies take additional protective measures. The groups have suggested letting grass grow tall around the towers to make prey on the ground less visible to birds and regrouping the towers in clusters that might reduce the number of rotor hits.

The return of gray wolves to Yellowstone National Park has helped revitalize other elements of that ecosystem, biologists with the National Park Service's Wolf Restoration Project reported in October 2003. "Wolves are to Yellowstone what water is to the Everglades," observed Doug Smith, director of the project, in an interview with the *Boston Globe.* The presence of the wolves helps maintain critical balance among various animal and plant populations in the park, according to project biologists.

Gray wolves were native to Yellowstone when the park was established in 1872. However, hunters eliminated the wolves over the next 50 years, mostly to protect livestock on nearby ranches. By the 1920's, Yellowstone no longer had any resident wolves.

In 1995 and 1996, U.S. and Canadian wildlife biologists captured gray wolves in Canada, tagged them with radio collars, and released them into the park according to a phased plan. At the same time, other wolves arrived in the area on their own. The wolves formed packs and began producing new litters in 1996.

As park biologists tracked and observed the radio-collared wolves, they discovered significant changes in the park's ecology. For example, Yellowstone's elk herd no longer linger in valleys along stream beds and other wet-

lands, where they feed on the tender willow branches. Now, because they would become easy prey for wolves in such places, the elk more often forage on grass at higher elevations. As a result, the heavily browsed willow thickets have revived and flourished, providing more habitat for birds. Yellow warblers, willow flycatchers, and warbling vireos are among the species benefiting from this change.

The number of beavers, which thrive on willow, has also increased. The beavers are building new dams and creating wetland areas in which moose, otters, frogs, ducks, and other species can find additional habitat.

Wolves may also be helping scavenger species such as ravens, magpies, and perhaps even grizzly bears, especially during winter. After eating large prey, a wolf pack leaves enough leftovers to attract these and other scavengers to the site.

The absence of the wolves over the past century badly disrupted the Yellowstone ecosystem, wildlife biologists and conservationists assert. The successful reintroduction of wolves in Yellowstone Park marks a milestone in ecological restoration in western North America, they said.

Salmon pollute lakes. Salmon transport industrial *toxins* (poisons) known as polychlorinated biphenyls (PCB's) over vast distances from the Pacific Ocean to lakes in Alaska, where the toxins accumulate, according to research published in September 2003. Biologist E. M. Krummel of the University of Ottawa in Canada headed a team that conducted the research on the salmon and the Alaskan lakes in which they spawn.

Salmon put on more than 95 percent of their body mass while at sea, building muscle and fat tissues that can retain and concentrate chemicals such as PCB's. The mature fish return upriver to spawn in the same lakes in which they hatched. When the salmon die after spawning, the PCB's in their bodies are released into the lakes.

Krummel's team measured the PCB concentrations in body tissues of the fish and sampled sediment cores from the bottoms of eight lakes to determine the PCB levels de-

CONSERVATION continued

posited by salmon carcasses. The researchers detected a sevenfold increase of PCB's in some of the spawning lakes. They also found a strong link between the density of the returning salmon and PCB concentration in the lake sediments. PCB levels in sediments from a lake where salmon do not spawn were far lower, the researchers discovered. Furthermore, the PCB pollution detected there was of a type that is transported through the atmosphere.

Krummel and his team concluded that returning salmon act as "biological pumps" that inadvertently contaminate their spawning areas with pollution acquired up to 1,000 kilometers (600 miles) away. The released PCB's may affect the crop of hatching salmon as well as the bears, eagles, and people that feed on the adult fish. Normally, nutrients released from salmon carcasses enrich the waters where young fish hatch, but industrial pollution widely dispersed in the oceans may threaten this natural system.

Human-ape Ebola link. Gorillas and chimpanzees face new threats from Ebola, a deadly virus that also infects human beings. Eric M. Leroy of the Research Institute for Development in the African nation of Gabon led a team

CREATURES FROM THE DEEP

With their huge eyeballs and body armor plates, these creatures from deep waters of the Tasman Sea live up to their name of goblin shrimp. The crustaceans were captured in June 2003 by researchers on the NORFANZ voyage, a research expedition that explored deep sea habitats and animal life in the ocean waters between Australia and New Zealand.

that linked Ebola epidemics in people and major reductions in ape populations in central Africa. The research, which was published in the January 2004 issue of *Science,* reported 264 human deaths resulting from five outbreaks of Ebola since the early 2000's. At one location, researchers reported that the human epidemics were accompanied by a 60-percent drop in gorilla populations and a 90-percent decline in chimpanzee numbers.

Human beings most often contract Ebola when hunters and villagers handle apes killed illegally for meat. People also may become infected with the virus when they encounter the carcasses of infected dead apes. However, the Ebola virus ceases to be infectious in dead animals after about four days. As a result, apes are less likely to contract the disease from one another because individual apes seldom have contact with apes from different groups. Epidemics of Ebola, therefore, probably do not spread wavelike across the Congo basin in a single outbreak but instead start separately at each location, the researchers said.

Some of the more recent epidemics in the Congo have occurred near Odzala National Park in Congo (Brazzaville). The park is the home for one of the world's largest popula-

tions of gorillas and chimpanzees. The source of the Ebola virus is not known, but scientists believe that a rodent or other species acts as a *reservoir* for the disease. A reservoir is an animal population in which a *pathogen* (germ) can exist as a source of infection and later spread to other populations. Conservationists feared in mid-2004 that an Ebola infection among ape populations could prove catastrophic for gorillas and chimpanzees.

Ebola epidemics occur abruptly and can eliminate local ape populations very rapidly. Because apes have a slow reproductive cycle, their populations cannot recover easily after attacks of deadly diseases. Conservationists theorized that the combined losses from Ebola and illegal hunting may completely eliminate gorillas and chimpanzees from much of central Africa.

Scientists believed that further research into the problem could also protect the human population in the area. The continued research could lead to warning systems and prevention programs for residents in central Africa, the study concluded. However, such systems would not protect the chimpanzee and gorilla populations.   ■ Eric G. Bolen

See also **ENVIRONMENTAL POLLUTION; OCEANOGRAPHY.**

DEATHS OF SCIENTISTS

Notable people of science who died between June 1, 2003, and May 31, 2004, are listed below. Those listed were Americans unless otherwise indicated.

Borel, Armand (1923–Aug. 11, 2003), Swiss-born mathematician who exerted a profound influence on the study of mathematics in the second half of the 1900's. Borel applied his study of *Lie groups,* which are certain continuous collections of mathematical symmetries, to illuminate other fields of mathematical study, particularly profound patterns in the theory of numbers. In 1991, the American Mathematical Society awarded Borel the Steele Prize for providing "the empirical base for a great swath of modern mathematics .... His observations pointed out the structure and mechanisms that became central concerns of mathematical activity."

Brockhouse, Bertram (1918–Oct. 13, 2003), Canadian-born physicist who shared the 1994 Nobel prize in physics for the development of a technique in which materials are bombarded with subatomic particles called *neutrons* to determine their atomic structure. The technique—*neutron spectroscopy*—became an essential research tool for the scientific community, particularly in the study of solid state physics and organic chemistry. Brockhouse's experiments involving neutron scattering confirmed the existence of *phonons,* which are *quanta* (particles) of thermal energy in the form of sound or vibration.

Casals-Ariet, Jordi (1911–Feb. 10, 2004), Spanish-born *epidemiologist* (a person who studies epidemic diseases) who established the *taxonomy* (classification) of at least 10,000 viruses that affect all life forms on

DEATHS OF SCIENTISTS continued

Earth. Casals also identified a large number of previously unknown viruses, including the Lassa virus. Casals and his team of researchers at Yale University in New Haven, Connecticut, discovered the Lassa virus in 1969, after Casals contracted it during his study of the rare and often fatal Lassa fever.

Chase, Martha (1927–Aug. 8, 2003), researcher who played a pivotal part in identifying DNA (deoxyribonucleic acid) as the substance that transmits genetic information from one generation to another. In 1952, Chase assisted Alfred D. Hershey in an experiment to determine whether DNA or an associated protein carried the genetic information for the infection, growth, and development of a *phage* (bacterial virus). Using radioactive tracers to mark the DNA core and protein coat, Hershey and Chase placed the material in a food blender. After the blender separated the DNA and the protein, an examination showed that only the DNA could replicate the virus because only the DNA had entered the bacteria.

Martha Chase

Murie, Margaret (1902–Oct. 19, 2003), conservationist and Wilderness Society official who was dubbed the "grandmother of the conservation movement." Murie and her husband, naturalist Olaus Murie, spent years promoting legislation that ultimately led to the preservation of millions of acres of United States land, including Alaska's Arctic National Wildlife Refuge. For her lifelong commitment to conservation, Margaret Murie received the Presidential Medal of Freedom in 1998.

Oke, John Beverley (1928–March 2, 2004), Canadian-born astronomer who designed light-analysis equipment for the Hale, Keck, and Hubble telescopes, which have helped unlock many secrets of the cosmos. Oke devised mechanical systems that provided astronomers with detailed information about the solar spectrum of light. Most famously, he invented a way to accurately estimate the tem-

perature of stars, which provides information about how stars and galaxies are formed and how they generate energy.

Pake, George (1925?–March 4, 2004), physicist who helped lay the foundation for the modern computer industry. Pake persuaded the Xerox Corporation to establish a company research center. To encourage creativity, he located it in California, away from the corporate structure at Xerox headquarters in Stamford, Connecticut. As the first director of the Palo Alto Research Center, Pake recruited a team of computer researchers who, through the 1970's, invented a wide range of computing technologies. These inventions included the graphical user interface, laser printer, and office networking.

Pickering, William H. (1910–March 15, 2004), New Zealand-born engineer and scientist who supervised the 1958 launch of the first U.S. satellite. Under his direction, a team of engineers from the U.S. Army and the Jet Propulsion Laboratory in Pasadena, California, designed, built, and successfully launched Explorer 1 in just 83 days. Their speed was dictated by the U.S. drive to match the space program of the Soviet Union, which shocked the world in October 1957 by launching the Sputnik satellite into space. The 1971 launch of Mariner 9, the first spacecraft to successfully orbit Mars, was the last major mission completed under Pickering's direction at the Jet Propulsion Laboratory, which he headed until 1976.

Pople, Sir John A. (1925–March 15, 2004), English-born mathematician and chemist who pioneered the use of computers in the study of chemistry. Pople won the Nobel Prize in chemistry in 1998 for devising a computer program that describes the motion of molecules in chemical reactions. The program predicts whether molecules are stable; what colors of light they absorb or emit; and the speed of chemical reactions. Pople based his work on *quantum mechanics*, a theory that explains the behavior of molecules in terms of the motions and energies of electrons. The program, named Gaussian, was initially published in 1970 and remains in use by thousands of chemists around the world.

Safar, Peter (1924–Aug. 3, 2003), Austrian-born anesthesiologist and professor of

Peter Safar

resuscitation medicine at the University of Pittsburgh School of Medicine in Pennsylvania. After years of practicing as an anesthesiologist, Safar in 1979 founded Pittsburgh's International Resuscitation Research Center. There, he developed and refined *cardiopulmonary resuscitation* (CPR), the emergency procedure performed on cardiac-arrest victims. Safar's research and accomplishments in resuscitation, emergency and critical-care medicine, and disaster *reanimation* (life restoration) saved many lives.

Scribner, Belding (1921–June 19, 2003), medical professor who made long-term kidney dialysis possible, thereby saving the lives of millions of people suffering from kidney failure. *Kidney dialysis*—the process of mechanically filtering toxic substances left in the blood by failing kidneys—existed before 1960. However, patients could use it only a limited number of times because it severely damaged blood vessels.

Scribner solved this problem by developing a U-shaped tube, the Scribner shunt, that was designed to be permanently installed in the body to act as an artificial kidney. The shunt was made of a new engineering material, Teflon, that proved to be nonreactive with surrounding body tissue and so prevented blood clots. Believing that medical research and treatment should not be conducted for profit, Scribner did not patent the shunt. He subsequently founded a nonprofit dialysis center in Seattle, Washington, where thousands of physicians received training.

Teller, Edward (1908–Sept. 10, 2003), Hungarian-born physicist who was involved in the Manhattan Project, which built the first

atomic bomb, and who promoted and supervised the creation of the hydrogen bomb. Teller's role as the "father of the H-bomb" and his enthusiasm for nuclear weapons turned much of the scientific community against him. Nevertheless, his views, particularly his opposi-

Edward Teller

tion to the banning of nuclear testing, exerted considerable influence on U.S. government policy through much of the *Cold War* (the struggle between Communist and non-Communist nations that ended in 1991). Teller was responsible for the development of a second national laboratory, the Lawrence Livermore Laboratory in California.

Von Hippel, Arthur R. (1898–Dec. 31, 2003), German-born scientist who pioneered research in *materials science* (the study of the molecular structure of materials). He founded the Laboratory for Insulation Research at the Massachusetts Institute of Technology in Cambridge. There, researchers under his direction made major contributions to the development of radar during World War II (1939–1945). After the war, von Hippel became a leader of the then-relatively new field of study of materials science. The Materials Research Society established the Von Hippel Award as its highest honor in 1976 in recognition of his contributions to the field.

■ Scott Thomas

Arthur R. von Hippel

DRUGS

The United States Food and Drug Administration (FDA) approved some 37 new drugs in 2003 and early 2004. Among these drugs were treatments for asthma and HIV infections as well as medication to lower cholesterol.

New treatment for asthma. The FDA in June 2003 approved the use of omalizumab (sold as Xolair), the first *asthma* medication designed specifically to treat moderate to severe asthma. Asthma is a chronic, inflammatory lung disease. Individuals suffering from asthma experience such breathing difficulties as wheezing, coughing, and shortness of breath. Asthma affects approximately 17 million Americans, including nearly 5 million children, according to the National Institute of Allergy and Infectious Diseases.

Omalizumab works by blocking immunoglobulin E (IgE), a natural *antibody* (a substance produced by the body's immune system), in *allergic* asthma attacks. The majority of all asthma attacks occur in response to specific substances in the environment called *allergens.* Some common allergens include dust, molds, pollen, and animal *dander* (tiny particles of shed skin).

An allergy response is triggered when an antibody, such as IgE, comes into contact with an allergen to which the individual is sensitive. The antibody stimulates special cells called *mast cells* to release histamine and other chemicals. The histamine triggers such allergic responses as coughing, sneezing, and swelling of mucous membranes in air passages, including the *trachea* (windpipe) and bronchial tubes. By blocking IgE, omalizumab breaks this chain of events and short-circuits the allergy response that can lead to an asthma attack.

Omalizumab is a *monoclonal antibody*—a complex protein created through genetic engineering processes to target a specific substance, such as the IgE antibody. Because it is complicated to make, the drug, marketed in injectable form, carried a high price tag. Patients receiving omalizumab will require one to two injections per month, at an annual cost of up to $10,000.

New HIV treatments. In mid-2003, the FDA approved two new drugs for the treatment of HIV infection. HIV, which stands for *h*uman *i*mmunodeficiency *v*irus, causes AIDS. The new drugs are atazanavir sulfate (sold as Reyataz), approved in June, and emtricitabine (sold as Emtriva), approved in July.

Current HIV treatment guidelines issued by the U.S. Public Health Service recommend the use of combinations of anti-HIV drugs consisting of three or four different medications. These combinations of drugs are referred to as *highly active anti-retroviral therapy* (HAART), and are known popularly as drug "cocktails."

The HAART treatment strategy is highly effective in suppressing HIV activity and reducing the number of side effects experienced by patients. However, because HIV tends to become resistant to the effects of drugs over time, there is a continuing demand for new anti-HIV medications. Atazanavir sulfate and emtricitabine represent the latest offerings by the pharmaceutical industry in response to that demand.

Atazanavir sulfate belongs to the class of drugs known as *protease inhibitors*. These drugs block the action of *protease*, an enzyme used by HIV to assemble new copies of itself, which can then infect other cells. Emtricitabine belongs to a class of drugs known as *reverse transcriptase inhibitors*. These drugs interfere with *reverse transcriptase*, an enzyme used by HIV to inject genetic material into cells at an early stage of infection. Both drugs were designed to be incorporated into a HAART treatment regimen.

New Alzheimer's drug. Until 2003, treatment for Alzheimer's disease typically included drugs effective in managing some of the disease's mild to moderate symptoms such as disorientation. However, about 70 percent of diagnosed Alzheimer's patients have moderate to severe dementia, according to the Alzheimer's Association.

A new drug that became available in October was intended for the treatment of moderate to severe Alzheimer's disease. It was to help control such problems as loss of memory; problems with reasoning or judgment; disorientation; loss of language skills; and the inability to perform routine tasks. The new drug, memantine (sold as Namenda), is thought to quiet brain activity by blocking the

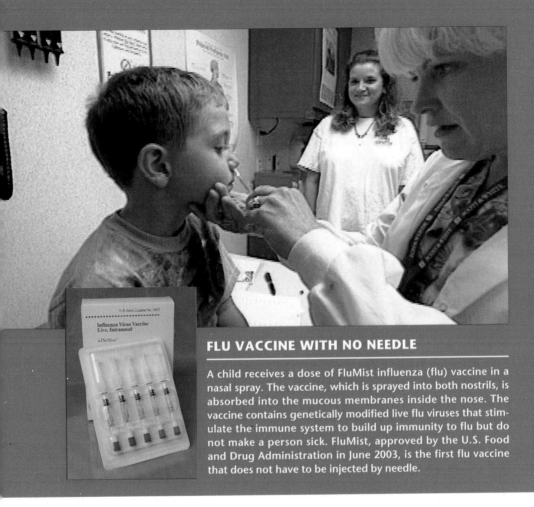

FLU VACCINE WITH NO NEEDLE

A child receives a dose of FluMist influenza (flu) vaccine in a nasal spray. The vaccine, which is sprayed into both nostrils, is absorbed into the mucous membranes inside the nose. The vaccine contains genetically modified live flu viruses that stimulate the immune system to build up immunity to flu but do not make a person sick. FluMist, approved by the U.S. Food and Drug Administration in June 2003, is the first flu vaccine that does not have to be injected by needle.

actions of *excitatory neurotransmitters* in the brain. In normal brain activities, small amounts of these neurotransmitters are released. Alzheimer's disease causes the neurotransmitters to be released too often, which leads to brain degeneration and dementia.

Memantine produces few side effects and is, therefore, a relatively safe drug. Some instances of dizziness, confusion, headache, and constipation have been reported in dementia patients. In addition, certain drugs may interfere with the actions of memantine. These drugs include Tagamet, Zantac, amantadine, ketamine, and certain diuretics.

New anti-cholesterol drug. In August 2003, the FDA approved rosuvastatin (sold as Crestor), the newest member of a family of drugs called *statins*. Statins can significantly lower cholesterol in patients who have higher-than-recommended blood levels of low-density lipoprotein cholesterol (LDL-C). LDL-C is the so-called "bad" cholesterol, which can form fatty deposits on the inner walls of arteries and veins. Such deposits increase a per-

son's likelihood of developing heart disease, strokes, blood clots, or other serious illnesses.

Several statins have been available in the United States for some time. They include atorvastatin (sold as Lipitor), fluvastatin (Lescol), pravastatin (Pravachol), and sinivastatin (Zocor). Clinical tests suggest that rosuvastatin is more powerful than these drugs and may be useful for patients who have not been able to lower their LDL-C levels sufficiently using the other statins.

Side effects of rosuvastatin may include constipation, headache, or upset stomach. Like other statins, rosuvastatin may cause more serious side effects, though these problems are rare. One such condition is rhabdomyolysis, in which muscle tissue breaks down, releasing products into the blood that, in turn, damage the kidneys. Another of these conditions is a type of liver damage. To check for signs of such problems, doctors may order periodic blood tests for patients taking rosuvastatin. ■ Thomas N. Riley

See also **MEDICAL RESEARCH.**

From DNA to Drugs

Pharmacogenetics became one of the most promising new fields of medical research in 2004. As the name suggests, pharmacogenetics combines *pharmacology* (the study of the effects of drugs) and *genetics* (the study of heredity—the passing on of biological characteristics from one generation to another). Pharmacogenetic researchers use modern genetic techniques to develop medicines and to enable physicians to predict which drugs will be safest and most effective for each of their patients.

The developing field of pharmacogenetics received a tremendous boost from the Human Genome Project, an ambitious scientific undertaking to map the entire human *genome* (the complete set of genetic information in human cells). The project aimed to help researchers pinpoint the genetic causes of disease and correct them through a technique called *gene therapy* (treating and preventing diseases by inserting genes into a patient's cells).

Pharmacogenetic researchers envision a day when physicians will prescribe medications tailored to the unique genetic makeup of each patient. This scenario offers a sharp contrast to the way physicians select medications today. Currently, doctors take several factors into account when prescribing drugs—a patient's age, weight, gender, general health, lifestyle, and use of other medicines. Settling on a new treatment often requires a frustrating amount of trial and error—sometimes involving several changes of medicine or dosage before an effective therapy is found. Some patients also unexpectedly develop serious side effects. An estimated 100,000 people die annually in the United States because of medication reactions.

One of the first scientific studies examining how a person's genetic makeup could account for a severe reaction to a medicine appeared in 1988. Geneticist Frank J. Gonzalez of the National Cancer Institute and his colleagues studied people who became ill when given a blood-pressure-lowering drug called debrisoquine. First, the scientists identified the human gene that is largely responsible for how the body handles the drug. The gene, later called CYP2D6, *codes for* (carries the instructions for producing) a *drug-metabolizing enzyme* (a protein that chemically transforms medications).

The researchers discovered that people who had bad reactions to debrisoquine had versions of the CYP2D6 gene that were slightly different from the usual form. These variants caused cells to produce inadequate amounts of the drug-metabolizing enzyme. As a result, people with these variants had difficulty eliminating debrisoquine from their body, and so a normal dose of the drug caused severe side effects.

Researchers by 2004 had identified and described more than a dozen genes like CYP2D6. All code for drug-metabolizing enzymes, and all have common variants that affect the way people react to medications. Some variants cause the body to eliminate certain drugs too slowly or too quickly. If a body eliminates a drug too slowly, levels may become dangerously high, causing severe side effects. If a drug is eliminated too quickly, a normal dose may not provide needed benefits. Each gene affects the body's handling of one or more prescription medications. The CYP2D6 gene helps metabolize more than 50 prescription medications, including the pain reliever codeine and drugs used to treat depression, schizophrenia, irregular heartbeats, high blood pressure, and high blood cholesterol.

While some pharmacogenetic researchers are studying genes for drug-metabolizing enzymes, others are focusing on genes involved in drug response. For example, researchers may study molecules that transport a drug or proteins involved in the disease being treated. By 2004, researchers had identified more than 20 such genes, including ApoE. A variant of this gene—ApoE4—increases a person's risk of developing the memory disorder Alzheimer's disease. Pharmacogenetic scientists found that tacrine, a medicine that helps some Alzheimer's patients, is ineffective in patients with ApoE4 variants.

Pharmacogenetic research likely will change the way drug companies test new medicines. Before allowing a new prescription drug to be sold in the United States, the Food and Drug Administration (FDA) requires that clinical research trials prove the drug is safe and effective. If a drug does not help many of the research subjects, or if it causes serious side effects, then the medicine may not receive FDA approval. In 2004, pharmaceutical companies tested increasing numbers of medicines in patients whose genetic makeup suggests they would benefit from the drugs and experience few side effects. This change should make it easier, faster, and cheaper to demonstrate that a new drug is safe and effective. The result, according to the pharmaceutical industry, will be more new drugs making it to market.

Pharmacogenetic research also will allow physicians to prescribe medicines based on each patient's genetic makeup. Scientists predict that physicians may one day order a "pharmacogenetic profile" for each patient. From a patient's blood cells, a laboratory technician would extract DNA (deoxyribonucleic acid, the chemical of which genes are made). Using a technique called a *polymerase chain reaction*, the technician would create multiple copies of drug-response genes, including genes for metabolic enzymes and for drug targets and transporters.

The technician would then apply the mixture to a small glass chip containing hundreds of thousands of bits of DNA that correspond to all known variants of drug-response genes. If a patient's genes precisely matched any of the DNA snippets, they would *bind* (attach), producing a distinctive pattern. The technician would use this pattern to prepare a pharmacogenetic profile report, listing genetic variants and suggesting safe and effective medicines for a variety of conditions.

As pharmacogenetic scientists tout the potential benefits of their research, medical ethicists ponder the risks. For example, will "pharmacogenetic profiling" be a test for only the wealthy or well insured? Will patients whose genetic makeup means that they are "hard to treat" be left out when new drugs are developed? Such concerns will loom larger as pharmacogenetics becomes an everyday part of medical practice.

■ Jinger G. Hoop

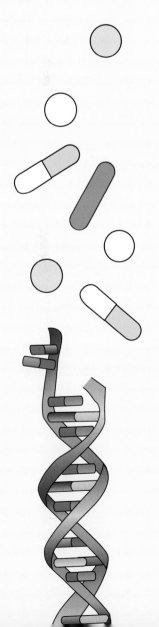

ECOLOGY

oral reefs may have a greater ability to adapt to—and survive—habitat destruction caused by human activities than previously believed, according to a study reported in August 2003 by Australian scientists. Coral reefs are large structures found in shallow tropical and subtropical waters around the world. They are the work of large colonies of small animals called coral *polyps.* The cylinder-shaped polyps remove calcium from seawater and deposit it as *calcium carbonate* (limestone) around themselves to form an external skeleton. Over time, the build-up of thousands of skeletons forms a reef. Reefs host a variety of animal life, including fish, shellfish, octopuses, and sea anemones.

Certain human activities, including overfishing and pollution, harm reef ecosystems. A number of reef studies have also revealed serious damage caused by rising sea-surface temperatures linked to *global warming,* a gradual increase in global temperatures that began in the late 1800's. Many scientists blame the rising temperatures on an increase in heat-trapping carbon dioxide and other so-called *greenhouse gases* released into the atmosphere by the burning of *fossil fuels* (oil, coal, and natural gas).

Marine biologists at James Cook University in Townsville, Australia, headed by Terence P. Hughes, analyzed several earlier reports predicting massive die-offs of coral reefs by about 2030 due to *bleaching.* In this phenomenon, coral polyps—under the stress of higher-than-normal water temperatures—expel tiny algae that live within their tissues. These algae normally provide the corals with nutrients as byproducts of *photosynthesis* (the use of energy from sunlight to make food). After expelling the algae, the corals turn a pale color and become weak. Although some corals recover from bleaching, others die.

Hughes said the studies underestimated the effects of many factors that make corals resistant to the damage from bleaching. For example, he pointed out that corals have a high degree of *genetic variability*—that is, different polyps have different forms of the same genes. The greater the variability between different animals, the greater the chance that some of them will fully recover from bleaching.

In addition, Hughes noted that many corals have migrated from waters that have experienced the most warming to cooler, more favorable waters. A coral has the ability to swim to a new location soon after it develops from an egg—before it settles down on a reef and builds its skeleton. Hughes also described fossil evidence showing that corals have survived for hundreds of millions of years through many earlier climate changes.

Hughes concluded that if sea-surface temperatures rise slowly, many of the world's coral polyps will be able to survive—though with a possible loss in their variety and numbers. Hughes called for more intense international efforts to ensure the survival of these amazing ecosystems.

Coral reef mucus. The *mucus* (slimy substance) on coral reefs plays a much more important role in reef ecology than scientists had realized. So reported a team of marine biologists led by Christian Wild of the Max Planck Institute for Marine Microbiology in Bremen, Germany, in March 2004.

During photosynthesis, the algae inside corals produce *organic* (carbon-containing) compounds for their own food. Scientists have long known that the corals excrete as much as half of this organic material as mucus. The mucus covers the external skeletons and helps protect the corals from drying out at low tide.

Wild and his colleagues showed that the mucus also aids in the corals' nutrition. The team studied the Great Barrier Reef, an enormous group of coral reefs along the northeast coast of Australia. The scientists observed that as the excreted mucus settles to the bottom of the reef, it traps bacteria, algae, and other particles that are suspended in the lagoon of the reef. The sand at the bottom of the lagoon, in turn, traps the particle-filled mucus. As the mucus chemically breaks down, the particles in it are released as nutrients for the coral polyps and the other animals of the reef.

Snake and pelican partners. A report in February 2004 described a previously unknown, mutually beneficial relationship between snakes and birds on Seahorse Key, a tiny island off the coast of Florida. Harvey Lillywhite, a *herpetologist* (reptile and amphibian expert) at the University of Florida in

"CRAZY ANTS" ALTER ISLAND ECOLOGY

On Christmas Island in the Indian Ocean, areas that are not infested with the yellow "crazy ant" (below) look radically different from areas that are infested with the alien ant species (below, bottom). In October 2003, ecologist Dennis O'Dowd of Monash University in Melbourne, Australia, described how the ant has caused a cascade of changes in the ecological makeup of the island. Hordes of the ants have killed off the seed-eating red land crab. As a result, more tree seedlings are surviving, leading to excess plant growth on the forest floor.

ECOLOGY continued

Gainesville, discovered why the island has huge populations of larger-than-normal cottonmouth snakes as well as many pelicans and other tree-nesting birds that feed on fish.

According to Lillywhite, the snakes usually live near the trees in which the birds nest. At night, the snakes feed on fish scraps that the birds drop from the trees. As a result, the island's snakes are healthy and well fed. Lillywhite suggested that by living near the nesting trees, the snakes, in turn, protect the birds from raccoons and other nest predators. This protection allows the bird populations to flourish.

Surviving on the Serengeti. Both hunting by meat-eating animals and food shortages help limit the populations of *ungulates* living on the grasslands of the Serengeti plains in East Africa, according to a study published in September 2003. Ungulates are hoofed, mainly plant-eating mammals. Biologists A. R. E. Sinclair, Simon Mduma, and Justin S. Brashares of the University of British Columbia in Vancouver, Canada, found that the weight of the ungulates chiefly determines which of these two forms of population control has a greater influence.

The Serengeti ecosystem has 28 species of ungulates and 10 species of large *predators* (animals that hunt other animals), including lions, leopards, and hyenas. For their study, the researchers analyzed 40 years of data on the populations of these African animals.

The zoologists reported that ungulates weighing less than 150 kilograms (330 pounds)—including antelopes, gazelles, and wart hogs—were more likely than others to be pursued by predators. As a result, predators played a major role in controlling the populations of these smaller animals. In contrast, ungulates weighing more than 150 kilograms—including wildebeest, buffalo, and giraffes—were less likely than the smaller ungulates to have predatory enemies. Because of this situation, the shortage of food ranked as the major factor controlling their populations. The researchers said that their conclusions should be useful for wildlife managers seeking to maintain a healthy balance among various species on the Serengeti. ■ Robert H. Tamarin

See also **BIOLOGY; CONSERVATION.**

FOREST FRAGMENTS

A tea plantation in India surrounds a fragment of tropical forest, which was preserved to give wildlife a sheltered environment and allow their movement to other fragments. Such forest fragments must be at least 10,000 hectares (24,700 acres) in size to ensure the protection of wildlife over a long period of time. This conclusion was reported in December 2003 by scientists with the Biological Dynamics of Forest Fragments Project, a long-term ecological study based in Manaus, Brazil.

ENERGY

The first successful flight of a wireless model aircraft powered solely by a ground-based *laser* took place in September 2003. (A laser is a device that produces a powerful beam of light.) The research team that developed the plane included scientists from the United States National Aeronautics and Space Administration's (NASA) Marshall Space Flight Center in Huntsville, Alabama; NASA's Dryden Flight Research Center in Edwards, California; and the University of Alabama in Huntsville. The aircraft was a radio-controlled model built primarily of balsa wood. It had a 1.52-meter (5-foot) wingspan and weighed only 310 grams (11 ounces).

The successful 2001 flight of the solar-powered aircraft *Helios* had encouraged scientists working to develop long-distance aircraft unburdened by fuel tanks. However, because solar power becomes unavailable after sundown, such planes still would need a backup, on-board power source for nighttime travel.

The flight took place inside a building at NASA's Marshall Space Flight Center. While one operator flew the radio-controlled plane, another beamed power from a 1,000-watt continuous wave infrared laser onto a panel of *photovoltaic cells* on the plane. (Photovoltaic cells are devices that convert light into electric energy.) The plane's tiny, 6-watt electric motor, which spun the propeller and powered the plane, used only a small portion of the laser's available power. After the plane flew a number of laps around the interior of the building, the operator turned off the laser beam, and the aircraft glided to the ground.

The researchers suggested several uses for aircraft powered by laser light. For example, such aircraft could serve as surveillance or telecommunications satellites. To prevent bad weather or other objects from interrupting the beam of light, lasers could be placed in several locations. The sites could "hand-off" the plane to each other much as cell phone towers do with telephone calls from moving vehicles.

Fuel cells powered by methane. The world's first *fuel cell* power plant fueled solely by methane gas emissions from a coal mine was dedicated in October 2003 by FuelCell Energy, Inc., of Danbury, Connecticut. The plant, which operated as a demonstration pro-

ject for six months, was built on the site of the company's abandoned Rose Valley coal mine in Hopedale, Ohio.

Fuel cells are devices that convert chemical energy into electric energy by means of chemical reactions. They work like large, continuously operating batteries that generate electricity as long as a fuel is supplied. Because the fuel is not burned, the process produces none of the pollution commonly associated with the combustion of such *fossil fuels* as coal and oil.

Methane is a dangerous gas that coal mines vent to keep miners safe from possible explosions. Scientists refer to methane as a *greenhouse gas,* a type of gas that traps heat in Earth's atmosphere. Many researchers believe that greenhouse gases contribute to *global warming,* a process that is gradually raising temperatures on Earth and that may have serious effects on agriculture, society, and the environment. Researchers estimate that both operating and abandoned coal mines annually produce methane emissions that equal the amount of pollution generated by 17 million automobiles.

The Rose Valley methane-powered fuel cells provided about 200 kilowatts of electric power, enough to supply the needs of 40 typical homes. American Electric Power, an electric utility company based in Columbus, Ohio, purchased the electricity and distributed it to customers. FuelCell Energy promoted its methane-powered fuel cells as a way to reduce U.S. dependence on foreign energy supplies as well as decrease air pollution.

Solar cells slim down. Researchers in Australia and Germany independently reported in December 2003 that they had made major improvements to solar photovoltaic cells. Such cells are part of solar power panels used to produce power for homes and businesses.

The main component of photovoltaic panels is crystalline silicon, an expensive material that accounts for most of the total cost of the panels. Obtaining the same performance from thinner slices of silicon would cut the cost of solar panels and help make solar energy more competitive in the world's energy market.

Origin Energy, an Australian company, reported that its engineers had developed a method to drastically slim down solar panels.

ENERGY continued

Origin's new solar cells are less than 70 microns thick (thinner than a human hair) and use 90 percent less silicon than other solar photovoltaic cells. Yet the cells match conventional cells in efficiency. A solar power panel using the new ultra-thin "Sliver" cells needs the equivalent of two silicon wafers to convert sunlight to 140 watts of power. A conventional solar panel requires about 60 silicon wafers to produce the same amount of power. The cells were developed with Australian National University's Centre for Sustainable Energy Systems.

Researchers at the Fraunhofer Institute for Solar Energy Systems in Freiburg, Germany, reported that they had produced a crystalline-silicon solar cell only 37 microns thick while achieving slightly better solar energy conversion efficiency. Fraunhofer engineers also developed a faster, less expensive way of attaching electrical connections to the cells. Nevertheless, the German researchers noted that their manufacturing techniques needed to be refined before the silicon wafers could be manufactured at an economical cost.

Ultra-clean fuel from natural gas. The U.S. Department of Energy (DOE) dedicated a new facility in October 2003 for the production of ultra-clean fuels from natural gas. The plant, located at the Port of Catoosa, near Tulsa, Oklahoma, was intended to pioneer the production of fuel that would significantly reduce tail pipe emissions from cars, trucks, and buses. In particular, such fuel would release less sulfur dioxide, a major pollutant.

The plant was built under a cooperative agreement between the DOE; Syntroleum Corporation of Tulsa; Marathon Oil Company of Houston; and Integrated Concepts Research

Sources: European Wind Energy Association; American Wind Energy Association.

GLOBAL WIND POWER

Wind turbines off the west coast of North Wales begin to produce power in spring 2004 in the largest offshore wind farm in the United Kingdom (right). By 2003 (the latest year for which data were available), facilities for harnessing wind power throughout the world were generating 39,294 megawatts of power (above). Ten countries accounted for 92 percent of the world's wind power generating capacity.

Corporation of Arlington, Virginia. The facility was to produce about 70 barrels of high-performance, environmentally friendly fuel per day once it reached peak capacity in November. Bus fleets operated by the Metropolitan Area Transit Authority in Washington, D.C., and the National Park Service in Denali, Alaska, were to test the fuel. The first shipment of ultra-clean diesel fuel left the plant in March 2004.

The Syntroleum plant uses a new, three-step process to convert natural gas to transportation fuel. First, the natural gas is changed into *synthesis gas,* a mixture of hydrogen and carbon monoxide. Then, the synthesis gas is converted into synthetic crude oil. Finally, a refining unit upgrades the synthetic crude oil to finished synthetic diesel fuel.

The DOE expected the new ultra-clean fuels facility to help diesel engine manufacturers and fuel suppliers meet new Environmental Protection Agency emissions standards. The standards, which were to be phased in between 2007 and 2010, called for reducing the sulfur content in diesel fuel by 97 percent.

■ Pasquale M. Sforza

ENGINEERING

The development of a window capable of withstanding the impact of hurricane winds traveling at 97 kilometers (60 miles) per hour was reported in September 2003 by its inventor, Sanjeev Khanna, a professor of mechanical and aerospace engineering at the University of Missouri in Columbia. The new window has two layers of heat-strengthened glass with four to five layers of a reinforcement material sandwiched between them. The material combines glass fibers and a *polymer* (a chemical compound in which each molecule contains two or more simpler molecules strung together). Khanna chemically treated the material to match the degree to which glass *refracts* (bends) light. The treatment makes the material transparent.

When an object slams into the window at high force—as it would in a hurricane—the glass fibers in the reinforcement material spread out the shock of the impact in different directions to disperse the energy. Khanna measured the strength of the window using a standard glass-industry test. He fired a 2-gram (0.07-ounce) missile at 257 kilometers (160 miles) per hour at the exact same spot on the window until it broke. The glass withstood 100 hits before shattering. Standard hurricane glass lasted for only 40 hits. The window may have applications for aircraft as well as for various types of buildings.

Carbon nanotubes. Researchers at the Brookhaven National Laboratory in Upton, New York, and the IBM T. J. Watson Research Center in Yorktown, New York, made an individual carbon *nanotube* (microscopic tube) that emits light. The development was announced at a meeting of the American Physical Society in Montreal, Canada, in March 2004.

The researchers achieved the feat through a process called *electron-hole recombination.* The scientists passed electricity through a carbon nanotube that had a diameter of only 1.5 *nanometers* (one-billionth of a meter). This action caused the current's electrons—which are negatively charged—to combine with positively charged *holes,* sites where electrons are missing. Electrons filling the holes caused the emission of light. The discovery marked a significant step toward using nanotubes for applications in electronics and display technologies, including such items as televisions and computer monitors.

Particle trap. In March 2004, Pratim Biswas, an engineering professor at Washington University in Saint Louis, Missouri, received a patent for a device that traps and deactivates microbes. Engineers believe that the device could be used to counter bioterrorism attacks as well as improve air ventilation in buildings and aircraft.

The device uses several components to destroy *biological agents* (cultivated microorganisms designed to create mass destruction to military and civilian populations). These components include an electrical field, *soft X rays* (weak X rays produced by low voltage), and *smart catalysts* (particles that radiation turns "on" and "off"). When viruses, for example, flow into the device, they develop charges and are trapped in the electric field. Tiny

ENGINEERING continued

chemical particles on the device's inner walls oxidize and eventually kill the organisms.

The device improves on similar systems that can trap contaminants of larger sizes but not viruses, which are only a few nanometers in diameter. In laboratory tests, Biswas and fellow scientists found that the device destroyed a strain of the polio virus with 99.99-percent efficiency.

Self-healing teeth. The development of a material that could promote the natural repair of defective teeth was reported by a team of biochemical engineers at the National Institute of Standards and Technology in Gaithersburg, Maryland, in June 2003. The material consists of calcium phosphate in a polymer.

The researchers discovered that, in the presence of a liquid similar to saliva, the material releases calcium and phosphate *ions* (atoms that have electric charges). This action, in turn, creates crystalline material similar to that present in teeth and bone.

The scientists also discovered that adding silica and *zirconia* (a compound that contains one zirconium atom and two oxygen atoms) to the material slowed the formation of calcium phosphate crystals. The release of the calcium phosphate over a longer period gives the teeth a better chance to heal.

Researchers hope to use the material in several types of dental applications. Among these are cavity-preventing liners to lie beneath conventional fillings.

A device for rail safety. A father-and-son team of researchers in the United Kingdom has developed a tiny device that may help prevent rail disasters, according to an announcement made in October 2003. The device is a miniature *data logger*, an electronic instrument that collects information over time. The device, called the Microlog, was made by Jarek Rosinski, a professor of engineering at the University of Newcastle upon Tyne, and his son Martin.

Although people have used data loggers since the 1980's, the Microlog is unique because of its size, which allows engineers to fit it in small areas such as train axles. Weighing less than 10 grams (0.35 ounce) and much smaller than a matchbox, Microlog can detect suspect areas on rail tracks where problems could lead to accidents. For example, sensors pick up information about the conditions of the tracks as the axles bend and twist under stress. Rail problems such as buckling of the lines due to excessive heat produce abnormal stresses. When it detects a problem, Microlog sends a warning signal to rail operators using satellite and mobile phone technology. Train operators will then be able to solve the problem as soon as possible, the researchers said.

Ultra-light magnets. Researchers in the Spanish cities of Barcelona and Zaragoza have created a new ultra-light transparent magnetic material. The finding, announced in November 2003, has potential applications in computer-related technology.

The material is a combination of silica aerogel—which is composed of 99 percent air—and fine magnetic particles containing the elements neodymium, iron, and boron. Because of the fineness of the particles, the material remains transparent and light. The magnetic particles are shaped like tubes and are each about 1 centimeter (0.39 inch) in diameter.

The new material is similar to a traditional magnet in that it retains the orientation of its magnetic field. This property makes it ideal for building memory devices, which rely on the stability of magnetic orientation in order to store information. Moreover, because the material is transparent, a laser beam could read memory devices made with it.

Bulletproof material. Researchers at the Technical Research Centre of Finland VTT in Espoo, Finland, announced the discovery of a material that is practically bulletproof. Scientists hoped that the material, announced in November 2003, would lead to the creation of a new type of civil and military vehicle.

A Transrapid train speeds through Shanghai, China (far left). In December 2003, the world's first commercial Transrapid began operation in that Chinese city, transporting riders between Long Yang Station and Pudong International Airport at speeds of up to 501 kilometers (311 miles) per hour. The Transrapid operates on a principle called *magnetic levitation*, or Maglev. A drawing (below) shows the parts of the technology. Magnets (red) mounted on the vehicle frame wrap around the track. The magnets work alongside the *stator* (green)—a stationary portion enclosing rotating parts in a motor—and cables (black) to levitate and propel the train.

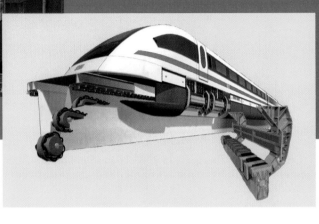

The compound is tougher than ceramic and is easy to mold into a desired shape. The material can also resist both high impact and high temperatures, which makes it a superior alternative to aluminum oxides and other ceramic materials used in everything from bulletproof vests to armored cars.

Self-lubricating material. The discovery of a material that is both tough and self-lubricating was reported by researcher Denis Music of Linkoping University in Linkoping, Sweden, in September 2003. The material could be used in a wide range of machine components and bearings in the manufacturing industry, which wants to cut down on the use of oils and lubricants that harm human health and the environment.

To make the material, the researchers used a method called *sputtering*. Sputtering involves changing atoms in a solid target material into a gas by bombarding the material with *energetic ions* (charged particles accelerated to high energies). Engineers use sputtering to create a wide variety of items, including alloys and granular materials.

"Seeing" through snow. Researchers have patented a design for a radar system that allows operators of snowblowers and snowplows to detect and avoid objects buried under snow. The discovery by researchers at the University of California at Davis was announced in February 2004.

Radar does not penetrate dense material such as snow easily. The layers of salt and dirt in snowbanks make radar penetration even more difficult. The new radar system "sees" up to 1.8 meters (6 feet) into a snowbank. According to the researchers, the radar system could help drastically cut down maintenance and repair costs for snowplows, which often bump into rocks and other buried objects.

The radar system also has potential applications for rescuing people buried in snow following an avalanche. Most avalanche-rescue systems depend on *transponders* that must be worn by skiers and other people venturing into snowy areas. Transponders are electronic devices that can receive radar or other signals and automatically transmit responses.

A new way to make chips. Researchers at Purdue University in West Lafayette, Indiana, announced in January 2004 a new method to create *microfluidic* chips quickly and inexpensively. Microfluidics combines the sciences of chemistry, engineering, physics, and biotechnology to study the properties and behavior of very small amounts of liquids. Microfluidic chips use very tiny channels through which scientists detect samples of various items.

Normally, scientists create microfluidic chips by etching patterns on glass or silicon with X rays. The Purdue researchers used minute quantities of liquids placed on a small surface area. Using glass microscope slides and tweezers, the researchers placed thin glass fibers—10 times thinner than a human hair— atop the glass. Then they pressed the polymer PDMS over the assembly. The sandwiched fibers acted as wicks, taking samples at one end and delivering results at the other.

ENGINEERING continued

By controlling the properties of the fiber, researchers can control which liquids flow through the channels and which liquids stick. Ultimately, the scientists can identify or separate different types of molecules, such as proteins, from fluids they send through the chip.

The potential applications of this type of technology are far-ranging. For example, microfluidic chips may allow researchers to detect potentially deadly molecules such as airborne *toxins* (poisons) and bioagents.

■ Yudhijit Bhattacharjee

ENVIRONMENTAL POLLUTION

Children whose mothers absorb high levels of methyl mercury during pregnancy by eating tainted seafood may suffer long-term damage to their nervous systems, according to reports published in February 2004. The studies, conducted by a team of international researchers, focused on women and their children on the Faroe Islands in the North Atlantic Ocean. Fishing dominates the islands' economy, and the inhabitants' diets are high in fish and pilot whale meat.

Methyl mercury is an *organic* (plant- or animal-based) form of elemental mercury, a common pollutant. Much of the mercury in the atmosphere comes from coal-fired power plants or is released as a by-product of industrial processes. Forest fires, volcanoes, and other natural sources release mercury as well.

The mercury pollution in the atmosphere usually ends up in oceans, rivers, and lakes. Fish and other aquatic animals convert elemental mercury to methyl mercury and other organic forms of the element that accumulate in body tissues. The mercury-containing compounds travel up food chains, becoming especially concentrated in large, predatory fish.

One of the Faroe Island studies measured the speed at which the brains of the islands' children and adolescents transmitted electrical signals. The researchers found a significant slowdown in transmission speed among children and adolescents who had been exposed to mercury as *fetuses* (developing babies). The second study found that fetal mercury exposure also interfered with the ability of the nervous system to regulate heart rate.

The studies also found that children and adolescents who absorbed mercury by eating mercury-tainted seafood suffered additional damage to their nervous systems. However, this damage affected different areas of the nervous system than those affected by mercury exposure as fetuses.

The researchers acknowledged that fish provide protein and other vital nutrients in a healthful diet. Because of the health dangers posed by mercury, however, the United States Department of Agriculture and health departments in several states have issued warnings asking people to avoid certain species or reduce their consumption of fish.

Some scientists argued that mercury may not be the main cause of the neurological problems found in the Faroe Islanders. They contended that high levels of polychlorinated biphenyls (PCB's)—perhaps in combination with mercury—may be responsible for the health problems. Scientific studies have shown that high concentrations of PCB's, which were banned by the U.S. government in 1979, may cause birth defects, cancer, liver damage, and disorders of the nervous system.

Space-age scrubber. A water purification system developed for the International Space Station (ISS) may help reduce airborne mercury emissions from coal-fired power plants on Earth, according to an August 2003 report from the University of Florida in Gainesville. The system may be less costly and more effective than filters containing activated carbon, a material commonly used to "scrub" emissions from coal-burning plants.

For their system, environmental engineering professors David Mazyck and Chang-Yu Wu used *silica* (the mineral in quartz) embedded in a *photocatalyst* (a light-sensitive material). Ultraviolet radiation in sunlight stimulates a chemical reaction in the photo-

PERSONAL POLLUTION EXPOSURE

A participant in a study of airborne pollutants called *volatile organic compounds* (VOC's) pumps gas while wearing a lapel-mounted air pollution sensor. The study, reported in January 2004 by researchers at the University of Minnesota in Minneapolis, found that the participants inhaled higher levels of VOC's than expected.

catalyst that, in turn, produces a chemical that captures and extracts the mercury.

In laboratory tests, the new technology proved to be 10 times more effective in reducing airborne mercury than the activated carbon process, the researchers reported. In addition, they found that the mercury removed from the silica can be recycled for use in such products as fluorescent light bulbs and camera batteries. Mercury removed by the activated-carbon process cannot be recycled.

Air pollution up close. People inhale considerably more air pollution of a type known as *volatile organic compounds* (VOC's) than previously estimated, according to a report published in January 2004. Researchers led by John Adgate, assistant professor of Environmental and Occupational Health at the University of Minnesota in Minneapolis, found that VOC's tend to collect in "envelopes" around people sitting in smoky rooms, driving in heavy traffic, or pumping gas.

VOC's include airborne chemicals from air fresheners, cleaning agents, and other household products; fumes from gas pumps and automotive products; and cigarette smoke. Some VOC's are suspected or known to cause cancer in people, according to the U.S. Environmental Protection Agency.

Typically, environmental agencies monitor urban air quality by taking outdoor samples from scattered locations and then averaging the results. To obtain data about personal exposure to VOC's, Adgate and his colleagues outfitted 71 nonsmoking volunteers with individual, lapel-mounted air sensors and set up sensors in volunteers' homes. They positioned other sensors in outdoor locations. The monitors registered the volunteers' exposure to 15 VOC's over a two-day period.

Study data revealed that the standard method of measuring VOC levels significantly underestimates actual human exposure. For example, the lapel sensors registered

levels of benzene, a cancer-causing chemical, that were 1.5 times as great as the levels detected by the home sensors and 2 times as great as those detected by the outdoor sensors. According to the researchers, such exposure raises the risk of developing cancer from 10 cases to 25 cases among 1 million people. Average personal concentrations of other VOC's ranged from 3 to 60 times as great as those found outdoors. The researchers concluded that the results of the study argue for closer monitoring of urban air pollution.

Pesticide delays puberty. Long-term exposure to the pesticide endosulfan may delay the onset of *puberty* (sexual maturity) in boys, according to research reported in December 2003 by Habibullah Saiyed of the National Institute of Occupational Health in Ahmedabad, India. Beginning in the 1980's, Indian farmers applied the pesticide widely to protect cashews and other commercial crops. The Indian government banned the use of endosulfan in 2000. Although the body excretes endosulfan fairly quickly, the pesticide may remain in the environment much longer.

The researchers examined 117 boys ages 10 to 19 in Padre, a village in India's cashew-growing region. The boys had been exposed to endosulfan throughout their lives, in the water they drank and in the fish they ate. Saiyed and his colleagues compared the Padre boys with a control group of boys living in an area of India where the pesticide had not been

ENVIRONMENTAL POLLUTION continued

used. The researchers found that, compared with the control group, the Padre boys had higher blood levels of endosulfan and lower levels of *testosterone*, a male hormone that stimulates puberty.

Pathway to the brain. Tiny airborne particles known as *particulates* may travel to the brain directly through the nose and *olfactory nerves* (nerves involved in smelling), by-passing the barriers that normally protect the brain from exposure to potentially harmful substances traveling through the blood-stream. This finding was announced in January 2004 by toxicologist Gunter Oberdorster and his colleagues at the University of Rochester in New York.

Oberdorster's team exposed rats for brief periods to air containing carbon atoms combined with a small amount of radioactive material. The scientists then checked the rats' olfactory nerves, lungs, and brains for traces of the particulate. They found that carbon levels in the *olfactory bulb* (the part of the brain most closely linked to nerve endings in the nose) rose in the hours after exposure. This indicated that the particulates were moving into the

brain along the olfactory nerves. In contrast, particulate levels in the lungs declined, indicating that mechanisms that remove the pollutants from this tissue were working normally.

The researchers concluded that particulates in air pollution may pose a more direct threat to brain health than previously thought. They also noted that increased knowledge about the nose-to-brain pathway might lead to the development of medications that could be administered directly to the brain by way of the nasal passages.

Fish fertility threatened. A synthetic form of *estrogen* (a female hormone) used in birth control pills for women may cause a significant decline in trout fertility. That finding was reported in June 2003 by researchers at the Battelle Marine Sciences Laboratory in Sequim, Washington.

Women taking birth control pills excrete estrogen residues in their urine, which ends up in sewage. The residues pass through sewage treatment plants and are returned to waterways, where fish and other aquatic organisms ingest them. The researchers exposed trout in the laboratory to three levels of ethinylestradiol (EE2) for two months. Male trout exposed to higher levels of EE2 suffered from excessive bleeding in their livers and kidneys. Male fish exposed to lower EE2 levels—lower than those commonly found in streams—fertilized about one-half of the eggs fertilized by normal, untainted fish.

■ Daniel D. Chiras

WHAT'S FOR DINNER?

Farm-raised salmon are more likely to contain dioxins and other cancer-causing pollutants than wild salmon are, according to a study published in January 2004. A team of United States and Canadian scientists said the salmon absorbed the pollutants from the fish oil used as feed. Other scientists, including officials at the U.S. Food and Drug Administration in Rockville, Maryland, argued that the pollutant levels found in the salmon were too low to cause harm.

ENVIRONMENTAL POLLUTION

The Aral Sea: Repairing an Ecological Disaster

During the 1960's, the Aral Sea was the world's fourth-largest inland body of water. The sea, which is actually a saltwater lake, lies on the border between the central Asian republics of Uzbekistan and Kazakhstan. Hundreds of thousands of people made a prosperous living from the sea's fishing and shipping industries. The sea was also a thriving ecosystem with hundreds of species of fish, reptiles, birds, and mammals.

By 2004, the Aral Sea ranked as one of the worst environmental disasters on Earth. Poorly planned agricultural irrigation projects had diverted vast amounts of water from the sea, which had lost 60 percent of its water volume. As a result, the Aral Sea had fallen to the tenth-largest inland body of water. Most species of fish had been killed off, resulting in the destruction of the local fishing industry. Hundreds of tons of salt blown off the sea's exposed salt bed had turned much of the surrounding farmland into a wasteland. Salt pollution of the air and drinking water, as well as pollution from chemical pesticides and fertilizers, led to high rates of cancer, tuberculosis, and other deadly diseases among the local population. The pollution also wiped out much of the region's wildlife.

In 2004, however, environmentalists were finding some hope in international projects aimed at reversing the ecological catastrophe of the Aral Sea. But it remained unclear whether these projects could save the sea.

The Aral Sea's many ecological problems began in the 1960's. The government of the Soviet Union, which controlled the region at the time, decided to diversify agriculture in the semi-desert region by growing cotton and rice. Unfortunately, both crops require large amounts of water, pesticides, and fertilizers. Soviet engineers built large-scale irrigation canals to carry fresh water from the two rivers feeding the Aral Sea to the cotton and rice plantations. The Syr Darya, which flows into the sea's northern section, provides most of the water entering the Aral. The more southerly Amu Darya contributes only a small amount of the lake's water supply.

The irrigation system cut the flow of water from both rivers dramatically, and the Aral Sea began to shrink. In the early 1960's, the Aral spread across 66,000 square kilometers (25,500 square miles). By 2004, it covered only 28,500 square kilometers (11,000 square miles). The maximum depth of the sea dropped from 68 meters (223 feet) to 35 meters (115 feet). Several fishing villages found themselves more than 100 kilometers (62 miles) from the sea. Some parts of the sea dried up completely.

By the late 1980's, the sea had split into two sections as an island grew between the larger "South Aral" and the smaller "North Aral." Each day, the wind blew tons of salt from this island and the sea's exposed shoreline as far as 480 kilometers (300 miles) away. The soil became so contaminated that many farmers gave up trying to grow crops. According to government statistics, the population of Kazakhstan's Aralsk region, northeast of the Aral Sea, dropped by about 10,000 between the early 1990's and early 2000's as farmers left to seek work elsewhere.

NO MORE FISHING

The Aral Sea, lying between Uzbekistan and Kazakhstan in central Asia (above), lost 60 percent of its water volume between the 1960's and 2004 because of irrigation projects. The sea's retreating shoreline has left many fishing villages and their boats tens of kilometers from the sea (below).

As the sea's water level dropped, the *salinity* (saltiness) of the remaining water more than doubled. In fact, the salinity grew to *toxic* (poisonous) levels for the fish, and such commercially important species as sturgeon and carp died out.

A failure to maintain the irrigation canals over the years has contributed greatly to the region's environmental problems. The World Bank, an international lending organization based in Washington, D.C., reported in 2003 that about 60 percent of the water that enters the irrigation system is lost because the canals are broken down and leaky. The water seeping into the ground has raised the *water table* (the level below which the ground is saturated with water). As the ground water rises, it carries salt from the deeper soil to the surface, polluting the soil even more.

The increased salinity of the ground water is just one cause of the deterioration in drinking water in the Aral Sea region. The drinking water is also dangerously contaminated with chemical pesticides from farms as well as *heavy metals* (toxic metal compounds) released into the environment by nearby military and aerospace facilities. In addition, improper water treatment processes have allowed harmful bacteria to contaminate the region's drinking water.

Health authorities blame the salt, agricultural chemicals, and other harmful substances in the drinking water and air for the region's high rates of disease. Cancer rates in Kazakh communities near the Aral Sea are three times higher than the national average for Kazakhstan. The local population also suffers from higher-than-normal rates of tuberculosis, asthma, bronchitis, birth defects, and infant mortality.

The shrinking of the Aral Sea and the pollution of the environment have devastated the region's wildlife. Local populations of muskrats, boar, deer, and egrets have fallen so low that their survival is threatened. Other endangered animals in the region include the giant bat, the honey badger, the hissing swan, and various species of eagles, pelicans, and lizards.

In 2004, the Aral Sea was the focus of a number of projects aimed at restoring its ecological balance and improving the management of its water resources. Most of these projects concentrated on the North Aral, giving up the rapidly drying South Aral as a lost cause. A June 2003 report by the Shirshov Institute of Oceanology in Moscow predicted that most of the South Aral would be completely dry by 2018.

Most scientists believed that the project with the best chance of saving the Aral Sea was being organized by the International Fund for Saving the Aral Sea (IFAS), a group made up of representatives from Kazakhstan,

Uzbekistan, and several other central Asian nations. In July 2003, engineers working with the IFAS began constructing a large concrete dam to permanently separate the northern and southern parts of the sea. The engineers expected that the dam, which is to be 13 kilometers (8 miles) long, would help keep the water from the Syr Darya inside the bed of the North Aral. They said the inflow should allow the water level in the North Aral to rise and spread across more than 520 square kilometers (200 square miles) that were dry ground in 2004. The IFAS plan also included restocking the sea's fish hatcheries to revive the region's once-productive fishing industry.

Russian scientists in mid-2004 were researching a massive project to construct a canal 2,500 kilometers (1,600 miles) long between the Aral Sea and Siberia. The canal would deliver water from the Ob and Irtysh rivers in western Siberia to the Amu Darya and Syr Darya. However, the plan aimed not to address the ecological problems of the Aral Sea but instead to improve irrigation for the cropland around the sea. Some environmentalists opposed

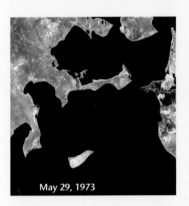

May 29, 1973

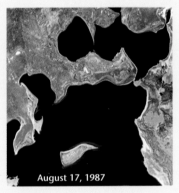

August 17, 1987

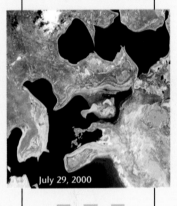

July 29, 2000

the plan, which had not yet been granted government approval as of mid-2004, because they feared it would create ecological problems in Siberia's Ob River basin.

Other Aral Sea projects underway in 2004 were attempting to reduce salinity in soils; improve the water supply and quality for the population; and train water managers in forecasting, analyzing, and exchanging water data. Major organizations providing technical and scientific assistance for these projects included the North Atlantic Treaty Organization, the United States Agency for International Development (a government agency that supports economic growth in other countries), and the Center for Research in Water Resources at the University of Texas at Austin.

Many scientists expressed concern that these projects would not do enough to save the Aral Sea. They noted that the efforts concentrated mostly on water management techniques rather than on ecological problems. These scientists called for greater commitments from central Asian governments to restore the Aral Sea's ecological balance.

Despite these concerns, scientists remained hopeful in 2004 that ongoing and future efforts would save the Aral Sea. If these efforts fail, the once-spectacular sea may disappear altogether. ■ Margaret A. Kilgore

FOSSIL STUDIES

The largest extinction of animal life in Earth's history may have been triggered by the collision of a massive meteorite with the planet some 250 million years ago. That theory was reported in November 2003 by a team of geologists led by Asish R. Basu of the University of Rochester in New York. The discovery off the coast of Australia of a large impact crater, dated to about 250 million years ago, provided additional evidence for the theory, researchers reported in May 2004.

At least 90 percent of animal species in the oceans died out about 248 million years ago, according to fossil evidence from rock lying at the boundary between the Permian Period (286 million to 248 million years ago) and Triassic Period (248 million to 213 million years ago), known as the *P-T boundary*. Many land-dwelling species also became extinct. Geologists have long debated the possible causes of this enormous extinction.

Basu's team analyzed 40 fragments of iron-rich rock excavated from Graphite Peak in Antarctica. They reported that the fragments, which were embedded in sedimentary layers dating from the P-T boundary, had the same ratios of iron and other metal compounds found in rocks from space known as *chondrite meteorites*. Geologists believe that such meteorites are leftover material from the formation of our solar system 4.6 billion years ago. This chemical analysis led the researchers to conclude that the fragments had come from a meteorite that hit Earth about the time of the Permian extinction.

The scientists proposed that about 250 million years ago, a mountain-sized object collided with Gondwanaland, the large southern landmass that existed during the Permian Period. The impact of such a collision and the resulting fires would have thrown a vast amount of dust and smoke into the atmosphere, blocking sunlight and causing surface temperature to plummet for many months. Any life on Earth would have found it very difficult to survive such catastrophic conditions.

A possible location for that crater was the subject of research published by geologist Luann Becker of the University of California at Santa Barbara and several colleagues. She reported finding mineral evidence of a meteorite

crater about 190 kilometers (120 miles) wide dating from the time of the P-T extinction. The crater is located off the northwest coast of Australia, which was part of Gondwanaland 250 million years ago.

Becker reported that sediment drilled from the so-called Bedout (*beh DOO*) Crater contained mineral fragments common in meteorites. She added that rocky crystals in the sediment showed chemical signs of having been melted by the intense heat created by the space rock's impact.

Earliest-known male. The oldest fossil evidence of a male animal was described in December 2003 by paleontologist David Siveter of the University of Leicester in England and several colleagues. The scientists said they had identified male *genitalia* (sex organs) in well-preserved fossils of *ostracodes* from volcanic deposits 425 million years old in England. Ostracodes are tiny relatives of shrimps and crabs that have hinged *bivalved* (two-part) shells, like those of clams.

The paleontologists explained that the ostracode specimens had remains of soft body parts preserved in *concretions* (cemented nodules of sediment) within the ash deposits. The researchers ground away thin slices of the concretions, taking digital photographs of the resulting cross sections at regular intervals—a technique sometimes called "shave and photograph." They then used computer software to combine the cross sections into detailed, three-dimensional images of the ostracodes. The images revealed the male genitalia of at least one of the animals.

Other pictures showed limbs for swimming and crawling, several pairs of gills, and an entire digestive tract. The tissue remnants preserved in these fossils were almost 200 million years older than the previous record-holder for earliest ostracode tissue. In addition, the fossilized genitalia were about 25 million years older than the earliest sex-organ fossils previously known.

From fish to amphibian. In April 2004, an analysis of the oldest-known fossil of a leg bone shed light on the evolution of fish fins into amphibian limbs during the Devonian Period (410 million to 360 million years ago). Paleontologist Ted Daeschler of the Academy of Natural Sciences in Philadelphia and colleagues at the University of Chicago found the ancient leg bone in the hills of north-central Pennsylvania. It lay in a layer of sediment, once part of an ancient riverbed, dated to about 365 million years ago.

The fossilized bone, which is about the length of two adult thumbs, was part of a *humerus* (upper front leg or upper arm). The bone has markings indicating that strong muscles were attached to it. The scientists could not determine if the bone originally ended in toes or *fin-rays* (flexible cartilage rods supporting the fins of many fish).

Daeschler said the shape of the bone and the way muscles were attached to it indicate that the bone was probably not used for walking. Instead, he theorized, it was most likely used to prop the animal upward, above the water level, so that it could look for predators or prey or breathe. The leg bone is approximately 2 million years older than any other animal leg ever found. Many paleontologists

agreed it was strong evidence that the first legs evolved for purposes other than walking.

Ancestral sauropod. Fossils that had been stored on shelves in a scientific institute for 20 years were described in July 2003 as the oldest specimen of Sauropoda, the group of enormous *herbivorous* (plant-eating) dinosaurs that includes such giants as *Apatosaurus* (also called *Brontosaurus*). Paleontologists Adam Yates and James Kitching of the Bernard Price Institute (BPI) for Paleontological Research in Johannesburg,

GIANT PREHISTORIC RODENT

A rodent the size of a buffalo had a riverside home about 8 million years ago in what is now northwestern Venezuela. That finding was based on an analysis of the animal's fossilized bones reported in September 2003 by paleontologist Marcelo R. Sanchez-Villagra at the University of Tubingen in Germany. The giant rodent, named *Phoberomys pattersoni*, weighed about 740 kilograms (1,630 pounds), dwarfing its modern relative, the guinea pig (inset).

FOSSIL STUDIES continued

South Africa, named the new dinosaur *Antetonitrus ingenipes.*

Kitching had unearthed the fossils in the early 1980's from Triassic Period rocks in central South Africa dating to 215 million years ago. Then, diverted by other projects, the scientist let the fossils sit in storage. Yates first realized the significance of the fossils while visiting BPI from the institute where he worked at the time.

The paleontologists said the fossils belonged to a *quadrupedal* (four-footed) dinosaur that measured about 10 to 12 meters (33 to 39 feet) in length and weighed about 1.8 metric tons (2 tons). As such, the fossils record the largest-known animal from the Late Triassic. The scientists concluded that *Antetonitrus* was probably a transitional form between the prosauropods—smaller, *bipedal* (two-footed) dinosaurs—and the larger, true sauropods. Although *Antetonitrus* walked on four legs, the bone structure of its front legs indicates that the dinosaur was capable of manipulating food with its front limbs.

New pterosaur. Paleontologist Paul Sereno of the University of Chicago reported in December 2003 the discovery of one of the best preserved fossils of *pterosaurs* known to science. Pterosaurs were large, flying reptiles that soared through the air during the Mesozoic Era (248 million to 65 million years ago), when dinosaurs walked on land.

Sereno found the fossils of the pterosaur, which had not yet been given a scientific name as of mid-2004, in the Sahara region of the African nation of Niger in 1997. The fossils were found in sediment that was 110 million years old, from the Cretaceous period. At that time, this region was the site of a large riverbed, according to scientists.

The fossils showed that the pterosaur had a wingspan of more than 4.8 meters (15.7 feet). It also had large jaws with a basketlike grouping of slender teeth that allowed it to scoop up fish while flying above the river.

Sereno noted that the new pterosaur resembles pterosaur fossils found in South America. This fact supports the theory that the sites lay near each other 110 million years ago.

Earliest land plants. Newly discovered fragments of *organic* (carbon-based) matter may re-date the origin of land plants, accord-

ing to a September 2003 report by paleontologist Charles Wellman of the University of Sheffield in England. Wellman identified the preserved specimens, each less than 1 millimeter (0.04 inch) in diameter, as parts of *sporangia,* sacs that hold reproductive cells called *spores.* He said he obtained the sporangia from a *core* (cylindrical drilled sample) of 475-million-year-old rock drilled in Oman, a country in the Arabian Peninsula.

Scientists had previously identified spores in rocks of this age in several places around the world. However, most *paleobotanists* (experts in fossil plants) believed those spores were from marine algae, organisms that are more primitive than true plants.

The earliest evidence of spores that were indisputably from land plants came from rock layers approximately 420 million years old. Because the type of sporangia described by Wellman is found only on true land plants, Wellman concluded that land plants arose more than 50 million years earlier than previously documented. Wellman reported that the structure of the spore sacs indicates that they came from a plant similar to modern *liverworts,* small mosslike plants that usually live in moist soil. These earliest plants would have formed a thin layer of green, filmy growth along the shores of ancient lakes and ponds.

Oldest vertebrate? A discovery reported in October 2003 may push back the record of *vertebrates* (animals with backbones) to about 560 million years ago. The find, by a team led by geologist James Gehling of the South Australian Museum in Adelaide, is some 30 million years more ancient than the oldest previously known vertebrate fossil. The scientists based their conclusion on a new analysis of fossils discovered in 1998 by a rancher in the Flinders Range, a mountainous territory in southern Australia. Gehling said the fossils, torpedo-shaped impressions in sandstone, each about 6.5 centimeters (2.6 inches) long, appear to be "primitive fishes." The impressions show evidence of a tail, a *dorsal* (back) fin, and V-shaped bands of muscles—all traits that scientists associate with vertebrates.

If these specimens are correctly identified, they indicate that the vertebrate lineage—to which human beings belong—extends back

FIRST "FISH" FOSSIL?

A fossil of what may be the oldest-known *vertebrate* (animal with a backbone) was described in October 2003 by paleontologist James Gehling of the South Australian Museum. Gehling said the fossil, which was discovered in southern Australia, is about 560 million years old—30 million years older than any other known vertebrate fossil. The animal represented by the fossil appears to be a "primitive fish" about 6.5 centimeters (2.6 inches) long, according to Gehling.

to a time known by many geologists as the Ediacaran Period (600 million to 543 million years ago). This would mean that vertebrates' roots stretch back almost as far as those of *invertebrates* (animals without backbones).

Fossil mystery solved? In December 2003, British investigators described fossilized features that appeared to resolve a long-standing scientific mystery that had involved the correct identity of very unusual fish fossils.

Paleontologists had long speculated about the identity of small fish fossils preserved in 385-million-year-old sandstone at Achanarras Quarry in Scotland. Scientists did not know whether the fish, named *Palaeo-spondylus gunni,* were shark relatives, bony fish, some other kind of fish, or even amphibian tadpoles. Because the specimens appear to lack jaws, some scientists had linked them with the group of jawless fishes that includes the modern lamprey and hagfish. However, unlike these fish, *P. gunni* appears to have had well-developed *vertebrae* (backbone segments).

A team led by Keith Stewart Thomson, a professor of natural history at Oxford University in England, analyzed the fossils using the "shave and photograph" technique. The images revealed details of the fish's anatomy never before observed. Most notably, the fossils showed nasal structures and bony projections at the back of the skull similar to those found in certain lungfish, a group of primitive jawed fishes that use both lungs and gills to breathe. But the absence of jaws in the fossils indicated that the *P. gunni* specimens were not fully developed lungfish.

Thomson's group concluded that the speci-

mens were most likely examples of *larval* (immature) lungfish. The scientists suggested that *P. gunni* was the larval form of a species named *Dipterus valenciennesi,* fossils of which were also found in the sandstone deposits at Achanarras Quarry.

Cave of fossils. During 2003 and 2004, an amazing collection of fossils discovered in an Australian cave in 2002 continued to provide new insights into animal life during the Pleistocene Epoch (2 million to 11,500 years ago). By early 2004, paleontologist John Long of the Western Australia Museum in Perth had identified several new species of large mammals and other animals among the fossils found in the cave, which lies in the Nullarbor Plains of western Australia. Many of the well-preserved skeletons are of huge, extinct *marsupials* (pouched mammals).

In addition to one of the best preserved examples of *Thylacoleo* (a large marsupial lion-like predator), Long identified at least five new species of kangaroo. These species included a giant measuring more than 3 meters (10 feet) in length that Long concluded was a juvenile. He also identified a kangaroo with bizarre hornlike structures on its head; a wombat the size of a pony; and a number of previously unknown birds similar to the emu.

■ Carlton E. Brett

See also **GEOLOGY.**

GENETICS

In a major advance in *therapeutic cloning*, scientists from South Korea and the United States announced in February 2004 that they had produced human *embryos* (organisms in the first stages of development) that survived longer and developed to a more advanced stage than any other embryos created in laboratory studies. The scientists were led by Woo Suk Hwang of Seoul National University in South Korea.

Therapeutic cloning is a process used to obtain embryonic *stem cells* (cells that can develop into any of the different cell types that make up the tissues and organs of the body). The goal of therapeutic cloning is completely different from that of reproductive cloning, which scientists might use to reproduce individuals. Scientists believe that stem cell research may help them find new treatments for spinal cord injuries and such diseases as multiple sclerosis and diabetes. However, many people oppose therapeutic cloning on moral grounds.

For their research, the scientists first collected 242 eggs from 16 women, ultimately producing 30 embryos. They used a cloning procedure called *nuclear transplantation*, in which the scientists removed the nuclei from individual eggs. They replaced these nuclei with nuclei from a *cumulus cell*, a type of cell that helps to nourish developing eggs. After allowing the cells to divide for several days, the scientists collected embryonic stem cells from one embryo and grew them in the laboratory. When the researchers placed the stem cells into mice, they formed cartilage, muscle, bone, and connective tissue.

Experts believe that several factors contributed to the researchers' success. First, they started with a greater number of eggs than any other therapeutic cloning project has. The researchers also developed a method of gently removing the nucleus from an egg, rather than using a needle. Needles, which are commonly used for this process, may damage the nucleus. The researchers also allowed the cells to rest for a short time after the nuclei were inserted and before they stimulated the cell masses to grow. Finally, both the egg cells and the new nuclei used in each case came from the same person. Introducing a nucleus from a different person could cause the host to reject it, just as a transplant patient may reject a donor's organ.

Stroke gene. The discovery of a gene connected to the most common form of stroke was announced in October 2003 by a team of scientists led by Solveig Gretarsdottir of deCode Genetics in Reykjavik, Iceland. This type of stroke, known as *ischemic stroke*, occurs because of an obstruction of the blood supply from arteries and accounts for 80 to 90 percent of stroke cases.

For their study, the scientists analyzed the genetic material of 867 people who had suffered strokes. They then compared this information to the genetic material from 908 people from the same region of Iceland who had not had a stroke. From this detailed comparison, the scientists identified one gene, called PDE4D, that seemed to be linked to the risk of having a stroke. In particular, the scientists found that people who had strokes produced lower levels of three *isoforms* (slightly different versions of a protein) that the gene *codes for* (carries the instructions for producing). The scientists also found that stroke victims had different combinations of genes in areas of the chromosome around the PDE4D gene. Scientists are not certain exactly how changes in the PDE4D gene may lead to a stroke.

Breast cancer risk. Women with *mutations* (changes) in genes that suppress tumors have a significantly greater risk of developing breast cancer than women without the mutations. This finding was announced in October 2003 by researchers led by Mary-Claire King, a professor of medicine and genetics at the University of Washington in Seattle.

The study included 1,008 women with breast cancer caused by genetic mutations. Within this group, 104 women—about 10 percent—had mutations in one of two genes, BRCA1 and BRCA2. Scientists knew that mutations in these genes increase the risk of developing breast cancer but were not certain of the degree of risk. The study showed that women carrying either of these mutations have, overall, an 82-percent risk of developing breast cancer by age 80.

The researchers also looked at the role

nongenetic factors may play in the development of this form of cancer. The researchers evaluated the women's reproductive histories, their level of exercise, body weight, and even hormone use. They found that women born after 1940 have a higher risk of developing the disease than women in the same family who were born before that date.

This finding strongly suggested that nongenetic factors could account for this difference. Scientists did not know the specific factors, but possibilities included obesity, lack of exercise, and age when giving birth. The researchers concluded that both genetic testing and maintaining a healthful lifestyle are important in helping women with BRCA1 and BRCA2 mutations avoid or delay the onset of breast cancer.

Genes and depression. Genetic makeup affects whether people in stressful environmental situations develop depression, according to a study reported in July 2003. The finding was announced by a team of scientists led by Avshalom Caspi, a social genetics professor jointly associated with King's College in London and the University of Wisconsin in Madison. The scientists studied about 1,000 individuals in New Zealand from age 3 until age 26.

The researchers questioned study participants between the ages of 21 and 26 about their history of such stressful events as the deaths of family members and friends and unemployment. Once the study participants turned 26, the researchers assessed whether the participants had experienced depression within the past year. They based diagnoses of depression on the results of interviews with study participants and information in questionnaires filled out by the participants' close friends. Overall, scientists found 17 percent of the people in the study had experienced depression.

The scientists looked for a genetic connection to depression based on the makeup of a gene called 5-HTT. Like most genes, 5-HTT comes in pairs, meaning that each person has two copies. Scientists had already known that there were "short" and "long" versions of this gene. As a result, each person carries either two copies of the short version, two of the long version, or one of each. The scientists found that after experiencing four or more stressful events, people with either one or two copies of the short version of the 5-HTT gene were much more likely to experience depression than those with two copies of the long version.

The 5-HTT gene plays an important role in the body's ability to use *serotonin* (a chemical that acts in the brain and nerve cells to influence many feelings, behaviors, and processes). People with the short version of the gene appear to produce fewer

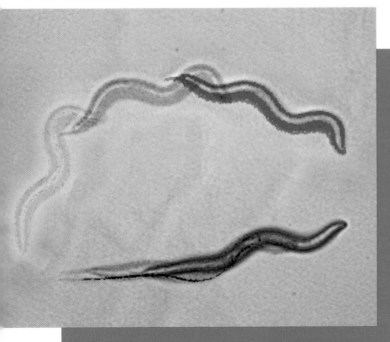

WORMS AND ALCOHOL

A time-lapse photograph of two worms reveals how differences in the worms' genes affect their behavior when exposed to alcohol. Researchers from the University of California at San Francisco reported in December 2003 that a normal worm (left, bottom) becomes noticeably less active when exposed to alcohol. However, a worm with a *mutation* (change) in the slo-1 gene (left, top) shows little effect from the alcohol and continues to move normally. Scientists hope the discovery may help in the development of drugs for treating alcoholism in people.

GENETICS continued

serotonin *transporters* (molecules that move other molecules) than people with the long version do. The scientists speculated that the reduced activity may affect the *uptake* (absorption) of serotonin by the nerve cells. Scientists praised the study as a demonstration of how environmental experiences and genetic factors affect behavior.

Blood vessel defect gene. Scientists have discovered a gene linked to the development of defective blood vessels found in a disorder known as *Klippel-Trenaunay syndrome*. This finding was announced in February 2004 by a group of scientists led by Xiao-Li Tian at Case Western Reserve University in Cleveland, Ohio.

Babies born with Klippel-Trenaunay syndrome have abnormally developed blood vessels. As a result, they face many serious medical problems, including bleeding as well as abnormally developed hands and feet. The disorder may also cause skin growths and fused or extra hands and feet.

While searching for the gene responsible for Klippel-Trenaunay syndrome, the researchers found a *chromosomal* abnormality in a patient with this disorder. Chromosomes are the structures that carry genes. Physical problems may occur if chromosomes become broken or rearranged during fetal development. The patient had a rearrangement in which part of one chromosome broke off and fused to another. The researchers found the VG5Q gene at the precise points where the restructuring occurred. They found that the amount of protein being produced was higher than normal. The scientists speculated that the production of too much protein from this gene

GENES DICTATE JOBS

A team of geneticists led by Gene Robinson of the University of Illinois in Urbana-Champaign announced in October 2003 that a honeybee's genes turn on or off in response to its role in the colony. The scientists reached this conclusion by using a computer chip with DNA sequences for approximately half of the bee genome to see which genes were active when the insects performed various tasks, including sharing nectar in a hive (right), taking care of younger bees, and gathering food.

could have a negative effect on the process of constructing blood vessels.

The scientists then examined genetic material from other patients with Klippel-Trenaunay syndrome to confirm the role that the gene might play. Although none of the other patients had the same chromosomal rearrangements, the researchers identified five people with the disorder who carried defective versions of the VG5Q gene. In comparison, an examination of genetic material from 200 control subjects revealed that none of them had defective versions of this gene.

Although their work showed that a defect in the VG5Q gene could explain some cases of Klippel-Trenaunay syndrome, the same defect was not found in all the patients with the disorder. This result indicated that more than one gene might cause the disease. Scientists hope to eventually control the abnormal blood vessel growth associated with the syndrome through *gene therapy* (inserting genes into a person's cells and tissues to treat a disease) involving VG5Q.

Rat genome sequence. A large international group of researchers participating in the Rat Genome Sequencing Project Consortium published the *genome sequence* of the rat in April 2004. A genome sequence is the entire layout of an organism's genes. Rats now join people and mice as the third group of mammals to have its genome sequence completed.

The researchers found that the rat genome is slightly smaller than the human genome and slightly larger than the mouse genome. They also found that up to 90 percent of the genes in the rat have human counterparts. This number is approximately the same as that between mice and human beings. The scientists also found, however, that the rat genome has many more genes involved in smell and breaking down *toxins* (poisons) than the human genome does. Finally, the researchers discovered that rats appear to be evolving faster than mice and human beings in terms of the number of changes found in their genetic material.

Purebred dogs and genes. The most thorough analysis of dog *DNA* ever conducted revealed that breeds differ in their genetic material as well as their physical appearance. (DNA [deoxyribonucleic acid] is the chemical genes are made of.) This finding was reported in May 2004 by a team of scientists headed by Elaine Ostrander, an associate professor of genome sciences and zoology at the Fred Hutchinson Cancer Research Center in Seattle.

The team of scientists analyzed the DNA of 414 dogs from the most popular breeds recognized by the American Kennel Club. The researchers looked at approximately 100 *microsatellites* (repetitive stretches of short DNA sequences) on the dogs' chromosomes. The team theorized that different microsatellites correspond to different dog breeds. A computer using microsatellite information correctly identified the breeds of 410 of the 414 dogs.

Using statistical techniques, the scientists also identified four clusters of breeds. The clusters include oldest, hunting, guarding, and herding dogs.

Scientists traced the ancestry of the oldest group of dogs to Asia and Africa. The scientists reported that the DNA of the oldest dogs is the most similar to wolf DNA. This diverse collection of breeds includes the Siberian husky, shar-pei, and *Akita*, a large dog originally bred in Japan. However, the Ibizan hound and Pharaoh hound, typically considered among the oldest dog breeds, did not fall into this ancient group. Dog breeders had thought these breeds descended directly from hounds pictured in 5,000-year-old Egyptian art.

The other groups of canines appear to have resulted from the efforts of Europeans to breed dogs for various purposes. The hunting dogs include such breeds as the bloodhound, golden retriever, beagle, and pointer. The mastiff, bulldog, boxer, rottweiler, and German shepherd are among the breeds in the guard dog category. Perhaps the most surprising group is the herding dogs, which includes not only the collie, sheepdog, and Saint Bernard but also the greyhound.

The researchers emphasized that they have not yet found genes that account for physical or behavioral differences between breeds, such as the gaze of a border collie or the spotted coat of a Dalmatian. But they now have a tool for studying genetic relationships between breeds. Researchers plan to use the data to improve dog health. By comparing the DNA of related breeds, scientists hope to determine the genes responsible for various diseases. Purebred dogs may contract at least 350 inherited disorders, including cancer, heart disease, and epilepsy.

■ David Haymer

See also **PSYCHOLOGY; SCIENCE AND SOCIETY.**

GEOLOGY

A study of rock from a chain of extinct underwater volcanoes stretching across the North Pacific Ocean has challenged long-held scientific theories about the formation of the Hawaiian Islands. The study was published in August 2003 by a team of researchers headed by geologist John A. Tarduno of the University of Rochester in New York. Specifically, the researchers suggest that, contrary to established belief, the *hot spot* that created the Hawaiian Islands drifted over time. (A hot spot is a column of *magma* [melted rock] that rises from deep inside Earth to form volcanoes on land or the ocean floor.)

The state of Hawaii consists of 132 islands that extend in a line approximately 2,900 kilometers (1,800 miles) to the northwest across the floor of the Pacific Ocean. The islands make up one segment of a lengthy chain of volcanoes that stretches some 5,800 kilometers (3,600 miles) from the Big Island of Hawaii to the Aleutian Islands, off the coast of Alaska. West of the Hawaiian Islands lies a series of *seamounts* (extinct volcanoes whose summits lie beneath the surface of the ocean.) At about 170° east *longitude* (the divisions used to mark east-west positions on Earth's surface), the direction of the seamounts turns abruptly northward. Those seamounts stretching to the north are known as the Emperor Seamounts.

Since the 1960's, scientists have believed that the Hawaiian Islands and Emperor Seamounts formed as the Pacific Plate slowly moved over a stationary hot spot. The Pacific Plate is one of about 30 rigid pieces, called *tectonic plates,* that make up Earth's outer surface. Many scientists believe that the island of Hawaii, which still has active volcanoes, sits above the hot spot now. They also believed the sharp bend in direction between the Hawaiian Islands and the seamounts resulted from a change in the orientation and direction of the Pacific Plate.

In an effort to obtain scientific evidence for this idea, Tarduno and his colleagues studied samples of volcanic rock collected from the Emperor Seamounts by the Ocean Drilling Program, a long-term international program that examines the composition of the ocean floor. To determine where the rocks formed,

SEE ALSO THE SPECIAL REPORT, **THE CORE: NEW FINDINGS ABOUT EARTH'S FINAL FRONTIER,** PAGE 76.

the scientists focused on the *paleomagnetism* of the rock samples. (Paleomagnetism refers to the orientation of magnetic minerals inside rock.) As lava cools, magnetic particles in the rock freeze in the direction of Earth's magnetic field at that time. By examining these minerals, geologists can plot the location of the rock's formation by longitude and *latitude* (the divisions used to mark north-south positions on Earth's surface).

Tarduno and his team theorized that if the Hawaiian hot spot had remained "fixed," all the volcanoes in the Emperor Seamounts would have formed at 19° north latitude, the present position of Hawaii's active volcanoes. However, they found that all the seamounts actually formed

HAWAIIAN HOT SPOT

The active volcanoes of the Hawaiian Islands (right) and the inactive volcanoes that form the Emperor Seamounts (far right) to the northwest of the islands were created by a *hot spot* as it drifted southward under the ocean floor, according to an August 2003 report by geologists at the University of Rochester in New York. A hot spot is a column of melted rock that rises from deep inside Earth to form volcanoes on land or the sea floor. Scientists had previously believed that hot spots remained relatively stationary.

farther north. For example, Detroit Seamount, now located just southwest of the Aleutian Islands, formed at about 35° north latitude.

Next, the scientists calculated the age of the lava samples by comparing their ratios of the elements potassium and argon. After volcanic rock solidifies, the potassium in the rock *decays* (breaks down and changes) into argon at a known rate. By comparing the ratio of these two elements in the rock, scientists can calculate the rock's age. The more argon a rock contains, the older it is.

The researchers found that the volcanoes sitting at the bend between the Emperor Seamount and Hawaiian Islands formed about 47 million years ago. They argued that if there had been a major change in the direction of

the Pacific Plate at that time, evidence showing a change in the orientation of magnetic minerals 47 million years ago should exist in the volcanic mountains along the edges of the Pacific Plate. However, rock samples from these mountains show no such evidence.

The investigators concluded that from about 81 million to 47 million years ago, the Hawaiian hot spot drifted south at a rate of about 4 centimeters (1.5 inches) per year. As it moved, it created the Emperor Seamounts. Then, for reasons still unknown to scientists, the hot spot stopped at 19° north latitude. It has remained relatively fixed at this location, creating the Hawaiian Islands.

Mountains and climate change. Climate change caused the rise of the High Andes, the highest section of the Andes Mountains, according to research published in October 2003 by earth scientists Simon Lamb of Oxford University in England and Paul Davis of the University of California at Los Angeles. The Andes Mountains stretch along the entire western coast of South America, from Cape Horn in the south to Venezuela in the north. The High Andes, which extend from Chile to Peru, make up the middle part of this mountain chain.

The Andes also lie along the western edge

WORLD BOOK map; image provided by National Oceanic and Atmospheric Administration, National Geophysical Data Center

GEOLOGY continued

of the South American Plate. Farther west lies the Peru-Chile Trench, a site where a tectonic plate is being *subducted* (forced down) into Earth's interior. This trench marks the boundary between the continental South American Plate and an oceanic plate called the Nazca Plate. At the trench, the Nazca Plate is being subducted under the edge of the South American Plate.

Lamb and Davis used a *computer model* (a digital simulation of natural processes) to analyze the geologic activity along the Peru-Chile Trench. The scientists theorized that the nature of the boundary between the Nazca Plate and South American Plate played a major role in determining the height of the Andes.

As an oceanic plate subducts beneath a continental plate, friction between the rubbing plates can push up rocky material along the plate boundary, forming mountain ranges. Lamb and Davis argued that if the Nazca Plate slid beneath the South American Plate with little friction, the resulting mountains would be low. However, a great deal of friction along the boundary would result in the formation of much higher mountains.

The two scientists reasoned that the amount of "lubricant" at the boundary would determine the amount of friction that would occur between the two plates. They proposed that the lubricant in this process was sediment carried into the Peru-Chile Trench by rainwater runoff from western South America. They theorized that the sediment would have formed a smooth layer that allowed the Nazca Plate to slide easily under the South American Plate.

Lamb and Davis suggested that the growth of ice sheets on Antarctica, beginning about 14 million years ago, caused a cooling of the Peru Current. This current flows northward along the western coast of South America from southern Chile to northern Peru. The cooling of the current would have resulted in a lower rate of evaporation from the ocean and less water vapor available in the atmosphere for precipitation. As a result, arid deserts developed in western South America.

According to the researchers, the dry desert climate provided little sedimentary runoff for the Peru-Chile Trench. Without sediment to serve as a lubricant, greater friction developed between the Nazca and South American plates. The increased friction caused the Peru-Chile section of the Andes to grow as much as 3 kilometers (1.8 miles) higher than the other sections of the Andes.

Slowest-spreading ridge. The first detailed description of the Gakkel Ridge, the slowest-spreading segment of Earth's *mid-ocean ridge,* has revealed surprising information about the segment's chemical composition. The findings were reported in June 2003 by a team led by geologist Peter Michael of the University of Tulsa in Oklahoma. The mid-ocean ridge is a chain of mountains that runs about 60,000 kilometers (37,000 miles) through Earth's oceans. These mountains build up as magma rises at the boundary between two tectonic plates. *Spreading* is a term used to describe the rate at which the material making up the plates on each side of the ridge moves apart.

The Gakkel Ridge lies north of Europe in the Arctic Ocean. The ultra-slow spreading rate in this area is about 0.6 centimeter (0.25 inch) per year. (Most segments of the mid-ocean ridge spread at a rate of a few centimeters per year.) The scientists used advanced *sonar* (devices that use sound waves to measure distance, direction, and speed) aboard research vessels to make detailed maps of the Gakkel Ridge. They also recovered samples from the ridge for study.

Michael's group concluded that the chemical composition of the Gakkel Ridge differs from that of other slow-spreading ridges. It consists mainly of *peridotite,* a greenish rock found in other slow-spreading ridges, and *basalt,* a black volcanic rock found in faster-spreading ridges. He also found that the Gakkel Ridge has much more *hydrothermal activity* than would be expected for a slow-spreading ridge. Hydrothermal activity results from seawater seeping down into the hot rocks of the mid-ocean ridge and then being expelled as hot springs on the sea floor.

Michael said his conclusions showed that the chemical composition and hydrothermal activity of mid-ocean ridges result from many factors in addition to the spreading rate. He added that further investigation of these factors will be necessary to better understand mid-ocean ridges.   ■ William W. Hay

See also **ATMOSPHERIC SCIENCE.**

MEDICAL RESEARCH

In 2003 and 2004, researchers continued to search for ways to prevent and treat Alzheimer's disease, AIDS, and the four most common cancers—lung, breast, prostate, and colorectal. They also uncovered an important clue about the process that leads to Parkinson disease and devised new tests to guide the use of antibiotics and to screen for ovarian cancer.

Gene therapy for Alzheimer's. A new treatment using *gene therapy,* reported in April 2004, may help slow the progression of Alzheimer's disease. (Gene therapy involves changing a person's hereditary material to cure an illness.) Alzheimer's is the most common form of dementia, causing memory loss, disorientation, and loss of reasoning abilities.

In 2000, about 4.5 million people in the United States had Alzheimer's disease, according to a study published in August 2003 by researchers at Rush University Medical Center in Chicago. The researchers expected that number to rise—to 13.2 million people by 2050—as the U.S. population ages.

For their treatment, neurologist Mark Tuszynski at the University of California in San Diego and his colleagues removed cells from the skin of eight patients with Alzheimer's disease. They inserted into the cells copies of a gene that *codes for* (carries the instructions for producing) a protein called nerve growth factor (NGF). Scientists believe that NGF protects *neurons* (nerve cells) in the brain from dying. Tuszynski's team then injected the cells modified with NGF directly into the patients' brains.

After about two years, the patients underwent *PET scans* and various psychological tests to detect any changes in the brain because of the therapy and the rate at which their thought processes declined because of Alzheimer's disease. (A PET—positron emission tomography—scan is a technique that uses small amounts of a radioactive chemical to track activity in various parts of the brain.) The PET scans showed that overall activity in the brains of all the patients had increased. In addition, the patients' mental decline had slowed to about 40 percent of the rate they experienced before the gene therapy was administered. The only other known treatment for Alzheimer's disease—medication—slows the rate of decline by only about 5 percent for a period of about six months.

SEE ALSO THE SPECIAL REPORT, **SEEING BENEATH OUR SKIN: IMAGING THE BODY,** PAGE 90. SCIENCE STUDIES, **WHY ARE WE GETTING FATTER? THE PUZZLE OF OBESITY,** PAGE 120.

Although the researchers were highly optimistic about the results of the trial, they cautioned that the group of patients they had studied was too small to declare the treatment a success with complete certainty. They planned to conduct additional trials with greater numbers of participants.

Clues to Parkinson disease. Excess copies of a normal form of a gene called alpha-synuclein may cause Parkinson disease. A group of researchers from several institutions, including the U.S. National Institutes of Health in Bethesda, Maryland, reported those findings in October 2003.

Parkinson disease, also called Parkinsonism, occurs when the brain cells that control movement are gradually destroyed. People with Parkinsonism experience tremors, rigid limbs, slowness of movement, and faulty balance and coordination. Parkinson disease affects more than 1 million people in the United States.

Researchers identified a link between Parkinson disease and *mutations* (changes) in the alpha-synuclein gene in 1996, in studies of families in which the disease was common. In the 2003 study, researchers analyzed blood sampled from another large family, many of whose members had a rare form of early-onset Parkinson disease. However, the researchers found no abnormalities in the alpha-synuclein gene among these family members.

When the investigators reexamined the second family's gene, located on *chromosome* 4, they found four copies of it, rather than the expected two. (Chromosomes are the threadlike structures that carry genes in cells. Each person inherits two chromosomes, one from each parent.) Three copies of the alpha-synuclein gene appeared on one chromosome 4, and one copy appeared on the other. This overabun-

MEDICAL RESEARCH continued

dance of the gene, which codes for a protein called synuclein, leads to an excess build-up of synuclein that the researchers believe causes Parkinson disease.

The researchers noted that the study provides clues to understanding other *neurological* (brain and nervous system) diseases as well. For example, people with Down syndrome have an abnormal amount of a protein called beta-amyloid, which also accumulates in the brains of people with Alzheimer's disease. Investigators believe that processes similar to those that cause the alpha-synuclein gene to multiply may underlie Down syndrome, Alzheimer's disease, and other diseases in which proteins accumulate in and around brain cells.

Blood test may cut antibiotic use. In February 2004, researchers at University Hospital in Basel, Switzerland, reported that a simple blood test may help physicians decide whether to prescribe antibiotics for people with common respiratory infections. The test, which produces results in less than one hour, may help to reduce the overuse of antibiotics. Researchers believe that overuse of antibiotics

allows bacteria present in the body to develop defenses against medications.

Nearly 75 percent of antibiotic prescriptions are written for such lower respiratory tract infections as bronchitis and pneumonia, which may be caused by either viruses or bacteria. Antibiotics, which are effective against many types of bacteria, do not work against viruses. However, many physicians prescribe antibiotics for patients with such infections because tests to determine whether a particular infection is caused by a virus or a bacterium is costly and time-consuming. In addition, viral infections may lead to bacterial infections.

The blood test used by the Swiss team measures levels of procalcitonin, a protein made by the body. Bacterial infections cause procalcitonin levels to rise significantly, while viral infections cause levels to rise only slightly.

During the study, researchers led by physician Beat Muller tracked 243 people who were treated at the University Hospital emergency room for respiratory tract infections. About half the patients received standard care, consisting of a physical examination, chest X ray, and

NEW TOOL FOR EMERGENCY MEDICINE

The use of a new tool for administering medication or performing a blood transfusion when a patient's veins have collapsed won approval from the U.S. Food and Drug Administration in March 2004. The tool, called the EZ/IO and manufactured by VidaCare Corp. of San Antonio, delivers medication or blood directly to the bone marrow. Although doctors have used such a technique in infants for years, emergency personnel could not use it in adults because adult bones are harder and much more difficult to penetrate. Physicians estimated that the EZ/IO would save thousands of lives by allowing emergency medical technicians and doctors to quickly administer necessary fluids to such patients as accident or heart attack victims (right).

After the patient has received a local anesthetic, a technician uses the EZ/IO device to place a hollow needle in the person's *tibia* (shin bone).

Once the needle is in place, the technician removes the device, leaving behind the hollow needle and a base to which the tubing carrying the fluid can be attached.

A technician can either administer medication or perform a blood transfusion by attaching tubing carrying the necessary fluid to the base imbedded in the bone.

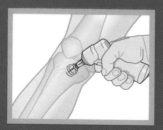

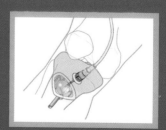

temperature check. The others received the blood test in addition to standard care. The researchers found that physicians who used the blood test prescribed antibiotics for only 55 out of 124 people. In contrast, they prescribed antibiotics for 99 out of 119 people who did not get the blood test. Both groups recovered at about the same rate. Patients who did not receive antibiotics did not suffer any ill effects. The researchers concluded that testing for procalcitonin levels can help reduce antibiotic overuse for lower respiratory tract infections.

HIV continues to spread. Human immunodeficiency virus (HIV), the virus that causes AIDS, continued to spread throughout the world in 2003 and 2004. According to estimates by the United Nations AIDS program (UNAIDS), 40 million people worldwide were living with AIDS in 2003. Also in 2003, 3 million people died of AIDS, and 5 million people were newly infected with the virus.

In the United States, the Centers for Disease Control and Prevention (CDC) in Atlanta, Georgia, reported that 900,000 people—the largest number ever—were living with HIV and 40,000 others became infected in 2003. However, the U.S. AIDS death rate during that year dropped to 16,000, mostly, researchers

believe, because of better treatment regimens introduced in 1996.

Antibody that fights HIV unraveled. In June 2003, an international team of scientists unraveled the structure of an *antibody* that is able to *neutralize* HIV (render it harmless). (Antibodies are proteins in the blood that fight infection.) The team was led by molecular biologist Ian Wilson and immunologist Dennis Burton at the Scripps Research Institute in La Jolla, California. Researchers had removed the antibody, called 2G12, in the early 1990's from a person who was HIV-positive but had never developed AIDS.

The researchers determined the structure of the 2G12 antibody by using a technique called *X-ray crystallography.* They forced the 2G12 protein to form a crystal and then deduced its structure by the way that X rays scattered when they hit the crystal's molecules. Unlike most antibodies, which are shaped like a Y with two outspread arms, the team found that 2G12 has arms that intertwine. Because of their shape, Y-shaped antibodies cannot bind to the sugar molecules that HIV uses to disguise itself from the immune system. The shape of 2G12, however, allows it to attach to the sugar molecules, blocking HIV from killing immune cells and using them as hosts in which to make more HIV.

The Scripps researchers planned to design an *antigen* that would trigger the body to produce 2G12. (Antigens are substances that prompt the immune system to fight off invading microorganisms.) Such an antigen may become the foundation of a vaccine against HIV.

Progress in HIV treatment. Other scientists in 2003 and 2004 continued to study the effectiveness of various treatments for people with AIDS. Researchers funded by the National Institute of Allergy and Infectious Diseases (NIAID) in Bethesda, Maryland, reported in December 2003 that the combination of anti-HIV drugs and the order in which they are given are important factors in treating people newly diagnosed with HIV.

Doctors who treat patients with HIV have long known that the most successful treatment regimens consist of combinations of anti-HIV drugs. Physicians use three or more drugs, from one or more different classes of anti-HIV drugs. Two of the most important classes are *reverse transcriptase (RT) inhibitors*, which prevent HIV from making copies of itself, and *protease inhibitors*, which block a later step in HIV reproduction. When effective, the therapy helps to

MEDICAL RESEARCH continued

suppress HIV's ability to multiply and, so, prevent the progression to AIDS and death. However, doctors have learned that, in many cases, the drugs become less effective over time, so patients must start taking new combinations of drugs. Until the NIAID study, doctors were not sure which drugs should be used first.

The first phase of the two-year study included 620 HIV-positive people in the United States and Italy who were receiving anti-HIV therapy for the first time. The study was led by clinical researcher Gregory K. Robbins at Massachusetts General Hospital in Boston. The researchers divided the patients into two groups, each of which received a specific combination of drugs. If the initial regimens did not work, the physicians prescribed all new anti-HIV drugs. The researchers measured success in time. The longer it took before a regimen ceased to work, the more successful the sequence was considered to be.

The second phase of the study was led by Robert W. Shafer, an assistant professor of medicine at Stanford University Medical Center in California. During this phase, researchers tested the effectiveness of four-drug versus three-drug regimens in 320 HIV-positive people who had never before received treatment.

The study results showed that all six drug combinations tested helped to control HIV infection. However, patients fared best for the longest period of time when they received the combination of zidovudine (also known as AZT), lamivudine (3TC), and efavirenz (EFV). All three drugs are RT inhibitors. AZT and 3TC belong to one subclass, while EFV belongs to another. The AZT-3TC-EFV combination also proved more effective than the four-drug regimens. The results of the study became part of the U.S Department of Health and Human Services HIV/AIDS treatment guidelines.

In April 2004, a three-year study of at least 1,100 patients revealed further evidence that the AZT-3TC-EFV combination is the most effective. The study was led by Roy M. Gulick, director of the HIV Clinical Trials Unit at Weill Cornell Medical College in New York City. Gulick's team showed that by using only RT inhibitors, patients avoided some of the dangerous side effects that may accompany the use of protease inhibitors, including liver damage and unsightly humps of body fat.

Cancer death rates. Death rates for the four most common cancers—lung, breast, prostate, and colorectal—declined in the United States in the late 1990's, according to a report released in September 2003 by the National Cancer Institute (NCI) in Bethesda, Maryland, a division of the National Institutes of Health. The report was based on research conducted by the CDC, the American Cancer Society, the North American Association of Central Cancer Registries, and NCI. The four cancers studied are responsible for more than half of all new cancer cases and deaths in the United States. Death rates for all cancers combined neither increased nor decreased during the late 1990's.

According to the researchers, trends in death rates and *incidence rates* (new occurrences) for the four most common cancers varied among men and women of different racial and ethnic groups. In black and white men, the death rate from lung cancer, the most common form of cancer, decreased throughout the 1990's. In women, the death rate continued to increase during the same period, but the rate of increase slowed. Researchers attributed the decreases to anti-smoking efforts.

Among both black and white women, breast cancer incidence continued to increase, although the rate of increase has slowed since 1986. Beginning in the early 1990's, death rates from breast cancer decreased, especially for white women. Decreases for black women were not as dramatic. Increased mammography screening and better treatments, according to the NCI, were at least partly responsible for the drop in breast cancer death rates and the increase in breast cancer incidence.

Although the incidence of prostate cancer has increased since 1995 in both black and white men, death rates from prostate cancer started to decline in 1994. Researchers are not sure why the incidence is increasing, but better screening may be one explanation. Prostate cancer rates increased sharply in the late 1980's after the introduction of the *prostate specific antigen test*, a blood test that indicates whether the prostate is enlarging. (An enlarged prostate may be a sign of cancer.)

Colorectal cancer death rates started to decline in the mid-1970's for both black and white men and women. Steeper declines oc-

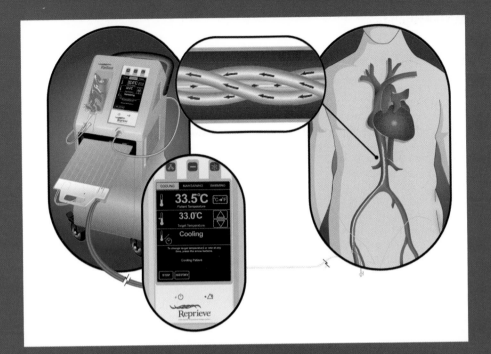

HOPE FOR HEART ATTACK VICTIMS

A treatment for heart attack victims that may significantly reduce the brain damage that often follows a heart attack won the endorsement of the American Heart Association (AHA) in July 2003. Brain damage can occur when a patient's heart stops beating and then begins to *fibrillate* (quiver), reducing the amount of oxygen being pumped to the brain. If the heart is not restarted quickly, the patient may experience brain damage or slip into a *coma* (a state of deep unconsciousness). The AHA recommended that physicians cool comatose patients, and then revive them slowly to lessen brain damage. One cooling method that has proven successful in tests on heart attack patients involves using a machine called the Reprieve Endovascular Temperature Therapy System, manufactured by Radiant Medical of Redwood City, California (above, left). Doctors insert a *catheter* (tube) into one of the body's largest veins (above, right). They then pump a cooling solution through the catheter (arrows, top center). The solution cools the blood around it to the desired temperature, which can be as much as 5 °C (9 °F) lower than a normal body temperature of 37 °C (98.6 °F).

curred in the 1980's. The decrease in the death rate among blacks lagged behind that for whites. Incidence rates of colorectal cancer decreased for all groups.

According to NCI Director Andrew C. von Eschenbach, the drop in the death rate for all four cancers shows that scientists' increased understanding of the disease, early screening programs, and improved treatments have led to more effective strategies for cancer control. Nevertheless, black men and women still do not experience the same screening and/or treatment as white men and women do. This disparity points out the need for new methods that will ensure that all people benefit equally from control strategies.

Early screening for ovarian cancer may become possible with a simple blood test. In October 2003, researchers led by oncologist Katherine R. Kozak at the University of California in Los Angeles reported on a highly accurate test that can be completed in 30 minutes using blood from a finger prick. The test was developed by Correlogic Systems, Incorporated, of Bethesda, Maryland.

Ovarian cancer has the highest death rate among all gynecological cancers. The cancer is often difficult for physicians to recognize until the disease has progressed. Physicians often confuse the bloating, stomach pain, and other symptoms of ovarian cancer with those for such digestive disorders as irritable bowel syn-

MEDICAL RESEARCH continued

drome. More than 85 percent of women with ovarian cancer are not diagnosed until the disease has progressed to a late stage. The five-year survival rate for those diagnosed early is greater than 90 percent. For those diagnosed when the disease has reached an advanced stage, the rate drops to less than 20 percent. According to the American Cancer Society, 23,000 women were diagnosed with ovarian cancer in 2002.

The Correlogic test measures previously undetectable changes in the levels of a wide range of proteins. Kozak's team analyzed the proteins in blood samples from 184 women using *mass spectrometry,* a technique that sorts proteins and other molecules based on their weight and electrical charge. Some of the patients had ovarian cancer; some had *benign* (noncancerous) tumors; and others were healthy. The researchers then used a computer program to analyze the patterns of proteins found in the women's blood, searching for patterns that appear during the early stages of ovarian cancer. They found that the Correlogic test identified the presence of ovarian cancer with 94-percent accuracy. The standard test for ovarian cancer, which measures levels of a protein called CA-125, is effective at detecting recurrences of ovarian cancer but detects only about half of new ovarian cancer cases.

In 2004, the Correlogic test became available to high-risk patients at the Lynne Cohen Cancer Screening and Prevention Project of High Risk Women at New York University and The Lynne Cohen Preventive Care Clinic for Women's Cancers at the University of Southern California in Los Angeles. In mid-2004, the widespread use of the test was awaiting approval by the FDA. ■ Renee Despres

See also **DRUGS.**

NOBEL PRIZES

The 2003 Nobel Prizes in science were awarded in October for discoveries of how molecules move through cell walls, research on substances with unique properties at supercold temperatures, and the development of a technique that allows physicians to see inside the human body with unprecedented clarity. Each of the prizes was worth about $1.3 million.

The Nobel Prize in chemistry was shared by biochemist Peter C. Agre of Johns Hopkins University in Baltimore and biophysicist Roderick MacKinnon of Rockefeller University in New York City. Agre and MacKinnon received the award for their work describing how proteins act as channels in the walls of living cells. These channels allow certain molecules to pass into and out of the cells while preventing other molecules from doing so. The movement of molecules through the channels helps cells perform such essential functions as filtering water from urine and producing electrical charges that make a heart beat.

Agre discovered a previously unrecognized protein in red blood cells and proved that the

 SEE ALSO THE SPECIAL REPORT, **SEEING BENEATH OUR SKIN: IMAGING THE BODY,** PAGE 90.

protein acts as a channel for water. He later produced a three-dimensional image of the protein that revealed how it acts as a filter for water molecules.

MacKinnon studied channels that filter *ions* (electrically charged atoms). Using a technique called X-ray crystallography, he determined the three-dimensional structure of a potassium ion channel. Agre and MacKinnon's research may lead to new treatments for such conditions as epilepsy and arrhythmia, in which the channeling processes are flawed.

The prize in physics was awarded to Vitaly L. Ginzburg of the P. N. Lebedev Physical Institute in Moscow; Alexei A. Abrikosov of Argonne National Laboratory in Argonne, Illinois; and Anthony J. Leggett of the University of Illinois at Urbana-Champaign. The three physicists contributed to an understanding of the unique properties certain ma-

2003 CHEMISTRY NOBEL PRIZE WINNERS

The 2003 Nobel Prize in chemistry was awarded for work describing how proteins act as channels in the walls of living cells, allowing certain molecules to pass in and out and preventing other molecules from doing so. The movement of the molecules helps cells perform such functions as filtering water from urine and producing electric charges that make a heart beat.

Roderick MacKinnon

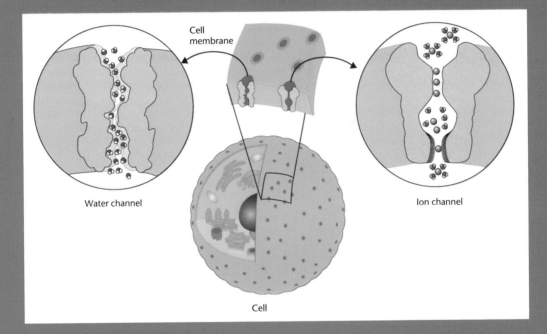

Cell membrane

Water channel

Ion channel

Cell

Peter C. Agre

The award was shared by biochemist Peter C. Agre (left) of Johns Hopkins University in Baltimore and biophysicist Roderick MacKinnon (top) of Rockefeller University in New York City. Researchers had long known that there must be openings in *cell membranes* (the walls that surround cells, above). Agre discovered a protein in red blood cells that acts as a channel or filter in the membrane for water (above, left) and provided three-dimensional images that showed how the protein functions. MacKinnon demonstrated how channels that filter *ions* (electrically charged atoms) work (above, right) and used a technique called X-ray crystallography to determine their structure. Both researchers learned that the channels are specific to a particular substance, such as a certain type of molecule or ion. That is, they allow only that particular substance to pass in or out of the cell and prevent other substances from doing so.

NOBEL PRIZES continued

terials and fluids exhibit at temperatures near absolute zero (–273.15 °C or –459.67 °F).

Ginzburg helped develop an equation that describes how *superconductors* behave in a magnetic field. (Superconductors are materials that conduct electricity without resistance at temperatures near absolute zero.) Ginzburg made his discoveries with Soviet physicist Lev Landau, who died in 1968.

Abrikosov built on Ginzburg and Landau's research, expanding the equation to show how one type of superconductor behaves at slightly higher temperatures. Leggett's work involved the related field of *superfluidity,* the study of the often-strange behavior of liquids at very cold temperatures. Supercold liquid helium, for example, flows with no resistance and so can travel up the side of a beaker.

The researchers' work contributed to such advances as the development of the medical technique called magnetic resonance imaging (MRI) and the design of fast-moving magnetically levitating trains. Such trains use magnetic forces to float above a fixed track.

The prize in physiology or medicine was shared by physical chemist Paul C. Lauterbur of the University of Illinois at Urbana-Champaign and physicist Sir Peter Mansfield of the University of Nottingham in the United Kingdom. The researchers received the award for discoveries that led to the development of modern MRI. (MRI is a diagnostic technique that allows medical personnel to view structures inside the human body and diagnose disease without performing surgery.)

Chemists first used MRI to see the structure of molecules. Lauterbur showed that because the human body contains so much water—a molecule made up of hydrogen and oxygen atoms—MRI, which detects the magnetic properties of hydrogen, could be used to create two-dimensional images of structures inside the body. Mansfield showed that using mathematics to analyze the MRI signals would speed the process, making the technique a more practical tool for diagnosis.

■ Kristina Vaicikonis

See also **CHEMISTRY.**

NUTRITION

Scientists using *genetic engineering* produced mice capable of converting a nutrient abundant in food into a related but less common nutrient known to help prevent heart disease in people. This finding was reported by J. X. Kang and colleagues from the departments of medicine and dermatology at Massachusetts General Hospital and Harvard Medical School in Boston in the February 2004 issue of *Nature.* Genetic engineering involves the altering of genes or genetic material to produce desirable new traits or eliminate undesirable ones in organisms.

The two nutrients are omega-3 and omega-6 fatty acids. Fatty acids are carbon-rich molecules that help form *lipids* (a group of organic compounds including fats and oils). The two types of fatty acids differ only slightly.

Mammals cannot produce either type of fatty acid, both of which are essential to

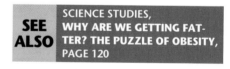

SEE ALSO SCIENCE STUDIES, WHY ARE WE GETTING FATTER? THE PUZZLE OF OBESITY, PAGE 120

health. They help stimulate skin growth, keep bones healthy, and regulate *metabolism* (the process by which the body converts food into energy). To ensure an adequate intake of omega-3 fatty acids, nutritionists recommend that people consume such foods as canola oil, walnuts, soybeans, and salmon. Omega-6 fatty acids are found mainly in meats, cereals, eggs, poultry, and most vegetable oils. In the United States, people generally follow a diet that contains more omega-6 fatty acids than omega-3 fatty acids.

The researchers already knew that the roundworm *Caenorhabditis elegans* carries a gene called fat-1 that *codes for* (carries the instructions for producing) a protein that converts omega-6 fatty acids into the more healthful omega-3 fatty acids. Human beings and most animals lack the fat-1 gene.

The scientists transferred the fat-1 gene into mice raised with control mice that did not receive the gene. Both groups of mice ate an identical diet that was high in omega-6 fatty acids but very low in omega-3 fatty acids.

When the researchers examined the two groups of mice, they found dramatic differences. Ninety-eight percent of the fatty acids in the tissues of the control mice consisted of omega-6 fatty acids, compared with 2 percent of omega-3 fatty acids. In contrast, the tissues of the mice with the fat-1 gene contained almost equal amounts of omega-3 fatty acids and omega-6 fatty acids. The researchers concluded that the *transgenic mice* (those with genes from another species) were able to change omega-6 fatty acids into omega-3 fatty acids.

The transgenic animals appeared to be normal and healthy. In addition, when the scientists bred these mice with one another, their offspring continued to produce high levels of omega-3 fatty acids for the four generations tested. The results showed that the inserted gene was active and capable of being passed on to future generations, the researchers said. The researchers noted that if farm animals could produce omega-3 fatty acids by means of genetic engineering, people could increase their intake of these acids without abandoning milk, eggs, meat, and other commonly eaten animal products.

Gene, diet, and atherosclerosis. A link between diet, genetics, and *atherosclerosis* (a disease characterized by fatty deposits on the walls of arteries) was reported in January 2004 by a group of scientists headed by James Dwyer, a professor of preventive medicine at the Keck School of Medicine at the University of Southern California in Los Angeles. The findings could lead to new dietary approaches for treating cardiovascular disease.

LOW-CARB CRAZE

In early 2004, several chains of fast-food restaurants started adding alternatives, such as burgers without buns, to their menus. The meteoric rise in popularity of such eating programs as the Atkins and South Beach diets—which stress eating high-protein, low-carbohydrate foods—prompted the change. Other changes included offering more salads as well as smaller portions of traditional items.

NUTRITION continued

Atherosclerosis involves an *inflammation* (a response by the body to injury or infection) of the arteries. Compounds called *leukotrienes* influence inflammation. An enzyme known as *5-lipoxygenase* (ALOX5) makes leukotrienes from polyunsaturated omega-6 fatty acids found in such foods as oils and eggs.

The scientists hypothesized that different forms of the ALOX5 gene *promoter* (which regulates gene activity) might influence the development of the disease. Because omega-6 fatty acids increase and omega-3 fatty acids reduce leukotriene formation, the researchers thought that diet might affect the number of leukotrienes ALOX5 eventually produces.

To test these hypotheses, the researchers examined 470 healthy middle-aged men and women for signs of atherosclerosis, including thickness in the arteries. The researchers also recorded each participant's diet over 18 months and measured fatty-acid buildup in their arteries. The diets had various amounts of omega-3 and omega-6 fatty acids. One as-

pect that the scientists considered was that the omega-3 fatty acids normally compete with other nutrients for the ALOX5 enzyme and reduce the production of leukotrienes.

The researchers discovered that people who did not have the common form of the ALOX5 gene were more likely to have thick artery walls, a sign of atherosclerosis. They also found that people with the high-risk form of the gene—about 20 percent of the participants—could reduce their level of leukotrienes and, consequently, decrease their risk of developing the disease by consuming more omega-3 fatty acids. Finally, the people who ate higher amounts of omega-6 fatty acids were more likely to develop atherosclerosis.

The scientists concluded that the ALOX5 gene is connected to atherosclerosis because it ultimately converts some fats into leukotrienes that can clog arteries. This discovery could lead to new treatments in fighting this disease. ■ Phylis B. Moser-Veillon

OCEANOGRAPHY

Scientists in 2003 and 2004 continued to gather evidence indicating that *global warming* (the gradual increase in the surface temperature of Earth) is altering fundamental systems on Earth. Such evidence came from oceanographic studies that measured changes in the ice surrounding Antarctica and in the salt content of waters in various regions of the Atlantic Ocean.

Sea-ice retreat. Australian researchers reported in November 2003 that the *sea ice* around Antarctica had shrunk by about 20 percent since 1950, apparently in response to warmer air and ocean conditions. Sea ice is frozen seawater that floats on the ocean surface. In contrast, glacial ice forms as snow piles up on land. The sea-ice finding was reported by oceanographers Mark Curran and Tas van Ommen of the Antarctic Climate and Ecosystem Cooperative Research Centre in Hobart, Australia.

The researchers based their conclusions

on an analysis of a gas called methanesulfonic acid (MSA), which is a byproduct of a chemical reaction carried out by sea-ice *phytoplankton*. Phytoplankton are masses of tiny photosynthesizing organisms—chiefly one-celled algae—that drift at or near the surface of oceans and other bodies of water.

The researchers compared samples of MSA found in a glacial ice core drilled from the Law Dome region of coastal eastern Antarctica with sea-ice data captured by Earth-orbiting satellites since the 1970's. They theorized that more extensive sea ice would harbor more MSA-producing phytoplankton and, thereby, introduce more of the gaseous chemical into the atmosphere. The researchers expected to find a direct connection between MSA concentrations in the glacial ice core and the extent of sea ice, and the ice core and satellite data confirmed this theory.

The researchers extended estimates of sea ice coverage backward in time using data

SQUID FLASHLIGHT

The finger-sized Hawaiian bobtail squid beams light below its body using a protein capable of reflecting light, according to a January 2004 study by researchers at the University of Hawaii in Honolulu. The light originates in microscopic bacteria that live on the squid. The researchers theorized that the squid illuminates water beneath its body to conceal its silhouette from potential predators.

from older segments of the ice core and the established mathematical proportion between the amount of sea-ice and ice-core MSA. Their analyses suggest that Antarctic sea ice remained stable from 1841 to 1950. After that time, however, sea ice began to disappear abruptly.

Atmospheric and oceanic warming—signs of climate change—could be causing the shrinkage of the sea ice, the scientists believe. Weather data show that air temperatures on the Antarctic peninsula have risen by 2.5 °C (4.5 °F) since the 1950's, for example.

Loss of sea ice could, in turn, accelerate global warming. Sea ice reflects sunlight, which helps limit the build-up of heat in the atmosphere. If polar regions held less ice, they might absorb more of the sun's warmth, and—in a self-reinforcing cycle—melt still more ice. Loss of sea ice could also disturb established ocean currents. Such changes could profoundly alter global climates because ocean currents strongly affect weather-producing conditions in Earth's atmosphere.

Salinity patterns in oceans. An oceanographic study jointly sponsored by scientific agencies in the United States and the European Union found that the *salinity* (saltiness) of vast regions of the Atlantic Ocean has changed dramatically since the 1960's. Uneven salinity in the oceans helps drive global systems of ocean currents, contributing to such climate patterns as the warming effect of the Gulf Stream on western Europe.

The study, published in the Dec. 18, 2003, issue of the journal *Nature,* showcased the research of physical oceanographers Ruth Curry of Woods Hole Oceanographic Institution in Falmouth, Massachusetts; Bob Dickson of the Centre for Environment, Fisheries, and Aquaculture Science in Lowestoft, United Kingdom; and Igor Yashayaev of the Bedford Institute of Oceanography in Dartmouth, Canada. Their analysis of ocean data collected since the 1960's revealed that tropical waters in the Atlantic Ocean have become saltier,

OCEANOGRAPHY continued

while polar waters have *freshened* (become less salty).

The researchers attributed the increase in salinity in the tropics to faster rates of evaporation caused by global warming. Warmer air evaporates water faster than cooler air does. According to the team's findings, the rates of evaporation in tropical and subtropical regions of the Atlantic have accelerated by 5 to 10 percent in the past 40 years. More intense evaporation concentrates salts in water.

Global wind patterns transport water vapor from the tropics to *higher latitudes* (areas closer to the poles than the tropics), forming clouds and producing *precipitation* (moisture such as rain or snow). The researchers theorized that heavier-than-normal precipitation, caused by the accelerated rate of water evaporation, has caused polar waters to freshen.

Other studies have revealed salinity changes in the Pacific and Indian oceans as well. Together with the Atlantic salinity data, these findings suggest that Earth is in the middle of a significant transformation in its *hydrological* (water) cycle. This transformation could have important implications for ocean current and precipitation patterns.

One effect of changes in ocean salinity patterns might be a weakening of the Gulf Stream. Normally, the sinking of relatively heavy, cold, salty water in the North Atlantic Ocean creates a "conveyor belt" effect, continually pulling warm waters from subtropical regions of the ocean northward.

That effect is responsible for the temperate climate of much of western Europe. Without Gulf Stream warmth, this vast region would be plunged into frigid winters. Disruption of ocean currents could also bring drought to world regions with productive agriculture.

MARINE CENSUS

A new species of scorpionfish, named *Scorpaenopsis vittapinna*, is one of a number of plant and animal species recorded by marine scientists in 2003. The effort to find and record plant and animal species in the world's oceans is part of an ongoing marine census project begun by researchers at Rutgers University's Institute of Marine and Coastal Sciences in New Brunswick, New Jersey, in the mid-1990's and now funded by governments and foundations around the world.

Dead dolphins in Florida. More than 100 dolphins washed up dead on beaches in the Florida Panhandle in March and April 2004. It was the largest dolphin kill since late 1999 and early 2000, when more than 160 dead dolphins washed up on beaches in the same region. In a normal year on the Florida Panhandle coastline, between 10 and 20 of the animals turn up dead.

In response, biologists with the National Oceanic and Atmospheric Administration in Washington, D.C., began testing some of the dolphin carcasses to search for a cause of death. They found that *toxins* (poisons) produced during a "red tide" had likely killed the dolphins. A red tide refers to a sudden massive increase in populations of one-celled organisms called *dinoflagellates*. Huge numbers of the organisms turn waters chocolate brown or red. (Red tides have nothing to do with the regular daily rhythm of tides in the world's oceans and other bodies of water.)

The dinoflagellates in red tides produce various chemicals that are toxic to a number of living organisms. Fish and other organisms feed on the dinoflagellates, accumulating toxins in their bodies. When sea birds and mammals such as dolphins eat contaminated fish, they get sick and die.

Scientists are unsure why red tides occur. Some scientists believe that pollution containing high levels of nitrogen and phosphorus spurs rapid growth of the dinoflagellates. Sources of this pollution include animal manure, paper mill waste, and lawn fertilizer. Other scientists have suggested that red tides are part of a normal cyclical pattern among dinoflagellate populations in the seas.

Ocean commission report. The preliminary report issued by the 16-member U.S. Commission on Ocean Policy in April 2004 called for sweeping changes in U.S. ocean policies to reverse decades of overfishing and pollution. The commission was created by Congress in 2000 and appointed by President George W. Bush. The commission submitted the draft report to the nation's 50 governors, a first step in a review process that was to involve the president and, finally, Congress.

The commission made nearly 200 specific recommendations for action by Congress, the executive branch, and state governments. Retired Admiral James D. Watkins, who chaired the commission, said the changes were urgently needed because the nation's ocean resources "are in trouble." Key among the commission's recommendations was a plan to streamline the activities of the many state and federal agencies that now attempt to manage ocean resources. Another key proposal suggested creating a Cabinet-level National Ocean Council to advise the president on ocean-related issues. Funding for ocean management under the new plan would come from royalties on offshore drilling profits earned by oil and gas companies.

The commissioners spent nearly three years reviewing local, state, and federal programs and agencies concerned with ocean management. They held 15 public meetings across the country to listen to concerns of environmentalists, fishing industry representatives, oil industry representatives, scientists, and other citizens and citizen groups. The commission's report represents the most comprehensive review of ocean policies in the United States since 1969.

Oceans and human health. Two leading science agencies in the United States in April 2004 announced the creation of four new centers to study the oceans and human health. The agencies are the National Science Foundation (NSF) in Arlington, Virginia, and the National Institute of Environmental Health Sciences (NIEHS) in Research Triangle Park, North Carolina. The NSF and the NIEHS pledged funding over a five-year period to support the new facilities at the University of Washington at Seattle; the University of Hawaii at Honolulu; the University of Miami in Florida; and Woods Hole Oceanographic Institution in Falmouth, Massachusetts.

The four centers are to study *microbial pathogens* (one-celled, disease-causing organisms) in ocean waters and toxins that can taint fish and shellfish eaten by people. Researchers will also investigate health risks of chronic water pollution on swimmers, divers, surfers, and others who have regular contact with coastal ocean waters.

Researchers at some of the centers will search for new medicines from the seas. The scientists plan to test compounds extracted from tropical sponges and other marine organisms for anti-cancer, anti-inflammatory, and germ-killing properties. Drug companies could develop new medicines from the researchers' findings. ■ Christina S. Johnson

See also **CONSERVATION; ENVIRONMENTAL POLLUTION.**

PHYSICS

The most precise limits yet achieved for the *mass* (amount of matter) of *neutrinos* were reported in September 2003 by physicists at the Sudbury Neutrino Observatory (SNO) near Sudbury, Canada. Neutrinos are any of three types of extremely light subatomic particles that have no electric charge. Physicist Arthur McDonald of Queen's University in Kingston, Ontario, headed the international team that measured these exotic particles. The measurements helped physicists fill in the details of the *Standard Model,* the theory which explains the behavior of all known subatomic particles. Among these gaps is the debate over whether neutrinos have mass, a topic of much discussion among physicists.

Neutrinos belong to a family of *fundamental* (basic) particles called leptons. Three members of this family carry an electric charge—the *electron* (any of the negatively charged particles that orbit the *nucleus* [central part] of an atom), the *muon,* and the *tau.* Muons and taus are also negatively charged but are much heavier than electrons. Each of these charged leptons has an electrically neutral counterpart—the electron neutrino, the mu neutrino, and the tau neutrino. Neutrinos are produced in nuclear reactions in stars and in the breakdown of some chemical elements.

Neutrino interactions. The interaction of neutrinos with other particles is governed by a force called the *weak interaction.* This force is so weak that vast numbers of neutrinos can pass through a massive amount of matter with hardly any of them interacting with the atoms in the matter.

On the rare occasions when a neutrino interacts with an atomic nucleus, the neutrino may be transformed into its charged companion lepton. This transformation allows scientists to identify which type of neutrino is present. For example, if an electron neutrino is present, a special apparatus in the neutrino observatory detects an electron.

A neutrino observatory's detector must be as massive as possible to maximize the chances that neutrinos passing through it will interact with the atoms in the detector. Even then, only a few neutrinos per trillion passing through the apparatus will interact and produce a detectable signal.

SEE ALSO THE SPECIAL REPORT, **THE SUPER-STRANGE WORLD OF SUPERSTRINGS AND EXTRA DIMENSIONS,** PAGE 106.

The sun is the most powerful source of the neutrinos that scientists can detect during their experiments. The sun produces energy through nuclear reactions in which hydrogen atoms are *fused* (combined) together into helium atoms. These solar reactions produce two electron neutrinos for every helium nucleus that they generate.

Neutrino detectors and oscillation. In the late 1960's, a research team led by physicist Raymond Davis of the Brookhaven National Laboratory near Upton, New York, became the first to detect these so-called "solar neutrinos." The team used a detector deep inside the Homestake gold mine in South Dakota's Black Hills.

Neutrino detectors must be deep underground to avoid interference from the continual hail of background radiation that is always present at and near Earth's surface. Davis, however, reported detecting fewer electron neutrinos than the researchers expected, based on the known rate at which the sun produces energy.

Continued research with underground detectors pointed to an inherent property of neutrinos called *neutrino oscillation* to explain the shortfall in electron neutrinos from the sun. Neutrino oscillation is the process by which neutrinos of one type are transformed into other types as they travel from their source to the detector. Physicists believe that, because of this process, some electron neutrinos produced in the sun change into mu and tau neutrinos before they reach detectors on Earth. According to the Standard Model, neutrino oscillations can take place only if neutrinos have mass and if the masses of the three types of neutrinos are different from one another. However, all attempts to measure neutrino masses directly have indicated that the particles are far too small to detect. In order to overcome this problem, the SNO team developed an indirect method to measure neutrino masses.

The heart of the SNO detector is a spherical

SCIENCE IS SWEET

Researchers at Princeton University in New Jersey reported in February 2004 that, when poured randomly into a large container, *spheroids* (partially flattened shapes like M&M candies) pack more densely than perfect spheres. Physicist Paul Chaikin (far left) and chemist Salvatore Torquato (left) explained that spheres cannot be rotated sideways by each other (below, left), so they are limited in their ability to make a tight fit. M&M-type shapes, however, can be rotated by each other (below, center), allowing more of them to come together into a dense packing (below, right). The scientists said this finding could have implications for the design of high-density ceramic materials.

tank containing 1,000 metric tons (1,100 tons) of *heavy water*—that is, water in which all the hydrogen nuclei consist of the *isotope* (form) hydrogen-2, also called deuterium. Deuterium nuclei contain both a *proton* (positively charged particle) and a *neutron* (electrically neutral particle). In contrast, "regular" hydrogen nuclei contain only a proton.

Neutrinos produce one of two reactions when they encounter deuterium nuclei. In the *neutrino absorption reaction*—which can be brought about only by an electron neutrino—an electron neutrino is converted into an electron. In the *deuteron breakup reaction,* the deuterium nucleus breaks up into a neutron and proton. All three types of neutrinos can produce this reaction.

The SNO detector can record the neutrino absorption reaction when the electron emits a faint flash of light as it passes through the heavy water. The light is detected by thousands of *phototubes,* sensitive electronic eyes

that convert the light energy into electrical signals. The signals are fed into a computer that identifies the reaction. SNO records the breakup reaction when the neutron is absorbed by the nucleus of another deuterium atom, resulting in a distinguishable flash of light.

The SNO team reasoned that the "missing" neutrinos were likely recorded in the deuteron breakup reaction. If that were the case, precise measurements of this reaction would shed light on the neutrino oscillation rates. And because neutrino oscillation rates depend on the squares of neutrino mass, the physicists hoped to arrive at a firm estimate of neutrino mass.

Unfortunately, the deuterium did not absorb all the neutrons from the breakup reaction, resulting in imprecise measurements of this reaction. To increase the accuracy of the measurements, the SNO researchers dissolved ordinary salt—sodium chloride—in the heavy

PHYSICS continued

water. A strong absorber of neutrons, the chlorine in the salt increased the number of neutrons absorbed during the breakup reaction. This, in turn, improved the accuracy of the measurements of the breakup reaction.

The SNO results provided the first reliable estimates of the oscillation rates. These rates indicated that electron neutrinos are at least 10 million times lighter than electrons, the lightest-known particles of matter whose mass had previously been measured.

The SNO researchers noted that much more precise measurements of neutrino masses would become possible when science develops a better understanding of the oscillations that take place between the types of neutrinos. In 2004, experiments focused on these oscillations were making the study of neutrino mass one of the most important research areas of fundamental physics and the Standard Model.

Playing DataTAG at CERN. A new record for high-speed data transmission was achieved in December 2003 by an international collaboration of physics laboratories—23.2 *gigabits* (billions of bits) per second. A *bit,* or *binary digit,* is any of the 0's or 1's that make up the digital language of computers. At this incredible rate, a computer user could download a full-length motion picture from the Internet in only two seconds.

At the forefront of this revolution in high-speed communication was CERN, the European physics laboratory near Geneva,

SCIENTISTS DISCOVER STRANGE NEW PARTICLE

Evidence for the existence of an exotic subatomic particle called the *pentaquark* was described in June 2003 by physicists at the Thomas Jefferson National Accelerator Facility in Newport News, Virginia. The physicists blasted the *nucleus* (central part) of a deuterium atom with gamma rays. The rays interacted with the nucleus's proton and neutron, which each consist of three subatomic particles called *quarks.* This led to the creation of a pentaquark, consisting of four quarks and one *antiquark* (which has the opposite charge to a quark). The pentaquark broke down into a neutron and a particle called a *meson.* Further support for the existence of the pentaquark came from other labs in 2003 and 2004.

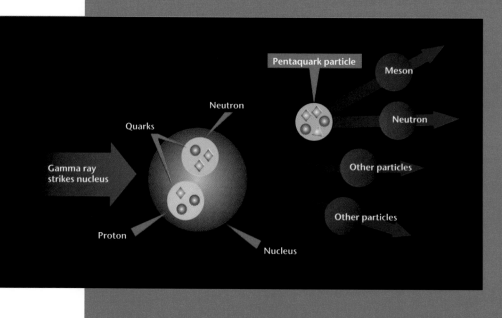

Switzerland, where British computer scientist Tim Berners-Lee developed the *World Wide Web* (Web, for short) in the early 1990's. (The Web is a system of computer files linked together on the Internet that includes sounds, pictures, and moving images as well as text.)

At CERN and similar laboratories, *particle accelerators* (machines that slam subatomic particles together or into a special target to create other particles) generate data at incredible rates. A single collision between two subatomic particles may generate many gigabits of data, and such collisions happen several times every second at CERN. The need to manage and share such complex data led Berners-Lee to develop the Web.

As particle physics research advanced and became increasingly complicated, CERN's data transmission needs grew. In the late 1990's, CERN and many other European and American institutions set out to create a faster, higher-performance Internet for the use of scientists. By 2003, an experimental data superhighway called "DataTAG" was setting new speed records every few months. Physicists set the latest record by using several *servers* (central computers that provide data to an interconnected group of computers) in the United States to send data to CERN and other sites in Europe, Asia, and the United States.

DataTAG works by fully exploiting a technology called *wavelength multiplexing*, in which scientists may insert many channels into a single *optical fiber* (a glass or plastic fiber that transmits information as rapidly flashing light). The light in each channel flashes a different wavelength. The speed of the data transmission increases with the number of wavelengths added to a fiber. Scientists believe that because an individual fiber should be able to handle hundreds of different wavelengths, transmission speeds may be virtually unlimited.

Researchers were still perfecting the DataTag network in mid-2004. However, many physicists believed that superfast networks of computers located around the world would, within a few years, make it much easier for them to attempt to solve some of the most complex, challenging computations in physics.

The smiling soprano. Opera fans often complain that it is hard to understand what the heroine, who is usually a *soprano*, is singing about—even when the opera is in the listener's language. (A soprano is a woman singer with the highest vocal range.)

In January 2004, physicists at the University of New South Wales in Sydney, Australia, described how this problem might result from a conflict between basic physics and the anatomy of the vocal tract. The three authors of the report are musicians as well as physicists: John Smith, a composer and woodwind player; Joe Wolfe, a double bass player; and Elodie Joliveau, a soprano.

Opera singers are trained to sing loud enough to be heard in a large concert hall without *amplification* (an increase in the strength of a sound). To do so, the physicists explained, the singers must exploit the *resonance* of the human voice—that is, the ability of the vocal tract to amplify sounds.

The vocal tract, which extends from the throat through the mouth, is shaped somewhat like an organ pipe. Its natural resonant *frequency* (the number of sound waves that pass a given point each second) depends on its length. The shorter the vocal tract (or the organ pipe) the higher the frequency and the more resounding the sound.

Singers can adjust the length of their vocal tract by changing the shape of their mouth. When a singer's mouth opens wide, the tract ends at the back of the mouth, producing the shortest length and, thus, the highest frequency. By altering the shape of her mouth with her lips and tongue, a soprano can extend her vocal tract forward, creating lower resonant frequencies.

According to the scientists, people ordinarily use these same lip and tongue movements to produce the distinct vowel sounds that make words understandable. When a soprano sings in the upper end of her range—the octave above high C—she usually opens her mouth wide and smiles to move the resonance up into the high octave. This action makes all the vowels sound more or less the same. As a result, listeners find it difficult to tell whether the singer is saying, for example, "hard," "hoard," "heard," or "who'd."

The physicists noted that technicians could resolve this problem by equipping sopranos with wireless microphones and training them to use their mouths differently. However, such changes would challenge centuries of opera tradition. To deal with this problem, many opera houses project the words being sung on a small screen above the stage.

Welcome element 110. The official list

PHYSICS continued

of named chemical elements gained a new member in August 2003, when the International Union of Pure and Applied Chemistry (IUPAC) in Research Triangle Park, North Carolina, approved the name *darmstadtium*—and the chemical symbol *Ds*—for element 110. IUPAC is the recognized world authority in crediting the discovery of elements and assigning names to them. A team headed by physicist Sigurd Hofmann first created the short-lived element at the Institute for Heavy Ion Research (GSI) in Darmstadt, Germany, in 1994.

Hofmann's group used a particle accelerator at GSI to produce an *ion* (electrically charged atom) beam of nickel-62, an isotope of nickel. The nickel-62 beam collided with a target of lead-208 atoms. The scientists adjusted the beam's energy so that the mutual electrical repulsion of the nickel and iron isotopes would slow the beam to zero *relative velocity* (the rate at which an object moves in relation to another object) when it neared the target. This action allowed the nuclei of the nickel and lead to combine into a single new nucleus—element

110. (The number *110* refers to the element's *atomic number*—that is, the number of protons in the nucleus of the atom.)

This heavy, combined nucleus was extremely unstable, immediately shedding a neutron. It then underwent a series of *radioactive decays,* in which one element changes into another element when the numbers of protons or neutrons in its nucleus change. The process of decay gives off a type of radiation, called alpha radiation, which can be measured to determine the mass and atomic number of the nuclei involved. These measurements pointed to the presence of element 110.

The same group of physicists that discovered element 110 also reported evidence in the 1990's for the existence of elements 111 and 112. As of mid-2004, however, these even heavier elements awaited confirmation by the strict standards of IUPAC, and names had not yet been approved for them.

■ Robert H. March

See also **ASTRONOMY; CHEMISTRY; ENGINEERING; NOBEL PRIZES.**

PSYCHOLOGY

Depression has a significant effect on the body's immune system, according to a multidisciplinary team of physicians, psychologists, and scientists at Ohio State University in Columbus. The team reported its findings in October 2003.

Researchers had known for more than a decade that depression is associated with higher-than-normal rates of *chronic* (long-term) medical illnesses, such as heart disease, Alzheimer's disease (a slow deterioration of thinking and memory functions), arthritis, and cancer. These illnesses are all related, by varying degrees, to *inflammation,* the body's reaction to infection or damage to its tissues.

Inflammation begins when, for example, we catch a cold or the flu or when we cut ourselves. Our bodies release chemicals called cytokines into the bloodstream or into tissues.

The cytokines attract immune cells to the area that was injured or invaded by bacteria or viruses. The immune cells attack the bacteria or viruses or send repairing substances into the damaged tissues.

Although immune responses are necessary for our health, inflammation that is either too severe or that lasts too long can damage the body and lead to illness. The research team at Ohio State had already begun studying the effects of stress on health in a group of older adults. The group decided to look more closely at the relationship between depression and the body's inflammatory response to influenza virus vaccination.

Normally, a vaccine triggers a small inflammatory reaction. The reaction stimulates the immune system to protect the body against infection by that particular virus. The researchers theorized that people who were more depressed might have a more severe and/or prolonged inflammatory reaction to the vaccine.

The study authors administered a regularly scheduled influenza vaccine to 119 adults whose average age was 71. The researchers took blood samples from the study participants before administering the vaccine and then again two weeks later to measure the amount of a cytokine called interleukin-6 (IL-6) in their blood. The adults also answered questions about symptoms associated with depression, such as sad mood, low energy, low appetite, and poor sleep.

The researchers found that people who reported more depressive symptoms also had higher levels of IL-6—both before and after receiving the vaccine—than people who reported fewer depressive symptoms. The researchers reasoned that even modest levels of depression in older adults may make the inflammatory response system more sensitive and, so, may lead to greater and more prolonged inflammation. They concluded that depression may lead to long-term medical illness by causing more chronic inflammation.

Genes, stress, and depression. Stress can cause depression in individuals who carry a particular form of a gene. That finding was reported in July 2003 by a team of researchers at the University of Wisconsin in Madison, King's College in London, and the University of Otago in Dunedin, New Zealand.

Researchers have long known that stressful life events lead to depression in some people, particularly those with a genetic *predisposition to* (tendency toward) depression. However, the genes involved in this predisposition were unknown. Because researchers had been unable to find a single gene that causes depression, they had presumed that many different genes act together to increase the risk of depression.

The international team studied a gene called 5-HTT as a possible candidate for creating a predisposition to depression. The 5-HTT gene produces a protein that transports an important chemical called serotonin across cells in the brain. Low levels of serotonin have been associated with depression. The team used a known *polymorphism* to distinguish two versions of the 5-HTT gene in a group of approximately one-thousand 26-year-olds from Dunedin, New Zealand. (A polymorphism is a subtle difference in the structure of copies of a gene either within one particular individual or between individuals.) Most people have two copies, called *alleles,* of each gene.

In the case of the 5-HTT gene, the researchers identified a short allele and a long al-

ANTIDEPRESSANTS MAY AFFECT BRAIN STRUCTURE

A three-dimensional image of the brain of a person with depression shows a *hippocampus* (indicated by arrows) that is about 10 percent smaller than the same brain structure in people without depression. (The hippocampus controls learning and memory.) Psychiatrist Yvette Sheline of Washington University in St. Louis, Missouri, and colleagues reported finding the size difference in August 2003. Sheline also discovered that the hippocampi of depressed people who had not been treated with medication were even smaller. The researchers concluded that antidepressants may work by preventing further depression-related damage to the brain, as well as by easing symptoms of depression.

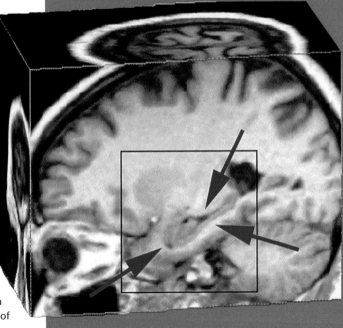

PSYCHOLOGY continued

lele. Approximately 20 percent of the study participants had two copies of the short allele; 50 percent had one short and one long copy; and 30 percent had two long copies. Several previous studies had demonstrated a link between the short allele and depressive features in animals. One study had shown such an association in people. However, no previous research had examined the relationship between short and long alleles, stress, and depression.

The researchers questioned the young adults about stressful events that had occurred in their lives during the preceding five years. These events included losing a friend, a job, or a home. The researchers also examined each study participant to determine whether that person had been depressed within the previous year. The researchers analyzed the responses using a statistical tool called *regression analysis,* which uses mathematical models to examine the relationship between pieces of data.

The researchers discovered that study participants who had experienced stressful life events and who had two copies of the short allele were much more likely to be depressed than those with two copies of the long allele. In fact, the young people with two copies of the long allele appeared to be resistant to the negative impact of stressful life events. The researchers concluded that stress plays a significant role in determining whether people born with a genetic predisposition to depression actually develop the illness.

The power of magnets. A group of researchers at Monash University in Melbourne, Australia, and at the Centre for Addiction and Mental Health in Toronto, Canada, reported in October 2003 on their studies of a novel treatment for depression. The treatment is called *repetitive transcranial magnetic stimulation* (rTMS). In rTMS, a physician places a strong magnet controlled by electricity near the head of the patient. The device creates a magnetic field that invisibly penetrates the person's head and affects the underlying brain tissue.

Researchers are still not sure how effective the treatment is, nor do they know what the proper dose of electric stimulation should be or how best to position the apparatus. Some researchers have found that slow pulses of magnetic energy applied to the right side of the brain are most effective for treating people with depression. Others have had success with fast pulses to the left side of the brain of depressed individuals.

The researchers in Australia and Canada designed a study that would test the effectiveness of both methods by randomly assigning people to one or the other treatment or to a similar-appearing treatment without the magnetic activity (a so-called "sham"). They wanted to determine whether the magnetic activity itself benefits patients, or whether the benefit comes from the interaction with the physician or the act of being placed near a piece of equipment. The team was particularly interested in studying people with treatment-resistant depression, those whose depression had not responded to several different anti-depressant medications.

Sixty patients with treatment-resistant depression were divided into three groups, composed of similar numbers of men and women. Each group received treatment with rTMS 10 times a day. The first group received a fast series of pulses from the magnet, applied to the left side of the head. The second group received a series of slow pulses to the right side of the head. A third group received a "sham" stimulation in which a physician held the equipment to their head but did not administer a magnetic pulse. A physician checked each person's degree of depression before and after the treatments.

After two weeks of treatment, depression in both groups receiving the magnetic stimulation had significantly lessened, compared with the "sham" group, though improvement was relatively modest in both treatment groups. Both treatment groups—those receiving fast pulses and those receiving slow pulses—improved to the same degree. After two additional weeks of treatment, both groups of patients improved even further.

The researchers interpreted these findings to mean that either fast or slow rTMS could help patients with depression, particularly those who had not been helped by anti-depressant medications. However, they noted that the slow rTMS had fewer side effects, such as scalp irritation, headaches, and seizures. ■ Michael Murphy

See also **GENETICS.**

Autism: Reaching for the Light

Daniel was a model baby. At 6 months, he could sit up and crawl. At 10 months, he could walk and say a few words. But at 18 months, Daniel began to withdraw from his parents. He stopped talking and interacting with anyone and avoided all eye contact. He preferred to be alone, spending hours spinning the wheels of a toy truck. When his mother or father tried to take the truck from him, he fought and screamed.

Daniel later became obsessed with lights and ran through the house flicking switches on and off. When his parents tried to stop him, he threw tantrums, biting and kicking them. When Daniel was 3 years old, a pediatric psychiatrist determined that the boy's problems stemmed from autism.

Autism is a complex, lifelong biological disorder. It is one of a spectrum of conditions called Pervasive Developmental Disorders. At least 1 million people in the United States have autism, according to estimates from the Centers for Disease Control and Prevention (CDC) in Atlanta, Georgia. The authors of a 1999 CDC review of scientific studies on autism concluded that the disorder affects 1 in every 1,000 children.

Several studies since then have suggested that the number of children with the disorder is increasing rapidly. In May 2003, the California Department of Developmental Services in Sacramento, for example, reported that the number of individuals receiving services for autism in that state increased by 273 percent from 1987 to 1998 and by 31 percent from 2003 to 2004. These increases affected all racial and ethnic groups. Some researchers have argued that the number of cases of autism only appears to be increasing. They believe that a growing awareness of autism and the establishment of clear criteria for diagnosing the disorder in 1994 may be fueling the increase. Other researchers attributed the increase to population growth. The California researchers and others, however, are convinced that the number of children with autism is actually rising, though they are unsure why this development is occurring.

HARD WORK, MORE HOPE

A special education teacher helps a student with autism improve her spelling skills with the aid of an assistive learning device. Such individualized treatment, when begun early, can significantly improve an autistic child's progress in school, many experts believe.

Symptoms of autism

In general, children with autism have difficulty communicating and interacting with others. However, the symptoms vary, depending on the stage of life. Infants with autism generally are withdrawn, avoid eye contact, and become limp when picked up. Some may become rigid and arch their backs when held. Instead of exploring their environment, autistic infants may prefer to be left alone and may remain fixated on a single item or activity. They often do not appear to crave attention or affection and may even resist cuddling and hugging.

Older children with autism have little understanding that other people have different ideas, experiences, or points of view. They have trouble expressing their feelings and reading the feelings of others. Facial expressions and body language may be meaningless to them.

About 50 percent of children diagnosed with autism are mute, and many remain so throughout their lives. Some infants may babble and coo during the first months of life but then stop making sounds, often abruptly. Others eventually begin talking but only as late as 5 to 8 years of age. Autistic children who do speak often use language in strange ways. For example, they may repeat the same word or phrase regardless of the situation. Others "parrot" words and phrases or scramble their words. Even those who develop functional speech may not be able or willing to discuss anything outside their immediate situation. They appear to talk "at," rather than "with," others.

Children with autism characteristically repeat motions—rocking their entire body back and forth, wringing their hands, or toying with objects in repetitive ways. Many insist on strict routines and have strong food preferences. Changes in routine or diet may trigger extreme reactions, even violent behavior. Touch, sound, and light appear to overwhelm some autistic children. Others seem to be unaffected by pain, even after a serious injury.

The teen-age years can be especially difficult for children with autism. They generally become more withdrawn and less communicative. Behavior problems may worsen. About 25 percent of teen-agers with autism experience seizures, probably because of hormonal changes, according to researchers at the National Institute of Mental Health.

The puzzling nature of autism

Leo Kanner, a psychiatrist at Johns Hopkins University in Baltimore, was the first physician to describe autism as a distinct condition. In 1943, he published an article about 11 children who exhibited similar severe behavioral, communication, and social problems. He called the condition *early infantile autism*, a name derived from the Greek word *autos,* meaning *self.* Kanner first categorized autism as a mental disorder related to *schizophrenia*, a severe mental disease characterized by unpredictable disturbances in thinking. He speculated that bad parenting, particularly by cold, aloof mothers, caused autism.

Although Kanner later decided that autism was a biological condition, the medical profession was slow to follow his lead. As late as the mid-1960's, the scientific community called the condition childhood schizophrenia. A 1964 book titled *Infantile Autism* changed that belief.

The author, psychologist Bernard Rimland, persuasively argued that autism was not caused by bad parenting, after observing his own son, who had exhibited the symptoms of autism from birth.

Autism remains one of the most puzzling of childhood disorders more than 60 years after Kanner identified the condition. Although it is not a mental illness, autistic children often have other mental disorders. About 70 percent are mentally retarded, some severely. Yet 10 percent have average or even above average intelligence, and a few—a group known as autistic savants—display extraordinary mental skills that approach genius level.

What causes autism?

Most health professionals agree that autism results from abnormalities in brain structure or function, and they agree that heredity appears to play a role. When autism occurs in identical twins—who develop from a single egg and share the same genetic makeup—both twins have the condition an average of 60 percent of the time. When autism occurs in fraternal twins—who develop from separate eggs—both have the condition only 3 to 6 percent of the time.

Researchers, however, do not know what causes the abnormalities in brain structure or function associated with autism. They have studied a variety of possible causes—infections or other problems during pregnancy; exposure to mercury and other pollutants; inoculation with childhood vaccines; and higher-than-normal levels of serotonin, a chemical that acts in the brain and other parts of the body to influence many feelings, behaviors, and processes. With one exception, none of the research produced definitive results. In May 2004, the Institute of Medicine (IOM), part of the National Academies of Science in Washington, D.C., declared that there is no demonstrated link between vaccinations and the neurological abnormalities that lead to autism. The IOM based its conclusion on large-scale studies conducted in the United States and other countries.

One of the most intriguing studies into the roots of autism grew out of Leo Kanner's original 1943 description of the disorder. He noted that children with the disorder appeared to have larger-than-normal heads. A research project published in 2003 bore out Kanner's observations. Eric Courchesne, a psychologist at the University of California at San Diego, concluded that the brains of autistic children are slightly larger and heavier than those of normal children. The skulls of autistic children also are, on average, larger in circumference than those of normal children.

Researchers under Courchesne's direction analyzed the medical records of 48 autistic children. They found that autism appears to be linked to small head circumference at birth, followed by a sudden, excessive growth of head size in the first 6 through 14 months of life. Courchesne concluded that the "burst of extreme growth" was primarily

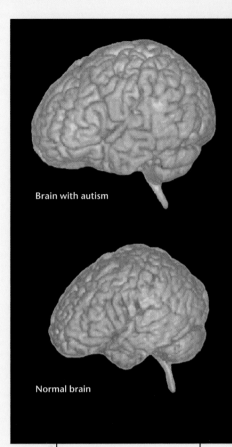

Brain with autism

Normal brain

BRAIN SIZE AND AUTISM

The brain of an autistic child (above, top) is larger than that of a normal child of the same age (above). In 2003, researchers at the University of California at San Diego reported that the heads of autistic children, on average, are smaller than normal at birth. However, such children experience excessive growth in head and brain size sometime between 6 and 14 months of age.

in the frontal cortex, which is the center of complex functions centered on perception, awareness, and the acquisition of knowledge. During the first year or so of life, brain cells develop in response and in proportion to a baby's first experience of the outside world. Courchesne speculated that too-rapid growth may produce so much "neural noise" that an infant might lose "the ability to make sense of the world and withdraw."

Reaching the autistic child

The Autism Society of America, an organization based in Bethesda, Maryland, that promotes lifelong access and opportunity for individuals with autism, provides information about treatments for children with autism. However, many professionals argue that only one type of treatment—applied behavior analysis (ABA)—produces comprehensive and lasting improvements that can be measured scientifically.

The ABA treatment developed from an experiment conducted in the late 1970's by O. Ivar Lovass, a professor with the Department of Psychology at the University of California at Los Angeles (UCLA). Lovass divided a group of children with autism into three groups. One was an experimental group, and the other two were control groups. The 60 children in the experimental group spent 40 hours a week in a highly structured program of behavior modification. The program involved constant repetition to enhance various skills—language and communication, social and play, learning, and independent living. UCLA students administered the therapy with the assistance of the children's parents. The children in the two control groups received only 10 hours of therapy a week, with no supplemental training by parents.

Lovass and his team compared the children in the three groups at ages 6 and 7. The researchers found that 47 percent of the children in the experimental group had been able to enter a standard grade school, complete normal first-grade classes, and earn promotion to the second grade. In contrast, only 2 percent of the children in the control groups could be placed in normal first-grade classes.

Lovass designed ABA in the belief that autism results from problems in the brain's *neurocircuits* (the nerve connections in the brain that transmit messages). He argued that the neurocircuits in the brains of autistic children do not work as efficiently as those in normal children. In the brains of normal children, neurotransmissions pass directly from points A to B to C. Lovass concluded that neurotransmission in the brain of an autistic child works indirectly—from points A to C to D before reaching B. He speculated that this inefficiency resulted in "excess neural noise," which blocks the development of social skills and learning. According to Lovass, when an autistic child learns a specific behavior through repetition, the therapy somehow teaches the brain to receive neurotransmissions that would otherwise be drowned out by the "excess noise." To be effective, however, ABA must be started early, conducted with sufficient intensity, and carried out with constant parental reinforcement of skills taught by therapists. ■ Renee Despres

PUBLIC HEALTH

A heat wave of historic proportions caused the deaths of an estimated 35,000 people in Europe during the first two weeks of August 2003. Climatologists at the University of Bern in Switzerland reported that the heat wave was the worst to affect Europe in at least 500 years. The Earth Policy Institute, an environmental research organization headquartered in Washington, D.C., stated that August 2003 was the warmest August on record in the Northern Hemisphere. Temperatures reached 38.5 °C (101.3 °F) in the United Kingdom; 40.8 °C (105.4 °F) in Germany; 41.5 °C (106.7 °F) in Switzerland; and 47.3 °C (117.1 °F) in Portugal. Some 11,000 people died in those four countries from heat-related causes.

SEE ALSO SCIENCE STUDIES, WHY ARE WE GETTING FATTER? THE PUZZLE OF OBESITY, PAGE 120

The greatest number of deaths, however, occurred in France, where more than 14,800 people died as the heat reached 42.6 °C (108.7 °F). The disaster overpowered France's health care system and caused a government scandal, as many hospital workers and most government ministers were away on month-long vacations when the crisis hit. Many of the victims were elderly people whose families were also out of town. Most French resi-

DON'T LET THE BEDBUGS BITE

Bedbugs crawl along the edge of a mattress (left). The pests had been all but eradicated in the United States by the mid-1900's. By the early 2000's, however, the tiny, bloodsucking bugs were back, attacking at night and leaving bite marks that appear as small, red, itchy bumps (below). According to the National Pest Management Control Association, headquartered in Dunn Loring, Virginia, an increase in foreign travel and decrease in the use of such pesticides as DDT have allowed the bugs to reestablish themselves and flourish. (DDT use was phased out in the United States after 1972 because of concerns that it endangered animals and contaminated the food supply.)

PUBLIC HEALTH continued

dences, businesses, and even hospitals do not have air-conditioning—which health care experts consider the best defense against heat-related deaths—because recorded temperatures had never before risen so high or remained elevated for so long in Europe. In November 2003, the French government announced that, beginning in July 2004, it would abolish one paid national holiday to fund a program to improve health care for the elderly.

The Intergovernmental Panel on Climate Change (IPCC) in Geneva, Switzerland, reported that Earth's surface temperature has risen by 0.6 °C (1 °F) since the 1970's. (The IPCC is an international group of scientists established in 1988 to assess the risks of climate change brought about by human activities.) The organization predicted that average temperatures—as well as severe heat waves and related deaths—would continue to rise through the end of the 2000's.

Teen pregnancies continue decline. By 2000, pregnancy rates among teen-agers in the United States had declined for the 10th straight year, according to a report published by the Alan Guttmacher Institute in February 2004. The institute, headquartered in New York City, conducts research and promotes education on sexual and reproductive health issues.

In 2000 (the latest year for which figures were available), 83.6 of 1,000 U.S. women under the age of 20 became pregnant, according to the institute. Although the decline from 1999 was small—only 2 percent—it continued a downward trend that began after teen pregnancy rates reached a peak of 116.9 per 1,000 young women in 1990. A similar drop occurred in the birth and abortion rates among teen-age women.

The researchers reported that the declines occurred among all groups of young women: black, white, and Hispanic. Teens in all 50 states were less likely to become pregnant, including those living in the District of Columbia, which had the highest rate of teen pregnancy at 128 per 1,000. (North Dakota had the lowest teen pregnancy rate at 42 pregnancies per 1,000 young women.)

The institute attributed the drop in teen pregnancy rates primarily to an increased use of effective contraception (responsible for about 75 percent of the drop) and, to a lesser degree (25 percent), to a decrease in sexual activity among teens.

Smoking and health. The rate of smoking among adults in the United States has decreased by nearly half since the first Surgeon General's Report on smoking and health was published in 1964. Julie Louise Gerberding, director of the Centers for Disease Control and Prevention (CDC) in Atlanta, Georgia, reported the development in January 2004. About 43 percent of U.S. adults smoked in 1965, compared with 23 percent—or 46.2 million people—in 2001 (the latest year for which figures were available).

Although tobacco use has dramatically declined, Gerberding pointed out that smoking remained the leading preventable cause of death in the United States, killing more than 440,000 people each year. In addition, at least 4,000 young people each day try cigarettes for the first time. According to CDC officials, cigarette smoking among high school students declined from 28 percent in 2000 to 22.9 percent in 2002. Nevertheless, among middle-school students, the percentage of those who smoked remained constant at 13.3 percent.

CDC researchers estimated that the economic costs of smoking in the United States average about $150 billion each year, including losses in productivity and in direct medical expenditures. About 8.6 million people are experiencing some type of smoking-related illness. The most common health problems linked to smoking were chronic lung diseases, followed by heart attacks.

Surveys conducted by the CDC noted that about 70 percent of people who smoke say they would like to quit. Nevertheless, fewer than 5 percent of smokers are actually able to stop smoking for 3 to 12 months.

Early influenza season. The 2003-2004 influenza season in the United States caused unusual anxiety among parents and health care workers alike. The illness began about one month earlier than usual—in October 2003—before many individuals had been immunized. In addition, the predominant strain of the flu, called the new Fujian strain, had not been included in preparations

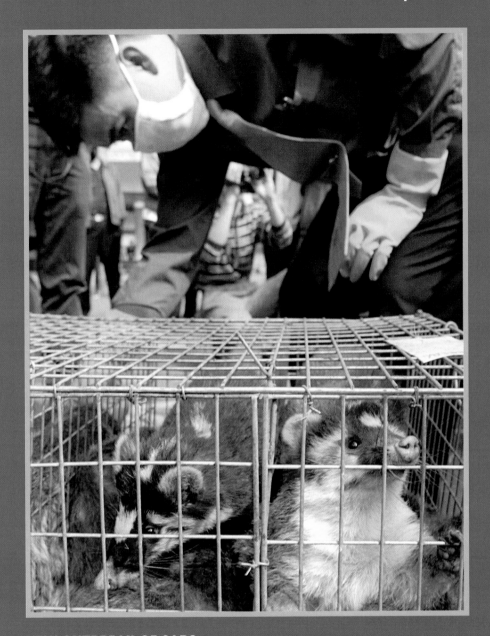

NEW OUTBREAK OF SARS

A health worker in Guangzhou, China, in January 2004 inspects confiscated masked palm civets. The animals, which resemble large weasels, are considered a delicacy in some parts of Asia, but *epidemiologists* (doctors who study the spread of diseases) suspect them of spreading the virus that causes SARS (severe acute respiratory syndrome). SARS is a *zoonotic* disease (one that can be passed from animals to people). It first appeared in China's Guangdong Province in November 2002. By the end of 2003, more than 8,000 people worldwide had contracted the disease and almost 800 of them had died of it. SARS is spread from person to person by respiratory droplets from a cough or sneeze or by touching an infected surface. Health care authorities had contained the spread of SARS by late 2003. The illness resurfaced briefly in Guangdong in December 2003 and January 2004.

PUBLIC HEALTH continued

of the annual vaccine. *Epidemiologists* (infectious disease experts) had suspected as early as February 2003 that the Fujian strain would be active in the coming flu season. However, it was already too late to include it in the formulations being prepared for the Northern Hemisphere. Manufacturers require at least eight months to produce a vaccine.

Early reports of children who had died of influenza in Texas and Colorado—among the first states to experience the new flu strain—spurred families in other parts of the country to demand the influenza vaccine. Normally, medical personnel administer about 80 million shots each year. Vaccine manufacturers usually prepare an additional 10 million. However, for the 2003-2004 season, vaccine manufacturers had cut back on the additional amounts of vaccine to save costs. The sudden rush and increased demand led to a shortage in some states.

In response to concerns over the deaths among children younger than 18 years, the CDC requested that state and local health departments report all fatal cases. By the end of the season, at least 143 children had died from influenza or its complications. In previous years, health authorities were not required to report influenza-associated deaths among children, so epidemiologists cannot accurately compare the 2003-2004 season toll to that of previous years. Nevertheless, some researchers estimate that an average of 92 children die of influenza each year. Public health officials estimate that influenza kills about 36,000 people, young and old, annually in the United States and sends 114,000 to the hospital.

In April 2004, CDC officials recommended that babies and toddlers receive annual flu shots because their immature immune systems leave them—as well as the elderly—particularly vulnerable to the illness. The American Academy of Pediatrics, based in Elk Grove Village, Illinois, and the American Academy of Family Physicians, based in Leawood, Kansas, had made similar recommendations in January.   ■ Deborah Kowal

SCIENCE AND SOCIETY

Charges of politically motivated interference in science swirled around Washington, D.C., during 2003 and 2004. A number of scientists and prestigious scientific journals accused the administration of United States President George W. Bush of suppressing or distorting findings of scientific studies on such politically controversial matters as climate change and abortion. Critics also charged the administration with appointing members of government science advisory committees on the basis of personal views or political affiliation rather than on scientific credentials.

On Feb. 18, 2004, the Union of Concerned Scientists (UCS), an environmental advocacy group headquartered in Cambridge, Massachusetts, issued a report entitled *Scientific Integrity in Policymaking*. The report alleged numerous incidences of the misuse of science. It included a statement calling on Congress to enact legislation that would restore integrity to the science used in making public policies. At least 60 prominent scientists, including 20 Nobel Prize winners, signed the statement.

John H. Marburger, III, President Bush's science adviser and director of the White House Office of Science and Technology Policy, defended the administration. He argued that the events cited in the report were not connected with one another and did not "add up to a big pattern of disrespect." D. Allan Bromley, who served as science adviser to President George H. W. Bush, father of George W. Bush, called the statement "politically motivated."

In August 2003, U.S. Representative Henry A. Waxman (D., California), a frequent critic of the administration, had issued a similar report prepared by the minority staff of the House of Representatives' Committee on Government

Reform. The Bush administration dismissed the report as political. Some political analysts suggested that the administration's actions were no different than those of previous administrations.

Stem cells and cloning. In a development that excited scientists but also reignited calls for a ban on all forms of human *cloning,* South Korean and United States researchers announced that they had succeeded in cloning some 30 human *embryos* and then extracting *stem cells* from one of them. (Cloning is the production of genetically identical organisms. Embryos are the initial stage of life. Stem cells are capable of developing into virtually any kind of human tissue.) The researchers described their achievement in the online version of the journal *Science* on Feb. 12, 2004. The announcement highlighted the ethical issues raised by cloning as well as the disadvantages faced by U.S. scientists in the intense international competition in this frontier of research.

The team of 15 scientists led by veterinary medicine professor Woo Suk Hwang of Seoul National University produced the clones using a technique known as *somatic cell nuclear transfer.* First the scientists removed the *nucleus* (the part that contains the genetic material) from the eggs of 16 women donors. Then they transplanted the nuclei from non-reproductive cells in the women's bodies to the eggs. They grew the embryos in culture for a week and then extracted embryonic stem cells from one of them.

Scientists are eager to explore the potential of stem cells for treating diabetes, heart disease, Parkinson disease, and other disorders. The advantage of creating stem cells by somatic cell nuclear transfer—also known as *therapeutic cloning*—is that researchers can produce stem cells that are genetically identical to a person's cells and, therefore, will not be rejected as some transplants are.

Some people are opposed to such research, however, because of concerns that it may one day lead to the development of techniques for *human reproductive cloning* (making babies that are exact genetic duplicates of cell donors). Other people object on ethical grounds because the embryos are destroyed in the process of extracting the stem cells.

The ethical debate over these issues has been ongoing in the United States since the late 1990's. Under a policy announced by President George W. Bush in 2001, embryonic stem cell researchers using federal funds are limited to *cell lines* (colonies) created before Aug. 9, 2001. Researchers in many other countries face no such limitations. The South Korean achievement led some U.S. scientists and policymakers to express concern that the federal restrictions may be undermining U.S. scientific preeminence and technological innovation. At the same time, some experts said, the United States may miss the opportunity to set ethical precedents.

Several states, meanwhile, had moved to promote stem cell research with non-federal funds under their control. The California legislature passed a law in 2002 permitting the use of state funds for stem cell research. In February 2004, New Jersey set aside $6.5 million in state funds as part of a public/private partnership that would support stem cell research there. Also in February, officials at Harvard University in Cambridge announced plans to create a stem cell research center with private funds. Researchers at other universities were conducting stem cell research with private funds by mid-2004.

Butler case. In December 2003, microbiologist Thomas Butler, an international authority on infectious diseases, won acquittal on charges of lying to federal authorities, though he was found guilty of several lesser charges. Butler had reported on January 13 that about 30 vials of *plague* bacteria were missing from his laboratory at Texas Tech University in Lubbock. (Plague is an infectious disease that has killed millions of people throughout history.) The next day, Butler signed a statement saying that he had accidentally destroyed the vials. Later, he claimed that he had been coerced by investigators into signing the statement and said that he had no idea what happened to the bacteria. The incident triggered an investigation by the Federal Bureau of Investigation and led to Butler's indictment on 69 federal charges stemming from the case. By mid-2004, authorities had not learned what happened to the vials.

Federal prosecutors initially charged Butler with 15 counts of lying to law enforcement officials. They later added other charges, including 44 counts of fraud, alleging he had kept for personal use payments from drug companies intended to fund clinical trials at the university.

SCIENCE AND SOCIETY continued

Many scientists supported Butler and established a legal defense fund for him. They believed that Butler had been indicted only because of the terrorist attacks of Sept. 11, 2001, on the United States and the letters containing *anthrax* (a bacterium that causes a potentially fatal disease) sent to several federal offices a few weeks later. These events heightened public concern about the threats posed by chemical and biological agents and led to the passage of laws imposing criminal penalties for mishandling such agents.

ENROLLMENT OF FOREIGN STUDENTS AT UNIVERSITIES IN THE UNITED STATES

A Chinese man hoping to study in the United States displays his passport, filled with numerous stamps that indicate his visa application has been denied by the U.S. Embassy in Beijing. The number of foreign students enrolled at universities in the United States during the 2002-2003 school year rose by only 0.6 percent (below)—the lowest since 1995, according to the Institute of International Education (IIE). The IIE is an organization located in New York City that monitors student exchange. Foreign students fill many research and teaching positions on U.S. campuses, particularly in the areas of science and engineering. Educators and administrators attributed the unusually small increase in foreign students to stricter visa guidelines after the Sept. 11, 2001, terrorist attacks on the United States. According to the IIE, lower enrollment by foreign students affects not only the number of candidates available for teaching positions, it also impacts universities financially—with a loss in the 2002-2003 academic year of about $12-billion in tuition and living expenses.

*Reflects change in number of students during the 2002-2003 academic year compared with number of students during the 2001-2002 academic year; latest figures available.

Source: Institute of International Education.

In December 2003, Butler was acquitted on the initial, most serious, charges. A jury found him guilty of 44 counts of defrauding the university and 3 counts related to his mishandling of plague samples sent to scientists in Tanzania with whom he was working. The Texas medical board suspended Butler's medical license, and he resigned his position at Texas Tech.

On March 10, 2004, a judge sentenced Butler to two years in prison, levied a $15,000 fine, and ordered him to pay restitution of $38,000 to the university. Butler's lawyers indicated they would appeal the verdict. Nevertheless, Butler's experience led several scientists to declare that they would be reluctant to engage in research related to bioterrorism for fear of similar repercussions.

U.S. science decline? Several public policy analysts expressed concern in May 2004 that the United States may be losing its position as a world leader in science. Analysts at the National Science Foundation (NSF) pointed out, for example, that U.S. inventors won only 52 percent of the patents awarded in the United States in 2003, down from 60 percent in 1980. The NSF is a federal agency headquartered in Arlington, Virginia, that promotes scientific research.

Diana Hicks, chair of the School of Public Policy at the Georgia Institute of Technology in Atlanta, noted the increase in patents and scientific papers by researchers in Asia and Europe. Rising standards of living around the world, as well as the difficulties foreign students and scientists encounter in getting *visas* (entry papers to the United States), are contributing to a decline in the number of researchers eager to live and work in the country, many experts believe.

In mid-2004, the United States still dominated many areas of science and technology. However, some analysts called for new efforts to address the declining interest in science among U.S. students. They also protested plans by the Bush administration to cut federal funding for areas of scientific research other than defense, national security, and the space program. ■ Albert H. Teich

See also **GENETICS.**

SPACE TECHNOLOGY

China joined Russia and the United States in the elite club of nations capable of sending human beings into space when it launched a pilot into orbit in October 2003 in a Chinese-built space capsule and rocket. Meanwhile, the United States took its first steps toward sending astronauts to Mars, even as it struggled to get its three remaining space shuttles into Earth orbit again by fixing the flaws that caused the shuttle Columbia to crash in February 2003. On the International Space Station (ISS), astronauts and cosmonauts performed science experiments and routine maintenance as they awaited the arrival of new components to complete the station.

During 2003 and 2004, the pace of unmanned space exploration quickened. Both the United States and Europe sent spacecraft to explore distant comets. Europe launched its first robotic probe to the moon and moved ahead on plans for both its own global positioning system and space shuttle. The United States launched a satellite to test aspects of

SEE ALSO

THE SPECIAL REPORTS,
FANTASTIC VOYAGE:
DISCOVERIES ON MARS,
PAGE 28.

FANTASTIC VOYAGE:
DISCOVERIES ON JUPITER,
PAGE 36.

the theory of relativity developed by German-born physicist Albert Einstein. On Mars, twin U.S. rovers named Spirit and Opportunity explored craters and drilled into rocks on opposite sides of the planet, while overhead, a new European orbiter called Mars Express returned spectacular pictures of the planet's surface.

First taikonaut in space. On Oct. 15, 2003, Yang Liwei, a Chinese air force pilot, became the first *taikonaut* (the Chinese word for *astronaut* or *cosmonaut*) in space. Yang orbited Earth 14 times in a Shenzhou spacecraft launched on a Long March 2F rocket.

SPACE TECHNOLOGY continued

(Shenzhou means *divine ship* or *magic vessel*.) Yang landed successfully in Mongolia 21 hours later, using parachutes and small retrorockets to cushion the capsule's impact.

Yang's spacecraft was a modernized version of Russia's Soyuz capsule, which can carry three crew members. China paid Russia, which in 1961 had sent the first person into space, to teach its taikonauts and engineers about space flight and then used that knowledge to develop its own space program. After Yang's flight, the Chinese government promised more missions with bigger crews as the Chinese gained experience and skill.

Columbia investigation. Scientists, engineers, and astronauts at the National Aeronautics and Space Administration (NASA) concentrated in 2003 and 2004 on getting the three remaining space shuttles—Discovery, Atlantis, and Endeavour—back into action. The first step was to determine what had gone wrong with Columbia and what changes were needed to prevent such a disaster from happening again.

In February 2003, NASA formed a panel of experts called the Columbia Accident Investigation Board (CAIB). Over the next six months, members of the CAIB examined all the technical data radioed back from Columbia in the final minutes before the spacecraft broke up over Texas and examined some 85,000 pieces of the shuttle picked up by thousands of volunteers on the ground. Board members also interviewed eyewitnesses who saw pieces falling away from Columbia as the shuttle streaked across the early-morning sky from California to Texas. CAIB investigators used computer simulations to test theories of why the shuttle failed after flying successfully 87 times.

The CAIB concluded that a piece of foam insulation about the size of a small suitcase fell from Columbia's big external propellant tank during launch on January 14. The foam struck the *leading* (front) edge of the shuttle's left wing 81 seconds after liftoff. The force of the blow damaged the space-

FIRST FLIGHT

China's first *taikonaut* (astronaut), Yang Liwei, greets well-wishers after stepping out of the space capsule in which he successfully completed 14 orbits around Earth. The spacecraft, called Shenzhou—which means *divine ship* or *magic vessel*—had been launched on Oct. 15, 2003, from China's Jiuquan launch site in the Gobi Desert. Twenty-one hours later, the capsule landed in Inner Mongolia, using parachutes and small retrorockets to cushion its fall. With Yang's flight, China became only the third nation—after Russia and the United States—to have launched a human being into space.

craft's thermal protection system, which consisted of curved panels of a special material designed to protect the aluminum shuttle wing from the intense friction-generated heat of reentry.

Although the impact had been filmed as it happened, engineers who studied the film and other images of the blow while Columbia was still in space mistakenly decided the foam had not damaged the shuttle. Crew members could not see the spot that had been struck by the foam and so could not check for damage themselves. As long as Columbia was in the airless vacuum of space, the damage did not cause any problems.

However, when the spacecraft reentered Earth's atmosphere over Hawaii at the beginning of what was to have been a long glide to its landing strip in Florida, Columbia quickly developed trouble. Superhot air worked its way through the damaged leading edge like a blowtorch and began to melt the wing from the inside. By the time Columbia was over Dallas, the wing was too weak to withstand the stress of traveling faster than the speed of sound through Earth's atmosphere, which thickened as the spacecraft descended. The wing fell off, sending the shuttle into a fatal tumble. Columbia broke apart, killing all seven astronauts aboard.

The CAIB, in its report released in August 2003, recommended many changes to prevent another such accident, and NASA officials promised to follow the recommendations before allowing the remaining shuttles to fly again. The CAIB, for example, recommended modifying the shuttle's big external tanks, which fall into the ocean as the shuttle reaches space, to prevent large pieces of foam from breaking away during launch. NASA agreed to strengthen the thermal protection panels to better withstand blows from foam or other debris that might hit them. New sensors installed on the inside of the leading edges of the wings would alert engineers to anything striking the crucial surfaces outside.

In addition, NASA said it would equip the shuttle's robot arm with a new boom that would allow the crew to inspect the underside of the shuttle and other hard-to-see places for damage. The astronauts would be able to repair most damage themselves using patches and tools that NASA engineers were to develop. If the damage was too severe, the crew was to move into the ISS until another shuttle could be launched to rescue them. For that reason, NASA said the shuttles would travel

SPACE TECHNOLOGY continued

only to and from the space station on their remaining flights and would no longer take on such missions as repairing the Hubble Space Telescope.

All three of the shuttles were to be retired in about 2010, after the station was finished. NASA engineers estimated that the shuttles would not be ready to fly again until the spring of 2005 at the earliest.

The International Space Station. The grounding of the shuttle fleet forced the 16 international partners in the ISS project to develop alternate plans for supplying the station.

The shuttles had served as the primary means of transporting cargo, new components, and astronauts to the space station. To conserve water and other supplies, station managers cut the crew size from three astronauts to two—one American and one Russian. Crews flew to and from the station in a Russian Soyuz spacecraft that became their "lifeboat" after they reached the station.

Russian cosmonaut Yuri Malenchenko and NASA astronaut Edward Lu, who had arrived at the station in a Soyuz in April 2003, were replaced in October. Their mission, which had

EUROPE IN SPACE

The European Space Agency (ESA) sent its first missions to Mars and to the moon in 2003. On June 2, the agency launched Mars Express (below) from Russia's Baikonur Cosmodrome in Kazakhstan. The mission was the first, since the U.S. Viking probes landed on the Red Planet in 1976, sent to determine whether life exists on Mars. On Sept. 27, 2003, SMART-1 (for Small Missions for Advanced Research and Technology, opposite page, top)—was launched to the moon from Kourou, French Guiana.

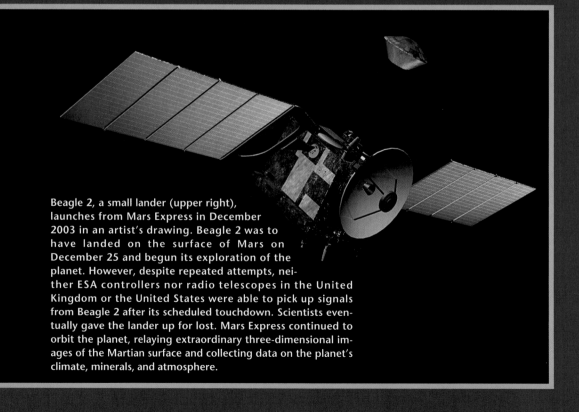

Beagle 2, a small lander (upper right), launches from Mars Express in December 2003 in an artist's drawing. Beagle 2 was to have landed on the surface of Mars on December 25 and begun its exploration of the planet. However, despite repeated attempts, neither ESA controllers nor radio telescopes in the United Kingdom or the United States were able to pick up signals from Beagle 2 after its scheduled touchdown. Scientists eventually gave the lander up for lost. Mars Express continued to orbit the planet, relaying extraordinary three-dimensional images of the Martian surface and collecting data on the planet's climate, minerals, and atmosphere.

been designated Expedition 7—the seventh crew aboard the station since it became continuously occupied in 2000—consisted of keeping station systems running and conducting a reduced science research program.

On Oct. 18, 2003, astronaut Michael Foale and cosmonaut Alexander Kaleri of Latvia flew to the station as Expedition 8, replacing Malenchenko and Lu. Foale became the first U.S. astronaut to have worked on both the International Space Station and on the Russian station Mir, which was allowed to fall out of or-

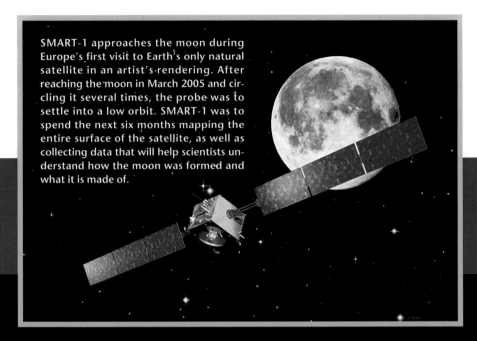

SMART-1 approaches the moon during Europe's first visit to Earth's only natural satellite in an artist's rendering. After reaching the moon in March 2005 and circling it several times, the probe was to settle into a low orbit. SMART-1 was to spend the next six months mapping the entire surface of the satellite, as well as collecting data that will help scientists understand how the moon was formed and what it is made of.

SMART-1's flight to the moon was to be the longest in duration ever taken, testing the capabilities of a relatively new type of engine. The probe was to fly a series of ever-lengthening orbits around Earth (below) before propelling itself into orbit around the moon. SMART-1 is propelled by a solar-powered *ion* engine. (An ion is an electrically charged atom.) The engine accelerates the spacecraft very slowly by separating electrons from the element xenon to create ions and ejecting them in a high-speed beam from the back of the probe. Although the thrust produced is tiny, the engine is extremely energy-efficient and, thus, would be useful for long journeys through space. Such an engine has been used once before, on NASA's Deep Space 1 probe to an asteroid in 1998.

SPACE TECHNOLOGY continued

bit in 2001. Foale and Kaleri were joined on the flight by Spain's Pedro Duque, a European Space Agency (ESA) astronaut who returned to Earth with Malenchenko and Lu.

Foale and Kaleri continued the maintenance and science work of their predecessors. On Feb. 26, 2004, they conducted a spacewalk to replace trays of scientific experiments that had been hanging outside the station for two years. The experiments measure the effects of space debris on the station. Foale and Kaleri also installed, on the outside of the station, a doll that was nearly life-sized. Sensors embedded in the doll were to measure the amount of solar radiation to which spacewalkers are exposed.

Foale and Kaleri's spacewalk was the first two-person EVA (extra-vehicular activity) conducted at the station without a third crew member inside to monitor the spacewalkers' safety. Russian cosmonauts had routinely conducted EVA's in this manner outside their Mir and Salyut space stations. Flight controllers in Houston, however, were concerned that there would be no one inside the station to oversee its systems or to help Foale and Kaleri after they returned. As it turned out, Kaleri's spacesuit malfunctioned, and the spacewalk was cut short. One of the tubes in the suit's water-cooling system had bent, causing the spacesuit to become very warm and a film of water to form inside the suit. The spacewalkers returned to the station to prevent Kaleri's body from overheating.

As a new crew prepared to replace Foale and Kaleri in April, the Russian space agency proposed prolonging missions to the space station from six months to one year. By doing so, the Russians could sell the extra seat on Soyuz resupply ships to space tourists to defray the cost of their program. (Although each Soyuz can seat three people, only two are needed to fly the spacecraft.) However, NASA rejected the idea, claiming its astronauts were not prepared to spend a full year in space. Russian cosmonaut Valery Polyakov had completed a record 438 uninterrupted days in space, primarily on Mir, in 1995. However, the longest continuous time ever spent by a U.S. astronaut in space was 196 days, a record set by Carl Walz and Daniel Bursch in 2002.

On April 19, 2004, the Expedition 9 crew

blasted off in a Soyuz vehicle from the Russian launch site in Kazakhstan, along with ESA astronaut Andre Kuipers of the Netherlands. The Dutch astronaut conducted life sciences experiments on a cargo of 4 million worms before returning to Earth with Foale and Kaleri on April 30. Cosmonaut Gennady Padalka and astronaut Michael Fincke remained aboard the station for a six-month mission that was to include at least three spacewalks.

The end of Hubble? Scientists and educators expressed dismay on Jan. 16, 2004, when NASA administrator Sean O'Keefe announced that space shuttles would not be used for a fifth servicing mission to the Hubble Space Telescope. The telescope, which was launched in 1990 and has provided researchers with spectacular views of both the early and current universe, could stop working by 2007 or 2008 as its batteries and *gyroscopes* (devices that use rotation to produce a stable direction in space) wear out. Because the ISS is the only safe haven for a shuttle crew in space, NASA had decided not to visit the telescope again to install new instruments and maintain the orbiting observatory. Astronomers argued that too much remains to be learned from the telescope to abandon it. In mid-2004, NASA engineers were exploring the possibility of using robots rather than astronauts to perform the servicing mission.

Chasing comets. In January 2004, NASA controllers guided a rugged spacecraft called Stardust through the head of a comet called Wild 2. Special panels aboard the vehicle collected thousands of bits of comet dust during the 12-minute encounter, and the probe's cameras radioed back pictures of the comet's surprisingly battered surface. The probe then began its return trip to Earth. The samples from the comet were to parachute to Earth in 2006, giving scientists their first chance to examine unaltered material dating from the formation of the solar system more than 4 billion years ago. The images sparked debate about the nature of comets among scientists, who had expected a much smoother surface on the comet's *nucleus* (center).

Astronomers expected a European spacecraft launched on March 2, 2004, to contribute data for these discussions, but not until 2014. The Rosetta probe left the ESA's spaceport on

Kourou, French Guiana, for a 10-year journey to the comet Churyumov-Gerasimenko. Rosetta was to orbit the comet's nucleus and send a small lander to its surface. To reach the comet, Rosetta must first make three flybys of Earth and one of Mars, using the two planets' gravity like a slingshot to gather enough energy to achieve its distant target. In 2014, Churyumov-Gerasimenko will be so far from the sun—675 million kilometers (420 million miles)—that it will be inactive, without the dramatic tail created as comets approach the sun.

Europe's first trip to the moon. The ESA also sent a spacecraft to a much closer

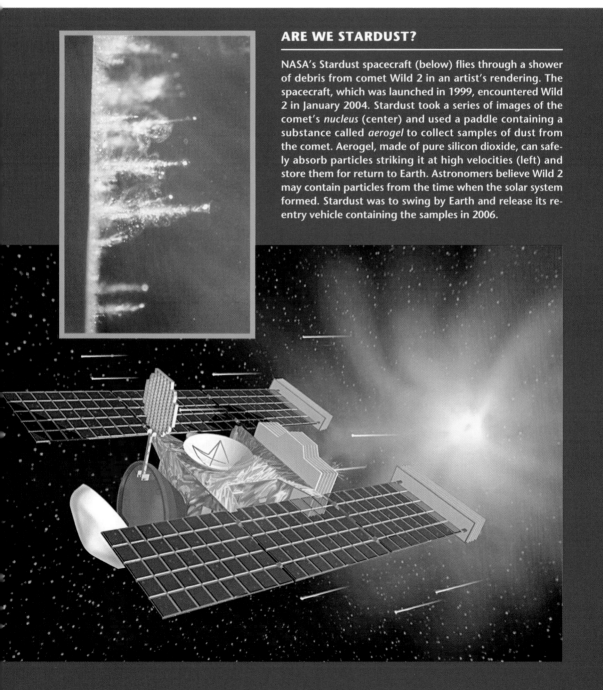

ARE WE STARDUST?

NASA's Stardust spacecraft (below) flies through a shower of debris from comet Wild 2 in an artist's rendering. The spacecraft, which was launched in 1999, encountered Wild 2 in January 2004. Stardust took a series of images of the comet's *nucleus* (center) and used a paddle containing a substance called *aerogel* to collect samples of dust from the comet. Aerogel, made of pure silicon dioxide, can safely absorb particles striking it at high velocities (left) and store them for return to Earth. Astronomers believe Wild 2 may contain particles from the time when the solar system formed. Stardust was to swing by Earth and release its re-entry vehicle containing the samples in 2006.

SPACE TECHNOLOGY continued

target—the moon. The SMART-1 probe (for *Small Missions for Advanced Research and Technology*) took off from Kourou on Sept. 27, 2003. The probe had two missions—to test technology that will be used for more challenging future missions and to perform valuable scientific investigations after reaching orbit around Earth's only natural satellite.

Launched on an Ariane 5 rocket along with two big communications satellites, SMART-1 got its power from an innovative engine. Electricity from SMART-1's solar panels strips *ions* (electrically charged atoms) from xenon gas and propels them through a nozzle, generating thrust that is weak but extremely energy efficient. Over time, the engine will nudge the little probe into higher and higher Earth orbit, until it is close enough to the moon to shift into lunar orbit.

Once in lunar orbit, SMART-1 was to map the composition of the lunar surface, analyzing the subtle differences in light and X rays reflected from different minerals below. The mineral maps and other data may help scientists pick the best places for people to land on the moon.

Was Einstein right? NASA launched a spacecraft called Gravity Probe B (GP-B) on April 21, 2004, to test a puzzling aspect of Einstein's theory of relativity. According to this theory, celestial objects such as Earth *warp* (distort) the fabric of *space-time.* (Space-time is a combination of the dimension of time and the three dimensions of space—length, width, and height.) GP-B was designed to measure two aspects of this distortion that Einstein predicted: the extent to which Earth warps space-time and whether Earth drags space-time along as it rotates.

After GP-B reached orbit, NASA engineers aligned it with the star IM Pegasi. The probe contains four gyroscopes. NASA planned to monitor the probe over the course of 18 months for evidence that Earth has effected a small but measurable change in the probe's alignment.

Galileo. Europe moved ahead in 2004 on its own version of the U.S. Global Positioning System (GPS), a constellation of satellites that broadcast radio signals that enable ships, aircraft, and even hikers to find their location on Earth's surface. A meeting between U.S. and European delegates in February addressed U.S. concerns that the new system could interfere with GPS signals.

Called Galileo, after the Italian astronomer and physicist of the late 1500's, the system was to consist of 30 satellites orbiting at an altitude of 23,616 kilometers (14,674 miles). The ESA and the European Union, partners in the project, planned to build the $4.5-billion system so that Galileo's ground receivers would be compatible with signals from the GPS satellites and Russia's Glonass navigation satellites. The ESA planned to launch the first satellite in its system, to test the Galileo hardware, in 2005. The full constellation was expected to be operational by 2008.

A European space shuttle. A prototype for a new European space shuttle flew successfully for the first time on May 6, 2004. The shuttle, called Phoenix, was dropped by a helicopter from an altitude of 2,400 meters (7,900 feet) at the North European Aerospace Test Range in Kiruna, Sweden, 1,240 kilometers (770 miles) north of Stockholm. Phoenix glided to a landing after a 90-second flight. At about 7 meters (23 feet) in length and with a wingspan of 4 meters (13 feet), the prototype was about one-sixth the size of the projected space vehicle. Phoenix was built by the European Aeronautic Defense and Space Company (EADS), the largest aerospace company in Europe. EADS engineers expected to complete an actual shuttle between 2015 and 2020.

New U.S. plans for space. On Jan. 14, 2004, U.S. President George W. Bush ordered NASA to begin planning a long-term space exploration program that would use the moon to test equipment for a landing on Mars and other places beyond Earth's orbit. The president's plan called for a 5.6-percent increase in NASA's budget for 2005, to $16.2-billion, with annual 5-percent increases over the next five years. Congressional leaders reacted to the proposal with concern over the high cost of the program, especially in light of the nation's increasing federal deficit. However, many scientists noted that the challenge may provide encouragement to a new generation of scientists, engineers, and astronauts. ■ Frank Morring, Jr.

See also **ASTRONOMY.**

SUPPLEMENT

New encyclopedia articles are devoted
to the following topics:

Comet is an icy body that releases gas or dust. Most of the comets that can be seen from Earth travel around the sun in long, oval orbits. A comet consists of a solid *nucleus* (core) surrounded by a cloudy atmosphere called the *coma* and one or two tails. Most comets are too small or too faint to be seen without a telescope. Some comets, however, become visible to the unaided eye for several weeks as they pass close to the sun. We can see comets because the gas and dust in their comas and tails reflect sunlight. Also, the gases release energy absorbed from the sun, causing them to glow.

Astronomers classify comets according to how long they take to orbit the sun. *Short-period comets* need less than 200 years to complete one orbit, while *long-period comets* take 200 years or longer.

Astronomers believe that comets are leftover debris from a collection of gas, ice, rocks, and dust that formed the outer planets about 4.6 billion years ago. Some scientists believe that comets originally brought to Earth some of the water and the carbon-based molecules that make up living things.

Parts of a comet. The nucleus of a comet is a ball of ice and rocky dust particles that resembles a dirty snowball. The ice consists mainly of frozen water but may include other frozen substances, such as ammonia, carbon dioxide, carbon monoxide, and methane. Scientists believe the nucleus of some comets may be fragile because several comets have split apart for no apparent reason.

As a comet nears the inner solar system, heat from the sun vaporizes some of the ice on the surface of the nucleus, spewing gas and dust particles into space. This gas and dust form the comet's coma. Radiation from the sun pushes dust particles away from the coma. The particles form a tail called the *dust tail*. At the same time, the *solar wind*—that is, the flow of high-speed electrically charged particles from the sun—converts some of the comet's gases into *ions* (charged particles). These ions also stream away from the coma, forming an *ion tail*. Because comet tails are pushed by solar radiation and the solar wind, they always point away from the sun.

Halley's Comet becomes visible to the unaided eye about every 76 years as it nears the sun.

Lick Observatory

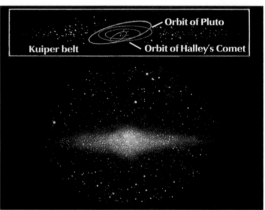

WORLD BOOK diagram by Terry Hadler, Bernard Thornton Artists

Where comets come from

Comets that pass near the sun come from two groups of comets near the outer edge of the solar system, according to astronomers. The disk-shaped *Kuiper belt* contributes comets that orbit the sun in fewer than 200 years. The Kuiper belt lies beyond Pluto's orbit, which extends to about 4.6 billion miles (7.4 billion kilometers) from the sun. The *Oort cloud* provides comets that take longer to complete their orbits. The outer edge of the Oort cloud may be 1,000 times farther than the orbit of Pluto.

Most comets are thought to have a nucleus that measures about 10 miles (16 kilometers) or less across. Some comas can reach diameters of nearly 1 million miles (1.6 million kilometers). Some tails extend to distances of 100 million miles (160 million kilometers).

The life of a comet. Scientists think that short-period comets come from a band of objects called the Kuiper belt that lies beyond the orbit of Pluto. The gravitational pull of the outer planets can nudge objects out of the Kuiper belt and into the inner solar system, where they become active comets. Long-period comets come from the Oort cloud, a nearly spherical collection of icy bodies about 1,000 times farther away from the sun than Pluto's orbit. Gravitational interac-

Famous comets

Name	First recorded sighting	Period of orbit (years)
Halley's Comet	About 240 B.C.	76
Comet Swift-Tuttle	69 B.C.	130
Comet Tempel-Tuttle	1366	33
Tycho Brahe's Comet	1577	unknown
Biela's Comet	1772	6.6
Encke's Comet	1786	3.3
Comet Flaugergues	1811	3,100
Great Comet	1843	513
Great September Comet	1882	759
Comet Ikeya-Seki	1965	880
Comet Bennett	1969	1,678
Comet Kohoutek	1973	unknown
Comet West	1975	558,300
Comet Shoemaker-Levy 9	1993	*
Comet Hale-Bopp	1995	2,380
Comet Hyakutake	1996	63,400

*Comet Shoemaker-Levy 9 was in a two-year orbit around Jupiter before it collided with that planet in July 1994.

tions with passing stars can cause icy bodies in the Oort cloud to enter the inner solar system and become active comets.

Comets lose ice and dust each time they return to the inner solar system, leaving behind trails of dusty debris. When Earth passes through one of these trails, the debris becomes meteors that burn up in the atmosphere. Eventually, some comets lose all their ices. They break up and dissipate into clouds of dust or turn into fragile, inactive objects similar to asteroids.

The long, oval-shaped orbits of comets can cross the almost circular orbits of the planets. As a result, comets sometimes collide with planets and their satellites. Many of the impact craters in the solar system were caused by collisions with comets.

Studying comets. Scientists learned much about comets by studying Halley's Comet as it passed near Earth in 1986. Five spacecraft flew past the comet and gathered information about its appearance and chemical composition. Several probes flew close enough to study the nucleus, which is normally concealed by the comet's coma. The spacecraft found a roughly potato-shaped nucleus measuring about 9 miles (15 kilometers) long. The nucleus contains equal amounts of ice and dust. About 80 percent of the ice is water ice, and frozen carbon monoxide makes up another 15 percent. Much of the remainder is frozen carbon dioxide, methane, and ammonia. Scientists believe that other comets are chemically similar to Halley's Comet.

Scientists unexpectedly found the nucleus of Halley's Comet to be extremely dark black. They now believe that the surface of the comet, and perhaps most other comets, is covered with a black crust of dust and rock that covers most of the ice. These comets release gas only when holes in this crust rotate toward the sun, exposing the interior ice to the warming sunlight.

Another comet nucleus that has been seen by spacecraft cameras is that of Comet Borrelly. During a flyby in 2001, the Deep Space 1 spacecraft observed a nucleus about half the size of the nucleus of Halley's Comet. Borrelly's nucleus was also potato-shaped and had a dark black surface. Like Halley's Comet, Comet Borrelly only released gas from small areas where holes in the crust exposed the ice to sunlight.

In 1994, astronomers observed a comet named Shoemaker-Levy 9, which had split into more than two dozen pieces, crashing into the planet Jupiter. One of the most active comets seen in more than 400 years was Comet Hale-Bopp, which came within 122 million miles (197 million kilometers) of Earth in 1997. This was not an especially close approach for a comet. However, Hale-Bopp appeared bright to the unaided eye because its unusually large nucleus gave off a great deal of dust and gas. The nucleus was estimated to be about 18 to 25 miles (30 to 40 kilometers) across.

Donald K. Yeomans

Additional resources

Bonar, Samantha. *Comets.* Watts, 1998. Younger readers.
Levy, David H. *Comets: Creators and Destroyers.* Simon & Schuster, 1998.
Verschuur, Gerrit L. *Impact! The Threat of Comets and Asteroids.* Oxford, 1996.

How an impact crater forms

An impact crater forms when a comet, asteroid, or other small body collides with a larger body, such as a planet or moon.

WORLD BOOK illustrations by Paul Turnbaugh

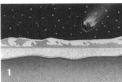

An asteroid approaches the surface of a planet or a moon at high speed.

The asteroid penetrates the surface, releasing energy in the form of shock waves.

The shock waves destroy the asteroid and push material away from the impact site.

The crater's center rebounds to form a peak and its walls collapse, creating terraces.

Crater is a bowl-shaped depression on the surface of a planet, moon, or other solid body. A variety of forces can produce craters.

Most craters on planets and moons in our solar system are *impact craters.* Impact craters form when an asteroid, comet, or other solid body strikes the surface of a larger body, such as a planet or moon, at high speed. Such an impact releases a tremendous amount of energy in the form of *shock waves.* Shock waves are waves of energy that travel away from the impact. The shock waves travel through the surface until their energy is used up. As they travel, they push material away from the impact site, forming the crater. The shock waves force some of this material upward and outward to form the wall of the crater. The impact also tosses some of the material into the air. This material, called *ejecta,* settles around the crater in a layer called the *ejecta blanket.*

Small impact craters are often bowl-shaped. Larger impact craters tend to have flatter bottoms and more complex features. After the impact, the center of the crater can bounce back up, producing a central peak. The steep walls can collapse under the force of gravity, forming terraces.

Astronomers study impact craters to learn more about the surfaces of heavenly bodies. The number of craters on a surface gives astronomers some idea of the surface's age. The depth and shape of craters provide scientists with clues about the materials that make up the surface.

Volcanic activity creates most of the craters on Earth. A volcanic explosion can make a crater by blasting away dirt and rock. Inactive volcanoes can collapse to leave craters called *calderas.* Other craters form when water dissolves away underground rock. This can cause the ground above to collapse, forming a crater called a *sinkhole.*   Nadine G. Barlow

Gravitation is the force of attraction that acts between all objects because of their *mass.* An object's mass is its amount of matter. Because of gravitation, an object that is near Earth falls toward the surface of the planet. An object that is already on the surface experiences a downward force due to gravitation. We experience this force on our bodies as our weight. Gravitation holds together the hot gases that make up the sun, and it keeps the planets in their orbits around the sun. Another term for gravitation is the *force of gravity.*

People misunderstood gravitation for centuries. In the 300's B.C., the Greek philosopher and scientist Aristotle taught the incorrect idea that heavy objects fall faster than light objects. People accepted that idea until the early 1600's, when the Italian scientist Galileo corrected it. Galileo said that all objects fall with the same *acceleration* unless air resistance or some other force acts on them. An object's acceleration is the rate of change of its *velocity* (speed in a particular direction). Thus, a heavy object and a light object that are dropped from the same height will reach the ground at the same time.

Newton's law of gravitation

Ancient astronomers measured the movements of the moon and planets across the sky. However, no one correctly explained those motions until the late 1600's. At that time, the English scientist Isaac Newton described a connection between the movements of the celestial bodies and the gravitation that attracts objects to Earth.

In 1665, a falling apple caused Newton to question how far the force of gravity reaches. Newton explained his discoveries in 1687 in a work called *Philosophiae Naturalis Principia Mathematica (Mathematical Principles of Natural Philosophy).* Using laws of planetary motion discovered by the German astronomer Johannes Kepler, Newton showed how the sun's force of gravity must decrease with the distance from the sun. He assumed that Earth's gravitation decreases in the same way with the distance from Earth. Newton knew that Earth's gravitation holds the moon in its orbit around Earth, and he calculated the strength of Earth's gravitation at the distance of the moon. Using his assumption, he calculated what the strength of that gravitation would be at Earth's surface. The calculated result was the same as the strength of the gravitation that would accelerate an apple.

Newton's law of gravitation says that the gravitational force between two objects is *directly proportional* to their masses. That is, the larger either mass is, the larger is the force between the two objects. The law also says that the gravitational force between two objects is *inversely* (oppositely) proportional to the distance between the two objects *squared* (multiplied by itself). For example, if the distance between the two objects doubles, the force between them becomes one-fourth of its original strength. Newton's law is given by the equation $F = m_1 m_2 / d^2$, where F is the gravitational force between two objects, m_1 and m_2 are the masses of the objects, and d^2 is the distance between them squared.

Until the early 1900's, scientists had observed only one movement that could not be described mathematically using Newton's law—a tiny variation in the orbit of the planet Mercury around the sun. Mercury's orbit— like the orbits of the other planets—is an *ellipse,* a geometric figure with the shape of a flattened hoop. The sun is not at the exact center of the ellipse. So one point in each orbit is closer to the sun than all other points in that orbit. But the location of the closest point changes slightly each time Mercury revolves around the sun. Astronomers refer to that variation as a *precession.*

Scientists used Newton's law to calculate the precession. The calculated amount differed slightly from the observed amount.

Einstein's theory of gravitation

In 1915, the German-born physicist Albert Einstein announced his theory of space, time, and gravitation, the *general theory of relativity.* Einstein's theory completely changed scientists' way of thinking about gravitation. However, it expanded upon Newton's law, rather than contradicting it.

In many cases, Einstein's theory produced results that differed only slightly from results based on Newton's law. For example, when Einstein used his theory to calculate the precession of Mercury's orbit, the result agreed exactly with the observed motion. That agreement was the first confirmation of Einstein's theory.

Einstein based his theory on two assumptions. The first is related to an entity known as *space-time,* and the second is a rule known as the *principle of equivalence.*

Space-time. In the complex mathematics of relativity, time and space are not absolutely separate. Instead, physicists refer to space-time, a combination of time and the three dimensions of space—length, width, and height. Einstein assumed that matter and energy can *distort* (change the shape of) space-time, curving it; and that gravitation is an effect of the curvature.

The principle of equivalence states that the effects of gravity are equivalent to the effects of acceleration. To understand this principle, suppose you were in a rocket ship so far from any planet, star, or other celestial object that the ship experienced virtually no gravitation. Imagine that the ship was moving forward, but not accelerating—in other words, that the ship was traveling at a constant speed and in a constant direction. If you held out a ball and released it, the ball would not fall. It would hover beside you. But suppose the rocket accelerated by increasing its speed. The ball would appear to fall toward the rear of the ship exactly as if gravity had acted upon it.

Predictions of general relativity

In the years since the calculation of Mercury's precession confirmed Einstein's theory, several observations have verified predictions made with the theory. Some examples include predictions of the bending of light rays and radio waves, the existence of gravity waves and black holes, and the expansion of the universe.

Bending of light rays. Einstein's theory predicts that gravity will bend the path of a light ray as the ray passes near a massive body. The bending will occur because the body will curve space-time. The sun is massive enough to bend rays by an observable amount, and scientists first confirmed this prediction during a total eclipse of the sun in 1919.

Bending and slowing of radio waves. The theory also predicts that the sun will bend radio waves and slow them down. Scientists have measured the sun's bending of radio waves *emitted* (sent out) by *quasars,* extremely powerful objects at the centers of some galaxies. The measurements agree well with the prediction.

Researchers measured a delay of radio waves that pass near the sun by sending signals between Earth and the Viking space probes that reached Mars in 1976. Those measurements still represent one of the most precise confirmations of general relativity.

Gravitational waves. General relativity also indicates that massive bodies in orbit around each other will emit waves of energy known as *gravitational waves.* Scientists have confirmed the existence of gravitational waves indirectly by observing an object known as a *binary pulsar.* A binary pulsar is a rapidly rotating *neutron star* that orbits a similar, but unobserved, companion star. A neutron star consists mostly of tightly packed *neutrons,* particles that ordinarily occur only in the nuclei of atoms.

A pulsar emits two steady beams of radio waves that flow away in opposite directions. As the star rotates on its own axis, the beams sweep around in space like searchlight beams. If one of the radio beams periodically sweeps over Earth, a radio telescope can detect the beam as a series of pulses. By closely observing changes in the pulse rate of a binary pulsar, scientists can determine the pulsar's *orbital period*—the time it takes the two stars to completely orbit each other.

Observations of the binary pulsar called PSR 1913 + 16 indicate that its orbital period is decreasing, and astronomers have measured the amount of the decrease. Scientists have also used equations of general relativity to calculate the amount by which the orbital period would decrease if the binary pulsar was radiating away energy as gravitational waves. The calculated amount agrees with the measured amount.

In addition, the pulsar's orbit precesses as the pulsar revolves around the companion star. General relativity predicts the precession rate, and measurements match the prediction with great precision.

Black holes. Einstein's theory predicts the existence of objects called *black holes.* A black hole is a region of space whose gravitational force is so strong that not even light can escape from it. Researchers have found strong evidence that most very massive stars eventually evolve into black holes, and that most large galaxies have a gigantic black hole at their centers.

Expansion of the universe. In a paper published in 1917, Einstein applied general relativity to *cosmology,* the study of the universe as a whole. The theory showed that the universe must either expand or contract. At that time, scientists had not yet found evidence of expansion or contraction. To prevent his theory from contradicting the available evidence, Einstein added a term, the *cosmological constant,* to the theory. That term represented a *repulsion* (pushing away) of every point in space by the surrounding points, preventing contraction.

But in 1929, the American astronomer Edwin Hubble discovered that distant galaxies are moving away from Earth and that, the more distant a galaxy, the more rapidly it is moving away. Hubble's discovery indicated

that the universe is expanding. In response to Hubble's discovery and confirming observations by other astronomers, Einstein abandoned the cosmological constant, calling it his greatest blunder.

The discovery of the expansion of the universe, together with other observations, led to the development of the *big bang* theory of the origin of the universe. According to that theory, the universe began with a hot, explosive event—a "big bang." At the beginning of the event, all the matter in the part of the universe we can see was smaller than a marble. Matter then expanded rapidly, and it is still expanding.

Dark energy. Although Einstein called the cosmological constant his greatest blunder, it may turn out to be one of his greatest achievements. Measurements reported in 1998 suggest that the universe is expanding more and more rapidly. Furthermore, the rate of expansion has been increasing as predicted by general relativity with a cosmological constant.

Astronomers have concluded that the increase in the expansion rate is due to an entity that presently opposes gravitation. That entity could be a cosmological constant or something much like it called *dark energy.* Scientists have not yet developed theories to account for the existence of dark energy, but they know how much of it probably exists. The amount of dark energy in the universe is about twice as much as the amount of matter.

The matter in the universe includes both visible matter and a mysterious substance known as *dark matter.* Scientists do not know the composition of dark matter. But measurements of the motion of stars and gas clouds in galaxies have led scientists to believe that it exists. Those measurements show that the masses of galaxies are many times larger than the masses of the visible objects in them. These and other observations suggest that the universe has at least 30 times as much dark matter as visible matter.   Joel R. Primack

Related articles include:
Antigravity
Big bang
Black hole
Dark energy
Dark matter
Einstein, Albert
Falling bodies, Law of
Force (Kinds of force)
G (symbol)
Galileo
Gravity, Center of
Kepler, Johannes
Mass
Newton, Sir Isaac
Observatory (Gravitational observatories)
Pendulum
Planet (How planets move)
Pulsar
Quasar
Relativity
String theory
Weight

Additional resources

Blair, David, and McNamara, Geoff. *Ripples on a Cosmic Sea: The Search for Gravitational Waves.* Addison Wesley Longman, 1997.
Wheeler, John A. *A Journey into Gravity and Spacetime.* Scientific Am. Lib., 1990.

Human being has the most highly developed brain of any animal. The human brain gives people many special abilities, the most outstanding of which is the ability to speak. Language has enabled human beings to develop *culture,* which consists of ways of behaving and thinking. These ways are passed on from generation to generation through learning. Culture also includes *technology*—that is, the tools and techniques invented by people to help satisfy their needs and desires. The richness and complexity of human culture distinguish human beings from all other animals.

The human brain helps make people the most adaptable of all creatures. They behave with the most flexibility and in the greatest variety of ways. The human body is highly adaptable because it has few specialized features that could limit its activities. In contrast, a seal has a body streamlined for swimming, but it has difficulty moving about on land. People cannot swim as well as a seal, but they can also walk, run, and climb. Human adaptability enables people to live in an extremely wide variety of environments—from the tropics to the Arctic.

People are inquisitive and have long sought to understand themselves and their place in the world. Throughout much of human existence, religion has helped provide such understanding. Nearly all societies have assumed that one or more gods influence their lives and are responsible for their existence. Since ancient times, *philosophy* (the study of truth and knowledge) has also provided definitions of what it means to be human.

Today, religion and philosophy remain important parts of people's efforts to understand the nature of human existence. But many other fields of study also help human beings learn about themselves. For example, *anthropology* is the study of human cultures and of human physical and cultural development. Specialists in *psychology* study human and animal behavior and mental processes. *Sociology* deals with the groups and institutions that make up human societies, and history is the study of past human events.

This article describes the physical and cultural characteristics that distinguish human beings from other animals. It also traces human physical and cultural development. For more information on the life of early human beings, see Prehistoric people.

Characteristics of human beings

Scientific classification. Biologists classify all living things in groups, including *class, order, family, genus,* and *species.* Human beings belong to the class of animals called *mammals.* There are about 4,500 species of living mammals, including such animals as cats, dogs, elephants, and otters. All mammals have a backbone, hair, four limbs, and a constant body temperature. Female mammals are the only animals with special glands that produce milk for feeding their young.

Human beings, along with apes, monkeys, lemurs, and tarsiers, make up the order of mammals called *primates.* Scientists classify human beings and apes together in the superfamily *Hominoidea.* Scientists have compared the anatomy and *genome* (the complete set of genes in an organism) of the African great apes with modern human beings. They determined that chimpanzees and gorillas are the closest living relatives to human beings. In fact, scientists have determined that

AP/Wide World

Human beings, as shown by this crowd enjoying the excitement of a baseball game, display an amazing degree of diversity within a single species. The richness and complexity of human culture distinguishes human beings from all other animals.

about 98 percent of the genes of living people are identical to those of chimpanzees.

Within the Hominoidea, the family *Hominidae* consists of human beings and their closest prehuman ancestors. Species in this family are often referred to as *hominids.* Human beings are the only living members of a genus called *Homo,* the Latin word for human being. This genus consists of one living species—*Homo sapiens*—and several extinct human species that are known only through fossil remains. The Latin words *Homo sapiens* mean *wise human being.* All existing peoples belong to the subspecies *Homo sapiens sapiens.*

Physical characteristics. Human beings and the other primates share many physical features. For example, all primates rely on their excellent vision for much of their information about the environment. They have large eyes, sensitive retinas, and *stereoscopic vision* (the ability to perceive depth). Human beings and apes also have a highly developed nervous system and a large brain. Human beings and many other primates have long, flexible fingers and *opposable thumbs,* which can be placed opposite the fingers for grasping. In addition, their fingers and toes have nails instead of claws.

Many of the physical characteristics that distinguish human beings from other primates are related to the ability of people to stand upright and walk on two legs. This ability requires long, powerful legs. The human rump has strong muscles that propel the body forward and balance the trunk alternately on each leg when a person walks. In contrast, apes spend most of their time climbing and swinging in trees or walking on all four limbs. Their rumps have relatively weak muscles, and their arms are longer and stronger than their legs.

Physical differences between human beings and apes

The bodies of human beings are suited to walking on two feet. On the other hand, the bodies of apes are suited to walking on four limbs or climbing. Some of the resulting physical differences between people and apes are shown below.

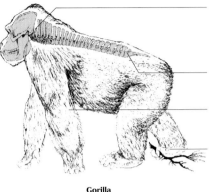

The human head rests on the spinal column. A gorilla's head hangs from the end of the spinal column.

Human beings have a curve in the lower spine to absorb the stress of walking on two feet. A gorilla's lower spine is straight.

A human being has shorter arms than legs. A gorilla's arms are longer than its legs.

The human foot is used chiefly for support of the body. A gorilla's feet can grasp things as well as support the animal's body.

Gorilla

Human being

WORLD BOOK illustration by Anthony Saris

The human spine, unlike the spine of any other animal, has a curve in the lower back. This curve helps make upright posture possible by placing the body's center of gravity directly over the pelvis. The human foot is also specially adapted for walking on two legs. Apes use all four limbs to support their weight, and they can grasp objects almost as well with their feet as with their hands. In human beings, however, the feet support the entire weight of the body, and the toes have little ability to grasp or to move independently.

The human brain is extremely well developed and at least twice as large as any ape's brain. Because of the brain's size, the human skull is rounder than any other primate's skull.

Human beings live longer and develop more slowly than other primates. The human life span varies from an average of about 40 years in some countries to more than 70 years in most industrial nations. A human infant is born completely helpless and depends on its parents for many years. Most human beings reach full maturity only between 18 and 25 years of age. Slow growth and development allow for a much longer period of learning and brain growth than exists in any other species.

Cultural characteristics. Some animals have simple aspects of culture. For example, young chimpanzees learn from older members of their group how to make some tools. They catch termites by peeling a twig and inserting it into a termite mound. They also chew leaves to make sponges for soaking up water to drink. Certain animals, including apes and monkeys, communicate by making a wide variety of sounds. These sounds express emotion and may communicate simple messages, but they apparently do not symbolize any object or idea. Language distinguishes human culture from all forms of animal culture. Through elaborate use of symbols, language enables people to express complex ideas and to communicate about objects and events that are distant in time and place. By using language, human beings have developed the ability to reason and to solve problems on a far higher level than any other animal.

Language also enables human beings to pass on knowledge and complex skills from generation to generation.

Human physical development

The Bible describes how God created the world and all its living things, including the first human beings, in six days. Many people accept this description as fact.

Evidence from fossils has convinced most scientists that human beings developed over millions of years from ancestors that were not completely human. But the fossil record does not yet provide enough information to trace human development in detail. As a result, not all experts agree on how human beings developed. This section describes human physical development as a majority of anthropologists believe it occurred.

Prehuman ancestors. Anthropologists believe human beings, chimpanzees, and gorillas all developed from a common ancestor that lived between about 7 million and 10 million years ago. During this time, the ancestral population that leads to modern human beings *diverged* (split) from the populations that gave rise to modern gorillas and chimpanzees. This divergence represents the beginnings of the family Hominidae. Because chimpanzees and gorillas are native to Africa and the earliest known hominid fossils are limited to Africa, scientists believe the human family originated there.

Anthropologists have discovered fossil remains of the earliest hominids at sites in Africa. The oldest known species, *Sahelanthropus tchadensis* (pronounced *suh hehl AN throh puhs cha DEHN sihs*), lived about 7 million years ago in what is now the central African nation of Chad. Another species, *Orrorin tugenensis* (*aw RAWR ihn too juh NEHN sihs*), is known from fragmentary fossil remains found in eastern Africa. This species lived about 6 million years ago. The fossil bones of *Ardipithecus ramidus* (*AR duh PIHTH uh kuhs RAM uh duhs*), another humanlike creature, were uncovered in the east African nation of Ethiopia. This species lived between $5\frac{1}{2}$ million and $4\frac{1}{2}$ million years ago. Like other hominids, this species walked upright. However, fossil hunters have found only a small number of bones of these earliest hominids. Scientists know little about the biology of these creatures and their relationship to later hominids.

More than 4 million years ago, a more advanced form of humanlike creature called *Australopithecus (aw STRAY loh PIHTH uh kuhs)* appeared in Africa. Anthropologists recognize at least six different species of *Australopithecus* from fossil remains. Members of the *genus* (group of species) *Australopithecus* are called *australopithecines.* Fossil remains of the australopithecine skeleton indicate that these creatures stood fully erect and walked on two legs. The australopithecines were about $3\frac{1}{2}$ to 5 feet (110 to 150 centimeters) tall. They had large, strongly developed jaws and large *molars* (back chewing teeth). These hominids had a brain about one-third the size of a modern human brain.

Early human beings. Primitive human beings appeared about 2 million years ago in Africa. Anthropologists believe that these early human beings developed from the australopithecines. By 1,800,000 years ago, fossil evidence suggests, several different species of early human beings lived in Africa. They are all placed in the same genus as living people, *Homo.* One species, *Homo erectus* (upright human being), had a larger brain and a more humanlike face and teeth than the other species. From the neck down, *Homo erectus* resembled human beings of today. But, like other species of early *Homo,* it had a large, projecting face and a low forehead with a large *browridge,* a raised strip of bone above the eyes.

Homo erectus made and used a variety of stone tools. About 1,800,000 years ago, these early people began to migrate out of Africa. Fossil sites indicate *Homo erectus* migrated to Asia and later to Europe. By 600,000 years ago, *Homo erectus* had migrated as far as northern China. The Chinese fossil sites show evidence that *Homo erectus* there made controlled use of fire and butchered large animals.

Human beings of today. Scientists today are uncertain about precisely how modern human beings developed from earlier species of *Homo.* Some anthropologists suggest that modern human beings evolved directly from earlier *Homo erectus* populations who had spread from Africa through Europe and Asia. In this view, living people are the culmination of a long history in various geographic areas. For example, modern Asian peoples are seen as the descendants of the *Homo erectus* populations that reached Asia more than 1 million years ago.

Most anthropologists, however, support a different theory. This theory suggests that modern human beings are descendants of a single population of *Homo sapiens* that originated in Africa. Anthropologists who share this view cite genetic evidence that suggests *Homo sapiens* originated between 100,000 and 200,000 years ago. This population may have migrated from Africa, replacing populations of early human beings that existed in Africa, Europe, and Asia. Although scientists continue to debate the question of the exact origins of living people, genetic studies clearly indicate that all human beings today are closely related.

Human cultural development

Human culture has developed in three major phases. These phases have been based on (1) hunting and gathering societies, (2) agricultural societies, and (3) industrial societies.

Hunting and gathering societies. For almost the entire prehistoric period of human existence, people lived by hunting game and gathering fruit, nuts, roots, seeds, and other plant foods. Evidence suggests that the hunters and gatherers lived in widely separated groups of 25 to 50 persons. These people roamed over large areas in search of food. They lived in harmony with their environment and used their natural resources efficiently.

The first inventions probably included weapons and cutting tools for butchering animals, plus containers for gathering plant foods. As people improved their hunting skills, they obtained big amounts of meat by killing large mammals, including elephants.

Agricultural societies became possible after people began to domesticate wild animals and plants about 10,000 years ago. These farming activities greatly increased the amount of food available in any area. Permanent villages appeared, and then towns and cities developed. The larger and more dependable supply of food supported a continually increasing population.

Agriculture made it unnecessary for everyone to help in the production of food. Some people became specialists in other fields, such as manufacturing or trade. Governments were established, and systems of writing were created. Thus, the invention of farming opened the way for the development of civilization.

Industrial societies appeared in their modern form during the A.D. 1700's, after people learned to run machinery with energy from coal and other fuels. Today, petroleum, coal, natural gas, and nuclear fuel furnish most of the energy used by industrial societies. These fuels have brought a great expansion of technology.

The processes and products developed by industry have greatly improved the standard of living for countless people. These developments have also helped make possible many other advances, including tremendous increases in human knowledge. But not all nations and economic classes have received the full benefits of industrial progress. Millions of people throughout the world continue to live without modern medicine, electric power, clean water, and sanitation. Industrial technology has produced many harmful side effects as well. Its wastes have polluted the environment, and its production methods have sometimes created monotonous, unfulfilling jobs.   Alan E. Mann

Related articles. See Prehistoric people and its list of *Related articles.* See also the following articles:

Ape	Human body
Civilization	Primate
Culture	Races, Human

Additional resources

Ehrlich, Paul R. *Human Natures: Genes, Cultures, and the Human Prospect.* Shearwater Bks., 2000.
Harris, Marvin. *Culture, People, Nature.* 7th ed. Longman Pub. Group, 1997.
Jolly, Alison. *Lucy's Legacy: Sex and Intelligence in Human Evolution.* Harvard Univ. Pr., 1999.
Merriman, Nick. *Early Humans.* 1989. Reprint. Dorling Kindersley, 2000. Younger readers.
Tattersall, Ian. *Becoming Human: Evolution and Human Uniqueness.* Harcourt, 1998.
Tudge, Colin. *The Time Before History: 5 Million Years of Human Impact.* Scribner, 1996.

A petroleum refinery is a vast area of towers, tanks, pipes, pumps, and valves. Towers called *fractionating towers* separate crude oil into its different useful parts or *fractions.* Large tanks hold crude oil and various petroleum products.

Petroleum

Petroleum is a valuable substance, used as a fuel and as a raw material, that comes from rocks far beneath the ground. The word *petroleum* comes from Greek words meaning *rock oil.* Petroleum comes in two forms—a liquid and a gas. Liquid petroleum is commonly called *crude oil.* Gaseous petroleum is often referred to as *natural gas.* The remainder of this article uses *petroleum* to mean both crude oil and natural gas. For more information on natural gas, see **Gas** (fuel).

Petroleum consists of a mixture of different chemicals that can be separated into a number of useful substances. Many petroleum products are used as fuels. Gasoline supplies fuel for transportation, and fuel oil burns to generate electric power in power plants. Natural gas heats houses and other buildings and provides fuel for electric generators. Other petroleum products serve as raw materials in manufacturing. Some serve as lubricants, while others are a basic component in the making of plastics.

Most geologists believe petroleum developed from the remains of plants and animals that died long ago. These remains became buried deep below the ground. There, heat and pressure transformed them into petroleum. Over time, this petroleum moved through rock to the areas where it is found today. Petroleum deposits also moved as Earth's surface shifted.

Geologists use their knowledge of how petroleum forms and *migrates* (moves through rock) to find underground petroleum deposits. They also search for petroleum using special equipment, including magnetic sensors, devices that vibrate the ground, and instruments that measure tiny variations in Earth's gravity.

Engineers and drilling crews use special equipment to drill a well to a petroleum deposit. The well serves as a passageway through which petroleum flows to the surface. From the well, pipelines and ships transport the petroleum to a *refinery,* a vast area of towers, tanks, pipes, pumps, and valves where petroleum is converted into various products.

Petroleum supplies about two-thirds of the world's energy. All countries use petroleum, and nearly 100 countries produce it. Most of the world's richest countries, including the United States, Japan, and several nations in Western Europe, use much more petroleum than they produce. On the other hand, a small number of relatively poor countries, many of them in the Middle East, produce much more petroleum than they consume. The need of wealthy countries to import large amounts of petroleum has led to global economic and political problems and even to war.

The widespread use of petroleum has given rise to a number of environmental problems. During the production, transportation, and use of petroleum, some of it spills or seeps onto the land and into the water. The burning of petroleum produces waste particles and gases that pollute the air. Burning petroleum produces carbon dioxide (CO_2) gas, which some scientists believe is causing Earth's surface to become warmer.

People have used petroleum for thousands of years. Petroleum did not become a major energy source, how-

Michael J. Economides, the contributor of this article, is Professor of Chemical Engineering at the University of Houston.

Crude oil from Saudi Arabia

Crude oil from Australia

Crude oil from Venezuela

Tar sands from Canada

Oil shale from the United States

Top three photos, BP; bottom two, WORLD BOOK photos

Petroleum is found below the ground in many different forms. Liquid petroleum, called *crude oil,* varies in color and thickness from a clear, thin fluid to a dark, tarlike substance. Petroleum can also be found as a colorless gas called *natural gas* and as a solid in certain sands and rocks.

ever, until the mid-1800's. At that time, the invention of the kerosene lamp and, later, the automobile created an enormous demand for kerosene and gasoline—two fuels derived from petroleum. Today, the petroleum industry is one of the largest in the world.

Earth has a limited supply of petroleum. As more and more is used, what remains will become increasingly expensive to *produce* (remove from the ground). Improved production methods, increases in fuel efficiency, and conservation may allow petroleum to remain the world's primary source of energy for some time. Eventually, however, other energy sources will have to replace petroleum.

The composition of petroleum

Petroleum consists mainly of a mixture of molecules called *hydrocarbons.* Hydrocarbons are combinations of two chemical elements, carbon (C) and hydrogen (H). Carbon atoms combine readily with one another, forming molecules shaped like chains, branches, and rings. Hydrogen atoms attach to the carbon atoms in these structures. The simplest hydrocarbon, called *methane* (CH_4), consists of four hydrogen atoms attached to a single carbon atom. Complex hydrocarbons can have 30 or more carbon atoms. Some petroleum deposits include hundreds of different kinds of hydrocarbons. See **Hydrocarbon.**

Different hydrocarbons in a petroleum deposit may exist as gases, liquids, or solids, depending on the temperature and pressure inside the deposit. Small molecules, such as methane, tend to exist as gases. These gases can be found at the top of a petroleum deposit or may be dissolved in liquid. Hydrocarbons with molecules that contain five or more carbon atoms are often found as liquids. Hydrocarbons with extremely large

molecules tend to exist as solids.

Each petroleum deposit contains a unique mixture of hydrocarbons. This mixture determines the *viscosity* (resistance to flow) of the deposit's crude oil. Some crude oils, called *light crudes,* have a relatively low viscosity— that is, they flow rather easily. Light crudes consist mainly of smaller hydrocarbon molecules and contain large amounts of dissolved gases. Crude oils that contain a high proportion of large hydrocarbon molecules are called *heavy crudes.* Heavy crudes have a relatively high viscosity. Light crudes can be produced, transported, and refined more cheaply and more easily than heavy crudes. Some heavy crudes are too thick to be produced at a profit.

In addition to hydrocarbons, all crude oils contain impurities, such as metallic compounds and sulfur. These impurities can make up as much as 5 percent of the weight of some crude oils.

Uses of petroleum

Petroleum has a greater variety of uses than perhaps any other substance in the world. Mixtures of different hydrocarbons give special characteristics to various *fractions* (parts) of petroleum. People use some fractions of petroleum, such as gasoline and kerosene, in their natural state. Other fractions must be further processed or combined with different substances before they can be used. Petroleum companies process most petroleum into gasoline, heating oil, and other fuels. The rest is converted chiefly into industrial raw materials and lubricants.

Petroleum as a fuel. Petroleum fuels ignite and burn readily and produce a great amount of heat in relation to their weight. They are also easier to handle, store, and transport than such other fuels as coal and wood. Petroleum is the source of nearly all the fuels used for trans-

Petroleum terms

Barrel is the standard unit used to measure crude oil and most petroleum products. One barrel equals 42 gallons (159 liters).

Benchmark crudes are crude oils, considered to be of average value, used in setting petroleum prices.

Completed well is a well that has been lined with pipe and sealed off from the surrounding rock formations.

Crude oil is liquid petroleum as it occurs naturally in a reservoir.

Derrick is a tall structure that holds the equipment used to drill an oil well.

Directional drilling is the use of special equipment to drill a well that turns or branches.

Drilling mud is a special fluid used to lubricate the drill bit during the drilling of a well.

Dry hole is a well that fails to produce a significant amount of oil or gas.

Fraction is any of the groups of hydrocarbons that make up crude oil. Fractions are separated during refining.

Gusher is a well that produces a large amount of oil without pumping.

Heavy crudes are less valuable crude oils that consist mostly of heavier fractions.

Hydrocarbon is a chemical compound made up of the elements hydrogen and carbon.

Light crudes are more valuable crude oils that consist mostly of lighter fractions.

Liquefied natural gas (LNG) is natural gas that has been turned into a liquid by cooling.

Mature fields are fields where petroleum production has slowed and become more expensive.

Migration is the movement of petroleum through layers of rock.

Natural gas is petroleum found in the form of a gas.

Offshore wells are wells drilled in oceans, seas, or lakes.

Oil tanker is a ship designed to carry large amounts of crude oil.

Perforator is a device that uses explosives to punch holes in a completed well, allowing petroleum production to begin.

Petrochemicals are chemicals processed from oil and gas.

Petroleum field is an area that contains one or more reservoirs.

Petroleum trap is an underground rock formation that blocks the movement of petroleum and so seals off a reservoir.

Primary recovery is a method in which the natural pressure in a reservoir is used to bring oil into a producing well.

Production rate is how rapidly a well can produce petroleum.

Refinery is a vast area of tanks and towers where crude oil is converted into various products.

Reservoir is an accumulation of petroleum below Earth's surface. It consists of crude oil and natural gas that collect in the pores of such rocks as limestone and sandstone.

Rig consists of the derrick, hoisting machinery, and other equipment used in drilling a petroleum well.

Roughneck is a worker on a drilling crew.

Thousands of cubic feet (Mcf) is the standard unit used to measure natural gas. One Mcf equals 1,000 cubic feet (28 cubic meters) of gas at a set temperature and pressure.

Well log is a record of different rock formations encountered during the drilling of a well.

Wildcat well is a well drilled in an area where no oil or gas has been found.

---

portation and of many fuels used to produce heat and electric power.

Fuels for transportation include gasoline, diesel fuel, and jet fuel. Most light motor vehicles and all piston-engine airplanes use gasoline. Nearly all trains, ships, buses, and large trucks use diesel fuel. Diesel fuel requires less refining and is cheaper than gasoline. Jet airplanes burn jet fuel, which is either pure kerosene or a mixture of gasoline and kerosene.

Other petroleum fuels are used to generate heat and electric power. Such fuels include *distillate oils* and *residual oils*. Distillate oils are lighter oils, most of which are used to heat houses and small business places. Residual oils are heavier, thicker oils. They provide power for electric utilities, factories, and large ships. Residual oils are also used to heat large buildings.

Where access to a natural gas pipeline is available, many homes use natural gas for cooking and heating. People who do not have access to a pipeline, including many people who live on farms or in mobile homes, often use *liquefied petroleum gas* (LPG) for heating and cooking. LPG is a gas produced during petroleum refining that has been compressed until it forms a liquid. LPG is used in industry for cutting and welding metals and on farms for operating some kinds of equipment.

Petroleum as a raw material. Other petroleum fractions serve as raw materials in manufacturing. Many of these fractions are converted into chemicals called *petrochemicals*. Petrochemicals serve as a basic ingredient in the manufacture of *polymers*. Polymers are large molecules formed by the chemical linking of many smaller molecules into a long chain. Manufacturers use

---

Some uses of petroleum products

Fuels

For transportation

Aviation gasoline	Gasoline
Diesel fuel	Jet fuel

For heating and energy production

Distillate oils	Natural gas
Kerosene	Residual oils
Liquefied petroleum gas (LPG)	

Raw materials

Asphalt	Petroleum coke
Carbon black	Tar
Industrial hydrogen	Wax
Naphtha	

Miscellaneous oils

Lubricating oils and greases	Road oils
Medicinal oils	Technical oils

Petrochemicals

Alcohol	Food additives
Ammonia	Gasoline additives
Candles	Ink
Cosmetics	Insecticides
Drugs	Paint
Dyes	Plastics
Explosives	Resins
Fertilizers	Solvents
Fibers	Synthetic rubber

polymers to create plastics and other synthetic fibers for a wide variety of products, including food packaging, sewing thread, and computer casings and parts. Petrochemicals also form an ingredient in many cosmetics, detergents, drugs, fertilizers, and insecticides, and in hundreds of other products.

By-products of petroleum refining also serve as raw materials in certain industries. These by-products include asphalt, the chief roadbuilding material; and wax, an essential ingredient in such products as candles and furniture polish.

Other uses. Factories convert other petroleum fractions into lubricants or industrial oils. Lubricants reduce friction between the moving parts of equipment. They range from the thin, clear oil used in scientific instruments to the heavy grease applied to aircraft landing gear. Specialized industrial oils include cutting oils and electrical oils, which are used in manufacturing.

How petroleum deposits form

Most geologists believe petroleum developed from the remains of tiny plants and animals that died hundreds of millions of years ago. Those organisms once lived in the waters of river deltas and along coastlines. As they died, their remains settled to the sea floor and became trapped in *sediment* (particles of sand, mud, clay, and other materials). The remains consisted mostly of water molecules and organic materials rich in carbon and hydrogen. Over time, new layers of sediment piled up. As the sediments containing the remains became buried deeper and deeper, they were exposed to more intense heat and pressure. These forces compressed the sediment into rock. At the same time, chemical reactions changed the organic material into a waxy substance known as *kerogen.* Further heating caused the kerogen to separate into crude oil and natural gas.

Most petroleum did not remain where it was formed. It migrated through rock and was transported as Earth's outer layers shifted.

Migration occurred as petroleum traveled through *porous* rock. Porous rock contains tiny holes, or *pores,* that allow fluids to flow into and through the rock. Petroleum flowed differently into different kinds of rock. It flowed most easily through porous rocks called *sand-*

Pride International

An offshore drilling rig can drill to a petroleum reservoir deep beneath the ocean floor. This type of rig, called a *semisubmersible rig,* floats on legs filled with air.

stones and *carbonates.* These rocks are called *permeable* rocks because they have interconnected pores that allowed petroleum to pass through them.

Petroleum migrated because water was present in the porous rock where petroleum formed. Water, which is denser than petroleum, flowed slowly downward through the rock. The water displaced petroleum and forced it to flow upward. Natural gas is less dense than crude oil. Therefore, in deposits where petroleum included undissolved gas, the gas migrated even farther upward. Eventually, the crude oil settled on top of the

© Sal Maimone, SuperStock

Derricks and beam pumps crowd a California oil field. Derricks are tall steel structures that support the equipment used to drill for petroleum. Beam pumps, which feature a long beam that rocks back and forth, help draw crude oil to the surface.

water. If gas was present, it settled on top of the oil.

As petroleum migrated upward, it tended to flow into areas of more permeable rock. Thus, it may have moved several miles or kilometers from where it originally formed. Eventually, the petroleum migrated to a place where it was surrounded by rock with few or no pores. This rock, called *impermeable* rock, prevented the petroleum from moving upward. Such an area is called a *petroleum trap.* The petroleum collected below the trap in an area of porous rock is called a *petroleum reservoir.*

The most common kinds of petroleum traps are *anticlines, faults, stratigraphic traps,* and *salt domes.* An anticline is an archlike formation of rock under which petroleum may collect. A fault is a fracture in Earth's rocky outer shell. Rock can shift along a fault, moving an impermeable layer of rock next to a permeable one that contains oil. Most stratigraphic traps consist of layers of impermeable rock that surround oilbearing rocks. In a salt dome, a cylinder- or cone-shaped formation of salt pushes up through sedimentary rocks, causing the rocks to arch and fracture in its path. Petroleum may accumulate above or along the sides of such a formation.

Shifting of Earth's surface changed the position of the ancient deltas and coastlines where petroleum formed. Earth's surface is made up of about 30 huge, rigid slabs called *tectonic plates.* The plates slide around over a layer of rock that is so hot that it flows, even though it remains solid. The continents are embedded in the tops of plates, so as those plates move, they carry the continents along with them. See **Plate tectonics.**

The shifting of the plates moved some of the deltas and coastlines where petroleum had formed. Some of these areas moved inland. Others sank into much deeper waters, in some cases to depths of more than 2 miles (3.2 kilometers). In some places, a single deposit of petroleum appears to have split where two plates broke apart and drifted away from each other, carrying the petroleum with them.

Finding petroleum

Until the 1990's, drilling for petroleum was a major financial risk. A success rate of 20 percent—finding 2 producing wells for every 10 wells drilled—was considered normal. Since then, however, scientists and engineers have developed technology that has raised this success rate to about 70 percent. Prospectors are able to conduct geological studies to locate areas where petroleum will likely be found. Geophysical studies help prospectors confirm the presence of petroleum and learn more about the deposit.

Geological studies. Petroleum geologists study rock formations on and below Earth's surface to determine where petroleum might be found. They may begin by selecting an area that seems favorable to the formation of petroleum. Geologists then make a detailed map of the surface features of the area. They may use photographs taken from airplanes and satellites in addition to their ground-level observations. The geologists study the map for signs of possible oil traps. For example, the appearance of a low bulge on an otherwise flat surface may indicate the presence of a salt dome, a common petroleum trap.

If the site looks promising, geologists may use a drill to obtain *cores,* cylindrical samples of the underground

Petroleum in the Middle East

This map shows major oil fields and oil-producing areas in the Middle East. The region contains most of the world's petroleum reserves.

△ Giant oil field
450 million to 5 billion barrels

△ Supergiant oil field
5 billion to 100 billion barrels

△ Megagiant oil field
More than 100 billion barrels

Major petroleum-producing area

WORLD BOOK map

layers of rock. The geologists analyze the cores for chemical composition, structure, and other factors that relate to the formation of petroleum.

Geologists may also study *well logs.* A well log is a record of the rock formations encountered during the drilling of a well. Well logs describe such characteristics as the radioactivity, density, and fluid content of the rocks. Geologists use well logs from a certain area to estimate the location and size of other possible petroleum deposits in the same area.

Geophysical studies help prospectors confirm the presence of petroleum in an area or determine new areas for petroleum exploration. Scientists called *geophysicists* search for petroleum by measuring gravity and magnetism. They also conduct *seismic studies,* studies of vibrations in the ground.

Gravity measurements help prospectors locate porous rocks deep below the ground. The pull of gravity is slightly stronger at places on Earth's surface where underground rocks are more dense. Likewise, the pull of gravity is slightly weaker where underground rocks are less dense. Porous rocks are much less dense than nonporous rocks. Also, petroleum is less dense than water, so porous rocks that contain petroleum are less dense than those that contain water. Geophysicists can locate low-density rocks that may contain petroleum by finding areas where gravity's pull is relatively weak.

Geophysicists measure Earth's gravity using a device called a *gravity meter* or *gravimeter.* The meter consists of a weight hanging from an extremely sensitive spring. Tiny changes in Earth's gravity cause the spring to lengthen or shorten. The meter measures the length of the spring to determine the pull of gravity.

Magnetic measurements help scientists locate petroleum deposits that were transported as Earth's crust shifted. Each rock formation has its own *magnetic field,* an invisible region of magnetic force that is *aligned* (lined up) in a certain direction. The strength and align-

Petroleum around the world

This map shows the world's largest oil fields, based on the total amount of recoverable oil, as well as other major oil-producing regions. Petroleum is found on every continent and in many offshore areas. Petroleum is produced on every continent except Antarctica.

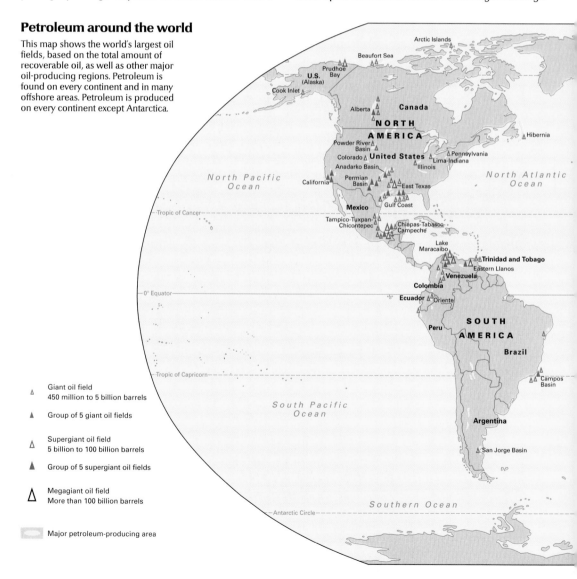

△ Giant oil field
   450 million to 5 billion barrels

▲ Group of 5 giant oil fields

△ Supergiant oil field
   5 billion to 100 billion barrels

▲ Group of 5 supergiant oil fields

△ Megagiant oil field
   More than 100 billion barrels

▭ Major petroleum-producing area

ment of the magnetic field depends on where the rock originally formed. By measuring the rock's magnetic field, scientists can determine where a formation originated. For example, magnetic analysis might indicate that a particular formation was at an ancient river delta or ocean coast when the rock formed. Such a formation might contain petroleum.

Geophysicists measure the magnetic field using a device called a *magnetometer*. The magnetometer measures both the *declination* (compass direction) and the *inclination* (up-and-down direction) of the magnetic field. Scientists can take these measurements from the air or on the surface.

Seismic studies help scientists locate deposits of petroleum below the ground. During a seismic study, scientists use special equipment to generate a *seismic event,* a miniature earthquake in which waves of vibration travel downward through the ground. These waves travel to different layers of underground rock and

bounce back. By studying the waves that bounce back, scientists can determine the depth and density of different layers of rock. This allows them to locate potential petroleum traps. Sensitive measurements can even reveal direct evidence of petroleum trapped in the rock. Seismic studies require a great amount of work and special equipment. For this reason, petroleum companies often limit such studies to areas of fewer than 40 square miles (100 square kilometers).

In the early days of seismic studies, petroleum prospectors used several thousand pounds of explosives to create a seismic event. Today, special *thumper trucks* create the vibrations by hammering the ground. The reflected waves are recorded by a group of sensors called *geophones.*

To search for petroleum deposits beneath the ocean floor, a ship equipped with devices called *air guns* shoots highly pressurized air into the water. The air generates a wave of energy that travels to the ocean floor.

Where petroleum is found
Most petroleum lies in underground formations called *traps.* In a trap, crude oil collects in the pores of certain kinds of rock. Natural gas and water are also present in most traps. The most common types of traps are *anticlines, faults, stratigraphic traps,* and *salt domes.*

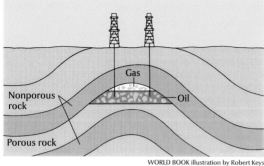

WORLD BOOK illustration by Robert Keys

An anticline is an archlike formation.

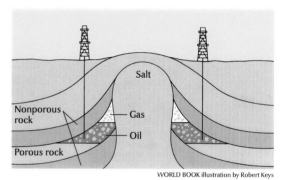

WORLD BOOK illustration by Robert Keys

A fault is a fracture in Earth's rocky outer shell.

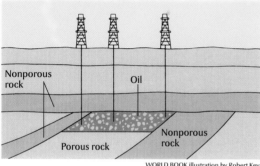

WORLD BOOK illustration by Robert Keys

A stratigraphic trap consists of horizontal layers of rock.

WORLD BOOK illustration by Robert Keys

A salt dome is formed by a large mass of salt.

When the wave strikes the floor, it creates a seismic event, sending waves of vibration traveling downward through the rock. Sensors called *hydrophones* record the vibrations reflected by different layers.

Geophones and hydrophones transmit their data to a computer. The computer can display the data mathematically or produce an image of the underground rock formations. Data from a single seismic event can generate a two-dimensional view called a *cross section* of the rock layers beneath the surface. Often, the truck or boat will move, generating several seismic events as the geophones or hydrophones follow it. This generates a series of cross sections that the computer can combine to form a three-dimensional model of rock formations beneath the ground.

Seismic studies have revolutionized petroleum exploration. Many petroleum engineers believe advances in seismic exploration have brought about much of the improvement in the success rate of well drilling. Three-dimensional seismic models have reduced the uncertainty involved in drilling a new well. They have also enabled prospectors to identify previously overlooked deposits.

Seismic models have also helped petroleum companies produce petroleum more efficiently. Engineers and geologists can use seismic models to determine the best place to drill into a deposit. In this way, seismic models reduce the number of wells needed and greatly speed the process of producing petroleum. These ad-

vances have made petroleum production faster and cheaper, allowing companies to produce petroleum from deposits that were once considered too small to be profitably mined.

Petroleum companies can also conduct seismic studies of a deposit as petroleum is extracted. Geologists use this information to monitor the petroleum remaining in a deposit. This technique has allowed more petroleum to be extracted from reservoirs where production had ceased.

Drilling for petroleum

Once prospectors have located a potential petroleum deposit, a drilling crew must drill a well to the suspected reservoir. New wells are called *wildcat wells,* reflecting the uncertainty of finding petroleum. Drilling crews use a giant drill called a *rotary drilling rig* to bore a hole down to the petroleum. They also can drill a well using special equipment that turns at an angle or even travels sideways, a technique called *directional drilling.* Drilling a well allows geologists to test and evaluate a petroleum deposit.

A rotary drilling rig consists of a powerful drill and the machines and structures that allow it to operate. The drill is mounted on a tall structure called a *derrick.* The derrick supports the *drill pipe,* a length of pipe that descends into the well as it is drilled. The drill pipe consists of smaller sections of pipe attached end to end. A large drill bit is attached to the bottom of the drill pipe.

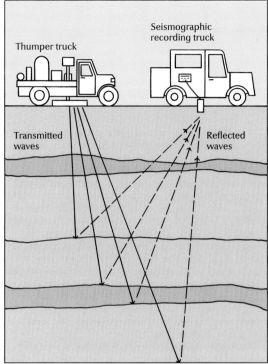

WORLD BOOK illustration by Steven Liska

Seismic studies help prospectors locate underground rock formations that might contain petroleum. A special truck called a *thumper truck* strikes the ground. This generates a *seismic event,* a miniature earthquake in which waves of vibration travel through the ground. The waves bounce off the layers of underground rock. Another truck records the reflected waves. These data can be used to map underground rock formations.

A turntable on the floor of the derrick rotates the drill pipe, causing the bit to grind through soil and rock. As the bit drills deeper, the drill pipe is lowered into the ground. When the drill pipe cannot be lowered any farther, workers attach another length of pipe to the top of the drill pipe and continue drilling.

Workers raise and lower the drill pipe using a hoisting mechanism called the *draw works.* The draw works operates somewhat like a fishing rod and reel. Steel cable is unwound from a motorized wheel called the *hoisting drum.* The cable is then threaded through two *blocks* (sets of pulleys)—the *crown block,* at the top of the rig, and the *traveling block,* which hangs inside the derrick. The workers attach the upper end of the drill pipe to the traveling block with a giant hook. They can then lower the pipe into the hole or lift it out by turning the hoisting drum.

Workers use a special fluid to lubricate the drill bit. This fluid, called *mud,* is a complex artificial mixture with many ingredients. Workers pump mud down through the drill pipe. At the bottom of the pipe, the mud flows out and lubricates the drill bit. The mixture then flows up around the outside of the drill pipe and out of the well. The mud carries away the bits of rock that the drill has broken loose, keeping the well free from debris.

Workers continue to add length to the drill pipe until the well reaches the petroleum reservoir. Working in

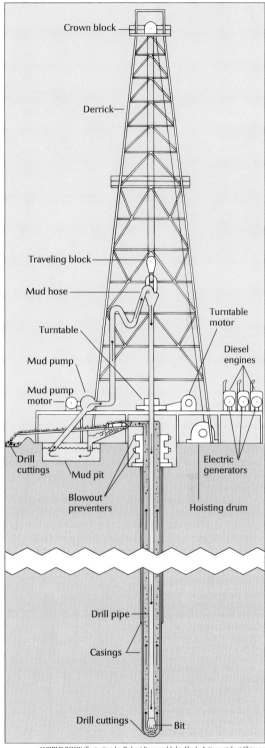

WORLD BOOK illustration by Robert Keys and John Fleck, Artisan etalent-Chicago

A rotary drilling rig includes a derrick and the machinery used to raise and lower the drilling equipment. As the drill pipe is lowered, a turntable rotates it, causing the bit to bore through the ground. A fluid called *mud* is pumped into the well to lubricate the bit and bring up *cuttings* (pieces of rock).

A drill bit must be changed when it becomes dull or when a different type of bit is needed. Workers attach the new bit to the drill pipe before lowering the pipe back into the well.

this manner, drilling crews have drilled experimental wells more than 9 miles (14 kilometers) deep. Petroleum wells often measure 5,000 to 20,000 feet (1,500 to 6,100 meters) deep.

Special drilling rigs can be used to drill for oil beneath the ocean floor. These rigs may be mounted on a stable platform, on a floating platform, or on a special boat called a *drillship*. Drillship crews use small computer-controlled propellers called *thrusters* to keep the ship steady over the well.

Directional drilling. Most wells are drilled straight down. Some drilling crews, however, use directional drilling equipment to drill wells that turn to one side as they penetrate the rock. These wells may even turn so much that the drill bit moves horizontally. Directional

drilling requires special drills. These drills are powered by the pressure of mud, water, or air flowing through the drill bit.

Directional drilling can help a well reach deeper into the petroleum reservoir. This exposes more of the well's length to reservoir rock, speeding the rate at which the well produces petroleum. Directional drilling also enables petroleum companies to drill wells that branch off from a single vertical well. This allows several wells to be drilled without moving the drilling rig.

Some directionally drilled wells are *multilateral wells*. These wells have branches that leave the main well at about the same level. Other directionally drilled wells are *multilevel wells*. Branches in these wells leave the main well at two or more levels. Some extremely long horizontal wells travel sideways for several miles or kilometers. Some complex wells have several branches extending hundreds of feet or meters from the main shaft.

Special tools and instruments enable crews to take measurements while drilling and to track the bit as it advances. As drilling proceeds, the crew makes continuous measurements and compares them with knowledge obtained from seismic measurements and information from previously drilled wells. The crew uses this information to steer the drill. This technique, known as *geosteering,* allows the crew to pinpoint exact locations inside a petroleum reservoir.

Reservoir evaluation. Once a well has been drilled, scientists test and evaluate the petroleum deposit. Using data from seismic studies, they calculate the volume of natural gas, crude oil, and water in the reservoir. They analyze drill cores, well logs, and *mud logs* to find out how porous and permeable the reservoir rock is. Mud logs are records of different types of rock and other substances carried to the surface by drilling mud. Scientists test samples of petroleum from the new well to determine its viscosity and chemical composition. They also measure the amount of pressure the petroleum is under.

Evaluation allows scientists and engineers to predict the well's *production rate*—that is, how rapidly the well can produce petroleum. Testing the petroleum can help determine how difficult it will be to extract and refine. Petroleum companies use this information to determine if the petroleum can be produced at a profit.

Directional drilling

Petroleum companies can use special equipment to drill wells that turn or branch to reach different parts of a petroleum deposit. *Multilateral wells* have multiple branches that leave the main well at the same level. *Multilevel wells* have branches that leave the main well at more than one level. Wells that travel sideways for a long distance are called *horizontal wells.* Horizontal wells enable petroleum companies to reach petroleum beneath sensitive wilderness areas, under buildings, or below other areas where setting up a drilling rig would be undesirable or impossible.

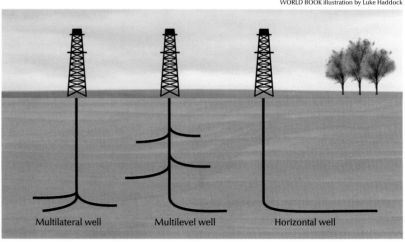

Multilateral well   Multilevel well   Horizontal well

Offshore drilling   Petroleum companies can drill offshore wells using *jack-up rigs, semisubmersible rigs,* or *drill-ships.* A jack-up rig, which can be raised or lowered to various heights, has legs that rest on the ocean floor. A semisubmersible rig floats on legs filled with air. A drillship has drilling equipment mounted on its deck and a special opening in its hull through which the drill pipe is lowered.

WORLD BOOK illustration by Robert Keys

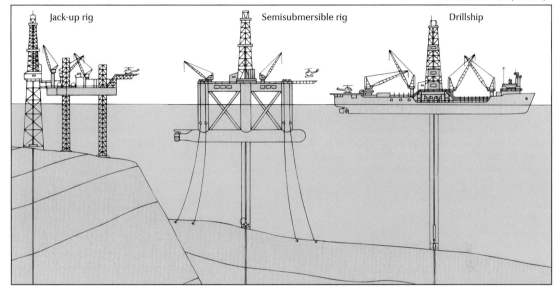

Jack-up rig   Semisubmersible rig   Drillship

Producing petroleum

If testing indicates that the petroleum in a deposit can be profitably extracted, workers prepare the well for production. This process is called *completing* the well. Once the well has been completed, it can begin producing petroleum.

Completing the well. Wells are completed as soon as possible because a well that is left open can quickly develop problems. A well in brittle rock might fill up with debris or even collapse. An open well shaft can allow other fluids to mix with the petroleum, complicating the extraction and refining process. An open well can also allow petroleum to leak into *aquifers* (reservoirs of water in the rock), contaminating the local water supply. Open wells can decrease the pressure inside a petroleum reservoir, making the petroleum difficult or impossible to extract.

Workers begin by lining the well with metal pipes called *casing.* They then fill the space around the casing with concrete to seal different rock formations from one another. When the concrete has hardened, workers lower a device called a *perforator* to the bottom of the well. The perforator uses explosives to blast holes in the casing that will allow petroleum to flow into the well. Workers then lower a thinner pipe called *tubing* that will carry the petroleum to the surface. They remove the drilling rig and place a device called a *Christmas tree* over the well. A Christmas tree is a series of pipes and valves that controls the flow of petroleum.

Stimulating production. The oil in the reservoir is under pressure. This pressure drives petroleum into the well. However, the drilling process often damages the reservoir rock near the well, decreasing its permeability. This can slow the flow of petroleum or even prevent it from entering the well. Drillers use *stimulation* techniques to restore or increase the flow of petroleum.

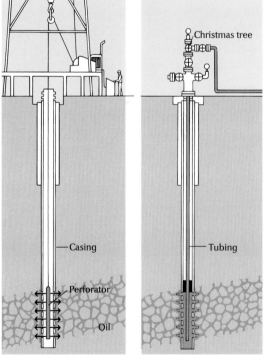

WORLD BOOK illustration by Robert Keys

Completing a well. After lining the well with pipes called *casing,* the crew lowers an instrument called a *perforator* into the well. The perforator punches holes in the casing through which oil can enter, *left.* Then the crew installs the *tubing,* a string of smaller pipes that conducts the oil to the surface; and a *Christmas tree,* a set of valves that controls the flow of oil, *right.*

Some stimulation techniques use chemicals. Engineers can flush solutions of hydrochloric acid and hydrofluoric acid down the well to dissolve particles of drilling mud and natural clay that tend to accumulate around the well. They may use a hydrocarbon called *toluene* and other organic solvents to remove solid fractions of petroleum, such as *paraffins* (waxes) and *asphaltenes* (hard, brittle particles of asphalt), which can also gum up the rock near the well.

Another stimulation technique, called *hydraulic fracturing,* creates a crack in the reservoir by injecting highly pressurized fluids into the well. The fracturing fluids carry particles known as *proppants* that "prop open" the fracture. Proppants include synthetic materials and clean sand of uniform particle size. The proppants can be hundreds of thousands of times more permeable than the reservoir rock, allowing petroleum to flow easily into the well and increasing the rate of production.

Primary recovery. During the early stages of production, the natural pressure of the petroleum deposit will force crude oil into the well. This stage is called *primary recovery.*

Over time, removing crude oil from a reservoir reduces the pressure in the reservoir. As reservoir pressure drops, the well's production rate slows. If the reservoir contains liquid petroleum with almost no dissolved gas, removing a relatively small amount of fluid can rapidly reduce the reservoir pressure. Recovery of as little as 5 percent of the initial crude oil can make the reservoir pressure equal to the pressure at the bottom of the well. When this happens, the reservoir pressure no longer drives the oil into the well, stranding about 95 percent of the original oil in the reservoir.

Most reservoirs, however, hold crude oil that contains a significant amount of dissolved gases. As the pressure in such a reservoir decreases, more gas comes out of solution, helping to maintain pressure within the reservoir. In this type of reservoir, up to 30 percent of the original petroleum can be recovered before the pressure in the reservoir equals the pressure in the bottom of the well.

In many deposits, underground water also pushes against petroleum. The more water a reservoir contains, the more crude oil the water can drive to the surface. Water pressure can help wells extract 35 to 50 percent or more of the crude oil in a reservoir.

As reservoir pressure declines, engineers must take steps to help the petroleum reach the top of the well. They can extract gas from the top of the reservoir and

How oil is recovered   A completed well will begin to produce crude oil. As more oil is produced, what remains in the ground becomes increasingly difficult to recover. Oil production is typically divided into three stages called (1) primary recovery, (2) secondary recovery, and (3) tertiary recovery.

WORLD BOOK illustrations by Robert Keys

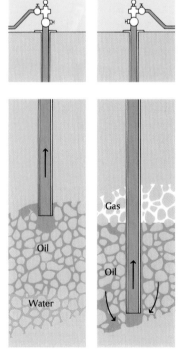

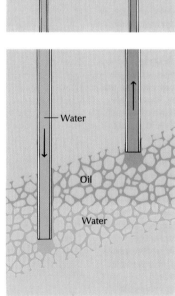

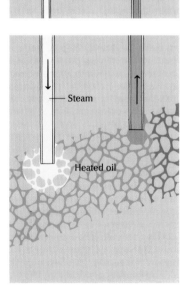

Primary recovery relies on natural pressure to drive oil into the well. Water rising at the bottom of the deposit can push oil up into the well. Gas at the top of the deposit presses down on the oil, forcing it into the well.

Secondary recovery involves restoring some of the pressure that is lost as oil is recovered. In the most common method, called *waterflooding,* water is injected into the bottom of the deposit. The rising water forces more oil into the well.

Tertiary recovery includes a variety of methods for recovering more oil from a deposit. In one such method, steam is injected into the deposit. The steam heats the oil and makes it thinner, enabling it to flow more freely into the well.

inject it into the bottom of the well. The gas dissolves into the crude oil at the bottom of the well, reducing its density. Less pressure is required to drive the less dense fluid to the surface.

Engineers can also use a pump to reduce the pressure inside the well, drawing more petroleum to the surface. The most common pumping device is the *beam pump.* This device gets its name from a long steel beam that rocks like a seesaw as the pumping mechanism connected to it goes up and down inside the well.

Eventually, water will seep into the well. The most expensive activity in petroleum production is the removing and disposing of water. Crews usually dispose of water by injecting it into another underground reservoir.

Eventually, the production rate of an oil well will drop dramatically. Lower production may result from many factors, including a drop in permeability or reservoir pressure, or the increased production of water. A petroleum reservoir is said to be *mature* when production at its wells slows and becomes more expensive.

Secondary and tertiary recovery. A mature petroleum reservoir, however, still contains most of its original petroleum. Engineers use many techniques to coax more petroleum from the wells. All of these techniques involve injecting fluids into strategically placed wells to stimulate the flow of oil into producing wells.

The most common technique used to produce oil from a mature reservoir is called *secondary recovery* or *waterflooding.* In this technique, the drillers inject water into the bottom of a reservoir. As water levels at the bottom of the reservoir rise, they force petroleum into the producing wells. Secondary recovery often uses water that has been recovered from the reservoir during primary recovery.

Other techniques called *tertiary recovery* or *enhanced oil recovery* methods extract crude oil that remains trapped in the rock. Tertiary recovery techniques are often too expensive to produce a profit.

In tertiary recovery, engineers often inject chemicals called *surfactants* into the well. Surfactants are soaps that literally wash oil from reservoir rocks. A similar technique treats the reservoir with *miscible floods,* injections of polymers mixed into water. The polymers make the water viscous enough to sweep liquid petroleum toward the producing wells. If the water were not so viscous, it would push through the petroleum and flow into the producing wells.

The most common and successful tertiary recovery technique is called *thermal recovery.* In thermal recovery, engineers pump hot water or steam into a mature oil reservoir. Engineers use this technique to produce heavy crude oils that are so viscous that they do not flow. The steam or water reduces the viscosity of the oil, allowing it to flow into the producing wells.

Natural and artificial recovery techniques still leave a large part of the original petroleum in place. In even the most mature and heavily produced reservoirs, more oil may remain than has been brought to the surface. Production ceases when extracting the oil becomes too expensive to be profitable.

Transporting petroleum

After petroleum reaches the surface, devices called *separators* separate crude oil from natural gas. Other devices remove water from both substances.

Some petroleum companies inject unwanted natural gas back into the reservoir. Other companies pump natural gas into a pipeline for transportation to a processing facility. If a pipeline is unavailable or inadequate, the natural gas may be converted into a liquid by cooling it. Gas that has been liquefied in this way is called *liquefied natural gas* (LNG). LNG may take up $\frac{1}{600}$ as much storage space as the same amount of unliquefied gas. For more information on how natural gas is transported and processed, see **Gas** (fuel).

Crude oil travels over land from the oil well to the refinery through pipelines. Pipelines may carry the oil from a few miles or kilometers to hundreds of miles or kilometers. One of the best-known pipelines, the Trans-Alaska Pipeline, stretches about 800 miles (1,300 kilometers) from oil fields on Alaska's North Slope near the Arctic Ocean to the port of Valdez on the coast of the Pacific Ocean. In Canada, the Enbridge Pipeline system carries oil about 3,300 miles (5,300 kilometers) from Edmonton, Alberta, to Montreal, Quebec. The Friendship Pipeline system, which measures about 1,625 miles (2,615 kilometers), carries oil from the Ural Mountains in Russia to other countries in Europe.

Where oceans and seas are available, special ships called *tankers* carry petroleum. Some tankers can hold more than 1 million barrels of petroleum. A petroleum barrel holds 42 gallons (159 liters). Tankers carry most of the oil transported between nations.

Refining petroleum

Crude oil arrives at a petroleum refinery, a maze of towers, tanks, and pipes. Refineries hum with activity day and night. They can operate continuously for years before being shut down for repairs. Refineries range in size from small plants that process about 150 barrels of crude oil a day to giant complexes with a daily capacity of more than 600,000 barrels.

A refinery converts crude oil into useful products by separating it into its various fractions. The fractions are then chemically changed and treated with other substances. The refining process includes (1) separation, (2) conversion, and (3) chemical treatment.

Separation. The first stage in petroleum refining is *fractional distillation.* Fractional distillation separates crude oil into some of its fractions. Additional fractions may be separated from these fractions by processes called *solvent extraction* and *dewaxing.*

Fractional distillation is based on the principle that different fractions have different boiling points. As crude oil is heated, each fraction *vaporizes* (turns into a gas or vapor) at its boiling point. For example, some kinds of gasoline vaporize at about 90 °F (32 °C), while some of the heavy fuel oils have boiling points higher than 600 °F (316 °C). As a vaporized fraction's temperature falls below its boiling point, it *condenses* (turns into a liquid).

In fractional distillation, crude oil is pumped through pipes inside a boiler and heated to temperatures of over 650 °F (343 °C). The resulting mixture of hot gases and liquids then passes into a vertical steel cylinder called a *fractionating tower* or *bubble tower.* A fractionating tower is divided into several different levels. The bottom level of the tower is the hottest. Each level above the bottom is slightly cooler than the one below. As vapor-

**How oil is
transported**

Petroleum and petroleum products are transported by a variety of methods during their journey from the oil field to the consumer. A device called a *separator* separates natural gas from crude oil. Pipelines then carry the crude oil to a tanker or directly to a refinery. Petroleum products travel from the refinery to market by tanker, truck, railroad tank car, or pipeline.

WORLD BOOK illustration by Robert Keys

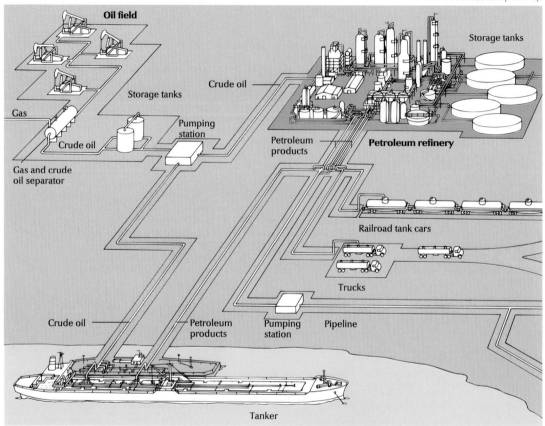

ized petroleum rises through the tower, fractions condense when the temperature drops below their boiling point. Heavy fuel oils condense in the lower sections. Lighter fractions, such as gasoline and kerosene, condense in the middle and upper sections. At each level, condensing fractions collect in trays and are drawn off by pipes along the sides of the tower.

Some fractions do not cool enough to condense. They pass out of the top of the fractionating tower into a collection tank called the *vapor recovery unit.* Other fractions, which vaporize at temperatures higher than those in the furnace, remain as liquids or semisolids. These *residues* are recovered from the bottom of the tower and refined into such products as asphalt and lubricating oils.

Fractions produced by fractional distillation are called *straight-run products.* Almost all must undergo conversion and chemical treatment before they can be used.

Solvent extraction separates additional fractions from certain straight-run products. A chemical called a *solvent* either dissolves some of the fractions or causes them to separate out as solids. The principal solvents used include *furfural* and *phenol.* Many refineries improve the quality of gasoline, kerosene, and lubricating oils by solvent extraction.

Dewaxing, also called *crystallization,* is used chiefly to remove wax and other semisolid substances from heavy fractions. The fractions are cooled to a temperature at which these heavier substances form crystals or solidify. They are then put through a filter that separates out the solid particles.

Conversion. Although nearly all petroleum can be refined into useful products, some fractions are much more valuable than others. Gasoline, for example, accounts for nearly 50 percent of the crude oil used in the United States. Gasoline, however, makes up only a small percentage of the straight-run products. Many less valuable fractions make up a higher percentage of crude oil.

Scientists have developed several methods to convert less useful fractions into more valuable fractions. These methods fall into three main groups: (1) cracking processes, (2) combining processes, and (3) reforming processes. Conversion allows refiners to produce about half a barrel of gasoline from each barrel of crude oil.

Cracking processes convert heavy fractions into lighter ones, mainly gasoline. These processes not only increase the quantity of gasoline obtained from oil but also improve the quality. Gasoline produced by cracking has a higher *octane number* than straight-run gasoline. Octane number is a measure of how smoothly fuel

How petroleum is refined A device called a *fractionating tower* separates the various *fractions* (useful parts) of petroleum. A boiler heats the oil, vaporizing some of the fractions. The vapors cool as they rise through the tower. As each fraction cools below its boiling point, it condenses into liquid and collects on a tray. Heavier fractions are often separated under reduced pressure, which lowers their boiling points.

WORLD BOOK illustration by Jay E. Bensen

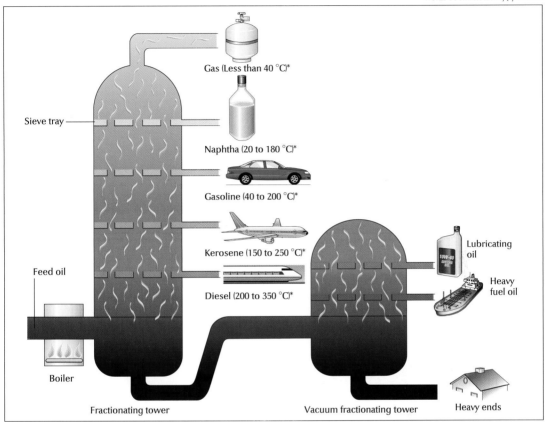

Gas (Less than 40 °C)*

Sieve tray

Naphtha (20 to 180 °C)*

Gasoline (40 to 200 °C)*

Kerosene (150 to 250 °C)*

Feed oil

Diesel (200 to 350 °C)*

Lubricating oil

Heavy fuel oil

Boiler

Fractionating tower

Vacuum fractionating tower

Heavy ends

*Boiling temperatures vary for different crude oils, end products, and refining processes.

burns in an engine. See **Octane number.**

There are two principal types of cracking processes—*thermal cracking* and *catalytic cracking.* In thermal cracking, heavy fractions are subjected to intense heat and pressure to weaken the bonds that hold large, complex molecules together. The heat and pressure *crack* (break down) these molecules into the simpler ones that make up light fractions.

In catalytic cracking, a *catalyst* is used to accelerate the thermal cracking process. A catalyst is a substance that sets off or speeds up a chemical reaction without being changed by the reaction. In this form of cracking, the fractions of petroleum are heated and then passed over minerals called *zeolites* or other catalysts. The combination of heat and catalytic action causes the heavy fractions to crack into lighter ones. Catalytic cracking is more widely used than thermal cracking alone because it requires less pressure and produces higher-octane gasoline.

During cracking, hydrogen may be added to the fractions. This procedure, known as *hydrocracking,* further increases the yield of high quality gasoline and other useful products.

Combining processes do the reverse of cracking. They combine simple gaseous hydrocarbons to form more complex fractions. As a result, many of the gases produced by distillation and cracking are converted into high-octane liquid fuels and valuable chemicals. The major combining processes include *polymerization* and *alkylation.*

In polymerization, gases are subjected to heat and pressure in the presence of a catalyst. The hydrocarbon molecules unite to form polymers. Polymers are effective ingredients in high-octane gasoline. Alkylation is similar to polymerization. It produces a fraction called *alkylate,* which is used in both aviation fuel and gasoline.

Reforming processes use heat and a catalyst to rearrange the molecules of a fraction so that they form different hydrocarbon groups. Instead of breaking the molecules apart or combining them, reforming changes their structure. Reforming produces high-octane fuels and *aromatics,* which are chemicals used in making explosives, plastics, food preservatives, and many other products.

Chemical treatment. Nearly all fractions are chemically treated before they are sent to consumers. The method of treatment depends on the type of crude oil and on the intended use of the petroleum product.

Many fractions are treated to remove impurities. The most common impurities are sulfur compounds, which can damage machinery and pollute the air when burned. Treatment with hydrogen is a widely used method of removing sulfur compounds. In this method, called *hydrotreating,* fractions are mixed with hydrogen, heated, and then exposed to a catalyst. The sulfur in the fractions combines with the hydrogen, forming the gas hydrogen sulfide. The hydrogen sulfide is then trapped in a vapor recovery unit.

Some fractions perform better if they are blended or combined with other substances. For example, refineries blend various lubricating oils to obtain different degrees of viscosity. Gasoline is blended with chemicals called *additives,* which help it burn more smoothly and give it other special properties.

Once refining processes are complete, such fractions as gasoline and kerosene are shipped to fueling stations. Other fractions are sent to factories for use in manufacturing. These products travel from the refinery by pipeline, truck, railroad, or ship to their final destinations.

Environmental problems

The production and use of petroleum has given rise to several environmental problems. Toxic crude oil can be spilled on land or in water, poisoning plants and animals. The burning of fuels derived from petroleum releases toxic gases that pollute the air. Some scientists even believe that the burning of petroleum fuels contributes to global climate change.

Spills and seeps. Petroleum can spill during many stages of its production, transportation, and consumption. Petroleum can leak from wells on land or in the sea. Pipelines can break, causing petroleum to spill during transportation. Oil tankers may collide or sink, releasing huge loads of crude oil into the water. Accidents or disasters can cause toxic petroleum products to spill from power plants, refineries, and even gasoline stations. Some petroleum also seeps naturally from openings in the sea floor.

Spills and seeps release about 15 million barrels of crude oil into the environment each year. This amount makes up only about $\frac{1}{5}$ of the oil consumed in one day. About 10 percent of this oil seeps naturally from the ocean floor. Petroleum companies spill about 28 percent of this oil during production and transportation. The remaining 62 percent is released in spills during industrial and private consumption.

Although only a small fraction of petroleum produced is spilled, petroleum spills are a major environmental problem. Most of the chemicals in petroleum are toxic to living things. Petroleum spills can poison plants, animals, and even people. They can also be difficult and expensive to clean up. Large petroleum spills, such as those caused by accidents involving giant oil tankers, often provoke public anger at oil companies. Such an angry outcry occurred in 1989, when the tanker *Exxon Valdez* struck a reef off southeastern Alaska, spilling nearly 11 million gallons (42 million liters) of crude oil.

Air pollution. The burning of petroleum fuels generates exhaust gases and particles that pollute the air. Petroleum fuels burned to power vehicles, heat homes and businesses, and generate electric power are a leading cause of air pollution in many countries.

Burning petroleum fuels generates gases, such as carbon monoxide, sulfur dioxide, and nitrogen oxides. These gases are poisonous to plants, animals, and people. Sulfur dioxide and nitrogen oxides can combine

with water in the atmosphere, raising the water's acidity. This water can then fall back to the surface, where it can damage property and pollute the environment. This phenomenon is known as *acid rain.* Since the 1970's, many industries have taken steps to reduce the emissions of these gases. However, these forms of pollution remain a problem in some areas.

In general, burning liquid fuels derived from petroleum produces less pollution than burning an equivalent amount of coal. Burning natural gas creates much less pollution than burning liquid petroleum fuels. Burning natural gas produces no sulfur dioxide and no solid particles.

Global warming. Some scientists consider petroleum use to be a major factor in global climate change. Since the late 1800's, the average temperature of Earth's surface has risen about 0.7 to 1.4 °F (0.4 to 0.8 °C). These scientists believe increasing concentrations of *greenhouse gases* are responsible for some or all of this warming. Greenhouse gases, such as methane and carbon dioxide, trap heat from the sun and hold it near Earth's surface.

Carbon dioxide makes up the largest portion of waste gases produced by burning petroleum. The concentration of carbon dioxide in the atmosphere has risen by 30 percent since the beginning of the Industrial Revolution of the late 1700's to the mid-1800's. This was a period when people began burning large amounts of petroleum and coal as power-driven machinery largely replaced hand labor.

Some experts do not believe that human activities, such as the burning of fossil fuels, have significantly contributed to global warming. They believe that the warming trend may be part of a natural cycle of climate change. Scientists who believe human activities contribute to global warming, however, are concerned that warming will continue or even accelerate if fossil fuel consumption continues to grow.

The price of petroleum

Because petroleum is such an important source of energy, the price of petroleum is often a major concern. Petroleum prices rise and fall according to supply and demand.

How prices are set. Petroleum prices are determined in a special market called a *commodity exchange.* In such an exchange, buyers bid on contracts called *futures contracts.* A futures contract is an agreement by a petroleum producer to deliver a certain amount of petroleum on a certain date at a prearranged price. The auctioning of futures contracts determines fair market prices for petroleum, which are then published.

Futures contracts measure crude oil and natural gas in standard units. Crude oil is measured in *barrels.* One barrel equals 42 gallons (159 liters) of petroleum. Natural gas is measured in *thousands of cubic feet* (Mcf). One Mcf equals 1,000 cubic feet (28 cubic meters) of natural gas at a set temperature and pressure.

Crude oils vary greatly in quality and value. For this reason, crude oil prices are based on *benchmark crudes,* crude oils considered to be of average value. Two commonly used benchmark crudes are West Texas Intermediate Crude and Brent Crude. West Texas Intermediate Crude is a blend of oil from fields in western

Texas. Brent Crude comes from the North Sea. A barrel of light crude often sells for higher than the benchmark price. Barrels of heavy crude often sell for less.

How prices change. Petroleum prices rise and fall according to demand for petroleum and the supply available to meet that demand. In general, an increase in demand causes prices to rise. An increase in supply can cause prices to fall.

As petroleum prices rise, petroleum companies invest more money in exploration. They may also begin producing petroleum from reservoirs that were once considered unprofitable. These activities increase the supply of petroleum, causing prices to fall. As prices fall, petroleum companies slow exploration and stop producing petroleum from some wells. Eventually, the supply begins to fall, and prices rise once again.

Other factors, such as news of wars, natural disasters, civil unrest, or terrorist attacks, can also influence the price of petroleum. Such news may convince investors that the supply of petroleum could be interrupted. Investors then buy more petroleum, causing prices to rise. Prices may fall again when a conflict or disaster ends.

Petroleum and international relations

The world's petroleum resources are not distributed equally. Some countries, especially those in the Middle East, tend to produce much more petroleum than they can use. On the other hand, the United States, Japan, and several countries in Western Europe use far more petroleum than they can produce. These countries must import most of the petroleum they use. The economies of all countries depend to some degree on the import or export of petroleum. For this reason, petroleum can complicate international relations and lead to disagreements, conflicts, or even war.

The petroleum gap. The countries that consume the most petroleum are also the world's wealthiest and most industrialized. Petroleum-producing nations tend to be, in general, smaller and poorer. This inequality can create resentment and mistrust between petroleum-producing and petroleum-consuming nations.

As with any valuable resource, petroleum can also create political and social instability where it is found. In a petroleum-producing region, the people who control the petroleum are often richer and more powerful than the people who do not. This inequality can anger people who feel that petroleum resources and profits are distributed unfairly.

Petroleum and diplomacy. For countries that depend on imported petroleum, the security of the petroleum supply is a major concern. Petroleum may be produced in one country, be refined in another, and pass through several nations before it arrives at its final destination. The need to maintain friendly relationships with all of the countries along this petroleum pathway is a major challenge in international relations.

At any point during production or consumption, petroleum may pass through areas made unstable by political unrest, ethnic and religious strife, or disputes between neighboring countries. When situations like these threaten the petroleum supply, the nations that depend on petroleum can find it difficult or even impossible to resist becoming involved in such conflicts.

Petroleum and war. Historians have argued that petroleum influenced the course of many modern wars. For example, during World War II (1939-1945), rival petroleum-consuming nations fought battles for the control of petroleum-producing regions.

More recent conflicts have pitted petroleum-producing nations against one another and against petroleum-consuming nations. These include the Iran-Iraq War (1980-1988) and the Persian Gulf Wars of 1991 and 2003. All of these wars had causes not directly related to petroleum. Political scientists have argued, however, that the need to secure the petroleum supply helped persuade the opposing countries to engage in these conflicts.

Petroleum and security. Since the 1970's, many people have become concerned about the link between petroleum and national security. Many modern terrorists come from petroleum-producing countries in the Middle East. These terrorists include those directly involved in the Sept. 11, 2001, attacks on the World Trade Center in New York City and the Pentagon near Washington, D.C. Some people worry that dependence on petroleum from the Middle East will complicate efforts to find and arrest terrorists. Other people express concern that petroleum profits support oppressive or hostile governments.

Many people also worry that the need to secure the petroleum supply influences petroleum-consuming countries to intervene too much in conflicts between petroleum-producing nations. Some fear that this intervention could incite the hatred of terrorists.

Environmental issues also pose a challenge to international relations. Efforts to reduce pollution often require the cooperation of many different nations. For example, in 1997, many nations drafted an agreement called the Kyoto Protocol. The agreement called upon industrial nations to reduce greenhouse gas emissions in an effort to control global warming. The United States refused to approve the protocol, causing widespread disagreement among countries.

History of petroleum use

People have used petroleum for thousands of years. Before the 1850's, people relied on the relatively small amount of crude oil that seeped to Earth's surface naturally or was extracted during salt mining. They used this oil to make construction materials, adhesives, lubricants,

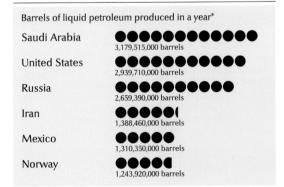

Leading petroleum-producing countries

Barrels of liquid petroleum produced in a year*

Country		Barrels
Saudi Arabia	●●●●●●●●●●●●	3,179,515,000 barrels
United States	●●●●●●●●●●●	2,939,710,000 barrels
Russia	●●●●●●●●●●	2,659,390,000 barrels
Iran	●●●●●(	1,388,460,000 barrels
Mexico	●●●●●	1,310,350,000 barrels
Norway	●●●●(	1,243,920,000 barrels

*One barrel equals 42 gallons (159 liters).
Figures are for 2001 and include crude oil, natural gas liquids, and other liquids.
Source: U.S. Energy Information Administration.

Petroleum 299

ointments, and fuel for lamps.

Beginnings of the petroleum industry. Most historians trace the beginning of the petroleum industry to 1859. In that year, "Colonel" Edwin L. Drake, a former railroad conductor, drilled an oil well near Titusville, Pennsylvania. Drake used equipment designed to drill saltwater wells that were used in the production of salt. His well reached $69\frac{1}{2}$ feet (21.2 meters) deep.

The petroleum industry soon filled the growing demand for kerosene to fuel lamps. In the 1850's, kerosene had begun to replace more expensive lamp fuels, such as *camphene* (a product of turpentine) and whale oils. At first, kerosene was produced by extracting it from coal and shale. Refining crude oil produced kerosene much more efficiently. The demand for kerosene drove oil prices to about $15 per barrel at the beginning of 1860. By the end of 1861, extensive drilling had produced much more oil than people could use. Prices plunged to 10 cents per barrel.

Growth of the petroleum industry. Prospectors soon discovered that other states had large oil deposits, too. By the mid-1870's, commercial production of oil had begun in California, New York, Ohio, and West Virginia. Several more states followed in the 1880's. In 1901, prospectors opened the first well at what came to be known as the Spindletop oil field in eastern Texas. The well gained fame as a *gusher,* an oil well that produces a great amount of oil without pumping. During the 1890's and early 1900's, California and Oklahoma joined Texas as the leading oil-producing states. Annual U.S. oil production rose from 2,000 barrels in 1859 to nearly 64 million barrels in 1900.

Interest in commercial oil production spread rapidly throughout the world. European countries began importing crude oil from the United States. Belgium, France, Germany, the Netherlands, and the United Kingdom opened refineries in the late 1860's. Other countries, including what are now Canada, India, Indonesia, Myanmar, Poland, Romania, and Russia, also began producing oil in the late 1800's.

Around 1900, two trends dramatically changed the petroleum industry—the replacement of kerosene lamps with electric lights and the increasing popularity of the automobile. The automobile created a strong demand for gasoline as the demand for kerosene declined. At that time, however, only a small amount of gasoline could be produced from a barrel of crude oil. The introduction of the thermal-cracking process in 1913 helped solve the problem. Within five years, refiners had more than doubled the amount of gasoline that they could produce from a barrel of crude oil.

World War I (1914-1918). Industry developed rapidly in the early 1900's, creating an increased demand for petroleum. Some countries, such as the United States and Russia, had their own petroleum reserves. Other nations, such as the United Kingdom and the Netherlands, imported oil from colonies or other areas under their control. Still other industrial countries, such as Germany, lacked access to large reserves of petroleum. Competition between industrialized powers for petroleum-producing colonies helped contribute to the outbreak of World War I.

Petroleum also affected the outcome of World War I. For the first time, motorized vehicles powered by petroleum competed against the power of steam, horses, and human muscles. By the end of the war, battleships, armored vehicles, and aircraft provided a huge military advantage, especially to nations, such as the United States and the United Kingdom, that had access to large stores of petroleum. The British Navy, powered by petroleum, proved

© Hulton Archive from Getty Images

"Colonel" Edwin L. Drake, *wearing the top hat,* confers with an engineer at his oil well near Titusville, Pennsylvania. Drake, a former railroad conductor, used equipment designed to drill saltwater wells to reach an underground petroleum deposit in 1859. The well reached a depth of $69\frac{1}{2}$ feet (21.2 meters). Many historians consider the drilling of Drake's well to mark the beginning of the petroleum industry.

World production and consumption of petroleum

This graph shows the amount of petroleum produced and used in various regions of the world. The Middle East, Latin America, and Africa produce more petroleum than they use, while other areas use much more petroleum than they can produce.

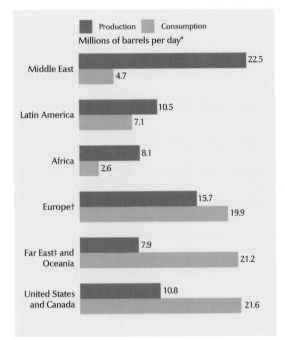

*Includes crude oil, natural gas liquids, and other liquids.
†Includes both European and Asian parts of Russia.
‡Excludes Russia.
Figures are for 2001. Source: U.S. Energy Information Administration.

World petroleum reserves

This graph shows the amount of petroleum remaining in various regions of the world. The Middle East has more petroleum than all the other regions combined. Reserves can increase as companies develop new ways to locate and produce petroleum.

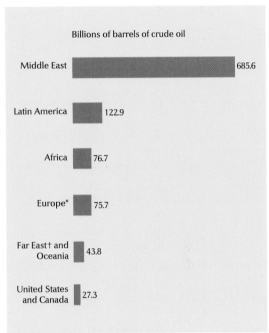

*Includes both European and Asian parts of Russia.
†Excludes Russia.
Figures are for 2001. Data based on petroleum that can be extracted using current technology.
Sources: U.S. Energy Information Administration; *Oil and Gas Journal.*

faster and more flexible than the coal-driven German navy. Petroleum-powered vehicles on land, air, and sea helped bring victory to the United States, the United Kingdom, France, Russia, and their allies.

Between the wars. After World War I, the use of petroleum brought about major changes on farms. More and more farmers began to operate tractors and other equipment powered by petroleum. Petroleum power had become an important part of nearly every industry.

The first important petroleum discoveries in the Middle East had occurred in Iran in 1908. Prospectors located huge petroleum deposits in Iraq in 1927, in Bahrain in 1932, and in Saudi Arabia in 1938. Large petroleum deposits were later found in other Middle Eastern nations. The Middle East eventually became the most important petroleum-producing region in the world.

World War II (1939-1945). Petroleum also strongly influenced the course of World War II. During the war, petroleum from the Middle East helped fuel the Allied war effort. Allied and Axis forces fought military campaigns for control of oil resources in the Middle East and other parts of the world.

When the war began, Germany lacked control of significant petroleum resources. The country's need for petroleum was one of the major causes of a disastrous attempt to invade the Soviet Union. In 1942, German forces drove toward oil fields in the Caucasus Mountains, then in the Soviet Union, now in Azerbaijan. Soviet forces defeated the

Germans at the Soviet city of Stalingrad (now Volgograd) in one of the bloodiest battles in history. Many historians cite Germany's lack of petroleum as a major cause of that country's defeat.

Petroleum also helped lead to war in the Pacific. Japan's economy had grown rapidly during the early 1900's. In 1931, the country's increasing demand for petroleum and other resources led it to seize Manchuria, a region of China rich in natural resources. By 1941, Japan had seized other petroleum-producing areas of China and Southeast Asia. In response, the United States stopped exporting petroleum to Japan.

In 1941, Japan attacked U.S. military bases at Pearl Harbor in Hawaii. The United States responded by declaring war against Japan. The two nations fought many battles for control of the petroleum supply. To obtain petroleum from the Dutch East Indies (now Indonesia), Japanese forces occupied that colony in 1942. In that year, the U.S. Navy had begun attacking Japanese oil tankers. Allied forces had completely cut off Japan's oil supply by early 1945. Petroleum shortages severely crippled Japan's ability to wage war.

The postwar period. After World War II, increased industrialization and rapid population growth created new and greater demands for petroleum. In the United States, a boom in sales of single-family houses, electrical appliances, and motor vehicles led to great increases in the consumption of petroleum. By the end of the 1960's, the

United States accounted for more than 30 percent of the world's petroleum consumption.

During the 1960's, prospectors discovered significant amounts of petroleum in northern Alaska and in the North Sea off northwestern Europe. The new reserves, however, were not large enough to satisfy the increasing demand. Increasingly, industrialized nations relied on petroleum produced in the Middle East.

For much of the history of the petroleum industry, American and European companies owned or operated the petroleum industry in many Middle Eastern countries. In 1951, Iran became the first such country to take over the holdings of foreign firms. By the mid-1970's, most nations in the Middle East either fully controlled or held a majority interest in their petroleum industry.

In 1960, Iran, Iraq, Kuwait, Saudi Arabia, and Venezuela formed the Organization of the Petroleum Exporting Countries (OPEC). OPEC is a group of nations whose economies depend on the export of petroleum. Several more countries have joined OPEC since then. OPEC nations seek to control petroleum prices by controlling the amount of petroleum they produce.

The energy crisis. Adjusting for inflation, the price of oil remained largely stable from 1870 to 1970. During the late 1960's and early 1970's, political instability in the Middle East disrupted the flow of oil to the major industrialized countries. In 1971, OPEC's member nations, which held most of the world's petroleum reserves, acted to raise the price of oil by reducing production. Political instability and production cuts pushed oil prices from less than $3 per barrel in 1973 to a peak of $34 per barrel in 1981.

This steep price increase forced many countries to begin energy-conservation programs. In addition, petroleum exploration increased throughout the world. Prospectors discovered new petroleum reserves in Angola, Brazil, and Papua New Guinea.

Falling prices. Conservation and exploration helped to increase the petroleum supply. This led prices to fall by about 50 percent between 1985 and 1986. The price decline created economic problems in developing countries whose economies relied on the export of petroleum. Many economists believe that falling petroleum prices also contributed to the collapse of the Soviet Union in 1991. The Soviet economy had relied heavily on petroleum exports to the West. For the most part, oil export prices remained low throughout the 1990's.

In the late 1990's, an economic downturn in Asia reduced the demand for petroleum, causing prices to drop below $12 per barrel in 1998. OPEC responded by reducing exports, causing prices to double by 2000.

Persian Gulf wars. In 1990, Iraq invaded Kuwait, in part in an attempt to gain control of the country's petroleum reserves. The Iraqi government also desired better access to shipping ports used to transport petroleum. The United Nations (UN) responded by banning the import of most Iraqi products, including oil. In 1991, a coalition organized by the United States and the UN expelled Iraqi forces from Kuwait. This conflict became known as the Persian Gulf War of 1991.

In 2003, a coalition of nations led by the United States and the United Kingdom invaded Iraq in an effort to oust Iraqi president Saddam Hussein. Following the collapse of Hussein's government, many nations lifted their ban on imports of Iraqi oil. The coalition vowed to use profits from Iraq's petroleum to help rebuild the country.

In 2002 and 2003, political unrest and a series of strikes reduced petroleum production in Venezuela. The reduction, along with the Persian Gulf War of 2003, helped to keep oil prices relatively high.

The future of petroleum

The world's petroleum supply will not last forever. A limited amount of petroleum exists beneath the ground, and petroleum companies probably cannot extract all that is there. At current rates of consumption, the world's recoverable crude oil reserves could run out in the mid-2000's.

Increasing use of natural gas could help extend the petroleum supply. Some petroleum experts believe that switching to natural gas for much of our energy needs could help the petroleum supply last until about 2200. In addition to being mined from petroleum deposits, natural gas can be extracted from coal. Natural gas also exists in the form of *natural gas hydrates,* frozen deposits of methane and water ice found in cold regions and beneath the ocean floor. Improved methods for extracting natural gas and crude oil could extend the petroleum supply until about 2300.

Eventually, alternative energy sources will have to replace petroleum. Renewable energies, such as solar power, wind power, and water power, may replace petroleum in some areas. But many scientists believe that only nuclear power can fully replace the vast amounts of energy that petroleum provides. This power may come from the splitting of atoms, called *fission,* or the combining of atoms, called *fusion.*

In the early 2000's, many people were concerned about fission power, mainly because it creates radioactive wastes that can remain dangerous for thousands of years. Fusion, if perfected, could provide a cleaner and more efficient power source than fission. Fusion power, however, requires hydrogen. At present, producing a usable form of hydrogen from water, natural gas, or other sources is too expensive. Scientists are working on affordable ways to produce hydrogen for fusion.

Michael J. Economides

Additional resources

Level I
Aaseng, Nathan. *Business Builders in Oil.* Oliver Pr., 2000.
Bredeson, Carmen. *The Spindletop Gusher: The Story of the Texas Oil Boom.* Millbrook, 1996.
DuTemple, Lesley A. *Oil Spills.* Lucent Bks., 1999.
Pampe, William R. *Petroleum: How It Is Found and Used.* Enslow, 1984.

Level II
Burger, Joanna. *Oil Spills.* Rutgers, 1997.
Conaway, Charles F. *The Petroleum Industry: A Nontechnical Guide.* PennWell Bks., 1999.
Krueger, Gretchen D. *Opportunities in Petroleum Careers.* Rev. ed. VGM Career, 1999.
Shojai, Siamack, ed. *The New Global Oil Market.* Praeger, 1995.

Robot is a mechanical device that operates automatically. Robots can perform a variety of tasks. They are especially suitable for doing jobs too boring, difficult, or dangerous for people. The term robot comes from the

Universe consists of all matter and all light and other forms of radiation and energy. It includes everything that exists anywhere in space and time.

The universe includes Earth, everything on Earth and within it, and everything in the solar system. The solar system contains nine major planets along with millions of smaller bodies, such as comets, asteroids, and meteoroids. The solar system also includes the sun, the star around which the planets revolve.

All stars, including the sun, are part of the universe. Some other stars also have planetary systems. In addition to planets, stars, and other bodies, the universe contains gas, dust, *magnetic fields* (areas of magnetic force), and high-energy particles called *cosmic rays.*

Stars are grouped into *galaxies.* The sun is one of hundreds of billions of stars in a giant spiral galaxy called the Milky Way. This galaxy measures about 100,000 *light-years* across. A light-year is the distance that light travels in a vacuum in a year—about 5.88 trillion miles (9.46 trillion kilometers).

Galaxies tend to be grouped into *clusters.* Some clusters appear to be grouped into *superclusters.* The Milky Way is part of a cluster known as the Local Group. This cluster measures about 3 million light-years in diameter. The cluster also includes two giant spirals known as the Andromeda Galaxy and M33 and about 30 small galaxies called *dwarf galaxies.* The Local Group is part of the Local Supercluster, which has a diameter of about 100 million light-years.

On an even larger scale, galaxies are grouped into huge networks made up of stringlike regions of galaxies called *filaments.* Relatively empty regions of space called *voids* surround these filaments.

Size of the universe

No one knows for sure whether the universe is *finite* (limited) or infinite in size. Observations of the sky with optical telescopes indicate that there are at least 100 billion galaxies in the observable universe. Measurements show that the most distant galaxies observed to date are about 12 billion to 13 billion light-years from Earth. They appear in every direction across the sky.

Among the most distant objects ever observed are tremendously bright objects called *quasars.* Individual quasars are as much as 1,000 times brighter than the entire Milky Way. Evidence suggests that the centers of quasars may each contain a giant *black hole.* A black hole is an object whose gravitational force is so strong that nothing—not even light—can escape from it. Matter falling into a massive black hole could produce the radiation *emitted* (given off) by quasars.

Astronomers can determine the distance to a faraway object by measuring the object's *redshift.* Redshift is a stretching of the wavelength of light or other radiation emitted by an object. Wavelength is the distance between successive crests of a wave. The stretching is called *redshift* because red light has the longest wavelength of any visible light. Objects farther away from Earth have larger redshifts.

Redshift occurs when the object emitting light is moving away from the observer. Objects moving away more rapidly have a larger redshift. Astronomers interpret the large redshifts of faraway ob-

Arnold Zann, Black Star

Robots efficiently perform a wide variety of tasks that are boring, hard, or dangerous for people, including welding automobile body parts, *shown here,* and assembling electronic circuits.

Czech word *robota,* meaning *drudgery.* Robots efficiently carry out such routine tasks as welding, drilling, and painting automobile body parts. They also do such jobs as making plastic containers, wrapping ice cream bars, and assembling electronic circuits. The science and technology that deals with robots is called *robotics.*

A typical robot performs a task by following a set of instructions that specifies exactly what it must do to complete the job. These instructions are stored in the robot's control center, a computer or part of a computer. The computer, in turn, sends commands to the robot's motorized joints, which function much like human joints to move various parts of the robot.

Robots vary in design and size, but few resemble the humanlike machines that appear in works of science fiction. Most are stationary structures with a single arm capable of lifting objects and using tools. Engineers have also developed mobile robots equipped with television cameras for sight and electronic sensors for touch. These robots are controlled by stored instructions, feedback from sensors, and remote control. Scientists have used such robots to explore the sea floor on Earth and the surface of Mars.

Kazem Kazerounian

Additional resources

Menzel, Peter, and D'Aluisio, Faith. *Robo Sapiens: Evolution of a New Species.* MIT Pr., 2000.
Wickelgren, Ingrid. *Ramblin' Robots.* Watts, 1996.

jects as evidence that the universe is expanding—that is, every point in the universe is moving away from every other point. This expansion does not cause the matter within a particular object to expand, however, because attraction among its atoms and molecules holds the object together. Similarly, the force of gravity prevents the stars in a galaxy from moving away from one another. But the galaxies are moving away from one another. The expansion of the universe is a basic observation that any successful theory of the universe must explain.

Changing views of the universe

In ancient times, people from many cultures thought that the universe consisted of only their own locality, distant places of which they had heard, and the sun, moon, planets, and stars. Many people thought that the heavenly bodies were gods and spirits. But the Polish astronomer Nicolaus Copernicus suggested in 1543 that Earth and the other planets revolve around the sun. Later astronomers showed that the sun is a typical star.

Knowledge of the universe increased with the development of the telescope, the photographic plate, and the *spectroscope* (an instrument that analyzes light). Astronomers discovered that the sun is moving within a large system of stars, the Milky Way. About 1920, astronomers realized that not all of the *nebulae* (fuzzy patches of light seen in the night sky) are part of the Milky Way. Rather, many of these objects are actually other galaxies. The discovery of the redshift of distant galaxies led to the theory of the expanding universe.

The *big bang theory* provides the best explanation of the basic observations of the universe. According to the theory, the universe began with an explosion—called the *big bang*—13 billion to 14 billion years ago. Immediately after the explosion, the universe consisted chiefly of intense radiation and hot particles. This radiation, along with various kinds of matter and energy, formed a rapidly expanding region called the *primordial fireball.* After thousands of years, the fireball cooled.

In time, the matter broke apart into huge clumps. The clumps became galaxies, many of them grouped into clusters, superclusters, and filaments. Smaller clumps within the galaxies formed stars. Part of one of these clumps became the sun and the other objects in the solar system.

Strong evidence for the big bang theory comes from observations of faint radio waves coming from all directions in space. Scientists believe this radiation, called the *cosmic microwave background* (CMB) *radiation,* is all that remains of the primordial fireball.

The *steady state theory* offers another explanation for the expansion of the universe and other observations. According to this theory, the universe has always existed in its present state. As the galaxies move apart, new matter appears between them and forms new galaxies. However, the existence of the CMB radi-

ation and detailed studies of galaxies and *supernovae* (exploding stars) have cast strong doubts on the steady state theory.

Studies of nearby stars, distant galaxies, and the CMB radiation give scientists an idea of the types of matter and energy that make up the universe. These studies suggest that the universe consists of about 4 percent ordinary matter and radiation. The matter consists mainly of hydrogen and helium. The radiation includes light, radio, and other waves as well as cosmic rays. The rest of the universe is made up of matter and energy that scientists cannot directly observe. About 23 percent of the universe is *dark matter,* matter that does not emit, reflect, or absorb observable light or other radiation. The remaining 73 percent of the universe is composed of *dark energy.* Dark energy is a little-understood form of energy that is apparently making the universe expand more and more quickly.

Observations of supernovae and the CMB radiation suggest that the present age of the universe is about 13.7 billion years. This estimate agrees with studies of the ages of stars in groups called *globular star clusters,* which contain the oldest stars found in the Milky Way.

The future of the universe

Many studies indicate that the universe will continue to expand. Measurements of the brightness and redshift of supernovae in distant galaxies suggest that at the present time the expansion of the universe is accelerating. Observations of the CMB radiation provide evidence that the universe has the appropriate mixture of matter and energy to continue expanding. Both of these types of studies give similar predictions for the rate at which the universe is expanding.

Theories of the universe based on the German-born physicist Albert Einstein's theory of general relativity allow for the possibility that all of the matter in the universe could come back together again in a *big crunch.* This would happen if the matter's gravitational pull was strong enough to overcome its expansion. The entire universe would eventually collapse and then explode, entering a new phase that might resemble the present one. However, studies of the CMB radiation strongly suggest that the universe has an infinite mass and volume and that it will expand forever.

Kenneth Brecher

Related articles include:

Astronomy
Big bang
Black hole
Cosmology
Dark energy
Dark matter
Galaxy
Gravitation
Quasar
Redshift
Relativity

INDEX

How to use the index

Each index entry gives the page number or page numbers—for example, **Catarina, Hurricane,** 183. This means that information on this topic may be found on the page indicated.

The indications (il.) or (ils.) mean that the reference on this page is to an illustration or illustrations only, as in **Cells** (biology).

A page number in italic type means that there is an article on this topic on the page or pages indicated. For example, there is an Update article on **Chemistry** on pages 194–197. The page numbers in roman type indicate additional references to this topic in other articles.

When there are many references to a topic, they are grouped alphabetically by clue words under the main topic. For example, the clue words under **China** group the references to that topic under several subtopics.

The "see" and "see also" cross-references refer the reader to other entries in the index. For example, information on **Cigarettes** and **Conservation** will be found under the headings indicated.

An entry followed by "reprint" refers to a new or revised encyclopedia article in the supplement section, as in **Craters.** This means that there is a reprint article on page 277.

A

Abrikosov, Alexei A., 242, 244
Absorption of water, 195-196
Acheulian culture, 172
Acquired immune deficiency syndrome. See **AIDS**
Acropora (coral), 188
Additives, Food, 151
Adequate Intakes (nutrition), 160
Adipocytes (cells), 132-133
Adolescents
    autism, 258, 260
    obesity, 122-124, 128-131
    pregnancy, 262
Adrastea (moon), 39 (il.)
Advanced Camera for Surveys, 177
Africa, ungulates, 214
Agate Basin, 172
Aggressive mimicry, 62, 71
Agre, Peter C., 242-243
Agriculture, *163-165*
    environmental impact, 223-225
    vulture deaths, 187
    See also **Genetic engineering; Pesticides**
Agriculture, U.S. Department of, 130, 135, 149, 151, 154, 163
AIDS, 208, 239-240
Ainu, 167 (il.)
Air batteries, 144
Air pollution, 221-222
Aircraft and airplanes. See **Aviation**
Alaska, 168-169
Alcoholism, 231 (il.)

Alkaline batteries, 144-145
Alleles, 255-256
Allergies, 208
ALOX5 (enzyme), 244-245
Alpha-synuclein gene, 237-238
Alzheimer's disease, 208-209, 237, 238
Amalthea (moon), 39 (il.)
American Obesity Association, 124
Americas, Early. See **Native Americans**
Amino acids, 194-195
AMP-activated protein kinase (enzyme), 140
Amphibians, 226-227
Andes Mountains, 235-236
Angiotensin, 133
Animals
    book, 193
    early hunting, 166
    See also **Agriculture; Biology; Cloning; Conservation; Ecology; Extinctions; Fossil studies;** and specific animals
Anisotropic molecules, 78, 81, 84 (il.)
Anode, 144
Antarctica, 192
    global warming, 246-247
Antetonitrus ingenipes (dinosaur), 228
Anthrax, 266
Anthropology, *165-169*
Antibiotics, 238-239
Antibodies, 155, 239
Antidepressants, 255 (il.)
Antigens, 239
Antioxidants, 161
Antiquarks, 252 (il.)

Antiquities, Looting of, *12-27*
Antiquities Act of 1906, 22
Ants, 213
    fire, 189
ApoE (gene), 211
Appetite, 125-127
Apple Computer, Inc., 200
Arachnids, 62-75
Arachnology, 62
Aral Sea, *223-225*
Archaeological Resources Protection Act (U.S.), 22
Archaeology, *169-174,* 191
    antiquities looting, *12-27*
Arctic region, 183-184
Arteries. See **Heart disease**
Arteriosclerosis, 133
Arthritis, 134
Artifacts, Looting of, *12-27*
Aseptic packaging, 151
Asthma, 208
Astronauts. See **Space technology**
Astronomy, *175-182*
    books, 191
    See also **Planets; Stars; Sun; Universe**
Atazanavir sulfate (drug), 208
Atherosclerosis, 244-245
Atkins diet, 136
Atlantic Ocean, 52-53, 183, 247-248
Atmospheric pressure, 52, 54 (il.)
Atmospheric science, *183-186*
    extreme weather, *44-59*
    See also **Climate**

ACKNOWLEDGMENTS

The publishers gratefully acknowledge the courtesy of the following artists, photographers, publishers, institutions, agencies, and corporations for the illustrations in this volume. Credits are listed from top to bottom, and left to right, on their respective pages. All entries marked with an asterisk (*) denote illustrations created exclusively for this yearbook. All maps, charts, and diagrams were staff-prepared unless otherwise noted.

6 Jacques Desclioitres, MODIS Land Rapid Response Team, NASA/GSFC

7 Dale Debolt*

8 AP/Wide World; NASA/JPL/Cornell University/Maas Digital

9 © Stone/Getty Images

10 Chandler Wilkerson, Institute for Molecular Design, University of Houston

12-13 © Behrouz Mehri, Agence France Presse/Getty Images; PhotoDisc

15 © Frances M. Roberts, Getty Images

16 © ZENG NIAN, Gamma Presse

18 Royal Geographical Society, London, UK /The Bridgeman Art Library

20 © Thomas Hester; Anne Fritzinger*

21 © Michael B. Collins

23 © Kate Brooks, Corbis

24 © Brad Rickerby, Reuters New Media/Corbis

25 © Thomas Hester

26 © Lowell Georgia, Corbis

28 NASA/JPL/Cornell University; ESA/DLR/FU Berlin (G. Neukum) NASA/JPL/Cornell University/Maas Digital

30 NASA/JPL/Cornell University; NASA/JPL/ASU/Cornell University

31 NASA/JPL/ASU

32 NASA/JPL; NASA/JPL/Cornell University

33 NASA/JPL/Cornell University

34-35 ESA/DLR/FU Berlin (G. Neukeum)

36-37 NASA/JPL

38 NASA/JPL; NASA/JPL/WFPC2

39 NASA/JPL/CalTech; NASA/JPL/Cornell University

40-41 NASA/JPL

42 NASA/JPL/Arizona State University; NASA/JPL/DLR

43 NASA/JPL; NASA/JPL/DLR

44-45 © A & J Verkaik, Corbis; NOAA News Photo/FEMA; © David Silverman, Getty Images; EPA/AP/Wide World

46 © Carl Juste, Miami Herald

47 Geophysical Fluid Dynamics Laboratory/NOAA; Historic NWS Collection/NOAA; © Mario Villafuerte, Getty Images

49 Dr. Paul Stackhouse Jr., NASA/LaRC; Luke Haddock*

50 Bob McMillan, FEMA News Photo

53 NESDIS/National Climatic Data Center/NOAA

54 © William Thomas Cain, Getty Images

56 © Lionel Bonaventure, AFP/Getty Images

60-61 © R. B. Suter, Vassar College

62 © Samuel Zschokke

63 John F. Eggert*

65 © Gail Stratton, University of Mississippi; © Eileen Hebets, University of California at Berkeley; © Gail Stratton, University of Mississippi

67 Steve Karp*

68 © MCB Andrade, photo by Ken Jones

69 © Bertram G. Murray, Animals Animals; © Mark Stowe, University of Florida, Gainesville

70 © Joe McDonald, Corbis; Wayne Maddison*

71 © Norman Larsen

72 © Robert Jackson

74 © George Uetz

75 © Eric Stashak, Susquehanna University

77 © PhotoDisc/Getty Images

78 Raymond Perlman and Steven Brayfield, Artisan-Chicago*

79 Debbie Mackall*

80 © Iris Passcal Instrument Center at New Mexico Tech/Earthscope; Debbie Mackall*

81 © Miaki Ishii, created with Geomap software courtesy of Weijia Su

82 J. Harlan Hunt*; NASA/JPL/Anne Fritzinger

84 © Michael W. Davidson, Florida State University

85-88 Debbie Mackall*

91 © Scott Camazine, Photo Researchers

93 Given Imaging Ltd.

94-96 GE Medical Systems; Siemens AG

97 © Sellem-Demri-Voisin/Photo Researchers

98-99 Siemens AG; GE Medical Systems

100 Siemens AG; Philips Medical Systems

102 Siemens AG; © Wellcome/Photo Researchers

103 © Charing Cross Hospital/Photo Researchers

104-105 Siemens AG

106-107 Brenda Tropinski*

109-111 Luke Haddock*